Developing Windows 10 Applications with C#

Sergii Baidachnyi

ISBN: 1522894918
ISBN-13: 978-1522894919
Library of Congress Control Number: 2015921254
CreateSpace Independent Publishing Platform, North Charleston, SC

Table of Contents

Preface 10

Part I Introduction to the Universal Windows Platform

Chapter 1 What Is the Universal Windows Platform? 13

One Core, One Application Platform, One Store 14

Tools and Languages 17

Cross-Platform Development and Bridges 21

Our First Application 24

Chapter 2 XAML Basics 31

What Is XAML? 32

Basic Syntax 33

Namespaces in XAML 38

Code-Behind Pages and Event Handlers 39

Markup Extensions 43

Dependency Properties 44

Chapter 3 Layouts 47

Canvas 48

StackPanel 49

Common Properties and Panel Class 50

Grid 53

RelativePanel 57

ScrollViewer 60

Chapter 4 Common User Controls 63

Some Words about Hierarchy 64

Buttons 65

Working with Text 68

RangeBase Controls 73

ProgressRing 74

ToolTip User Control 74

Working with Collections 75

SplitView 81

Chapter 5 User Interaction 85

Chapter 6 Styles, Resources, and Themes 93

Introduction to Styles 94

BasedOn Styles 97

Resources 98

Resource Dictionaries 100

Themes 101

How to Localize Your Application 105

Chapter 7 Graphics, Transformation, and Animation 109

Graphic Primitives 110

Brushes 114

SolidColorBrush 114

LinearGradientBrush 115

ImageBrush 116

WebViewBrush 116

Geometric Shapes 118

Transformations 119

Basic Types of Transformations 119

CompositeTransform 122

3-D Transformation 122

Introduction to Animations 125

Basic Animation Types 125

How to Run Storyboards 127

Animation Using Key Frames 128

Easing Functions 129

Embedded Animations 130

    Transitions 130

    Theme Animations 133

Chapter 8 Data Binding..135

Element-to-Element Binding 136

Binding in Code 139

Element-to-Object Binding 140

Converters 151

Binding to Collections 154

Chapter 9 Navigation and Windowing...159

Pages and Navigation...160

Back Button Is Everywhere 163

Application Life Cycle...165

Windowing..169

    ApplicationView Class 169

    Title Bar...170

    How to Handle Window Size Changes 173

    Working with Additional Views.....................................173

Chapter 10 How to Create Adaptive Interfaces..............................179

What Do We Already Know about Adaptive Interfaces?.................180

VisualStateManager...181

Setters...183

Adaptive Triggers 184

How to Create Different Views 188

Chapter 11 Tiles and Notifications...191

Live Tiles..192

Toast Notifications 201

Scheduled Notifications 206

Periodic Notifications...206

Chapter 12 How to Publish Applications to the Store 209

Create a Publisher Account..210

Get Ready to Publish Your Application 212

Publishing..218

Part II Common Features and Extensions

Chapter 13 Introduction to MVVM...225

Chapter 14 How to Work with Files and Settings 233

Working with Files and Folders..234

Working with Settings and Temporary Data.........................237

Local Storage..238

Roaming Storage..239

Temporary Storage 240

File Pickers..240

Known Folders 241

File-Type Associations..243

Chapter 15 App-to-App Communications 245

How to Implement Drag-and-Drop Functionality 246

Clipboard 249

Data Sharing...250

How to Launch External Applications Based on URL Protocol...................253

Publisher Cache 260

Chapter 16 Application Services and Background Tasks 263

Background Tasks 264

Application Services 270

Chapter 17 Networking 277

Network Information 278

Working with Data 280

How to Work with RSS Feeds..281

Using the WebAuthenticationBroker Class............................282

Chapter 18 Audio and Video 287

Media Controls 288

MediaElement...288

Adaptive Streaming 296

Captions 298

Template for Media 298

Media Casting 301

Media Editing and Transcoding 304

Chapter 19 Camera API...305

Using CameraCaptureUI Dialog 306

Media Capture API..311

Chapter 20 Speech Recognition and Cortana 315

Text to Speech 316

Speech Recognition 319

Cortana 322

Chapter 21 Maps 331

Chapter 22 Inking 339

Chapter 23 Sensor API 345

Chapter 24 Platform Extensions 351

Chapter 25 How to Publish Web Applications to the Store..................357

WebView 358

Project Westminster...367

Chapter 26 How to Make Money in the Store.......................................371

Paid Applications 372

Twins...372

Trial Mode...373

Sale! 376

Promo Codes..377

Free Applications 377

Advertising 377

In-App Purchases 380

Part III Advanced Features

Chapter 27 Windows Notification Service 385

Chapter 28 Sending Notifications Using Azure 391

"Native Development" Scenario...392

Introduction to Notification Hub 394

Creating a Simple Notification Hub...396

Mobile Service API vs. Notification Hub API 402

Tables...403

How to Send Notifications from the Server 405

"Operator" application 406

Windows Notification Service and Windows Runtime 407

Server Side for Windows Runtime Application 408

Interface of Our Application 409

.NET Back End 416

Other Mobile Services Features...422

Tags 422

Templates 422

Jobs 424

Custom API...425

Chapter 29 How to Build Your Own User Controls 427

Templates 428

User Controls 431

Templated Controls 433

Chapter 30 Testing and Debugging...437

Emulators and Simulators..438

Live Visual Tree in Visual Studio 441

Profiling and Debugging Tools in Visual Studio 2015..................................444

XAML Tools in Visual Studio 2015..447

Chapter 31 Win2D: How to Use Graphics without Deep DirectX Knowledge 451

Chapter 32 Composition API...465

Chapter 33 How to Use Blend 475

Overview to Blend 476

How to Create Animations in Blend..477

States and State Triggers and Blend 479

Chapter 34 Internet of Things...483

Overview of Microboards 484

Arduino 484

Arduino and Visual Studio..488

Netduino 489

Raspberry Pi 2 491

How to Create Schemas...491

Windows 10 IoT Core..493

IoT Extensions 494

Analog and PWM on Raspberry..500

Chapter 35 How to Build Windows 10 Games in Unity3D...............................505

Visual Studio Tools for Unity...506

Publishing a Unity Game to the Store...512

How to Create a Plug-In for Unity...515

About the Author...519

Preface

In 2015 Microsoft released Windows 10 Operating System that has the common core for a large range of hardware, from PCs and tablets to phones and gaming devices. For the first time, the code written for any one of those devices will be able to work without any porting on all of them. At the same time, you can publish applications you've created in the Store, and make them accessible to the broad user audience. Maybe you can even become a millionaire from selling your software!

This book provides a complete reference to Windows 10 development using modern native object-oriented application platform. It is a step-by-step guide for creation of rich performant and secure applications on the Universal Windows Platform. The author covers many important controls and their properties, methods, events as well as cross-platform development capabilities.

Developing Windows 10 Applications with C# is, quite likely, the most comprehensive Windows 10 reference as of this date. This is not a C# language tutorial, however, anyone with basic knowledge of C# should read this book to progressively learn how to properly and effectively use C# language tools to develop UWP applications. Even if you have previous Windows 8 and Windows Phone development experience, this manuscript will still be a very useful reference to new features and controls in Windows 10. The book will cover user interface basics, design principles, templates, and more. It will teach you how to publish your app into the Store and monetize it. You will also learn how to monitor your app performance with Windows Dev Center Dashboard.

I have personally known Sergii Baidachnyi for over ten years, even before he joined Microsoft, and I am always captured by his passion and ability to explain most complex things in a nice simple manner. His original personality and vast knowledge of the subject area result in a unique writing style. I have enjoyed reading the book myself, and hope that you will not regret time spent on learning Windows 10 intricacies from the expert.

Dmitriy Nikonov

Vice President of Technology

VIAcode Consulting, LLC

Part I

Introduction to the Universal Windows Platform

This page intentionally left blank

Chapter 1

What Is the Universal Windows Platform?

One Core, One Application Platform, One Store

Prior to Windows 10, you could develop applications for Windows desktops, tablets, phones, Xbox, and embedded devices, and usually you had to use different approaches for each type of device. For example, to develop modern Windows 8.x applications, you had to use Windows Runtime. To develop Windows Phone 8.x applications, you had to use Silverlight and, later, Windows Runtime. To develop Internet of Things (IoT) applications for Galileo boards, you needed to use C++ and a subset of the Win 32 API; Xbox application developers were required to have access to a special private SDK. Therefore, it was not easy to develop something universal for all Windows devices. Additionally, Microsoft introduced Stores for Windows and Windows Phone, and developers had to support these two different Stores instead of just one.

The Windows 10 release changed everything. Today, when we talk about Windows 10 modern applications, we mean applications that work on desktops, tablets, Xbox, phones, HoloLens, and IoT devices. As you read this book, you will learn how to develop applications for all of them and publish your applications to the Store, at least for desktops, tablets, and phones. Let's see how you can do it.

First of all, we should mention that the Windows Core is the same for all the different versions of Windows SKUs. So even if you can see some differences in Windows interfaces between IoT devices and phones, they all have the same core, which contains standard communication protocols, universal driver models, application-platform interfaces, and so on. Based on this core, Microsoft can create different versions of Windows by adding some device-specific features and components. That is why Windows for desktops supports desktop and tablet modes, but IoT Core versions just support the ability to run your applications.

Today Microsoft supports several Windows SKUs for different device families, such as Desktop for desktops and tablets, Mobile for phones and small tablets, and so on.

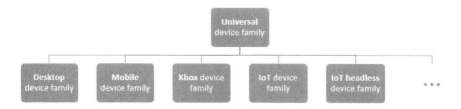

You can look at the different Windows SKUs as different sets of settings of the same Windows. This is important especially for developers because thanks to One Core, we can talk about the same application platform to develop applications for all possible types of devices. This platform is called Universal Windows Platform (UWP), and it is the main topic of the book. If you know how to build applications using UWP, you know how to build applications for all Windows 10 devices.

If you want to target some features of a specific device family, you can do so as well, because UWP supports a special mechanism called extensions, which allows you to include some device-specific features in your application, and even check in run time whether the particular feature is available, to make your application universal.

UWP is the next generation of Windows Runtime; it was introduced for Windows 8, and it is a native and object-oriented platform for developers. Since Windows Phone 8.1, Microsoft has brought Windows Runtime to Windows Phone and finally made it usable everywhere. UWP is not just a rebranding of Windows Runtime, owing to global availability on all devices. UWP is independent of Windows versions. The first version of Windows Runtime was announced for Windows 8.0, and the first update was announced for only Windows 8.1. In the case of UWP, Microsoft can update it independently of Windows updates. You can find some of those updates earlier than the next update of Windows, but other updates are accessible later. So the idea is similar to .NET Framework updates. I still know some developers who target the .NET Framework 2.0. Therefore, you can target an older version of UWP, and your application will still work everywhere, or you can target the latest one to use some of the new features.

To better understand UWP, look in **<disk>:\Program Files (x86)\Windows Kits\10** and find all SDK-related files. You will find a lot of **10.0.10240.0** subfolders. 10240 is a build of Windows that was released to the public and was an initial point for the first version of UWP. Once a new version of UWP is released, you will be able to find more subfolders that are related to that particular version of UWP. If you visit the **Platforms\UAP** subfolder, you can find a **Platform.xml** file, which should contain information about a particular platform:

```xml
<?xml version="1.0" encoding="utf-8"?>
<ApplicationPlatform name="UAP" friendlyName="Windows 10"
    version="10.0.10240.0">
    <MinimumVisualStudioVersion>14.0.22213.01
```

```
    </MinimumVisualStudioVersion>
    <ContainedApiContracts>
        <ApiContract
            name="Windows.Foundation.FoundationContract"
            version="1.0.0.0" />
        <ApiContract
            name="Windows.Foundation.UniversalApiContract"
            version="1.0.0.0" />
        <ApiContract
            name="Windows.Networking.Connectivity.WwanContract"
            version="1.0.0.0" />
    </ContainedApiContracts>
</ApplicationPlatform>
```

There you can see the full version, the user-friendly name, the main API contracts, and so on. Later we will discuss how to select a particular platform in Visual Studio.

In the XML file above, you can see that the Universal Windows Platform includes three contracts by default. A contract is a library that contains classes and metadata in separate files. Sets of contracts form extensions for UWP applications and UWP itself. If you want to see all available contracts, you can visit the **References** subfolder to find metadata for all available contracts.

The idea of metadata is simple. Because Windows Runtime and now UWP are native platforms, developers have the same problem they had when working with COM components—nobody knows what is inside a component. This problem was resolved in the .NET Framework, where all components/assemblies contain metadata information, but it is not easy to extend the existing COM model to add metadata. That is why Microsoft decided to put metadata in separate files. Visiting the **References** subfolder, you can find **WINMD** files, which contain metadata. Using this metadata, you can easily understand what is inside a selected contract, and tools such as Visual Studio can use metadata to provide IntelliSense support and other features.

If you want to open the metadata, the best way to do so is using the **ildasm** tool. This tool works for the .NET Framework, but Microsoft added the ability to read Windows Runtime metadata as well. To run **ildasm**, open the Developer Command Prompt for VS 2015 and type **ildasm**. Once the tool is running, you can open any of the metadata files in the **References** subfolder:

Now we know that the Windows 10 release brought One Core and One Application Platform. The last topic that I want to discuss is One Store. Starting with Windows 10, Microsoft announced One Store for all Windows 10 applications. Developers can publish the same package to the Store, and users can install it on any Windows 10 device, including phones, desktop, tablets, and so on. Thanks to this, you will not spend a lot of your time promoting your applications in different Stores to reach the maximum number of customers.

In the next chapter, I am going to discuss the Store in detail.

Tools and Languages

Of course, the best tool to develop Windows 10 applications is Visual Studio 2015. There are several editions, but Microsoft provides a free edition—Visual Studio 2015 Community edition. You can simply visit http://visualstudio.com and download the product from the main page. If you have fewer than five developers in your team, you can use Community for free, without any specific limitations.

Community edition substitutes Express versions, but in fact, it contains all the features that you could find in Professional Edition, including plug-in support, all languages and projects in the same IDE, integration with Git and Visual Studio, and so on.

In case you are working in an enterprise and cannot install Community Edition on your work machine, to avoid any licensing violations, you can continue to use the Express version of Visual Studio for Windows. Of course, you will have some limitations, but it should be enough to start learning Windows 10 development.

In general, to develop Windows 10 applications, you need to install Windows 10 on your computer. Visual Studio 2015 allows you to build Windows 10 applications on Windows 8.x and even Windows 7. Of course, in this case, you are not able to run and test your applications directly on your computer, but in the case of Windows 8.x, you can use a Windows Phone emulator and see how your application works at least on mobile devices. In both cases you can use a remote Windows 10 device to test and debug.

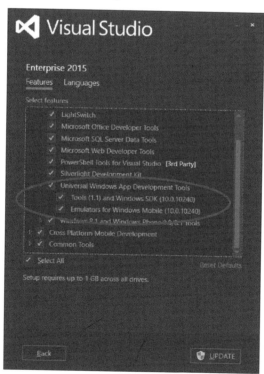

When installing Visual Studio 2015, you need to make sure that you install Universal Windows App Development tools. By default, they can be unselected, so it's better to use custom installation.

Once Visual Studio 2015 is installed, you can start developing Windows 10 applications. Before creating a solution, you need to decide what language you are going to use.

The Universal Windows Platform supports four languages that allow you to create Windows 10 applications: C#, VB.NET, C++, and JavaScript.

C++ is traditionally native for Windows platforms and allows you to create really native applications for Windows. If you want to build Windows 10 applications, it is better to use C++ with extensions (C++/CX) that provide some standard features of C#, such as interfaces, properties, events, and so on.

C# and VB.NET code look much clearer than C++ for Windows applications, and you can use C# for many other application types as well, including game development. Of course, C# is a managed language, but in the case of Windows 10 applications, that is an advantage, because while using C#, you can continue to use basic classes from the .NET Framework that allow you to work with strings and collections, use LINQ, and so on. At the same time, Visual Studio uses .NET Native technology, which allows you to compile Windows 10 applications in the cloud. Before you create a release package, Visual Studio will make some optimizations for .NET Native, and once a user requests your application from the Store, it will be compiled to native code. Using C#, you should not have any problems with the performance. Note that in debug mode, Visual Studio continues to use the .NET Core CLR to enable all debug features.

When we discussed UWP, we said that it is a native API for Windows. But even if your C# code is compiled by a .NET Native compiler, you cannot use native libraries as easily as you can .NET Framework Core libraries. That is why Microsoft developed language projections for C# and VB.NET. In general, a language projection is a layer between a language and Windows Runtime that allows you to use Windows Runtime libraries, such as native .NET Framework libraries. Using managed languages, you will not have any trouble communicating with Windows Core.

Developing Windows 10 applications in C++, C#, or VB.NET, you will spend a lot of time implementing user interfaces. Of course, using programming languages is not the best way to implement interfaces. That's why developers use a second language for Windows 10 applications, XAML (eXtensible Application Markup

Language). In the next chapter, we will spend a lot of time discussing XAML. Usually, if you select C++, C#, or VB.NET as your primary language, you will use two technologies C++/XAML, VB.NET/XAML, C#/XAML. This is not true for JavaScript.

In the case of JavaScript, you can use HTML to create user interfaces. As in the case of C# and VB.NET, Microsoft developed a special language projection for JavaScript—WinJS. Using JavaScript and WinJS, you can continue to use standard HTML controls and popular JavaScript libraries, but additionally, you can use all features of UWP. So if you like JavaScript, you can use it as a language to create native Windows 10 applications.

In this book we will use C#/XAML to create Windows 10 applications. You can use some materials in this book if you develop your applications in C++, but this book is not useful for JavaScript developers.

Working with Visual Studio 2015, we will use templates in Visual C# category. If you install the Universal Windows App Development tools successfully, you can find a Windows/Universal subcategory there. In most cases we will use Blank App template:

Take special note that you will not be able to run your application by default, because Windows doesn't allow you to install modern (UWP) applications that are not from the Store. To enable custom applications on your computer, you need to open the Settings window and switch your device to developer mode:

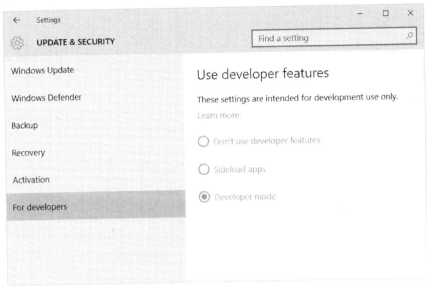

Once it's done, you can start creating your first application.

Cross-Platform Development and Bridges

Before going deeply into coding, I want to discuss one more topic, which is cross-platform development. It's a very important theme because customers use a lot of different devices, and some of them use not just Windows but Android or iOS operating systems. There are two topics to discuss: how to create from scratch a new application that will work on all available platforms, and how to migrate an existing Android and iOS applications to Windows 10. Let's discuss both questions.

If you want to create cross-platform applications but spend less time learning new languages, tools, and libraries, you can use one of three technologies that are already integrated into Visual Studio 2015: Xamarin, Apache Cordova, and C++.

To enable integration with Xamarin or/and Apache Cordova, you need to install the tools directly from the Visual Studio 2015 installer.

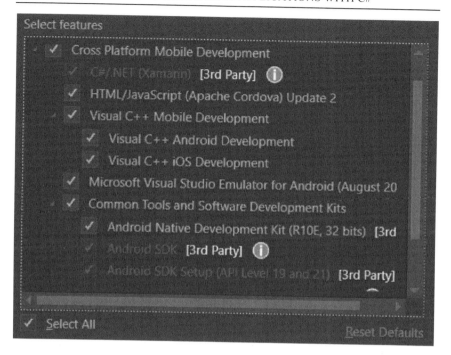

The installer contains everything that you need, meaning you can start developing applications right after Visual Studio installs and you do not have to think about Android SDK or something else.

The first tool, Xamarin, is built on an open-source implementation of the .NET Framework—Mono. If you use Xamarin, you can continue to use C# to develop applications for Android, iOS, and Windows. Xamarin is a paid product, but you can use Xamarin Starter Edition for free. The main idea is simple—implement language projections for Android and iOS in the same way as Microsoft has made the projection for Windows Runtime and C#. Today, you can find that 100 percent of Android and iOS API are implemented (wrapped) in managed classes, and there is nothing in Java and ObjectiveC/Swift that you cannot implement in C#. What is more important, Xamarin allows you to create native applications.

Using the Starter Edition of Xamarin, you can achieve two things: develop everything in C# and create a common business layer. Additionally, Visual Studio supports Android emulator and iOS and Android application designers, but you still need to create separate interfaces for each operating system. If you have a Xamarin license (starting at twenty-five dollars per month), you can create really universal applications. Xamarin Forms allow you to use universal set of controls and build universal UIs for all platforms, including Windows 10.

The second tool is Apache Cordova, which is free and allows you to use HTML and JavaScript to create applications for Windows, iOS, and Android. Applications that you can create with Apache Cordova are not truly native. In fact, Apache Cordova doesn't provide a lot of libraries, but it allows you to use the same code base (HTML and JavaScript) and pack it into application packages, using all embedded content as a source for a web control, which is available on each platform. For example, the web control in UWP is called WebView, and it allows you to present web content from the application package or using a URI. Similar controls are available in Android and iOS SDKs. There is a way to combine the content embedded in the application package and external content.

Using the standard set of HTML elements, you cannot use platform-specific features and components. That's why Apache Cordova supports plug-ins that allow you to aggregate different APIs and provide Apache Cordova developers a device-independent API. If you like JavaScript, you can use Apache Cordova as a universal platform for the most common operating systems.

Since Visual Studio 2015, Microsoft has included support for Android and iOS from C++. Right now you can use the same code base to create shared C++ libraries for Android and iOS directly from Visual Studio.

If you already have existing applications on other platforms, you can use special sets of tools and libraries called bridges. Microsoft announced three bridges that allow you to bring web, Android, and iOS applications to Windows. The first bridge we will discuss in detail in chapter 25. The next two bridges are still in development, but you can find some early betas.

The idea of a bridge for Android is to bring the native Android IDE some tools that will analyze your application, to find possible problems on Windows and provide recommendations to fix these problems. Once the application is ready, you can create the application package directly from Android IDE. So you do not have to rewrite any code.

In the case of iOS, you will be able to open your project in Visual Studio and compile your application there, continuing to add some functionality in ObjectiveC or Swift. If you have an application that you want to bring to Windows 10, contact a Microsoft representative in your region to get support with bridges.

Our First Application

We discussed the Universal Windows Platform, the tools, and cross-platform development. It's time to create your first Universal Windows Platform application.

To start, you can create a blank project as we discussed above, and Visual Studio will create all that you need:

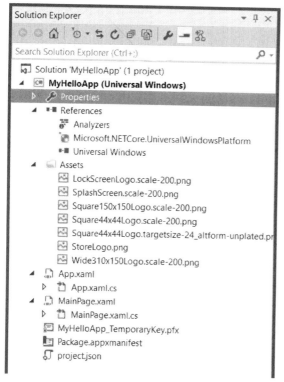

Let's open the Solution Explorer and see what Visual Studio creates for us.

First, bring your attention to the References folder, where you can find two references to the two frameworks.

The first one is Universal Windows—the common UWP contracts that implement all core features. That is all that you need to create Universal Windows Applications.

The second reference is Microsoft.NETCore.UniversalWindowsPlatform. As I mentioned before, C# is still a managed language, and it allows you to use core classes from the .NET Framework. That's why Visual Studio added the reference to .NET Core, allowing you to use collections, basic .NET types, LINQ, and so on.

If you want to see all classes that are included to the Universal Windows Platform and .NET Core, I would recommend using Object Browser. You can open this windows using the **View** menu item, and there is a way to filter all namespaces, selecting a particular framework or simply My Solution:

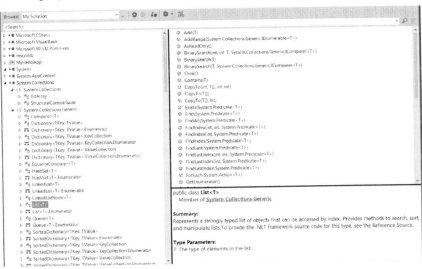

If you select My Solution, you can see the three UWP contacts that we discussed earlier and a lot of .NET Framework assemblies. Just open some of them to see the namespaces and classes there.

The next folder that you can see in the Solution Explorer is Assets. There you can find images that represent your application in the Store and on the Start screen.

Finally, you can see several files in the root folder:

- **MainPage.xaml** and **MainPage.xaml.cs:** These two files represent the main page of the application. By default, this page is empty, so you can leave it to start developing the first UI page there. The first file contains interface elements in XAML, and the second in C# code. There you can place event handlers and other page-related code.

- **App.xaml** and **App.xaml.cs:** These files represent the application itself. App.xaml.cs contains all the code that creates the infrastructure for your application and navigates it to the main page. Because the application object itself doesn't contain any interface elements the App.xaml file is empty. Later you can add application resources to it.

- **Project.json:** This file contains a list of packages that were included to the application using NuGet package manager. By default, there are no packages in it.

- **Package.appmanifest:** This is a very important file that contains all information about the application, including supported languages, tiles, splash screen, extensions, and so on.

- **.pfx:** Every application should be signed by a publisher's certificate, which you can get from the Store when you publish your application. At the beginning, however, you might not even have a Store account. That's why Visual Studio creates a temporary pfx file to sign your package. Once you associate your application with the Store entry, Visual Studio will change the pfx file to a real one.

Before you open the first page, I would recommend opening **Package.appmanifest** file. This file is in a XML format. Visual Studio supports a manifest designer, allowing you to edit almost all elements of the file:

In the manifest designer you can find six tabs, which contain different information about the application package:

- **Application:** Here you can find the basic information about the application, like the entry point for the application, description, supported orientation, and so on.

- **Visual Assets:** On this page you can find a list of supported tiles and links to image files that are linked with each of these tiles.

26

- **Capabilities:** All modern Windows 10 applications run in a way that limits their ability to get access to native Win32 API and system resources outside their own sandbox. If you try to use restricted APIs, your application will not pass the certification process in the Store. Even if the application is allowed in the Store, you still need to follow some rules. For example, if you want to use a camera, microphone, or location API, you need to notify users and their operating system about it, declaring appropriate capabilities. All these capabilities will be displayed to users on the Store page, and a user can decide whether they want to install the application based on this information. Even if the user installs your application, you need to check whether your application has the required permissions to use some declared features, because most capabilities users can turn them off by visiting the Privacy page in the Settings window.

- **Declarations:** Using this tab you can declare and set up some features that allow you to integrate your application with the operating system. Windows will use this part of the manifest to update the registry. For example, you can associate your application with some file types, and Windows will use it to open these files, or you can provide content for the lock screen.

- **Content URIs:** This tab allows you to make integrations with web content. We will discuss how to use this tab in chapter 25.

- **Packaging:** This tab contains information from the Store about the application's name and the certificate that will be used to sign your application. Usually you will not modify the information in this tab, because Visual Studio can fill it in automatically.

Before publishing your application, you will spend some time with the manifest designer to set everything up. However, as you currently have nothing to publish, you can finally open the MainPage.xaml to see the interface of the main page.

Using Visual Studio, you can edit the XAML file directly as a text file, or you can use design mode. Usually, I add XAML elements in the code editor and use design mode to preview my interface. It's very useful, especially if you use different layouts in design mode, to check how your interface looks on different devices:

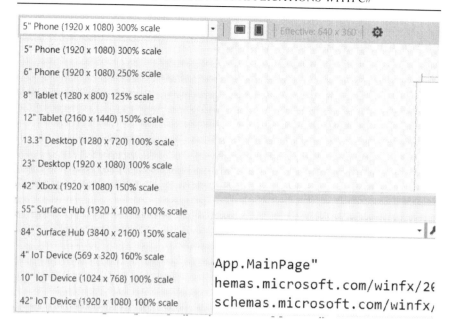

Inside the Grid element, let us add the following code:

```
<TextBlock Text="Hello World!" HorizontalAlignment="Center"
    VerticalAlignment="Center" />
```

Visual Studio provides several ways to run the application. If you are using Windows 10, you can run the application locally, you can also select a Remote Device to run and debug your application remotely, and finally you can use a Windows Phone device that is directly connected to your PC using a USB cable, or you can use a Windows Phone emulator:

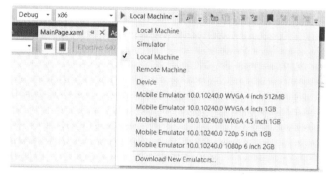

Select the best available method for you, and run the application. You will see the following window on the screen:

Congratulations! Your first Windows 10 application is done.

This page intentionally left blank

Chapter 2

XAML Basics

What Is XAML?

If you already have some experience in user interface development, you know that languages like C#, C++, Java, and JavaScript are not very suitable for declaring forms, styles, and resources. Let's look at some code from a Windows Forms application that creates a simple button:

```
this.myButton = new System.Windows.Forms.Button();
this.myButton.Location = new System.Drawing.Point(120, 60);
this.myButton.Name = "myButton";
this.myButton.Size = new System.Drawing.Size(110, 40);
this.myButton.Text = "Hello";
this.Controls.Add(this.myButton);
```

Creating the button took six lines of code! Usually a developer needs to set a lot more properties for each control, and additional forms can contain hundreds of controls and containers. So it is not easy to modify plain code there. Visual Studio and other IDEs support different types of visual editors, but in many cases developers need to go deep into the code and modify it directly. This is especially true if there is a need to create an adaptive interface that should be able to change the look in run time.

It is worth noting that web developers have had the solution to this problem for many years—HTML and JavaScript. HTML is used for declaring interfaces, and JavaScript for application logic. That's why almost ten years ago Microsoft introduced a language called XAML.

XAML (eXtensible Application Markup Language) is a special declarative language that is based on XML and is used primarily for creating interfaces.

XAML was introduced in the .NET Framework 3.0 as a part of Windows Presentation Foundation technology. Since that time developers have started using XAML in Silverlight, Windows Workflow, and Windows 8.x/Windows Phone 8.x development. Of course, we are going to use XAML in all Windows 10 applications in this book.

Let's review some simple code written in XAML that creates the same button inside a **Canvas** container:

```
<Canvas x:Name="LayoutRoot">
    <Button Content="Hello" Canvas.Top="60"
        Canvas.Left="120"
        Width="110" Height="40"
        x:Name="myButton">
```

```
    </Button>
</Canvas>
```

This code is much easier to understand because each element represents a control, and thanks to XAML editors in Visual Studio or Blend, you can easily understand the hierarchy of any interface. It's easy to locate any element in the interface tree, and to check properties of any control, you need to review attributes of an appropriate element.

Naturally, XAML not only can declare visual controls but is often used by developers to declare resources, styles, states of interface, and objects without visual representation. Additionally, XAML has markup extensions that extend simple XML and allow you to make bridges between XAML and C# code or between different parts of XAML. In this chapter we will review all aspects of this language.

Basic Syntax

If you are already familiar with XML, then you will be able to understand XAML without a problem. As in XML, each element is defined by a tag, which can contain attributes and child elements. Attributes are defined in **name="value"** pairs, where the value is any string and the attributes are located inside the start tag of an element.

```
<Canvas Name="LayoutRoot">
    <Button Content="Hello"
        Canvas.Top="60" Canvas.Left="120"
        Width="110" Height="40" Name="button1">
    </Button>
</Canvas>
```

The code above contains two elements: **Canvas** and **Button**. The **Canvas** element has only one attribute, the **Button** element has six attributes, and the button is located inside the **Canvas** element. As in XML, you can declare elements without any other elements inside using just an empty element tag:

```
<Button Content="Hello" Canvas.Top="60" Canvas.Left="120"
    Width="110" Height="40" Name="button1" />
```

In this case we don't use the end tag **</Button>**, but we close the start tag using **/>** instead of **>**.

Similar to XML, XAML is case sensitive, and this rule is important not just for element and attribute names but, in many cases, for attribute values as well. For

33

example, the following code declares two buttons with different names: button1 and Button1.

```
<Button Content="Hello" Canvas.Top="60" Canvas.Left="120"
    Width="110" Height="40" Name="button1" />
<Button Content="Hello" Canvas.Top="160" Canvas.Left="120"
    Width="110" Height="40" Name="Button1" />
```

Later we can use these names to get access to controls in C#.

XAML is very flexible and allows you to declare any code in several ways. For example, you can declare properties using not just attributes but child elements as well. The following two blocks declare the same button in different ways:

Block 1
```
<Button Content="Hello" Canvas.Top="60" Canvas.Left="120"
    Width="110" Height="40" Name="button1"></Button>
```

Block 2
```
<Button Content="Hello" Canvas.Top="60" Canvas.Left="120"
    Name="button1">
    <Button.Width>
        110
    </Button.Width>
    <Button.Height>
        40
    </Button.Height>
</Button>
```

To assign a control property using a child element, developers need to use the following notation: **<Element name>.<property name>**. Of course, this makes sense if you want to assign to a property a value that is a complex object and cannot be represented as a simple string. However, even if a value is too complex, in some cases you may use attributes. Let's review the following blocks:

Block 1
```
<Rectangle Width="100" Height="50" Fill="Red"></Rectangle>
```

Block 2
```
<Rectangle Width="100" Height="50">
    <Rectangle.Fill>
        <SolidColorBrush Color="Red" />
    </Rectangle.Fill>
</Rectangle>
```

This code assigns the **Fill** property for a rectangle. This property is very complex and can be assigned to an object of **SolidColorBrush** type. The second block helps us to understand all used types and their properties. In the first block, we used an easier way to assign the **Fill** property, owing to the attributes and a simple string. This is possible because of converters that are available for that property. In the case of data binding, you can create your own converters, which convert objects in memory to objects that can be assigned to control properties. For example, the following class allows you to convert a Boolean value to a **Visibility** enumeration type:

```
public sealed class BooleanToVisibilityConverter :
    IValueConverter
{
    public object Convert(object value, Type targetType,
        object parameter, string language)
    {
        return (value is bool && (bool)value) ?
            Visibility.Visible : Visibility.Collapsed;
    }

    public object ConvertBack(object value,
        Type targetType, object parameter, string language)
    {
        return value is Visibility && (Visibility)value ==
            Visibility.Visible;
    }
}
```

If you create your own control, you will be able to use attributes to define your own properties that accept string values. We will discuss this later in this book.

Let's look at two equivalent blocks of code:

Block 1
```
<TextBlock>
    Hello
</TextBlock>
```

Block 2
```
<TextBlock Text="Hello"></TextBlock>
```

You can see that in the first block, the **Text** property was assigned implicitly. This is possible because of the **ContentPropertyAttribute** attribute, which allows you to define a special content property for the control. Of course, each control may have just one content property, and in the case of **TextBlock** control, it is the **Text** property, but in the case of **Canvas**, it is the **Children** property.

You can visit MSDN to find out which content property was defined. In the case of **Canvas**, we need to check the base class **Panel** to review all attributes there.

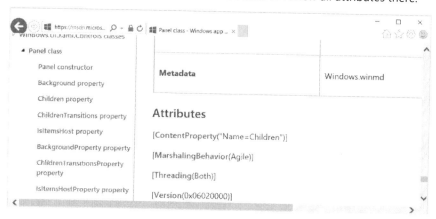

Additionally, you can use ildasm and review metadata in the winmd files. This approach is much better for third-party components.

At the end of this section, I want to show you how to define collections using XAML. Let's look at the following code:

```
<Rectangle Width="100" Height="50">
    <Rectangle.Fill>
        <LinearGradientBrush>
            <LinearGradientBrush.GradientStops>
                <GradientStopCollection>
                    <GradientStop Offset="0.0" Color="Red" />
                    <GradientStop Offset="1.0" Color="Green" />
                </GradientStopCollection>
            </LinearGradientBrush.GradientStops>
        </LinearGradientBrush>
    </Rectangle.Fill>
```

```
</Rectangle>
```

This code allows you to define a gradient brush for the rectangle. As you can see, **LinearGradientBrush** is a very complex object. It is not possible to define the **Fill** property using a simple string, because to define a gradient, you need to create a collection of **GradientStop** objects. But we can simplify this code.

First, note that **GradientStops** is a content property of the **LinearGradientBrush** object. So we can remove at least two lines in our XAML:

```
<Rectangle Width="100" Height="50">
    <Rectangle.Fill>
        <LinearGradientBrush>
            <GradientStopCollection>
                <GradientStop Offset="0.0" Color="Red" />
                <GradientStop Offset="1.0" Color="Green" />
            </GradientStopCollection>
        </LinearGradientBrush>
    </Rectangle.Fill>
</Rectangle>
```

Additionally, the XAML analyzer is smart enough to identify that **GradientStops** is a collection of **GradientStop** elements. We can modify our code in the following way:

```
<Rectangle Width="100" Height="50">
    <Rectangle.Fill>
        <LinearGradientBrush>
            <GradientStop Offset="0.0" Color="Red" />
            <GradientStop Offset="1.0" Color="Green" />
        </LinearGradientBrush>
    </Rectangle.Fill>
</Rectangle>
```

Even though this block, and the previous one, generate the same rectangle, these blocks are completely different. In the first block, we created the **GradientStopCollection** explicitly. It means we asked to construct a separate object in memory and assigned this object to the **GradientStops** property of our **LinearGradientBrush** object. We even could declare a name for **GradientStopCollection** and get access to this collection from C# code. The second block does not declare a **GradientStopCollection** object at all. Instead, it uses an existing empty collection that had already been created inside **LinearGradientBrush** and adds new members to it using the **Add** method.

In many cases we can initialize collections using the second approach only. For example, the following code will not work:

```
<StackPanel x:Name="LayoutRoot" Background="White">
    <StackPanel.Children>
        <UIElementCollection>
            <Button Width="100" Height="50"></Button>
        </UIElementCollection>
    </StackPanel.Children>
</StackPanel>
```

This code does not work because the **Children** property of the **Panel** class does not have a public **set** setter. There is no way to create a new collection of elements and assign it to the **Children** property. But developers can use the **Add** method (from ICollection) to add new elements to the existing collection. So the second approach will work fine:

```
<StackPanel x:Name="LayoutRoot" Background="White">
    <StackPanel.Children>
        <Button Width="100" Height="50"></Button>
    </StackPanel.Children>
</StackPanel>
```

Of course, we can simplify this code owing to content property there:

```
<StackPanel x:Name="LayoutRoot" Background="White">
    <Button Width="100" Height="50"></Button>
</StackPanel>
```

Namespaces in XAML

For C# developers, namespace is a fundamental concept. Thanks to namespaces, developers may create logical containers that contain classes. For example, the **Button** class is found in the **Windows.UI.Xaml.Controls** namespace together with other classes that define controls for developing user interfaces. The full name of the Button class is **Windows.UI.Xaml.Controls.Button**, but thanks to the **using** keyword, developers may declare namespaces in advance and avoid typing fully qualified names for classes.

XML also supports namespaces. However, there are two important distinctions from C# namespace support. First of all, you need to use URIs to declare namespaces. In some cases, it can be a web URI, but in the case of your own classes, it will be a **using** URI, as in C#. The second distinction is that you can declare only one default namespace. For all other namespaces, you can just declare a name, which you should use inside XAML to get access to your controls.

xmlns attributes are used to declare default or named namespaces. Usually xmlns is placed inside the root element of the document. For example, the following code declares namespace **my**:

```
xmlns:my="http://baydachnyy.com/schemas"
```

A default declaration of **Page** element usually contains five namespaces:

```
<Page
    x:Class="App33.MainPage"
    xmlns="http://schemas.microsoft.com/
        winfx/2006/xaml/presentation"
    xmlns:x="http://schemas.microsoft.com/
        winfx/2006/xaml"
    xmlns:local="using:App33"
    xmlns:d="http://schemas.microsoft.com/
        expression/blend/2008"
    xmlns:mc="http://schemas.openxmlformats.org/
        markup-compatibility/2006"
    mc:Ignorable="d">
```

The first two namespaces you can find in any WPF, Silverlight, or Windows Runtime applications. They allow developers to use standard controls and elements to declare UI. Because standard elements are widely used, the first namespace is declared as default.

The third namespace uses the **using** protocol to add access to classes. You can create them inside the default namespace of your application. Usually this is not needed, because developers like to create additional namespaces inside, but you can use this code as a reference.

The last two namespaces allow you to use objects and attributes that will affect the interface in design mode only. It is very valuable when you are using data binding but also want to see what the interface looks like in design mode.

Code-Behind Pages and Event Handlers

OK, we just finished with basic syntax of XAML, and it is time to see how to integrate XAML and C#. Let's open any XAML page and check the **Page** element there:

```
<Page
    x:Class="App33.MainPage"
    xmlns="http://schemas.microsoft.com/
        winfx/2006/xaml/presentation"
    xmlns:x="http://schemas.microsoft.com/
```

```
        winfx/2006/xaml"
   xmlns:local="using:App33"
   xmlns:d="http://schemas.microsoft.com/
        expression/blend/2008"
   xmlns:mc="http://schemas.openxmlformats.org/
        markup-compatibility/2006"
   mc:Ignorable="d">
```

The **Page** element contains an **x:Class** attribute used to declare a code-behind class for our **Page**. If your page is in a **MainPage.xaml** file, you can find the code-behind class inside **MainPage.xaml.cs**. So, thanks to the **x:Class** attribute XAML file, you can use any event handlers from a C# file. Of course, it's not enough, because we need a way to gain access to XAML from C# as well. Let's add a button to the page:

```
<Button Name="myButton" Width="100"
   Height="50">Hello</Button>
```

Once you add a button, you can open MainPage.xaml.cs and look inside. The code looks like this:

```
public sealed partial class MainPage : Page
{
    public MainPage()
    {
        InitializeComponent();
    }
}
```

Note that the class was defined as **partial** and contains a call to the **InitializeComponent** method. At the same time, you don't see any evidence of myButton button, but if you try to make changes to the button variable, you will see that Visual Studio provides the name of this variable in the IntelliSense system and allows you to work with it. Visual Studio tracks all changes in XAML and makes appropriate changes in the code-behind files.

Expand the **MainPage** class in Solution Explorer.

The **MainPage** class contains methods and data fields, including myButton and **InitializeComponent**.

If you click myButton, Visual Studio will navigate to **MainPage.g.i.cs**, which is another part of the **MainPage** class:

```
partial class MainPage :
global::Windows.UI.Xaml.Controls.Page
{

[global::System.CodeDom.Compiler.GeneratedCodeAttribute(
        "Microsoft.Windows.UI.Xaml.Build.Tasks",
        "14.0.0.0")]
    private global::Windows.UI.Xaml.Controls.Button
        myButton;
[global::System.CodeDom.Compiler.GeneratedCodeAttribute(
        "Microsoft.Windows.UI.Xaml.Build.Tasks",
        "14.0.0.0")]
    private bool _contentLoaded;

[global::System.CodeDom.Compiler.GeneratedCodeAttribute(
        "Microsoft.Windows.UI.Xaml.Build.Tasks",
        "14.0.0.0")]
[global::System.Diagnostics.DebuggerNonUserCodeAttribute()]
    public void InitializeComponent()
    {
        if (_contentLoaded)
            return;
        _contentLoaded = true;
        global::System.Uri resourceLocator =
            new global::System.Uri(
                "ms-appx:///MainPage.xaml");
        global::Windows.UI.Xaml.Application.LoadComponent(
```

```
        this, resourceLocator,
        global::Windows.UI.Xaml.Controls.Primitives.
          ComponentResourceLocation.Application);
  }
}
```

The myButton field is there, as well as the **LoadComponent** method, which helps build the XAML logical tree.

How do we declare event handlers in XAML? We use attributes to define an event and a value as the name of the method that will handle the event.

```
<Grid Background=
    "{ThemeResource ApplicationPageBackgroundThemeBrush}">
    <Button Name="myButton" Width="100"
        Height="50" Click="myButton_Click">Hello</Button>
</Grid>
```

If you have already defined an event handler in C# code, Visual Studio IntelliSense will select the method, filtering out all methods requiring prototypes. Alternatively, you can ask Visual Studio to create a new one and use **Peek Definition** or **Go To Definition** to navigate to the method in the **cs** file.

You can use the Properties window to review all available events and event handlers—just use the Event tab there:

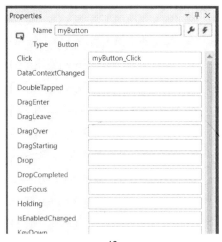

Finally, if you double-click the button in the design window, Visual Studio will generate an event handler for the Click event as well.

Markup Extensions

We already know how to declare the base interface, how to use event handlers in XAML from C#, and how to get access in C# to XAML elements, but there are still many scenarios that cannot be implemented using existing features of XML.

XAML extends XML and introduces markup extensions. The main purpose of markup extensions is to allow additional connections between C# objects and XAML, as well as between different elements in XAML. Therefore, thanks to markup extensions, you can assign attribute values in a nonstandard way.

The following XAML extensions are available for Windows 10 developers:

- **Binding:** Binds XAML properties to any objects in run time. You can use objects for reference that you created in memory or XAML objects.

- **StaticResource:** With this extension, you can use styles, templates, and objects defined in resources.

- **TemplateBinding:** Associates controls with templates defined in resources.

- **ThemeResource:** Similar to **StaticResource** but implements additional logic to select a resource based on the current theme.

- **RelativeSource:** Defines a source for binding in terms of a relative relationship.

- **x:Bind:** A new extension for a static binding that increases performance of applications. It can be used if you have strong-typed objects.

- **CustomResource:** Use this extension if you have your own storage for resources and want to implement custom logic.

In the following example, we use the **StaticResource** markup extension to apply btnStyle style from page resources to the myButton button:

```
<Page.Resources>
    <Style x:Name="btnStyle" TargetType="Button">
        <Setter Property="Background" Value="Green">
        </Setter>
    </Style>
</Page.Resources>
```

```
<Grid x:Name="LayoutRoot" Background="White">
    <Button Name="myButton" Width="100" Height="50"
        Style="{StaticResource btnStyle}" Content="Hello">
    </Button>
</Grid>
```

In the next piece of code, we work with the **x:Bind** markup extension. We bind the **Width** property of the **TextBox** control to the **Value** property of the **Slider** control.

```
<StackPanel x:Name="LayoutRoot" >
    <Slider Name="sld1" Width="300" Height="50"
        Minimum="100" Maximum="200" Value="10">
    </Slider>
    <TextBox Text="Hello"
        Width="{x:Bind sld1.Value, Mode=TwoWay}">
    </TextBox>
</StackPanel>
```

We will discuss all existing markup extensions in upcoming chapters in more detail.

Dependency Properties

Let's look at the following code:

```
<Canvas>
    <Button Content="Hello"
        Canvas.Top="60" Canvas.Left="120"
        Width="110" Height="40" Name="button1" />
</Canvas>
```

Note the **Canvas.Top** and **Canvas.Left** attributes of the **Button** element. They are not related to the **Button** class at all. Frankly speaking, **Button** should not know anything about possible containers. So how can one define two properties related to **Canvas**? This is possible owing to the **DependencyObject** and **DependencyProperty** classes. The first one brings **SetValue** and **GetValue** methods that support **DependencyProperty** objects as parameters. The main idea of these methods is to maintain a dynamic list of **DependencyProperty** objects inside any user control, and use this list to define new elements in the list like Canvas.Top. You can also assign dependency properties from C# code directly:

```
button1.SetValue(Canvas.TopProperty, 60)
```

Once **Canvas** places the button in the right position, it will use the **GetValue** method to extract the value for the **Top** and **Left** properties. We will create several dependency properties once we discuss custom user controls.

We have reviewed all basic features of XAML, and it is time to start using XAML to build real interfaces. In the upcoming chapters we will discuss containers and basic user controls. You will have more opportunities to practice with XAML.

This page intentionally left blank

Chapter 3

Layouts

Let's start our review of existing user controls with a special control type that allows you to create layouts. It is a very important set of controls because it defines how all other controls will be placed and how the interface of your application will look. In fact, developers start each page with layout controls.

You already know that all XAML pages contain a **Page** root element. The Page class is inherited from **UserControl**, which implements a **Content** property. Thanks to the **Content** property, you can place any **UIElement** inside a page, but you cannot place more than one element directly. That's why you need to start with a container, which will contain all other controls of the page and other containers.

It's almost impossible to design an interface inside only one container or using containers of the same type. So you need to understand all of them, and what is more important, you need to understand what you are going to implement. Therefore, it's very important to design all pages before you start developing anything.

In this chapter we will discuss the most common containers that are located in the **Windows.UI.Xaml.Controls** namespace and are inherited from the Page class: **Canvas**, **StackPanel**, **Grid**, and **RelativePanel**.

Canvas

Canvas is the "worst" layout container because it allows you to place inner controls using absolute positions inside the container. It violates the modern concept of Windows 10 applications—adaptive interface. If you freeze the positions of user controls, it's very hard to change something if the user changes the window size or switches his or her device from horizontal to vertical mode.

Nevertheless, you can find several scenarios when this container is useful. For example, if you develop a simple game where positions of all elements are critical, you can use **Canvas** together with **Viewbox**. Using **Canvas** you can draw anything, but using **Viewbox** you can resize the **Canvas** according to the window size.

Below you can see an example of how to declare a **Canvas** control and a button inside. To place inner elements in the right positions inside **Canvas**, you can use the **Canvas.Top** and **Canvas.Left** properties.

```
<Canvas>
    <Button Content="Hello" Canvas.Top="100"
       Canvas.Left="100">
```

```
    </Button>
</Canvas>
```

Once again, don't use this container unless you have a particular need.

StackPanel

One of the simplest layout controls is **StackPanel**. It places all user controls inside in one row or in one column. Let's look at the following code, which shows several buttons inside:

```
<StackPanel>
    <Button Content="Button 1"></Button>
    <Button Content="Button 2"></Button>
    <Button Content="Button 3"></Button>
    <Button Content="Button 4"></Button>
</StackPanel>
```

If you run this code, the StackPanel will show four buttons placed in one column.

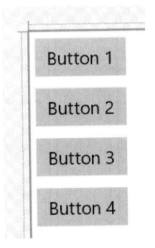

This is the default orientation for the **StackPanel** control. Despite the fact that **StackPanel** fills all space, the buttons do not use up all this space, but you can easily align buttons to the **StackPanel** width using the **HorizontalAlignment** property:

```
<StackPanel>
    <Button Content="Button 1"
      HorizontalAlignment="Stretch"></Button>
    <Button Content="Button 2"
      HorizontalAlignment="Stretch"></Button>
```

49

```
    <Button Content="Button 3"
       HorizontalAlignment="Stretch"></Button>
    <Button Content="Button 4"
       HorizontalAlignment="Stretch"></Button>
</StackPanel>
```

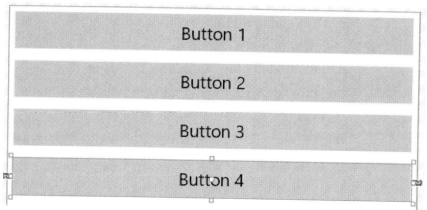

The **Stretch** value indicates that the button should fill all available space inside the container. If a **StackPanel** has a horizontal orientation, you can use the **VerticalAlignment** property and the **Stretch** value. Additionally, you can use values such as **Center**, **Right**, and **Left** for the **HorizontalAlignment** property and **Top**, **Bottom**, and **Center** for **VerticalAlignment**.

If you want to change the placement of user controls inside **StackPanel**, you can use the **Orientation** property:

```
<StackPanel Orientation="Horizontal">
    <Button Content="Button 1"></Button>
    <Button Content="Button 2"></Button>
    <Button Content="Button 3"></Button>
    <Button Content="Button 4"></Button>
</StackPanel>
```

Common Properties and Panel Class

When we worked with **StackPanel**, we used two properties of the **Button** class: **HorizontalAlignment** and **VerticalAlignment**. These two properties cannot satisfy all needs. But the common user controls additionally contains a lot of different properties that developers can use to align the controls within containers. Before we review these properties, let's open the **Panel** class in the Object Browser in Visual Studio:

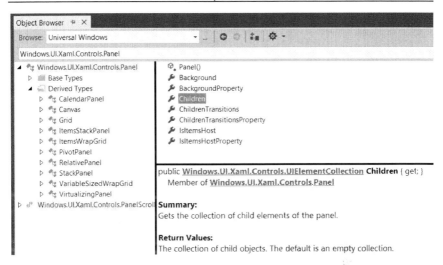

You can see that all classes for standard containers such as **StackPanel**, **Canvas**, **Grid**, and **RelativePanel** are inherited from the **Panel** class. This class has a special property called **Children**. We already mentioned that when developers place controls into a container, it affects the **Children** collection.

Of course, you can use the **Children** collection to add controls to a container from C#. Let's create an empty **StackPanel**:

```
<StackPanel Name="myPanel" />
```

We used the **Name** property to get access to the panel from C#. So to add a button from C#, you can modify the existing constructor for the main page of the application:

```
public MainPage()
{
    this.InitializeComponent();
    myPanel.Children.Add(new Button()
        { Content = "Hello" });
}
```

If you run this code, you can see that the panel contains the button with properties by default.

Let's look at the type of the **Children** property. It's a collection that can contain the **UIElement** objects inside. It's time to open the Object Browser once again:

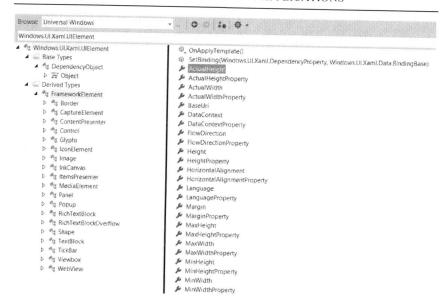

Thanks to the Object Browser, we know that **UIElement** has a **DependencyObject** as its base class. It's very important that the **DependencyObject** doesn't contain anything important for the layout. **UIElement** contains lots of properties, but they don't affect layout either. You can select just the **Visibility** property, which allows you to remove a control from the visual XAML tree if **Visibility** is **Collapsed**. You can see that the **UIElement** has just one derived type: **FrameworkElement**. So if we work with standard controls, we can guarantee that all controls have **FrameworkElement** in the hierarchy and all these controls have the same properties as **FrameworkElement**. The most important properties for layout are as follows:

- **Margin:** Allows you to define the space between a control and content outside the control. You can define **Margin** using just one number. In this case the distance will be the same between any side of the control and external control. You can define the space for each side. You can define **Margin** using the property editor in Visual Studio or in the XAML itself:

```
<Button Margin="10" Content="Hello"></Button>
<Button Margin="10,5,20,5" Content="Hello"></Button>
```

- **MinWidth:** Defines the minimum width of a control.

- **MinHeight:** Defines the minimum height of a control.

- **MaxWidth:** Defines the maximum width of a control.

- **MaxHeight:** Defines the maximum height of a control.

You may use the **Width** and **Height** properties as well, but it is best to avoid them if you can.

Additionally, if you check the **StackPanel**, **Grid**, and **RelativePanel** classes, you can find the **Padding** property there. This property allows you to set up the distance between the border of a panel and the content inside. Since the **Padding** property has different implementations for different containers, and some containers, such as **Canvas**, don't have **Padding** at all, Microsoft didn't include it in the **Panel** class.

Grid

The next container is **Grid**, which is the most powerful user control that allows building very complex layouts. Thanks to **Grid**, developers can divide all available space into cells, defining the number of rows and columns. Once columns and rows are declared, you can place other user controls inside, using rows and columns like dependency properties for **Grid**. Below you can find the code that shows you how to define columns and rows and place user controls inside:

```
<Grid>
    <Grid.RowDefinitions>
        <RowDefinition></RowDefinition>
        <RowDefinition></RowDefinition>
    </Grid.RowDefinitions>
    <Grid.ColumnDefinitions>
        <ColumnDefinition></ColumnDefinition>
        <ColumnDefinition></ColumnDefinition>
        <ColumnDefinition></ColumnDefinition>
    </Grid.ColumnDefinitions>
    <Button Content="Button 1" Grid.Row="0" Grid.Column="0"
        HorizontalAlignment="Stretch"
        VerticalAlignment="Stretch"></Button>
    <Button Content="Button 2" Grid.Row="0" Grid.Column="1"
        HorizontalAlignment="Stretch"
        VerticalAlignment="Stretch"></Button>
    <Button Content="Button 3" Grid.Row="1" Grid.Column="2"
        HorizontalAlignment="Stretch"
        VerticalAlignment="Stretch">
    </Button>
</Grid>
```

In this example we defined two rows and three columns and placed three buttons inside:

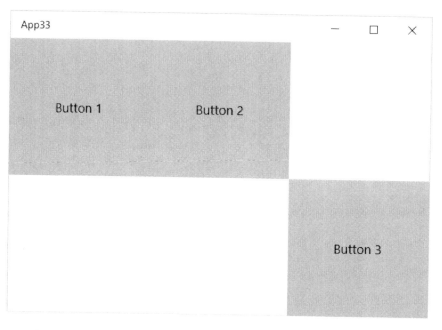

By default, Grid divides all available space equally between all rows and columns inside, but you can define the **Width** and **Height** properties for columns and rows accordingly. There are several ways to do this:

- Developers can declare sizes of columns and rows in effective pixels. You can use this approach to define headers, footers, or any cells that contain controls with fixed width and height.

- A better way to declare sizes of columns and rows, using adaptive interfaces, is using the **Auto** value or proportions. In the case of **Auto** value, **Grid** will provide as much space as needed for the controls inside. Let's look at the following example:

```
<Grid >
    <Grid.RowDefinitions>
        <RowDefinition Height="Auto">
        </RowDefinition>
        <RowDefinition Height="Auto">
        </RowDefinition>
    </Grid.RowDefinitions>
    <Grid.ColumnDefinitions>
```

```
        <ColumnDefinition Width="Auto">
        </ColumnDefinition>
        <ColumnDefinition Width="Auto">
        </ColumnDefinition>
         <ColumnDefinition Width="Auto">
        </ColumnDefinition>
    </Grid.ColumnDefinitions>
    <Button Content="Button 1" Grid.Row="0"
        Grid.Column="0"
        HorizontalAlignment="Stretch"
        VerticalAlignment="Stretch"></Button>
    <Button Content="Button 2" Grid.Row="0"
        Grid.Column="1"
        HorizontalAlignment="Stretch"
        VerticalAlignment="Stretch"></Button>
    <Button Content="Button 3" Grid.Row="1"
        Grid.Column="2"
        HorizontalAlignment="Stretch"
        VerticalAlignment="Stretch"></Button>
</Grid>
```

You can see that our interface is much more compact right now and the **HorizontalAlignment** and **VerticalAlignment** properties don't work at all, because **Grid** sets the space for buttons based on their default width and height.

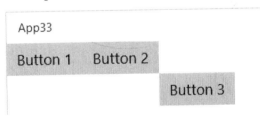

- In the case of proportional values, you can use the following example as a reference:

```
<Grid Background=
    "{StaticResource ApplicationPageBackgroundBrush}">
    <Grid.RowDefinitions>
        <RowDefinition Height="*"></RowDefinition>
        <RowDefinition Height="2*"></RowDefinition>
    </Grid.RowDefinitions>
    <Grid.ColumnDefinitions>
        <ColumnDefinition
            Width="*"></ColumnDefinition>
```

```
            <ColumnDefinition
                Width="2*"></ColumnDefinition>
            <ColumnDefinition
                Width="2*"></ColumnDefinition>
        </Grid.ColumnDefinitions>
        <Button Content="Button 1" Grid.Row="0"
            Grid.Column="0"></Button>
        <Button Content="Button 2" Grid.Row="0"
            Grid.Column="1"></Button>
        <Button Content="Button 3" Grid.Row="1"
            Grid.Column="2"></Button>
</Grid>
```

In this example Grid divides all available space for rows into three parts; one of these parts will be assigned to the first row, and two parts to the second one. In the case of columns, Grid divides all space into five parts: one part for the first row, and two parts for the second and third rows.

Let's look at the code below:

```
<Grid>
    <Grid.RowDefinitions>
        <RowDefinition Height="Auto"></RowDefinition>
        <RowDefinition Height="Auto"></RowDefinition>
        <RowDefinition Height="Auto"></RowDefinition>
        <RowDefinition Height="Auto"></RowDefinition>
        <RowDefinition Height="Auto"></RowDefinition>
    </Grid.RowDefinitions>
    <Grid.ColumnDefinitions>
        <ColumnDefinition Width="Auto"></ColumnDefinition>
        <ColumnDefinition Width="Auto"></ColumnDefinition>
    </Grid.ColumnDefinitions>
    <TextBlock Text="Employee" Grid.Row="0" Grid.Column="0"
        Grid.ColumnSpan="2" HorizontalAlignment="Center"
        FontSize="16" FontWeight="Bold" Margin="5">
    </TextBlock>
    <TextBlock Text="First Name:" Grid.Row="1"
        Grid.Column="0" Margin="5"></TextBlock>
    <TextBox Grid.Column="1" Grid.Row="1" MinWidth="100"
        Margin="5"></TextBox>
    <TextBlock Text="Last Name:" Grid.Row="2"
        Grid.Column="0"
        Margin="5"></TextBlock>
    <TextBox Grid.Column="1" Grid.Row="2" MinWidth="100"
        Margin="5"></TextBox>
    <TextBlock Text="EMail:" Grid.Row="3" Grid.Column="0"
```

```
    Margin="5"></TextBlock>
  <TextBox Grid.Column="1" Grid.Row="3" MinWidth="100"
    Margin="5"></TextBox>
  <Button Grid.Column="0" Grid.Row="4"
    Grid.ColumnSpan="2"
    Content="Send" Margin="5"
    HorizontalAlignment="Center">
  </Button>
</Grid>
```

In this code we used the **ColumnSpan** property, which allowed us to merge two columns in the row where user control is located. Similarly, we can use the **RowSpan** property to merge rows. If you run this code, you will see the following form:

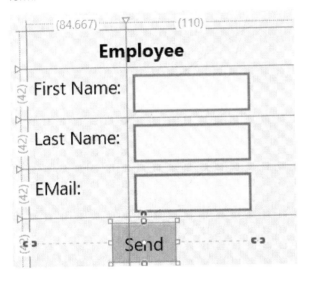

RelativePanel

Last, but not least, in layout controls is the **RelativePanel**. This is a new user control that was introduced in Windows 10 and is very useful for adaptive interfaces. For better understanding of the control, let's look at the following example:

```
<Grid>
  <Grid.RowDefinitions>
    <RowDefinition Height="Auto"></RowDefinition>
    <RowDefinition Height="*"></RowDefinition>
  </Grid.RowDefinitions>
  <Grid.ColumnDefinitions>
```

```
    <ColumnDefinition Width="Auto"></ColumnDefinition>
    <ColumnDefinition Width="*"></ColumnDefinition>
  </Grid.ColumnDefinitions>
  <TextBlock Text="This is a header" Grid.ColumnSpan="2"
    Style="{ThemeResource HeaderTextBlockStyle}">
  </TextBlock>
  <Image MaxWidth="800" Grid.Row="1"
    Source="Assets\drone.jpg" VerticalAlignment="Top">
  </Image>
  <TextBlock Text="This is a text about drones."
    Margin="10,0,10,0"
    TextWrapping="Wrap" Grid.Column="1" Grid.Row="1">
  </TextBlock>
</Grid>
```

In this example I implemented a simple layout, which uses the Grid element to place two text blocks and an image. So if you run this code, you can see something like this:

But there is a problem: Windows 10 allows you to change the size of windows, and additionally it allows you to run this application on phones. So it's easy to see that you will not have enough space to display the image and the text if you have a smaller window. Because I want to create a universal interface, I want change my layout dynamically if I don't have enough space. To do that, I simply need to place the text below the image, and for this purpose the best solution is to use the **VisualStateManager** (more information about this control can be found in next chapters). It allows you to change the interface during run time, based on a set of triggers or by request from C# code. I used the **Grid** container, which has two columns and two rows, and for a smaller display I need a grid with one column and three rows, which is virtually impossible to manage in **VisualStateManager**, even for my example. Real interfaces are much more complex. That's why when developers build universal applications for Windows 8.1, they duplicate some parts of the interface and simply work with the **Visibility** property inside **VisualStateManager**.

Starting with Windows 10, developers have a chance to use a new container, which allows you to avoid problems with **Grid**—it is the **RelativePanel**. Let's see the same example inside the **RelativePanel** control.

```
<RelativePanel >
    <TextBlock Text="This is a header" Name="header"
        Style="{ThemeResource HeaderTextBlockStyle}">
    </TextBlock>
    <Image Name="image" MaxWidth="800"
        RelativePanel.Below="header"
        Source="Assets\drone.jpg"></Image>
    <TextBlock Text="This is a text about drones."
        Margin="10,0,10,0"
        TextWrapping="Wrap"
        RelativePanel.AlignTopWith="image"
        RelativePanel.RightOf="image" Name="text">
    </TextBlock>
</RelativePanel>
```

You can see that in the case of **RelativePanel**, you can declare the position of inner controls using dependency properties. Because they are just properties, it is easy to reformat the layout using them in **VisualStateManager**. For example, you can use the following code to show the same interface in one row:

```
<VisualStateManager.VisualStateGroups>
    <VisualStateGroup>
        <VisualState x:Name="Normal">
            <VisualState.StateTriggers>
                <AdaptiveTrigger MinWindowWidth="900">
                </AdaptiveTrigger>
            </VisualState.StateTriggers>
        </VisualState>
        <VisualState x:Name="Mobile">
            <VisualState.Setters>
                <Setter Value=""
                    Target="text.(RelativePanel.AlignTopWith)">
                </Setter>
```

```
          <Setter Value="image"
           Target="text.(RelativePanel.Below)">
          </Setter>
          <Setter Value=""
           Target="text.(RelativePanel.RightOf)">
          </Setter>
          <Setter Value="0,10,0,10"
           Target="text.Margin">
          </Setter>
        </VisualState.Setters>
        <VisualState.StateTriggers>
          <AdaptiveTrigger MinWindowWidth="0">
          </AdaptiveTrigger>
        </VisualState.StateTriggers>
      </VisualState>
    </VisualStateGroup>
</VisualStateManager.VisualStateGroups>
```

Once the window is less than 900 pixels, the text is moved below the image. Pay careful attention to how to declare dependency properties in the **Target** attribute.

According to my experience, **RelativePanel** is now the most popular control for creating universal interface. Let's use this powerful control.

ScrollViewer

The next control is not a layout control, but I still decided to include it in this chapter because otherwise the story about layout controls would not be complete. To see how **ScrollViewer** works, just place lots of common controls inside **StackPanel**:

```
<StackPanel Orientation="Horizontal">
    <Button Content="Hello"></Button>
    . . . . .
</StackPanel>
```

If you add enough user controls, you can see that the **StackPanel** doesn't have a scroll bar, and some of the controls are placed outside the window without any ability to be used. To add a scroll bar, we simply need to place our **StackPanel** inside **ScrollViewer**:

```
<ScrollViewer HorizontalScrollMode="Enabled"
    HorizontalScrollBarVisibility="Auto"
    VerticalScrollBarVisibility="Hidden">
    <StackPanel Orientation="Horizontal">
```

```
   <Button Content="Hello"></Button>
   .  .  .  .  .
   </StackPanel>
</ScrollViewer>
```

The **ScrollViewer** user control is not just a scroll bar. With this control, you can apply scale functionality to your content. Here are several properties that can help you implement scaling:

- **ZoomMode:** activates scaling functionality,

- **MaxZoomFactor:** allows you to set up maximum zoom level,

- **MinZoomFactor:** allows you to set up minimum zoom level, and

- **ZoomSnapPoints:** allows you to set up snap points if you want to implement some scaling steps (1x, 1.5x, 2.0x, etc.).

OK. Let's finish with layouts and get an overview of common user controls.

This page intentionally left blank

Chapter 4

Common User Controls

Some Words about Hierarchy

Before we begin to work with common controls, let's take a look at the most important base classes and understand the hierarchy there. Of course, it's better to open Object Browser in Visual Studio and check the full hierarchy for any user control, so I would recommend using this approach later, but for now let's look at the image below:

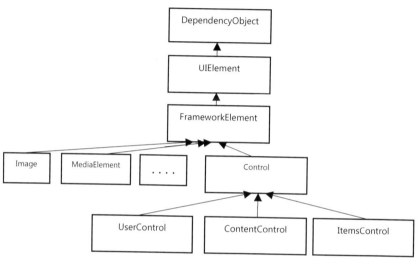

I didn't show the **System.Object** class to save some space, but it should be clear that all classes in C#/.NET Framework have this class as a base class at the top of the hierarchy.

The first important class on our image is **DependencyObject**. This class doesn't contain any specific properties for all other controls, but thanks to this class, all controls in hierarchy may contain dependency properties. Later, when we discuss our own user controls, we will see the important features that developers can implement thanks to the **DependencyObject** class.

The next class is **UIElement**, which declares events, properties, and methods related to basic input, including drag-and-drop functionality, basic pointer and keyboard events, and infrastructure for additional event handlers. You will not use this class directly. Even among standard classes in the Universal Windows Platform, you can find one class only, the **FrameworkElement** class, which has **UIElement** as its base class. Additionally, **UIElement** declares several common properties, such as **Opacity** and **Visibility**, but almost all common properties are defined in **FrameworkElement** class.

Therefore, the next class in the hierarchy is **FrameworkElement**. Thanks to this class all user controls support data binding, styles, and resources. Additionally, you can find some common properties such as **Width**, **Height**, **VerticalAlignment**, and **HorizontalAlignment**. So **FrameworkElement** has all needed elements to be in the XAML visual tree. And you can see that some user controls are inherited from **FrameworkElement** directly. For example, you can find user controls such as **InkCanvas**, **Image**, **TextBlock**, **WebView**, and **Panel**. Usually these controls display specific content and in some cases don't even have any visual representation. If a user control is inherited from **FrameworkElement** directly, you will not be able to change the control template, and it doesn't support different states.

The next control in the hierarchy is **Control**. Thanks to this class, user controls can support states and templates. Templates define the look and feel for user controls in XAML, they are separated from the C# code. It allows you to change the visual representation of any user control that supports templates (inherited from **Control**). User controls that are inherited from **Control** can be in focus or disabled, allowing you to create a fully new look and feel and support different states. We will discuss templates in a separate chapter, where I am going to show you how to create "almost" new controls just by changing templates without coding in C# at all.

The **Control** class is a base class for lots of different controls, such as **Hub**, **TextBox**, and **TimePicker**, but there are three more classes that are inherited from the **Control** class and extend its functionality: **UserControl**, **ContentControl**, and **ItemsControl**. The first one we will use just to create our own composite controls, which are built based on the existing set of user controls. **ContentControl** class is the base class for all user controls that can contain a single piece of content. In this case you can use anything as content and apply your own template there. **ItemsControl** class is a base class for all user controls that work with collections. It allows you to define a template for the item, set up a container for items, and bind to collections.

Later we will look at some of the properties of user controls in more detail.

Buttons

All buttons in the Universal Windows Platform are inherited from the **ButtonBase** class, which is inherited from **ContentControl**. Here is a screenshot that I made using Object Browser in Visual Studio:

◢ ᵃ⅌ ContentControl
　　▷ ᵃ⅌ AppBar
　　◢ ᵃ⅌ ButtonBase
　　　　◢ ᵃ⅌ Button
　　　　　　▷ ᵃ⅌ AppBarButton
　　　　▷ ᵃ⅌ HyperlinkButton
　　　　▷ ᵃ⅌ RepeatButton
　　　　◢ ᵃ⅌ ToggleButton
　　　　　　▷ ᵃ⅌ AppBarToggleButton
　　　　　　▷ ᵃ⅌ CheckBox
　　　　　　▷ ᵃ⅌ RadioButton

You can see that there are eight different buttons:

- **Button:** This is a classic button. Usually it looks like a rectangle with text box inside, however you can change the template for the button to your own liking. The most popular event here is **Click**.

- **AppBarButton:** A good example of how to change the look and feel of the classic button using templates and extend some functionality. **AppBarButton** is the same as the classic button, but it supports some additional properties and has the look and feel according to the design guidelines for UWP applications.

- **HyperlinkButton:** This button looks like a usual hyperlink in the browser (by default). Usually you will use it to navigate to other pages inside your application.

- **RepeatButton:** It's the same button, but if a user pushes it, the button can send **Click** events while it is being pushed. You can define an interval between **Click** events in milliseconds.

- **ToggleButton:** This is a button that has two states: Checked and Unchecked. Each click moves the button from one state to another.

- **AppBarToggleButton:** This control is similar to **ToggleButton** but has styles that are recommended for application-bar buttons.

- **CheckBox:** This button implements the simplest flag, which can show whether the button is checked. In fact, this button is the same as **ToggleButton**, but it uses a different template. **ToggleButton** and **CheckBox** can support a third state as well. This is an undefined state and can be set from the code only. It's needed if we want to make sure that a user makes a selection and does not miss the button.

- **RadioButton:** This control has two states as well, but it was designed to work together with other **RadioButton** objects. You can define as many controls in the group as you need and implement a single selection for the whole group without coding.

Additionally, I want to draw your attention to the **ToggleSwitch** control, which is not inherited from **ButtonBase**, but in fact is a button as well. With **ToggleSwitch**, you can implement **CheckBox** functionality, but using text, and the selector looks very unique. Let's look at the following example:

```
<ToggleSwitch OffContent="No" OnContent="Yes" />
```

The button shows a Yes or No message based on the state of the switch:

 Yes

Let's look at some examples related to buttons. In the next piece of code, I defined several RadioButton controls in a group to make a single choice:

```
<StackPanel>
    <RadioButton Content="Choice 1" IsChecked="True"
        GroupName="Group 1" Margin="5">
    </RadioButton>
    <RadioButton Content="Choice 1" IsChecked="False"
        GroupName="Group 1" Margin="5">
    </RadioButton>
    <RadioButton Content="Choice 1" IsChecked="False"
        GroupName="Group 1" Margin="5">
    </RadioButton>
    <RadioButton Content="Choice 1" IsChecked="False"
        GroupName="Group 1" Margin="5">
    </RadioButton>
</StackPanel>
```

Running this example, you can see the following group of controls:

Because all buttons, except **ToggleSwitch**, are inherited from **ContentControl**, they support any template for the **Content** property. Let's look at the code:

```
<Button Content="Hello">
    <Button.ContentTemplate>
        <DataTemplate>
            <Grid>
                <Ellipse Width="100" Height="50" Fill="Red" />
                <TextBlock Text="{Binding}"
                    HorizontalAlignment="Center"
                    VerticalAlignment="Center" />
            </Grid>
        </DataTemplate>
    </Button.ContentTemplate>
</Button>
```

In this example we use our own template using the **ContentTemplate** property. This property requires an object of the **DataTemplate** class, which we will use very often. Inside **DataTemplate** we can place just one control, but we can use a container and place anything else inside that container. In our case we used **Grid** and placed **Ellipse** and **TextBlock** inside the **Grid**. Note that we implemented a template but the button still has **Content** property that can be assigned outside template. To use this property, I use the **Binding** markup extension. That syntax allows you to use a **Content** property as the source for the **Text** property of the **TextBox** control. After running this code, you can see the following button:

Working with Text

Let's start our overview with the most common text-editing user control, **TextBox**. This control, just like all other text-editing controls, is inherited from the **Control** class and supports the **Template** property. If you visit msdn.microsoft.com, you even can find the template definition for this and other controls. Checking https://msdn.microsoft.com/en-us/library/windows/apps/xaml/jj710191.aspx, you can see that **TextBox** consists of **ContentPresenter**, **Border**, **ScrollViewer**, **ContentControl**, and even **Button**. Using **TextBox** you can allow users to edit plain text. Usually you can find this control in forms.

By default, **TextBox** will fill all available space inside a container, so you can use any of the available **FrameworkElement** properties to place it properly:

```
<TextBox Margin="10" HorizontalAlignment="Left"
   VerticalAlignment="Top" Width="150"></TextBox>
```

Running this code, you can see a typical text box:

If you start editing text, you can see a button at the end of the text box, which allows you to clear the text box all at once. That's why the button was included in the **TextBox** template. Try to enter more text, and you will see how **ScrollViewer** works, which is a part of **TextBox** template as well.

You can use the **TextBox** user control to edit more-complex text that contains several lines. In this case you need to use some properties. Let's list the most important properties:

- **AcceptsReturn:** This property allows you to make new lines inside the text.

- **IsReadOnly:** With this property, **TextBox** can display a text in read-only mode, without allowing the user to edit or enter it in the text box.

- **Header:** Allows you to assign a header. It can be plain text or something more complex based on **HeaderTemplate**.

- **InputScope:** Allows you to set up a default screen keyboard. For example, if **TextBox** should accept numbers, you can use Number as the **InputScope** value. Note that it's not a validator, and the user can switch the type of the keyboard in real time.

- **SelectedText:** Returns the selected text in the text box.

- **SelectionLength:** Returns the number of characters in the selection.

- **SelectionHighlightColor:** With this property you can define a brush that will be used for highlighting a selection.

- **SelectionStart:** Returns the position of the first character from the selection.

- **TextWrapping:** Allows you to define text behavior if a line of the text exceeds the width of the text box.

- **IsSpellCheckEnabled:** Allows the use of spell checker.

- **PlaceholderText:** Allows you to fill TextBox with a placeholder, which will be removed once the user start editing.

Let's see a short example with the **TextBox** user control:

```
<TextBox Margin="10" HorizontalAlignment="Left"
  AcceptsReturn="True" VerticalAlignment="Top"
  Height="150" Width="300" Header="Summary"></TextBox>
```

In this case we can enter several lines of text, and the text box has a header:

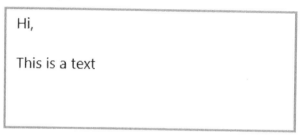

If you want to enter more text, you will see that you don't have a scroll bar to scroll the text quickly. To activate the scroll bar, you can use dependency properties and apply them to the internal **ScrollViewer** from the template.

```
<TextBox Margin="10"
  ScrollViewer.VerticalScrollBarVisibility="Auto"
  HorizontalAlignment="Left" AcceptsReturn="True"
  VerticalAlignment="Top" Height="150" Width="300"
  Header="Summary" />
```

The next text-editing control is **PasswordBox**. This is a standard control that allows the user to enter hidden plain text and usually is used for password input. It contains the following important properties:

- **Password:** Gets access to text that was entered to **PasswordBox**.

- **PasswordChar:** Allows you to define a character that will be shown instead of real input.

- **IsPasswordRevealButtonEnabled:** Allows you to hide or display a button that enables the user to toggle between real and password input.

Look at the following code to see an example of **PasswordBox**:

```
<PasswordBox Width="150" HorizontalAlignment="Left"
   VerticalAlignment="Top" PasswordChar="*" Margin="10"
   IsPasswordRevealButtonEnabled="True"></PasswordBox>
```

Running this code, you can see the following user control:

The next editing control is **SearchBox**. This control allows the user to enter and edit a plain text, but it's adapted for search queries. Of course, the most important advantage of this control is search-history support. You can allow the user to display history using the **SearchHistoryEnabled** property. Additionally, this control contains a special search button and supports some important events such as **QuerySubmitted**, **QueryChanged**, and **ResultSuggestionChosen**.

You can use the following code to display **SearchBox**:

```
<SearchBox Width="150" HorizontalAlignment="Left"
   VerticalAlignment="Top" Margin="10"
   SearchHistoryEnabled="True" />
```

Play with this control for some time, and you will see the suggestions:

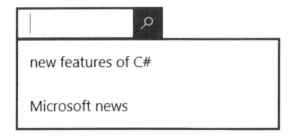

The last text-editing user control is **RichEditBox**. With this control, you can edit formatted text/rtf documents, which can include paragraphs, different fonts, images, and so on.

You can easily paste formatted text from Word or load an rtf document.

This control doesn't have any buttons to help the user edit and format text (just a context menu). So if you want to build a professional editor, you need to implement your own interface that extends the functionality of **RichEditBox**. For implementing your own editing buttons, you can get access to selection and formatting interfaces, using the **Document** property.

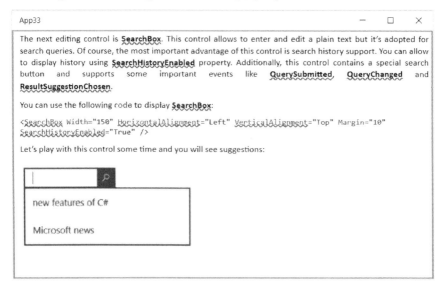

The Universal Windows Platform contains several user controls that allow you to display text only without the editing ability. All these controls are inherited from **FrameworkElement** directly, and do not support templates, but often, they themselves, are the basic building blocks for other controls.

The first control in the list is **TextBlock**, which allows you to display plain text. Using the **Text** property, you can assign any text to this control, and with properties such as **FontFamily**, **TextTrimming**, and **TextWrapping**, you can easily apply base formatting to the text. We will use the control often, so I don't want to spend much time on it right now.

Finally, I want to give an overview of the **RichTextBlock** user control. This control can display formatted text. In fact, this control is a container that contains special elements such as **Paragraph**, **Run**, **Span**, **Bold**, **LineBreak**, and so on. Let's see how to use these elements inside **RichTextBlock**:

```
<RichTextBlock HorizontalAlignment="Left"
    Name="rArea" VerticalAlignment="Top"
    Height="300" Width="400" >
```

```
    <Paragraph>
        <Bold>This is a bold text</Bold>
        <LineBreak></LineBreak>
        <Underline>This is an underline text</Underline>
        <LineBreak></LineBreak>
        <Italic>This is an italic text</Italic>
        <LineBreak></LineBreak>
        This is a button:
        <InlineUIContainer>
            <Button Content="Button"></Button>
        </InlineUIContainer>
    </Paragraph>
</RichTextBlock>
```

Running this code, you will see the following:

This is a bold text

This is an underline text

This is an italic text

This is a button: Button

Note that **RichTextBlock** can contain XAML elements as well.

RangeBase Controls

In this section we will discuss several user controls—scrollers, which are inherited from the **RangeBase** class: **Slider**, **ScrollBar**, and **ProgressBar**. Because **RangeBase** is inherited from the **Control** class, it supports all the main features and properties, including templates. The most important properties for all controls are these:

- **Minimum:** defines the minimum value of a scroll bar.

- **Maximum:** defines the maximum value of a scroll bar.

- **Value:** allows you to get or set current position of a scroll bar.

The difference between all these controls is that **Slider** and **ScrollBar** allow users to change the current value, but **ProgressBar** just displays the status.

The following code allows you to show all three bars:

```
<StackPanel>
    <ProgressBar Minimum="0" Maximum="100" Value="50"
    Margin="10"></ProgressBar>
```

```
<ScrollBar Minimum="0" Maximum="100" Value="50"
    Margin="10" IndicatorMode="MouseIndicator"
    Orientation="Horizontal"></ScrollBar>
<Slider Minimum="0" Maximum="100" Value="50"
    Margin="10"></Slider>
</StackPanel>
```

Running this code, you can see the following interface:

Note that **ScrollBar** has a vertical orientation by default and doesn't contain any scroll indicators. So we needed to change these properties.

ProgressRing

When you cannot display progress using **ProgressBar**, you can use the **ProgressRing** user control. This control shows that the application is doing something without giving any specific information about progress. To activate this control, you need to use the **IsActive** property, which is set to false by default.

```
<ProgressRing IsActive="True" Margin="10" Height="100"
    Width="100"></ProgressRing>
```

Using the **Width** and **Height** properties, you can define the size of the moving ring.

ToolTip User Control

The next interesting user control is ToolTip. This control allows you to display tooltips and can be assigned to any control and contain anything inside. Let's look at the code:

```
<Button Content="Detach" MinWidth="100" Margin="10">
    <ToolTipService.ToolTip>
        <ToolTip Placement="Right">
            <ToolTip.Content>
                <TextBlock Text="Any content here">
                </TextBlock>
            </ToolTip.Content>
        </ToolTip>
```

74

```
</ToolTipService.ToolTip>
</Button>
```

You can see that **ToolTip** has a content property that contains any container and controls inside. Additionally, we used the **Placement** property to select the best place for the tool tip.

Working with Collections

UWP contains several controls that allow you to present collections of elements. You will find that all these classes are inherited from **ItemsControl** and have similar features, but provide a different presentation of elements inside:

```
▲  Windows.UI.Xaml.Controls.ItemsControl
   ▷  Base Types
   ▲  Derived Types
      ▷  AutoSuggestBox
      ▷  CommandBarOverflowPresenter
      ▷  MenuFlyoutPresenter
      ▲  Pivot
      ▲  Selector
         ▷  ComboBox
         ▷  FlipView
         ▷  ListBox
         ▲  ListViewBase
            ▷  GridView
            ▷  ListView
```

Thanks to **ItemsControl**, all classes have at least the following properties:

- **Items:** Contains a collection of elements.

- **ItemsTemplate:** Using this property, you can define a **DataTemplate** that represents a view of a particular element.

- **ItemsSource:** With this property, you can bind a collection to the user control. We will discuss this property in later chapters.

- **ItemsPanel:** Allows you to define the type of layout that will be used to place elements inside the control.

In fact, you can use **ItemsControl** itself to present a collection of data. Let's declare the following interface:

```
<ItemsControl Name="itemsControl" Margin="50">
```

```
<ItemsControl.ItemsPanel>
    <ItemsPanelTemplate>
        <StackPanel></StackPanel>
    </ItemsPanelTemplate>
</ItemsControl.ItemsPanel>
<ItemsControl.ItemTemplate>
    <DataTemplate>
        <Grid>
            <Grid.RowDefinitions>
                <RowDefinition Height="Auto">
                </RowDefinition>
                <RowDefinition Height="Auto">
                </RowDefinition>
            </Grid.RowDefinitions>
            <TextBlock Text="{Binding NewsTitle}"
                Style=
                "{StaticResource TitleTextBlockStyle}">
            </TextBlock>
            <TextBlock Grid.Row="1" Text=
                "{Binding NewsTitle}"
                Style=
                "{StaticResource BodyTextBlockStyle}">
            </TextBlock>
        </Grid>
    </DataTemplate>
</ItemsControl.ItemTemplate>
</ItemsControl>
```

You can see that I am using StackPanel to present our data (vertical by default). Also I provided a data template for a particular element of the list, where I used several text blocks and a Grid as a container. Inside the data template, we are using the data-binding markup extension—you do not have to understand it right now.

Next, we need to declare a class that will contain data, and use this class to create a collection and bind it to the control.

You can create this class anywhere in your project:

```
public class NewsItem
{
    public string NewsTitle { get; set; }

    public string NewsDescription { get; set; }
}
```

To make it work, you need to implement the following method in the MainPage class:

```
protected override void OnNavigatedTo(
   NavigationEventArgs e)
{
     ObservableCollection<NewsItem> list =
       new ObservableCollection<NewsItem>();
     list.Add(new NewsItem() { NewsTitle = "News 1",
       NewsDescription = "News description 1" });
     list.Add(new NewsItem() { NewsTitle = "News 2",
       NewsDescription = "News description 2" });
     itemsControl.ItemsSource = list;
}
```

After running this code, you can see the following UI:

Of course, it's a very basic UI, and you cannot select any elements, it doesn't support animation, and so on. Therefore, you will use this element as a base class for your own controls. Let's use more advanced controls.

We modify our XAML file using the ListView control:

```
<ListView Name="itemsControl" Margin="50">
     <ItemsControl.ItemTemplate>
        <DataTemplate>
```

```
        <Grid>
            <Grid.RowDefinitions>
                <RowDefinition Height="Auto">
                </RowDefinition>
                <RowDefinition Height="Auto">
                </RowDefinition>
            </Grid.RowDefinitions>
            <TextBlock Text="{Binding NewsTitle}"
                Style=
                "{StaticResource TitleTextBlockStyle}">
            </TextBlock>
            <TextBlock Grid.Row="1" Text=
                "{Binding NewsDescription}"
                Style=
                "{StaticResource BodyTextBlockStyle}">
            </TextBlock>
        </Grid>
    </DataTemplate>
  </ItemsControl.ItemTemplate>
</ListView>
```

We removed **ItemsPanelTemplate** and just changed **ItemsControl** to **ListView**. As a result, you will get the same list of data on the screen, but the control provides the ability to select an element from the list, and it supports animation:

These things are possible thanks to the **Selector** class, which supports selection, and with the **ListViewBase** class, you can handle a click event on an item, reorder elements, use semantic zoom, define a header and a footer, and many other things. So if you want to present data in a vertical way, you can use the **ListView** class.

Let's change **ListView** to **GridView**:

```
<GridView>
    <GridView.ItemTemplate>
        <DataTemplate>
            <Grid>
                <Grid.RowDefinitions>
                    <RowDefinition Height="Auto">
                </RowDefinition>
                    <RowDefinition Height="Auto">
                </RowDefinition>
                </Grid.RowDefinitions>
                <TextBlock Text="{Binding NewsTitle}"
                Style="{StaticResource TitleTextBlockStyle}">
                </TextBlock>
                <TextBlock Grid.Row="1"
                    Text="{Binding NewsDescription}"
                Style="{StaticResource BodyTextBlockStyle}">
                </TextBlock>
            </Grid>
        </DataTemplate>
    </GridView.ItemTemplate>
</GridView>
```

In this case, data will be presented in rows and columns that can be scrolled horizontally:

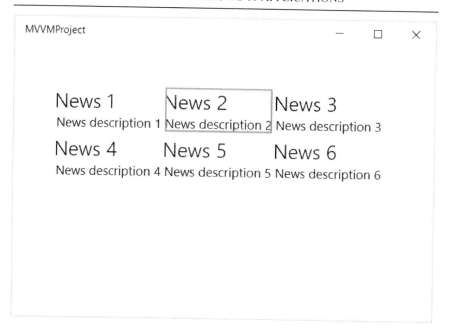

One more control that allows you to work with collections is **FlipView**. Unlike **ListView** and **GridView**, this control doesn't present all elements at the same time. Instead, **FlipView** presents them one by one and provides navigation controls. Usually you can find this element on websites. It presents collections of images, but in fact you can present anything, including your data:

```
<FlipView Name="itemsControl" Margin="50">
    <FlipView.ItemTemplate>
        <DataTemplate>
            <Grid>
                <Grid.RowDefinitions>
                    <RowDefinition Height="Auto">
                    </RowDefinition>
                    <RowDefinition Height="Auto">
                    </RowDefinition>
                </Grid.RowDefinitions>
                <TextBlock Text="{Binding NewsTitle}"
                    Style=
                    "{StaticResource TitleTextBlockStyle}">
                </TextBlock>
                <TextBlock Grid.Row="1" Text=
                    "{Binding NewsDescription}" Style=
                    "{StaticResource BodyTextBlockStyle}">
                </TextBlock>
```

```
        </Grid>
      </DataTemplate>
    </FlipView.ItemTemplate>
</FlipView>
```

Running this code, you can see the following UI:

SplitView

Another control that allows you to create adaptive interfaces is **SplitView**. Usually you will use this control to create menus, however **SplitView** allows you to declare two panels, **Pane** and **Content**, with any content inside. Particularly the **Pane** panel allows you to add some adaptive capabilities by supporting different display modes. The main syntax of **SplitView** is as follows:

```
<SplitView IsPaneOpen="False"
          DisplayMode="CompactInline"
          PaneBackground="Beige"
          OpenPaneLength="200"
          CompactPaneLength="30">
  <SplitView.Pane>

  </SplitView.Pane>
  <SplitView.Content>
```

```
    </SplitView.Content>
</SplitView>
```

Here the **DisplayMode** property can be set in one of the following values:

- **CompactInline:** The Pane panel supports compact mode. When it is expanded, all the content will be moved to provide enough space for the expanded panel.

- **CompactOverlay:** The same as the previous mode, but when panel is expanded, it doesn't affect any other content, because the panel will be placed above the content.

- **Inline:** Supported in expanded mode only. If it is displayed, then all other content will be moved to create enough space for the panel.

- **Overlay:** Supported in expanded mode only. It doesn't affect any other content, because the panel will be placed above the content.

With the help of **IsPaneOpen**, you can define whether the panel is displayed in standard mode or expanded (or compact) in compact mode. For example, if you set **IsPaneOpen** to false and the display mode is compact, then the panel will be displayed in compact mode. If you change **IsPaneOpen** to true, then the panel will be displayed in expanded mode.

You can see that **SplitView** doesn't have anything related to menus, but you can easily place something like **ListView** inside and declare menu items there. You can design the menu items in a way that users can see only icons in compact mode and all of the content in expanded mode, and implement **VisualStateManager**, which changes the **DisplayMode** and **IsPaneOpen** properties in run time.

I would advise you to follow these recommendations to design your own menu:

- Implement three states for your menu: Expanded, Compact, and UltraCompact for different screen sizes. If you have enough space, you can show the Pane in expanded mode without any problems, but if you have less space, you can show just icons in compact mode. Finally, if you don't have room at all (e.g., phone in portrait orientation), you should activate the UltraCompact state and hide your Pane completely.

- In Compact and UltraCompact states, add a bullet button above the menu that opens the Pane using Overlay modes. So you will be able to open the menu even in UltraCompact mode when the menu is hidden.

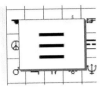

- Use **ListView** control for menu.

So your **VisualStateManager** can look like this (**CompactInline** as default and **IsPaneOpen** is true):

```
<VisualState x:Name="Expanded">
    <VisualState.StateTriggers>
        <AdaptiveTrigger MinWindowWidth="900">
        </AdaptiveTrigger>
    </VisualState.StateTriggers>
</VisualState>
<VisualState x:Name="Compact">
    <VisualState.Setters>
        <Setter Value="False"
            Target="splitView.IsPaneOpen">
        </Setter>
        <Setter Value="CompactOverlay"
            Target="splitView.DisplayMode">
        </Setter>
    </VisualState.Setters>
    <VisualState.StateTriggers>
        <AdaptiveTrigger MinWindowWidth="500">
        </AdaptiveTrigger>
    </VisualState.StateTriggers>
</VisualState>
<VisualState x:Name="UltraCompact">
    <VisualState.Setters>
        <Setter Value="False"
            Target="splitView.IsPaneOpen">
        </Setter>
        <Setter Value="Overlay"
            Target="splitView.DisplayMode">
        </Setter>
    </VisualState.Setters>
    <VisualState.StateTriggers>
        <AdaptiveTrigger MinWindowWidth="0">
        </AdaptiveTrigger>
    </VisualState.StateTriggers>
</VisualState>
```

If you implement a bullet button, you need to add logic that allows the user to expand the menu as well. You can implement all logic inside the code-behind, or you can try to create two more states and your own triggers. Later we will discuss triggers, adaptive interfaces, and **VisualStateManager** in more detail.

In this chapter we discussed the most common controls, but UWP contains many more controls and, additionally, you can find a huge number of third-party controls. Therefore, you should not have any problems with interface development.

In the next chapter, we will discuss how to implement interaction with users.

Chapter 5

User Interaction

Windows 10 works fine with different input methods, such as mouse/keyboard, pen, and gestures. Consequently, users can work with Windows 10 applications using different devices, including phones and tablets. But new features required changes inside the event model, and these changes were first introduced in Windows 8 when Windows Runtime was announced. If you have some experience with Windows Forms or Win32 API applications, you might be somewhat confused. For example, you will not find mouse events, because it's not important what users use for interaction—mouse, pen, or fingers. Otherwise, developers would have to implement different logic and event handlers for different input methods.

Windows 10 supports three groups of events related to interaction with users:

- events related to pushes,

- events related to gestures, and

- events related to pointer movement (pointers can be fingers as well as pen or mouse cursor).

Each of these groups allows you to use some common scenarios. For example, with clicks users can activate a context menu or send a click event to controls, such as buttons. Using gestures, users can scale the interface, make drag-and-drop actions, and move objects on the screen. Finally, pointer events allow the user to use the pointer to draw objects using pen, finger, or mouse. What is more important is that all these events are defined in the **UIElement** class, so all of them are available for all visual elements. Of course, in some cases you should not work with these events directly. For example, the **Button** class contains the **Click** event, which you should use because users can tap the button even if it is disabled.

Let's look at each of these groups of events in more detail.

The Universal Windows Platform defines four events related to pushes:

- **Tapped:** This event fires when a tap has occurred. In the case of a mouse, a tap can be generated by a left-button click, but in the case of pen and fingers, the user needs to touch and release the screen.

- **DoubleTapped:** This event is similar to the previous one, but fires when a double tap has occurred.

- **Holding:** Allows you to see whether the user is holding a finger or mouse cursor with the right mouse button pushed at the same place.

- **RightTapped:** This event fires when the user releases the right mouse button. In the case of pen and fingers, this event fires right after the Holding event, when the user releases the screen.

Note that these events can be disabled by default. If you want to handle these events, you need to enable them using the **IsTapEnabled**, **IsDoubleTapEnabled**, **IsHoldingEnabled**, and **IsRightTapEnabled** properties and set them to **true**.

Despite this universal approach, these events still allow you to understand which pointer type is used. Just check the parameters of the event handlers, and you can find the **PointerDeviceType** property, which can contain one of the following values: **Mouse**, **Pen**, and **Touch**. Therefore, you can always know for sure what the user has used for input.

Additionally, the **Holding** event has several holding states. Thanks to these states, you can always understand when the user starts to hold the pointer and when he or she finishes.

```
private void Grid_Holding(object sender,
    HoldingRoutedEventArgs e)
{
    switch (e.HoldingState)
    {
        case Windows.UI.Input.HoldingState.Started:
        . . . . .
        break;
        case Windows.UI.Input.HoldingState.Completed:
        . . . . .
        break;
        case Windows.UI.Input.HoldingState.Canceled:
        . . . . .
        break;
    }
}
```

The Canceled state is generated when a user moves the pointer outside of the control and continues to hold a finger or mouse button.

Note that all of these events are routed events. This means that if a user taps a control but the control doesn't handle the **Tapped** event, the event will be routed to the parent of the control, and so on. Even if you have an event handler for any of these events, you can throw it to containers using the **Handled** property of the second parameter of the event handler—just set it to false.

The second group of the events allows you to handle gestures. There are five events:

- **ManipulationStarting:** This event allows you to prepare for the beginning of the manipulation. Usually you can initialize some variables that can be used later.

- **ManipulationStarted:** This event signals that the user has started doing something with the object. So manipulation has started.

- **ManipulationDelta:** Usually you will handle this event. It allows you to understand which manipulation has happened. So you can check all needed parameters and apply them to the object.

- **ManipulationCompleted:** This event signals that manipulation has been completed.

- **ManipulationInertiaStarting:** This event is useful if you want to add some inertia effects. Using the parameters of the event handler for this event, you can calculate and apply animations that emulate inertia.

Of course, to understand the type of manipulation, you need to work with the parameters of the event handlers for these events, and the system will make all needed calculations and provide information on which manipulation has happened (see below). But all calculations related to manipulations are performance intensive. That's why they are disabled by default. So to collect information about manipulation for the selected controls, you need to initialize the **ManipulationMode** property. Once you do this, you can start working with manipulations using the **ManipulationDelta** event handler.

Using the **Delta** property of the parameter of the **ManipulationDelta** event handler, you can easily see which manipulation has happened:

- **Rotation:** Contains the angle of rotation in radians.

- **Expansion:** Contains the change in pixels between two touch points when two points are moving. This property can be used for scaling.

- **Translation:** Contains information about changes about the x- and y-axis.

- **Scale:** Contains the change in percentage between two touch points when two points are moving. This property can be used for scaling.

Once we know which manipulation happened, we can apply animations and transformations to the user control.

Look at the code below:

```
<Rectangle x:Name="rect" Width="300" Height="150"
    Fill="Green" ManipulationMode="All"
    ManipulationDelta="rect_ManipulationDelta">
    <Rectangle.RenderTransform>
        <CompositeTransform x:Name="transform">
        </CompositeTransform>
    </Rectangle.RenderTransform>
</Rectangle>
```

And the code-behind file:

```
private void rect_ManipulationDelta(object sender,
    ManipulationDeltaRoutedEventArgs e)
{
    transform.TranslateX = transform.TranslateX+
        e.Delta.Translation.X;
    transform.TranslateY = transform.TranslateY+
        e.Delta.Translation.Y;
}
```

This code shows you how to use manipulations to move a simple rectangle.

The last group of events is pointer events. There are eight events:

- **PointerPressed:** Fires when the pointer is pressed.

- **PointerReleased:** Fires when the pointer is released.

- **PointerWheelChanged:** Allows you to handle rotation of the mouse wheel.

- **PointerMoved:** Fires when the pointer is moved.

- **PointerEntered:** Fires when the pointer is moved inside the object.

- **PointerExited:** Fires when the pointer has left the object.

- **PointerCaptureLost:** Fires when the pointer has moved to another element (or application).

- **PointerCanceled:** Fires when there has been an abnormal loss of contact with the pointer.

These events are not very complex. Nevertheless, let's look at a short example to better understand them.

Just define the Canvas user control on the page:

```
<Canvas Name="LayoutRoot" Background="White"
    PointerPressed=" LayoutRoot_PointerPressed"
    PointerMoved=" LayoutRoot_PointerMoved"
    PointerReleased="LayoutRoot_PointerReleased">
</Canvas>
```

And implement the following code:

```
private void LayoutRoot_PointerPressed(object sender,
    PointerRoutedEventArgs e)
{
    startPoint = e.GetCurrentPoint(LayoutRoot).Position;
}


private void LayoutRoot_PointerMoved(object sender,
    PointerRoutedEventArgs e)
{
    if (startPoint != null)

    {
        Line l = new Line();
        l.X1 = ((Point)startPoint).X;
        l.Y1 = ((Point)startPoint).Y;
        startPoint =
            e.GetCurrentPoint(LayoutRoot).Position;
        l.X2 = ((Point)startPoint).X;
        l.Y2 = ((Point)startPoint).Y;
        l.Stroke = new SolidColorBrush(Colors.Red);
        LayoutRoot.Children.Add(l);
    }
}


private void LayoutRoot_PointerReleased(object sender,
    PointerRoutedEventArgs e)
{
    startPoint = null;
}
```

Thanks to this code, we can paint inside our Canvas element with the help of a mouse, a pen, or fingers.

If you want, you can add some instruments to this application and allow users to change color, line height, and so on.

This page intentionally left blank

Chapter 6

Styles, Resources, and Themes

Introduction to Styles

Style is a special approach that allows you to have common properties for a selected group of user controls in one place. If you open any application, you will see that even when the application has a very specific theme, all common user controls look the same. For example, buttons have the same color, the same font, and the same shape. To understand styles better, let's look at the following code:

```
<StackPanel>
    <Button Width="100" Height="50"
        Background="Green"
        Content="Button 1" Margin="5" FontFamily="Arial"
        FontSize="12" FontWeight="Bold"
        Foreground="Blue" BorderThickness="3">
    </Button>
    <Button Width="100" Height="50"
        Background="Green"
        Content="Button 2" Margin="5" FontFamily="Arial"
        FontSize="12" FontWeight="Bold"
        Foreground="Blue" BorderThickness="3">
    </Button>
    <Button Width="100" Height="50"
        Background="Green"
        Content="Button 3" Margin="5" FontFamily="Arial"
        FontSize="12" FontWeight="Bold"
        Foreground="Blue" BorderThickness="3">
    </Button>
    <Button Width="100" Height="50"
        Background="Green"
        Content="Button 4" Margin="5" FontFamily="Arial"
        FontSize="12" FontWeight="Bold"
        Foreground="Blue" BorderThickness="3">
    </Button>
</StackPanel>
```

You can see that we declared four buttons with a lot of common properties, such as **Background**, **Margin**, **FontSize**, and so on. There are two problems: First, it is a huge piece of code just for four buttons. Second, if we decide to change something, we need to visit each button to change the same attribute. That is why XAML supports a special element called **Style**.

The **Style** class is defined in the **Windows.UI.Xaml** namespace and contains four important properties: **BasedOn**, **Setters**, **TargetType**, and **IsSealed**. The **TargetType** property defines a type whose style can be applied, and **Setters** is a reference to a collection of **Setter** objects. Let us open the **Setter** class in **Object Browser**. You can find that **Setter** can store information about a property and its value. What is more important, is that the property should be **DependencyProperty**, and you cannot use any other properties. That is why when you create your own user control, it is important to inherit the **DependencyObject** class and register all public "visual" properties such as **DependencyProperty**. Therefore, when you create an object of the **Style** class, it should contain at least **TargetType** and a **Setters** collection. It is enough to move all common visual information from control of **TargetType** to Style. We are going to discuss **IsSealed** and **BasedOn** properties of the **Style** class later in this chapter.

OK. We have a way to pack information about some properties and their values inside one object, so it is time to think about how to apply this object to user controls. It is easy, and if you open **FrameworkElement** in Object Browser, you can find the **Style** property, which can accept an object of **Style** type. Therefore, technically, you can implement the following code:

```
Style st = new Style(typeof(Button));
st.Setters.Add(new Setter(Button.BackgroundProperty,
    Colors.Red));
mbutton.Style = st;
```

However, this approach is not very popular for XAML controls. Instead, you can declare **Style** objects in XAML. Since this element is not a part of the visual tree, we should include it in resources (see later in this chapter).

Let us see how to define the **Style** element for common button properties in our example:

```
<Page.Resources>
    <Style x:Key="buttonStyle" TargetType="Button">
        <Setter Property="Background" Value="Green">
        </Setter>
        <Setter Property="Margin" Value="5"></Setter>
        <Setter Property="FontFamily" Value="Arial">
        </Setter>
        <Setter Property="FontSize" Value="12"></Setter>
        <Setter Property="FontWeight" Value="Bold">
        </Setter>
        <Setter Property="Foreground" Value="Blue">
        </Setter>
        <Setter Property="BorderThickness" Value="3">
        </Setter>
```

95

```
        </Style>
    </Page.Resources>
```

We defined a style using **Page** resources—just place this element as an inner element of **Page**.

You can see that we used the **Style** tag with two properties: **TargetType** and **x:Key**. We just discussed the first one, but you can see that, because Visual Studio knows the type, it is possible to use the IntelliSense system to edit the **Style** element. The second one is the key of the style, and we will use this key to apply the style to the selected user controls.

Let us see how to apply our style to the buttons:

```
<StackPanel>
    <Button Width="100" Height="50"
        Style="{StaticResource buttonStyle}"
        Content="Button 1">
    </Button>
    <Button Width="100" Height="50"
        Style="{StaticResource buttonStyle}"
        Content="Button 2">
    </Button>
    <Button Width="100" Height="50"
        Style="{StaticResource buttonStyle}"
        Content="Button 3">
    </Button>
    <Button Width="100" Height="50"
        Style="{StaticResource buttonStyle}"
        Content="Button 4">
    </Button>
</StackPanel>
```

To apply the style, we used the **StaticResource** markup extension. It makes a reference to the local resources. We passed the style name as a parameter and assigned this construction to the **Style** property of the **Button**.

Once a style is assigned to any element in XAML, you cannot change it dynamically. The **IsSealed** property indicates whether you can still change the style. If **IsSealed** is **true** and you try to change something inside the style, the system will throw an exception.

You can declare an unnamed or implicit style without using the key property. In this case, the style will be applied to all controls of the target type, if you do not apply a different style explicitly. Therefore, we can remove even markup extensions from our code:

```
<Page.Resources>
    <Style TargetType="Button">
        <Setter Property="Background" Value="Green">
        </Setter>
        <Setter Property="Margin" Value="5"></Setter>
        <Setter Property="FontFamily" Value="Arial">
        </Setter>
        <Setter Property="FontSize" Value="12"></Setter>
        <Setter Property="FontWeight" Value="Bold">
        </Setter>
        <Setter Property="Foreground" Value="Blue">
        </Setter>
        <Setter Property="BorderThickness" Value="3">
        </Setter>
    </Style>
</Page.Resources>
<StackPanel>
    <Button Width="100" Height="50"
        Content="Button 1">
    </Button>
    <Button Width="100" Height="50"
        Content="Button 2">
    </Button>
    <Button Width="100" Height="50"
        Content="Button 3">
    </Button>
    <Button Width="100" Height="50"
        Content="Button 4">
    </Button>
</StackPanel>
</Grid>
```

BasedOn Styles

XAML styles support the special attribute **BasedOn**. Thanks to this attribute, you can extend existing styles for the same type of control:

```
<Style x:Key="baseStyle" TargetType="Button" >
    <Setter Property="Width" Value="100"></Setter>
</Style>
<Style x:Key="btnStyle"
    BasedOn="{StaticResource baseStyle}"
TargetType="Button">
```

97

```
        <Setter Property="Foreground" Value="Green"></Setter>
</Style>
```

This example is not very useful but demonstrates the idea.

You can change an already-assigned value if you declare **BasedOn** style:

```
<Style x:Key="baseStyle" TargetType="Button" >
    <Setter Property="Foreground" Value="Red"></Setter>
</Style>
<Style x:Key="btnStyle"
    BasedOn="{StaticResource baseStyle}"
    TargetType="Button">
    <Setter Property="Foreground" Value="Green"></Setter>
</Style>
```

If you now apply btnStyle to a button, it will have a green foreground.

Resources

When we discussed styles, we used the **Resource** property of the **Page** object. This property is available for all visual objects because it is defined in the **FrameworkElement** class. You can also find the **Resource** property in the **Application** class. Thanks to resources, you can define styles, templates, and separate objects inside any visual element and make a reference to them. If you open **FrameworkElement** in **Object Browser**, you can find that the **Resource** property has the **ResourceDictionary** type. The last one contains the property **ThemeDictionaries**, which is the reference to resources related to themes (see later), and the **MergedDictionaries** property, which contains a reference to a list of all other resource dictionaries. Thanks to **MergedDictionaries**, you can define resources not only inside a control or Application object but in separate files as well, and merge all these resources from different sources in one place.

As I mentioned earlier, you can use resources to store not just styles but also any other objects. Look at the following code:

```
<Page.Resources>
    <LinearGradientBrush x:Key="myBrush">
        <GradientStop Color="Red" Offset="0">
        </GradientStop>
        <GradientStop Color="Green" Offset="1">
        </GradientStop>
    </LinearGradientBrush>
</Page.Resources>
<StackPanel>
    <Button Width="100" Height="50"
```

```
            Background="{StaticResource myBrush}"
            Content="Button 1" Margin="5">
    </Button>
</StackPanel>
```

In this code we declared an object of the **LinearGradientBrush** type and used it as a background brush for the button. We used the same **StaticResource** markup extension as a universal way to gain access to resources.

If you declare resources inside an element, they will be available for the element itself as well as for any inner elements. We only need to know the key. Resources that are declared inside the **Application** element are available everywhere inside the application.

```
<StackPanel>
    <StackPanel.Resources>
        <LinearGradientBrush x:Key="myBrush">
            <GradientStop Color="Red" Offset="0">
            </GradientStop>
            <GradientStop Color="Green" Offset="1">
            </GradientStop>
        </LinearGradientBrush>
    </StackPanel.Resources>
    <Button Width="100" Height="50"
        Background="{StaticResource myBrush}"
        Content="Button 1" Margin="5">
    </Button>
</StackPanel>
```

In this code we used the **Resource** property of **StackPanel** instead of **Page**, and you can see that we used the same approach to access the **LinearGradientBrush** object. Therefore, the place of declaration only defines the scope of usage.

```
<Application
xmlns="http://schemas.microsoft.com/winfx/2006/xaml/present
ation"
xmlns:x="http://schemas.microsoft.com/winfx/2006/xaml"
xmlns:local="using:Application4">
    <Application.Resources>
        <LinearGradientBrush x:Key="myBrush">
            <GradientStop Color="Red" Offset="0">
            </GradientStop>
            <GradientStop Color="Green" Offset="1">
            </GradientStop>
        </LinearGradientBrush>
    </Application.Resources>
```

```
</Application>
```

In this example we declared the same object but with global scope. The object will be available for all user controls in all pages.

Resource Dictionaries

You can define resources in separate files. Visual Studio has a special template, **Resource Dictionary**, that allows you to work with external resources.

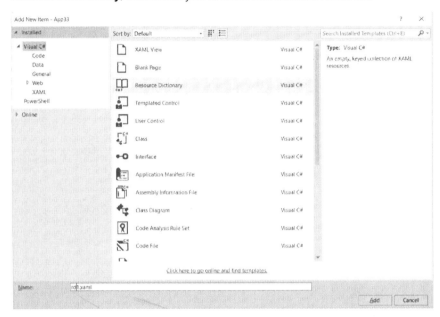

Because resources in separate files are not assigned to any controls yet, you need to use the root element **ResourceDictionary**:

```
<ResourceDictionary xmlns=
"http://schemas.microsoft.com/winfx/2006/xaml/presentation"
xmlns:x="http://schemas.microsoft.com/winfx/2006/xaml">
    <LinearGradientBrush x:Key="myBrush">
        <GradientStop Color="Red" Offset="0">
        </GradientStop>
        <GradientStop Color="Green" Offset="1">
        </GradientStop>
    </LinearGradientBrush>
</ResourceDictionary>
```

Once you declare all needed resource dictionaries, you can combine them inside any controls, including the Application object. Using the following code, you can include resource files in your application:

```
<Application xmlns=
"http://schemas.microsoft.com/winfx/2006/xaml/presentation"
xmlns:x="http://schemas.microsoft.com/winfx/2006/xaml"
xmlns:local="using:Application4">
    <Application.Resources>
        <ResourceDictionary>
            <ResourceDictionary.MergedDictionaries>
                <ResourceDictionary Source="RD1.xaml" />
            </ResourceDictionary.MergedDictionaries>
        </ResourceDictionary>
    </Application.Resources>
</Application>
```

In this code we used the **MergedDictionaries** property, which contains a list of all included dictionaries. Thanks to the **Source** properties, all we need to do is making a reference to our external file.

Of course, you can add as many files as needed, and you can mix them with explicitly defined objects:

```
<Page.Resources>
    <ResourceDictionary>
        <ResourceDictionary.MergedDictionaries>
            <ResourceDictionary Source="rd1.xaml">
            </ResourceDictionary>
            <ResourceDictionary Source="rd1.xaml">
            </ResourceDictionary>
        </ResourceDictionary.MergedDictionaries>
        <Style x:Key="mbuttonGreen" TargetType="Button">
            <Setter Property="Background" Value="Green">
            </Setter>
        </Style>
    </ResourceDictionary>
</Page.Resources>
```

In this code we added several dictionaries to **Page** resources. Of course, usually you will work with an **Application** object.

Themes

When you create a new page or an application from scratch, you can find a default Grid user control, which looks like the following example:

```
<Grid Background=
  "{ThemeResource ApplicationPageBackgroundThemeBrush}">
</Grid>
```

You can see that the background property points to something that we did not define in our code—**ApplicationPageBackgroundThemeBrush**. And to make this reference, the **ThemeResource** markup extension was used instead of **StaticResource**. Let's look at this construction in detail.

I suggest starting with **ApplicationPageBackgroundThemeBrush**. You can simply point to this name and call Peek Definition using the context menu in Visual Studio:

```
<Grid Background="{ThemeResource ApplicationPageBackgroundThemeBrush}"></Grid>
    <SolidColorBrush x:Key="ApplicationHeaderForegroundThemeBrush" Color="#FF000000" />
    <SolidColorBrush x:Key="ApplicationPageBackgroundThemeBrush" Color="#FFFFFFFF" />
    <SolidColorBrush x:Key="ApplicationPointerOverForegroundThemeBrush" Color="#CC000000
    <SolidColorBrush x:Key="ApplicationPressedForegroundThemeBrush" Color="#66000000" /:
    <SolidColorBrush x:Key="ApplicationSecondaryForegroundThemeBrush" Color="#99000000"
    <SolidColorBrush x:Key="BackButtonBackgroundThemeBrush" Color="Transparent" />
    <SolidColorBrush x:Key="BackButtonDisabledForegroundThemeBrush" Color="#66000000" /
```

You can see that **ApplicationPageBackgroundThemeBrush** was defined as a **SolidColorBrush** object inside resources in the **generic.xaml** file. In fact, the **generic.xaml** file is just a reference for designers, and all these objects, styles, and templates are a part of the Universal Windows Platform. So do not try to change **generic.xaml** in any case.

Just scroll through **generic.xaml**, and you will find a style for the **Button** user control, **CheckBox**, **TextBox**, and all other user controls that are inherited from the **Control** class.

```
<!-- Default style for Windows.UI.Xaml.Controls.Button -->
<Style TargetType="Button">
    <Setter Property="Background" Value="{ThemeResource SystemControlBackgroundBaseLowBrush}"
    <Setter Property="Foreground" Value="{ThemeResource SystemControlForegroundBaseHighBrush}'
    <Setter Property="BorderBrush" Value="{ThemeResource SystemControlForegroundTransparentBru
```

The Universal Windows Platform defines styles and templates for common user controls as well as lots of common control colors, fonts, brushes, and so on. Of course, you can use default styles and templates as an example for creating your own style, or you can simply rewrite the common objects.

```
<Page.Resources>
  <SolidColorBrush
    x:Key="ApplicationPageBackgroundThemeBrush"
```

```
        Color="Red" />
</Page.Resources>
```

If you want to make lots of changes to an existing style, it is better to get a copy of it from generic.xaml and modify it as you want. Visual Studio can help you create a copy of the template. Just select a control in the **Design** mode and use the context menu to make a copy:

Visual Studio will suggest selecting a container for the template, so you can select a user control, an application object, or a resource dictionary (you need to create an empty file for it):

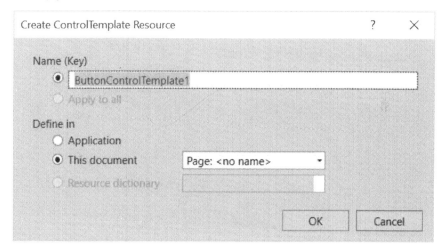

OK. Now we know what **ApplicationPageBackgroundThemeBrush** is, but it is still not clear what **ThemeResource** is. Let's open the App.xaml file and look at the root element:

```
<Application
    x:Class="App35.App" xmlns=
    "http://schemas.microsoft.com/winfx/2006/
        xaml/presentation"
```

```
xmlns:x="http://schemas.microsoft.com/winfx/2006/xaml"
xmlns:local="using:App35"
RequestedTheme="Light">
```

You can easy find the **RequestTheme** property, which is **Light** by default. The **RequestTheme** attribute can be applied to any user control and allows you to select a theme. Themes allow you to create the same set of objects but with different parameters. So the dark theme can declare a button template with white foreground color, but in the light theme this color can be defined as black. Let's scroll to the beginning of **generic.xaml**, where you will find the following code:

```
<ResourceDictionary.ThemeDictionaries>
  <ResourceDictionary x:Key="Default">
```

Instead of **MergedDictionaries**, another property, **ThemeDictionaries**, is used to declare several themes. These themes primarily contain colors, brushes, and simple objects, but all control templates defined outside themes simply use theme objects for their properties.

Let's look at the following code:

```
<StackPanel Orientation="Horizontal"
    VerticalAlignment="Top">
    <Grid RequestedTheme="Dark" Background=
    "{ThemeResource ApplicationPageBackgroundThemeBrush}">
        <Button Content="Hello" Margin="10"></Button>
    </Grid>
    <Grid RequestedTheme="Light" Background=
    "{ThemeResource ApplicationPageBackgroundThemeBrush}">
        <Button Content="Hello" Margin="10"></Button>
    </Grid>
</StackPanel>
```

We applied different themes to two grids inside the page, and these themes were applied automatically to all inner controls. What is more important, is the fact that the grids themselves have different backgrounds in run time, based on the theme.

So **ThemeResource** is a special markup extension that allows you to select the right object from resources based on the current theme. This markup extension works like **StaticResource** but contains some additional logic to allow controls to apply objects from the resources dynamically. Specifically, if you do not fix the theme for your application, and the user changes the theme using system settings, the new theme will be applied on the fly.

We will continue to discuss themes and templates in the chapter about custom user controls.

How to Localize Your Application

In this chapter we primarily discussed XAML resources that contain different objects such as styles and templates, but usually applications contain different types of resources, not just XAML resources. For example, images, icons, and videos, which you may include in the application package, are resources as well.

In this section I want to discuss special resources, such as separate files, that can contain text strings. This type of resource is used to localize applications.

Let's look at a simple button on a page:

```
<Button Content="Click me!"></Button>
```

The button contains the **Content** property that has the text in English. But what if I need to support several different languages in my application? For example, I want to have Ukrainian localization as well. In this case we need to think about resources.

To add resources to our application, we need to start with empty resource files. We need a way to show the system which resource file relates to which language. So we need to follow the rule: create folders inside your project with names mapped to language codes, and place a Resources.resw file in each folder.

You can create Resources.resw files using Visual Studio, but don't change the default name for the file:

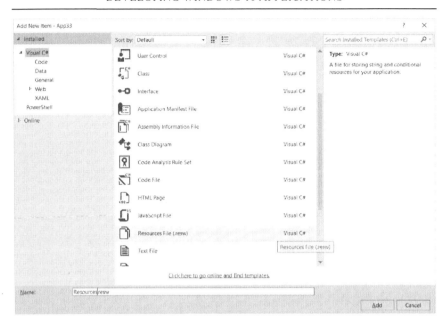

For English and Ukrainian languages, we will have the following structure:

▲ 📁 en-US
   📄 Resources.resw
▲ 📁 uk-UA
   📄 Resources.resw

It is time to edit these files and localize the content of the button. Open both files, and add the same name with localized strings:

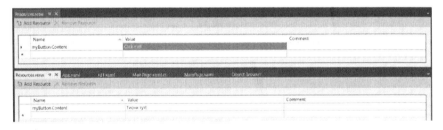

Note that you can use any name, but you need to add to it the exact same property name that you want to localize.

Modify our code in the following way:

```
<Button x:Uid="myButton"></Button>
```

We removed the content attribute from the button element and added an **x:Uid** attribute, which is a unique identifier of our resource string. The system will find all resource strings with **"myButton."** prefix and assign the properties that are declared there.

In the next step we need to change the manifest of our application to show which languages we support. Just locate the Resources element, and modify it in the following way:

```
<Resources>
    <Resource Language="en-US"/>
    <Resource Language="uk-UA"/>
</Resources>
```

That's all. From now on your application will support two languages (at least for the button).

To test different localizations of your application, you can use the **Language** dialog in the **Control Panel** window.

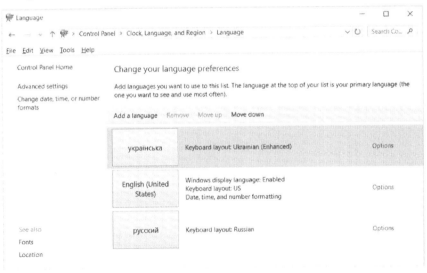

The first language in the list is your default language, and will be applied to the application.

Additionally, you can use resource files to declare simple strings that you can use in C# code. The following code will return the value of the string with myString name from the current resource file:

```
ResourceLoader rl = new ResourceLoader();
```

```
string s = rl.GetString("myString");
```

If you have lots of strings for localization and many languages for support, it can be difficult to translate the resource files and maintain them. That's why I would recommend downloading a special Multilingual App Toolkit, which extends Visual Studio and allows you to work with resw files using a more advanced interface. Just visit the blog of the team (http://blogs.msdn.com/b/matdev/) to check out the latest news about the tool and find the link for download.

Chapter 7

Graphics, Transformation, and Animation

Graphic Primitives

Lines, rectangles, ellipses—all these controls are fundamental for building other more complex user controls. That's why it is important to know all these graphic primitives, since you may use this knowledge to create a fully new shape for common user controls.

The Universal Windows Platform allows you to use the following graphic primitives: **Rectangle, Ellipse, Line, Polygon, Polyline,** and **Path**. All these primitives are inherited from the **Shape** class, which is inherited from **FrameworkElement**. Consequently, all graphic primitives can be located inside any container and have lots of properties that are common to all other user controls. Of course, the **Shape** class contains some specific properties, such as

- **Stroke:** allows you to define a brush for the outline of a shape,

- **Fill:** allows you to define a brush to paint the area inside a shape, and

- **Stretch:** defines how to fill the available space inside a container.

For the outline of a shape, the **Shape** class contains eight more properties, including StrokeDashArray and StrokeDashCap. With these properties you can customize the outline of a shape in many different ways. Look at the code below:

```
<StackPanel x:Name="LayoutRoot" Background="White">
    <Rectangle Width="300" Height="100" Stroke="Black"
        StrokeThickness="10"
        RadiusX="25" RadiusY="25" Margin="5"></Rectangle>
    <Rectangle Width="300" Height="100" Stroke="Black"
        StrokeThickness="10" RadiusX="25" RadiusY="25"
        StrokeDashArray="5,2,3,2" Margin="5"></Rectangle>
    <Rectangle Width="300" Height="100" Stroke="Black"
        StrokeThickness="10" RadiusX="25" RadiusY="25"
        StrokeDashArray="5,2,3,2" StrokeDashCap="Triangle"
        Margin="5"></Rectangle>
</StackPanel>
```

Upon running this code, you will see three rectangles with different outlines:

As you can see, to paint a rectangle, it's enough to define the **Width** and **Height** properties. But you can use the **MaxWidth, MaxHeight, MinWidth, MinHeight**, and **Stretch** properties to adapt your rectangles to different layouts. Additionally, you can find the **RadiusX** and **RadiusY** properties, which are defined in the Rectangle class directly. These properties allow you to define an ellipse that will be used to round the corners of the rectangle.

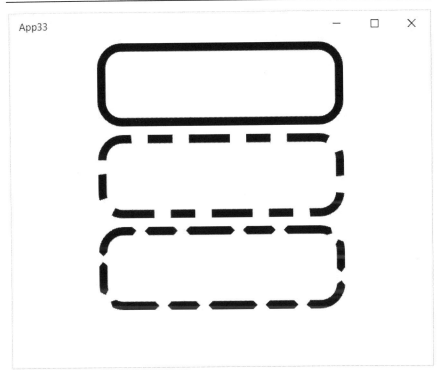

Using class **Ellipse**, you can paint an ellipse or a circle with the help of the Width and Height properties, which define the size of the ellipse:

```
<Ellipse Width="300" Height="100" StrokeThickness="10"
    Stroke="Black" Fill="Red">
</Ellipse>
```

In this example we used the **Fill** property to fill the ellipse in red, and we used **StrokeThickness** to define the height of the outline:

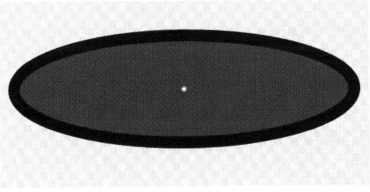

The next graphic primitive is Line, which allows you to paint a simple line using two points for beginning and ending the line:

```
<Line X1="0" Y1="0" X2="100" Y2="100" Stroke="Black">
</Line>
```

The most important question is, where is the origin? The origin is located in the top-left corner of the container. If you use **StackPanel** or **Grid**, these containers can draw a line without any problems, compared to the previous version of Windows Runtime.

The next example shows how to use the Polygon element, which allows you to create a closed contour:

```
<Polygon Points=
    "0,50,50,0,100,0,150,50,150,100,100,150,50,150,0,100"
    Stroke="Black" StrokeThickness="5">
</Polygon>
```

We used the **Points** property to define all corners of the shape. Note that the order of the corners is important.

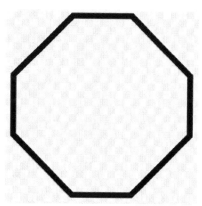

The Polyline element is similar to the previous one but doesn't close the contour automatically. Let's see how to work with a Polyline element that has the same set of points:

```
<Polyline Points=
    "0,50,50,0,100,0,150,50,150,100,100,150,50,150,0,100"
    Stroke="Black" StrokeThickness="5">
</Polyline>
```

You will see the following shape:

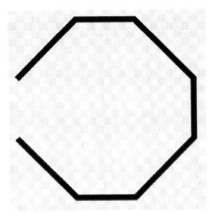

Finally, let's see the last graphic primitive—**Path**. With this element, you can paint lines with any complexity. This element contains only one important property—**Data**. Using this property, allows you to assign any geometric shapes (see below) or use special commands. Look at the following example:

```
<Path Stroke="Black" StrokeThickness="5"
    Data="M 10,100 C 10,300 300,-200 300,100">
</Path>
```

Upon running this code, you can see the following shape:

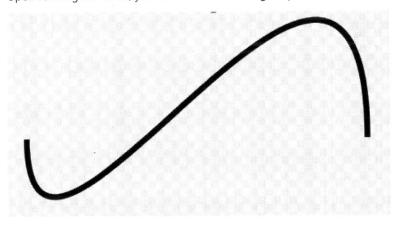

You can see that we used several commands, including M and C, to create this shape. Each command uses some parameters, which you need to place right after the command. The **Path** element supports the following commands:

- M: Allows you to move to the selected point.

- L: Paints a line from the current point to a defined point.

113

- H: Paints a horizontal line of the defined length from the current point.

- V: Paints a vertical line of the defined length from the current point.

- C: Uses three points as parameters and allows you to build a Bézier curve using the current and the third points. All other points are used as auxiliary.

- Q: Uses two points as parameters and allows you to build a quadratic Bézier curve using the current and the second point.

- S: You can pass two points as parameters to show a smoothed cubic Bézier curve.

- T: Allows you to build a smoothed quadratic Bézier curve.

- A: Allows you to build an elliptic curve using five parameters: radius, angle, type of segment (0 or 1), direction or angle (0 or 1), and ending point.

- Z: Closes the contour, making a line between the first point and the current one.

These are all the graphic primitives. Let's talk about brushes that you can use to fill an outline or the space inside the shapes.

Brushes

SolidColorBrush

In this and the previous chapters, we used some properties such as **Fill**, **Background**, and **Foreground**. All these properties were defined as properties of the **Windows.UI.Xaml.Media.Brush** type. This type is the base type for several classes. We are not going to use it directly, but we will use derived types, such as **SolidColorBrush** or **ImageBrush**. Let's start our overview with the simplest brush—**SolidColorBrush**.

SolidColorBrush is the simplest brush and allows you to define pure color using the **Color** property:

```
<Rectangle Width="300" Height="100" Fill="Red"></Rectangle>
<Rectangle Width="300" Height="100">
    <Rectangle.Fill>
        <SolidColorBrush Color="Red"></SolidColorBrush>
    </Rectangle.Fill>
</Rectangle>
```

```
<Rectangle Width="300" Height="100">
    <Rectangle.Fill>
        <SolidColorBrush Color="#FFFF0000">
        </SolidColorBrush>
    </Rectangle.Fill>
</Rectangle>
```

All three rectangles have the same color. But thanks to the embedded converters, you can define **SolidColorBrush** as a string, using a predefined string. You can do the same with the **Color** property, and finally, you can define color using ARGB notation.

If you want to see all of the predefined colors, just use Visual Studio IntelliSense or check the **Windows.UI.Colors** class.

Of course, you may create SolidColorBrush objects using C# code and assign them in run time:

```
rect.Fill = new SolidColorBrush(Colors.Red);
```

LinearGradientBrush

LinearGradientBrush allows you to create a brush based on a gradient. By default the gradient counts from the top-left corner to the bottom-right corner and creates a smooth transition from one color to another.

```
<Rectangle Width="300" Height="300">
    <Rectangle.Fill>
        <LinearGradientBrush>
            <GradientStop Color="Red" Offset="0">
            </GradientStop>
            <GradientStop Color="Green" Offset="1">
            </GradientStop>
        </LinearGradientBrush>
    </Rectangle.Fill>
</Rectangle>
```

The direction of the gradient can be easily changed using the StartPoint and EndPoint properties, but you need to remember that you should use a normalized rectangle:

```
<Rectangle Name="rect" Width="300" Height="300">
    <Rectangle.Fill>
        <LinearGradientBrush StartPoint="0,1"
            EndPoint="1,0">
            <GradientStop Color="Red" Offset="0">
```

```
        </GradientStop>
        <GradientStop Color="White" Offset="0.5">
        </GradientStop>
        <GradientStop Color="Green" Offset="1">
        </GradientStop>
      </LinearGradientBrush>
    </Rectangle.Fill>
</Rectangle>
```

This code will not only change the direction of the gradient but will add some more colors. So our gradient is changing from red to white and from white to green.

ImageBrush

You can not only use a color to fill your objects but images as well. To do this, you can use the ImageBrush element, which contains two main properties: ImageSource and Stretch. The first one you can use to point to an image, and the second one to specify how to fill the object.

```
<Ellipse Width="300" Height="100">
    <Ellipse.Fill>
        <ImageBrush ImageSource="Assets/drone.jpg"
            Stretch="UniformToFill">
        </ImageBrush>
    </Ellipse.Fill>
</Ellipse>
```

In this example we use the **UniformToFill** value for the **Stretch** property. It shows that we want to preserve proportions between the sides of the image but want to fill all the space inside of the object. You will see the following picture even in design mode:

WebViewBrush

One other brush is **WebViewBrush**, which can use a **WebView** control as the source of an image. This is not a popular user control today, but it is still there, so I decided to include it in the list as well. Let's look at the following code:

```
<Grid>
    <Grid.RowDefinitions>
        <RowDefinition></RowDefinition>
        <RowDefinition></RowDefinition>
    </Grid.RowDefinitions>
    <WebView Source="http://dev.microsoft.com"
        Name="webView"
        NavigationCompleted="webView_NavigationCompleted">
    </WebView>

    <Ellipse Width="600" Height="200"
        Margin="10" Grid.Row="1">
        <Ellipse.Fill>
        <WebViewBrush x:Name="webBrush"
            SourceName="webView" Stretch="UniformToFill">
        </WebViewBrush>
        </Ellipse.Fill>
    </Ellipse>
</Grid>
```

In the first row of the Grid, we created a **WebView** user control, and we used this control as a source for the **WebViewBrush**. But there is a problem: **WebView** needs time to download the content, and at that time **WebViewBrush** should be applied. So we need to redraw **WebViewBrush**. In this case it's better to implement a **NavigationCompleted** event handler:

```
private void webView_NavigationCompleted(WebView sender,
    WebViewNavigationCompletedEventArgs args)
{
    webBrush.Redraw();
}
```

Running this code, you can see the following picture:

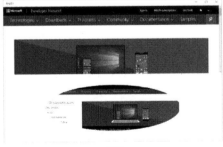

Geometric Shapes

The Universal Windows Platform defines a group of classes that you can use instead of complex commands to assign the **Data** property of **Path**. The simplest classes are these:

- **LineGeometry:** Uses two points to paint a line.

- **EllipseGeometry:** Defines an ellipse.

- **RectangleGeometry**: Allows you to paint a rectangle.

Look at the following code:

```
<Path Stroke="Black" StrokeThickness="2" >
    <Path.Data>
        <EllipseGeometry RadiusX="100"
            RadiusY="100" Center="100,100"/>
    </Path.Data>
</Path>
```

Running this code, you will see a simple circle.

For creating more-complex objects, you can use the **PathGeometry** element. This element allows you to define groups of simpler objects, or segments, which can be put in groups using the **PathFigure** element. The segments are represented by the following classes: **ArcSegment**, **LineSegment**, **BezierSegment**, **PolyBezierSegment**, **QuadraticBezierSegment**, and **PolyQuadraticBezierSegment**. Let's see how to use these objects in the code below:

```
<Path Stroke="Black" StrokeThickness="1" >
    <Path.Data>
        <PathGeometry>
            <PathGeometry.Figures>
                <PathFigure StartPoint="10,50">
                    <PathFigure.Segments>
                        <BezierSegment Point1="100,0"
                            Point2="200,200"
                            Point3="300,100"/>
                        <LineSegment Point="400,100" />
                        <ArcSegment Size="50,50"
                            RotationAngle="45"
                            IsLargeArc="True"
                            SweepDirection="Clockwise"
                            Point="200,100"/>
```

```
            </PathFigure.Segments>
          </PathFigure>
        </PathGeometry.Figures>
      </PathGeometry>
    </Path.Data>
</Path>
```

After running this code, you can see the following curve:

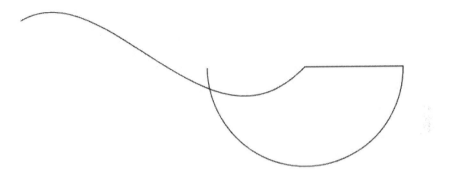

Additionally, if you want to group several geometries, you can use the **GeometryGroup** class.

Transformations

Transformations and animations are the coolest elements; they allow you to apply lots of different effects to the user control and help make your interface more responsive to the user. I am going to start this section with basic transformations and finish with embedded animations in existing controls.

Basic Types of Transformations

If you open Object Browser and look at the **UIElement** class, you can find the **RenderTransform** property, which is declared as a property of the **Transform** type. If you open this type, you can find several derived classes that allow you to apply basic transformations to user controls. Let's look at these classes:

- **RotateTransform**

- **ScaleTransform**

- **SkewTransform**

- **TranslateTransform**

- **MatrixTransform**

To apply any of these transformations, you simply need to create an object of the selected type and assign it to the **RenderTransform** property. If you want to assign several transformations at once, you can combine them using the **TransformGroup** class. Let's see a simple example:

```
<StackPanel x:Name="LayoutRoot" Background="White">
    <Rectangle Width="200" Height="100" Fill="Red">
        <Rectangle.RenderTransform>
            <TransformGroup>
                <RotateTransform Angle=
                    "{Binding Value,
                    ElementName=rotateSlider, Mode=OneWay}"
                    CenterX="100" CenterY="50">
                </RotateTransform>
                <ScaleTransform CenterX="100" CenterY="50"
                    ScaleX="{Binding Value,
                    ElementName=scaleXSlider, Mode=OneWay}"
                    ScaleY="{Binding Value,
                    ElementName=scaleYSlider, Mode=OneWay}">
                </ScaleTransform>
                <SkewTransform CenterX="100" CenterY="50"
                    AngleX=
                        "{Binding Value,
                        ElementName=skewXSlider,
                        Mode=OneWay}"
                    AngleY=
                        "{Binding Value,
                        ElementName=skewYSlider,
                        Mode=OneWay}">
                </SkewTransform>
                <TranslateTransform
                X="{Binding Value,
                ElementName=translateXSlider, Mode=OneWay}"
                Y="{Binding Value,
                ElementName=translateYSlider,Mode=OneWay}">
                </TranslateTransform>
            </TransformGroup>
        </Rectangle.RenderTransform>
    </Rectangle>
    <Slider Width="200" Name="rotateSlider" Minimum="0"
        Maximum="360">
    </Slider>
    <Slider Width="200" Name="scaleXSlider" Minimum="0"
```

```
      Maximum="100" Value="1">
  </Slider>
  <Slider Width="200" Name="scaleYSlider" Minimum="0"
      Maximum="100" Value="1">
  </Slider>
  <Slider Width="200" Name="skewXSlider" Minimum="-180"
      Maximum="180" Value="0">
  </Slider>
  <Slider Width="200" Name="skewYSlider" Minimum="-180"
      Maximum="180" Value="0">
  </Slider>
  <Slider Width="200" Name="translateXSlider"
      Minimum="-100" Maximum="100" Value="0">
  </Slider>
  <Slider Width="200" Name="translateYSlider"
      Minimum="-100" Maximum="100" Value="0">
  </Slider>
</StackPanel>
```

Running this code, you can see a rectangle and several sliders. Using these sliders, you can apply different types of transformations to the rectangle:

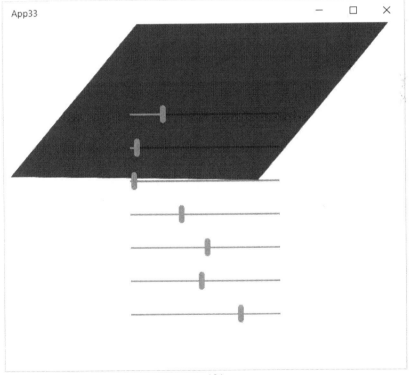

Note that the transformations don't affect the layout and that all containers will calculate the needed space based on initial values without applied transformations.

CompositeTransform

One other transformation type is **CompositeTransform**, which combines all of the transformation types. If you use several transformations, you can save time using this type. And, of course, all transformations should be applied around the same center. Just rewrite the previous Rectangle element using this type:

```
<Rectangle Width="200" Height="100" Fill="Red">
    <Rectangle.RenderTransform>
        <CompositeTransform CenterX="100" CenterY="50"
            ScaleX="{Binding Value,
            ElementName=scaleXSlider, Mode=OneWay}"
            ScaleY="{Binding Value,
            ElementName=scaleYSlider, Mode=OneWay}"
            Rotation="{Binding Value,
            ElementName=rotateSlider, Mode=OneWay}"
            SkewX="{Binding Value, ElementName=skewXSlider,
            Mode=OneWay}"
            SkewY="{Binding Value, ElementName=skewYSlider,
            Mode=OneWay}"
            TranslateX="{Binding Value,
            ElementName=translateXSlider, Mode=OneWay}"
            TranslateY="{Binding Value,
            ElementName=translateYSlider, Mode=OneWay}">
        </CompositeTransform>
    </Rectangle.RenderTransform>
</Rectangle>
```

3-D Transformation

If you develop applications for Windows Phone 8.1 or Windows 8.1, you can use the **PlaneProjection** class, which allows you to apply 3-D transformations to any UI elements. However, **PlaneProjection** is very limited and provides only a way to make a rotation. If you want to apply more-complex 3-D transformations, you need to use **MatrixTransform** and implement your own math algorithms.

Starting with Windows 10, you have a way to use these complex 3-D transforms with the help of new classes such as **PerspectiveTransform3D** and **CompositeTransform3D**. Let's look at the following code:

```
<RelativePanel HorizontalAlignment="Center">
```

```
<RelativePanel.Transform3D>
    <PerspectiveTransform3D></PerspectiveTransform3D>
</RelativePanel.Transform3D>
<Image Source="Assets\drone.jpg" Width="400"
    Name="image">
    <Image.Transform3D>
        <CompositeTransform3D CenterX="200"
            CenterY="100"
            RotationX=
                "{x:Bind sliderX.Value,Mode=OneWay}"
            RotationY=
                "{x:Bind sliderY.Value,Mode=OneWay}"
            RotationZ=
                "{x:Bind sliderZ.Value,Mode=OneWay}">
        </CompositeTransform3D>
    </Image.Transform3D>
</Image>
<Slider Maximum="360" RelativePanel.Below="image"
    Name="sliderX" Width="400" Margin="0,10,0,10">
</Slider>
<Slider Maximum="360" RelativePanel.Below="sliderX"
    Name="sliderY" Width="400" Margin="0,10,0,10">
</Slider>
<Slider Maximum="360" RelativePanel.Below="sliderY"
    Name="sliderZ" Width="400" Margin="0,10,0,10">
</Slider>
</RelativePanel>
```

If you execute the code, you will see the screen below, where you can rotate an image using three sliders:

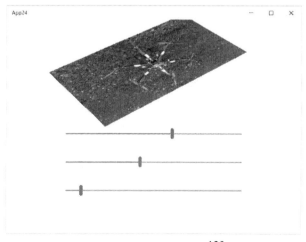

Frankly speaking, you would be able to make something like this using **PlaneProjection** as well, but with this example, we can understand the syntax for the new elements.

First of all, you need to use the **PerspectiveTransform3D** element and assign it to the **Transform3D** property, which is available for all the UI elements. **PerspectiveTransform3D** allows you to declare a common view port for all child elements. So you should think of it as a perspective camera. You can move the camera using the **OffsetX** and **OffsetY** properties, but this movement will not affect the position of your control inside the container—it just affects transformations because you have the same view port and any camera movement will add an angle that will only affect the projection. **PerspectiveTransform3D** has the **Depth** property as well, which declares the distance between the camera and the Z=0 plane. By default **Depth** is 1000, but you can change it; it only affects transformations as well. I have found that if you change **Depth**, you will see unpredictable effects.

Once you apply **PerspectiveTransform3D** to any container, you can use **CompositeTransform3D** to apply any transformations to elements inside the view port. You can scale, translate, and rotate UI elements.

However, I have discovered two disadvantages with this method.

First of all, **CompositeTransform3D** allows you to set the center of the transformation, but it requires you to use pixels. So if I want to make the transformation around the center of a control, I need to calculate the actual size. It's strange because even **PlaneProjection** allows you to set the center in relative coordinates ((0.5, 0.5)—center).

The second disadvantage is a problem with the correct placement of controls in the space—elements are rendered in XAML order, one by one. The elements that are closer to each other might be placed behind elements that are not so close. MSDN recommends using a workaround (**Canvas.ZIndex**), but it requires implementing complex code that should change **ZIndex** dynamically. Additionally, there are lots of tasks where **ZIndex** doesn't help. So in the current version, you cannot use these classes for more-complex scenarios.

If you need to build complex 3-D models, I would recommend using **WebView** and implementing your model there, using CSS 3D. Starting with Windows 10, **WebView** is based on Microsoft Edge and supports a preserve-3d value for 3-D transformation.

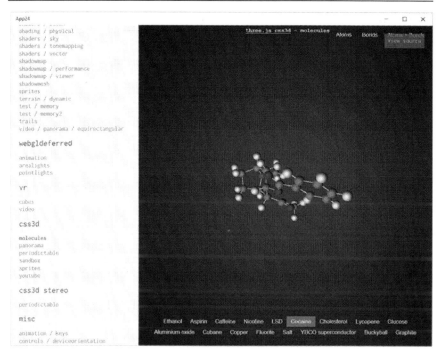

Introduction to Animations

Basic Animation Types

Using animations, you can create beautiful visual effects, animating any dependency property of user controls. And you can do it almost without coding in C#.

Let's see an overview of the basic animation types:

- **DoubleAnimation:** You can use this animation for animating properties of the **double** type. The most important properties are **From** and **To**, which allow you to declare the initial and final value of the animated property.

- **ColorAnimation:** You can use this animation type for animating properties of the **Color** type. Usually you will apply this animation type to brushes.

- **PointAnimation:** This animation type allows you to animate a point. You can use the **From** and **To** properties to assign initial and final points.

125

Regardless of the animation type, all animation objects have the following properties:

- **Duration:** This property allows you to initialize the duration for the animation. The format for the timeframe is hh:mm:ss (00:00:03 is three seconds). All animating properties will be changed evenly during the defined timeframe.

- **BeginTime:** If you are not going to start a particular animation in a group at once, you can set this property, which allows you to define a timespan in which the animation should start. It uses the same time format.

- **SpeedRatio:** Using this property, you can increase (decrease) the speed of the animation by **n** times, where **n** is **double**. By default **SpeedRatio** is equal to one.

- **AutoReverse:** Using this property, you can play the animation in both directions. So if you set **AutoReverse** to **true**, the whole process will contain two parts: all properties will be animated from initial (**From**) to final (**To**) values; then all properties will be animated from final (**To**) to initial (**From**) values.

- **RepeatBehavior:** Using this property, you can tell the animation to repeat by defining one of the following values: time in seconds over which the animation should be repeated; **Forever**—allows you to specify an infinite number of executions; or Count—allows you to define a number of cycles (you can specify it as Nx where N is number of cycles).

Of course, to create good effects, usually you need to use several types of animations together, or at least use the same animation for different properties. That's why animations don't contain any methods that would allow you to start or stop them, and you will not be able to place animations as separate objects. All animations should be packed into a special object, which you can create with the **Storyboard** class. Additionally, animations use **Storyboard.TargetName** and **Storyboard.TargetProperty** as attached properties to define the name of the object and its property to animate. Let's see how to define a simple animation:

```
<Canvas >
    <Button Name="myButton" Content="Hello">
        <Button.Resources>
            <Storyboard x:Key="buttonAnimation"
                x:Name="buttonAnimation">
```

```
        <DoubleAnimation
            Storyboard.TargetName="myButton"

        Storyboard.TargetProperty="(Canvas.Left)"
        To="200" Duration="0:0:5" AutoReverse="True"
        />
        </Storyboard>
    </Button.Resources>
  </Button>
</Canvas>
```

You can see that we used resources to store the Storyboard object. Because Storyboard is not a visual object, there is no way to include it in a visual tree, but resources work fine for any nonvisual objects.

How to Run Storyboards

There are two ways to run Storyboard:

- Run animations from C# code.

- Run animations from XAML when the object is loaded.

In the case of C#, you can simply call the **Begin** method of Storyboard. It's a universal approach because you can store animations as resources and call **Begin** as soon as you want.

```
protected override void OnNavigatedTo(
    NavigationEventArgs e)
{
    buttonAnimation.Begin();
    base.OnNavigatedTo(e);
}
```

Additionally, you can use the **Stop** and **Pause** methods, which are reasonable for long-running animations. If you want to run some code when Storyboard completes execution, you can create an event handler for the **Completed** event.

I have never used the second approach, but it still exists, so I cannot ignore it. You can place an animation inside a special object of the **EventTrigger** class. In fact, this object implements some sort of trigger, which will fire once user control is loaded. We can rewrite our code using **EventTrigger** in the following way:

```
<Canvas >
    <Button Name="myButton" Content="Hello">
        <Button.Triggers>
            <EventTrigger RoutedEvent="UserControl.Loaded">
```

```
            <BeginStoryboard>
                <Storyboard x:Name="buttonAnimation">
                    <DoubleAnimation
                    Storyboard.TargetName="myButton"
                    Storyboard.TargetProperty=
                        "(Canvas.Left)"
                    To="200" Duration="0:0:5"
                    AutoReverse="True" />
                </Storyboard>
            </BeginStoryboard>
        </EventTrigger>
    </Button.Triggers>
  </Button>
</Canvas>
```

Animation Using Key Frames

All standard animation types allow you to change user-control properties evenly, but if you want to change properties using complex algorithms, then it's better to use the following animations:

- **DoubleAnimationUsingKeyFrames**

- **PointAnimationUsingKeyFrames**

- **ColorAnimationUsingKeyFrames**

You can see that the names of these classes are similar to standard animation names but with a "UsingKeyFrame" suffix. The idea of these animations is that you can divide the full time frame into several intervals and give each interval of time its own parameters and even its own animation algorithm. Let's look at the following example:

```
    <Button Name="myButton" Content="Hello">
        <Button.Resources>
            <Storyboard x:Key="buttonAnimation"
                x:Name="buttonAnimation">
                <DoubleAnimationUsingKeyFrames
                    Duration="0:0:5"
                    AutoReverse="True"
                    Storyboard.TargetName="myButton"
                    Storyboard.TargetProperty=
                    "(Canvas.Left)">
                    <LinearDoubleKeyFrame KeyTime="0:0:2"
                        Value="70"></LinearDoubleKeyFrame>
                    <LinearDoubleKeyFrame KeyTime="0:0:5"
```

```
                           Value="100"></LinearDoubleKeyFrame>
                    </DoubleAnimationUsingKeyFrames>
                </Storyboard>
            </Button.Resources>
        </Button>
</Canvas>
```

As you can see, we divided the time frame into two intervals (two and three seconds in length) and used **LinearDoubleKeyFrame** objects to define the animation algorithm. Additionally, you can use **DiscreteDoubleKeyFrame** and **SplineDoubleKeyFrame**. The first one allows you to define a discrete animation, and the second one – a Bézier curve.

One more animation type in this group is **ObjectAnimationUsingKeyFrame**. This type allows you to change any user-control properties. Because the property type is unknown, it's possible to use discrete frames only.

Easing Functions

Even with key-frame animations, we need to write lots of code to create something complex. For example, if I want to paint a ball that is dropped on the ground, I need to use a huge number of **LinearDoubleKeyFrame** objects. This is because the ball in real life does not immediately stop on the ground. Instead, it bounces several times. That's why the Universal Windows Platform supports several classes that allow you to implement "easing" animations. The code below shows how to implement a bouncing ball:

```
<Canvas x:Name="LayoutRoot" Background="White">
    <Canvas.Resources>
        <Storyboard x:Name="sb1">
            <DoubleAnimation From="0" To="250"
                Storyboard.TargetName="el1"
                Storyboard.TargetProperty="(Canvas.Top)"
                Duration="0:0:5">
                <DoubleAnimation.EasingFunction>
                    <BounceEase Bounces="10"
                        EasingMode="EaseOut"
                        Bounciness="2">
                    </BounceEase>
                </DoubleAnimation.EasingFunction>
            </DoubleAnimation>
        </Storyboard>
    </Canvas.Resources>
    <Ellipse Fill="Blue" Width="50" Height="50"
```

```
x:Name="ell"></Ellipse>
</Canvas>
```

In this case we used the **BounceEase** element, which allows you to implement a "bouncing" function. The UWP supports eleven types of easing functions: **ExponentialEase**, **PowerEase**, **QuadraticEase**, **BackEase**, **BounceEase**, **CircleEase**, **CubicEase**, **ElasticEase**, **QuarticEase**, **QuinticEase**, and **SineEase**.

Embedded Animations

Basic animations work fine, but the Universal Windows Platform contains a special group of embedded animations that can be applied to user controls relative to other controls inside a collection. You can use these animations with any containers and user controls, which work with collections.

Transitions

The first group of these animations is related to transitions and allows you to define an appearance mechanism of the control when it's added to the collection or moves inside the collection. There are eight different classes:

- **AddDeleteThemeTransition:** Allows you to customize the appearance of a user control when it is added to or removed from the collection.

- **ContentThemeTransition:** This animation will work when a new value is assigned to the **Content** property. It will work at the first appearance of the control because Content is assigned for the first time.

- **EntranceThemeTransition:** Works when the user control is shown for the first time. You can apply this transition to individual objects or to containers. In the case of containers (panels), all child controls will be animated one by one.

- **ReorderThemeTransition:** Allows you to define an animation that will work if the element changes its position in the collection, usually as the result of a drag-and-drop operation.

- **RepositionThemeTransition:** Allows you to define an animation if a move occurred but there are no controls in the context.

- **EdgeUIThemeTransition:** Allows you to define transitional behavior from the edge of the window.

- **PaneThemeTransition:** Allows the user to slide panels.

- **PopupThemeTransition:** Allows you to define transitions for pop-in components of controls.

Let's see several examples of these animations. I will start with **ContentThemeTransition**. Because this type relates to content movement, it has two properties, **HorizontalOffset** and **VerticalOffset**. These attributes allow you to start moving the control to the final position using the offset. Look at the following code:

```
<Grid>
    <Button Content="Hello">
        <Button.Transitions>
            <TransitionCollection>
                <ContentThemeTransition
                    HorizontalOffset="100"
                    VerticalOffset="100"/>
            </TransitionCollection>
        </Button.Transitions>
    </Button>
</Grid>
```

This code allows you to animate a button when it appears on the screen (or changes Content). You can see that we applied the animation using the **Transitions** property of the button. In fact, this property is a collection, and you can add as many elements as you want. Thus, it is easy to combine several animation types.

If you have a container that has user controls and you want to assign the same animation to all of them, you can use the **ChildrenTransition** property. The next example works like the previous one:

```
<Grid>
    <Grid.ChildrenTransitions>
        <TransitionCollection>
            <ContentThemeTransition
                HorizontalOffset="100"
                VerticalOffset="100"/>
        </TransitionCollection>
    </Grid.ChildrenTransitions>
    <Button Content="Hello">
    </Button>
</Grid>
```

Transitions work fine for graphic primitives also. The following code allows you the user to see a "growing" rectangle:

131

```
<Grid>
    <Rectangle Height="100" Width="100" Fill="Red">
        <Rectangle.Transitions>
            <TransitionCollection>
                <AddDeleteThemeTransition/>
            </TransitionCollection>
        </Rectangle.Transitions>
    </Rectangle>
</Grid>
```

This transition doesn't have any special properties; the control just appears from nowhere.

The next example shows you how to work with **EntranceThemeTransition**:

```
<Grid>
    <Rectangle Height="100" Width="100" Fill="Red">
        <Rectangle.Transitions>
            <TransitionCollection>
                <EntranceThemeTransition
                    FromHorizontalOffset="300"
                    FromVerticalOffset="300" />
            </TransitionCollection>
        </Rectangle.Transitions>
    </Rectangle>
</Grid>
```

Let's work with some transition types dynamically. Just create a simple page:

```
<Grid>
    <StackPanel Name="stk">
        <Rectangle Width="100" Height="100" Fill="Red">
        </Rectangle>
        <Button Click="Button_Click">Click Me</Button>
    </StackPanel>
</Grid>
```

And implement the following event handler:

```
private void Button_Click(object sender, RoutedEventArgs e)
{
    Rectangle r = new Rectangle()
    {
        Height = 100,
        Width = 100,
        Fill = new SolidColorBrush(Colors.Red)
    };
    r.Transitions = new TransitionCollection();
```

```
    r.Transitions.Add(new ReorderThemeTransition());
    stk.Children.Insert(1, r);
}
```

When we click the button, while running this example, the application will create a rectangle and assign **ReorderThemeTransition** to it.

You can define transitions as styles using resources:

```
<Page.Resources>
    <Style x:Key="DefaultButtonStyle" TargetType="Button">
        <Setter Property="Transitions">
            <Setter.Value>
                <TransitionCollection>
                    <EntranceThemeTransition/>
                </TransitionCollection>
            </Setter.Value>
        </Setter>
    </Style>
</Page.Resources>
```

Theme Animations

The previous group of embedded animations allows you to implement base effects with minimum changes from the developer's side. But the next group allows you to control many more parameters, including the start time. Let's see what classes we have:

- **DragItemThemeAnimation:** Allows you to apply effects to a control that is ready to be dragged.

- **DragOverThemeAnimation:** Allows you to apply effects to controls over which something is being dragged.

- **DropTargetItemThemeAnimation:** Allows you to indicate that the control can be a source for dropping.

- **FadeInThemeAnimation:** Allows you to configure opacity when the control is displayed.

- **FadeOutThemeAnimation:** Allows you to configure opacity when the control disappears.

- **PopInThemeAnimation** and **PopOutThemeAnimation:** These animation types can be used with expandable controls.

- **RepositionThemeAnimation:** Allows you to apply effects for controls

133

that are changing their positions.

- **SplitCloseThemeAnimation** and **SplitOpenThemeAnimation:** Usually you can see these animations in complex scenarios when the user "splits" the content using two fingers.

- **TapDownThemeAnimation** and **TapUpThemeAnimation:** Allows you to apply effects on a Tapped event.

- **SwipeHintThemeAnimation:** Usually you can see this effect when swiping the control.

- **SwipeBackThemeAnimation:** Allows you to define the behavior of the control when swiping is finished.

To launch all these animations, you need to create a Storyboard. From one side, it's a disadvantage because you need to create additional code, but from the other side, it's good because you can control the animation time and use it for your own scenarios. Let's see a short example:

```xml
<StackPanel>
    <StackPanel.Resources>
        <Storyboard x:Name="myStoryboard">
            <FadeOutThemeAnimation
                Storyboard.TargetName="myRectangle" />
        </Storyboard>
    </StackPanel.Resources>
    <Rectangle PointerPressed="Rectangle_Tapped"
        x:Name="myRectangle"
        Fill="Red" Width="100" Height="100" />
</StackPanel>
```

This code declares the Storyboard, but to run it, we need to implement the following event handler:

```csharp
private void Rectangle_Tapped(object sender,
    PointerRoutedEventArgs e)
{
    myStoryboard.Begin();
}
```

Looks like that's all for animations, transformations, and graphic primitives—the longest chapter in the book.

Chapter 8

Data Binding

We already know how to create base interfaces using common user controls, and it's time to discuss how to use these controls to display real data. Of course, "display" is not the right word, because usually we have to implement much more complex tasks than just displaying data from memory, such as these:

- Display a current snapshot of the objects in memory. In this case, we are not going to track what happens with the objects later.

- Display the up-to-date data stored in memory objects. In this case, if some objects are updated, we need to update the interface as well.

- Allow users to change something through the interface. All changes should affect objects in memory and change their states and fields.

- Change the state of some user controls in the interface based on other user controls on the same page.

- Change the event handlers and templates based on states of objects in memory.

- Implement some ways to convert object properties to a more readable format when we display them on the page. If the user changes data using the interface, we need to guarantee backward conversion.

To achieve all these tasks, we need to look at the markup extensions, where the Universal Windows Platform supports extensions such as **Binding** and **x:Bind**. Both extensions have similar syntax and almost the same set of features, but we need to know that the first one makes bindings at run time using reflection to find all the needed fields and properties, while the second one works for strong types, such as static binding, which allows you to apply lots of rules at compilation. Obviously, **x:Bind** has better performance than the **Binding** extension, so it's better to use it if you have a choice. In any case, we are going to discuss both extensions.

Element-to-Element Binding

Let's start our journey with the basic binding, which allows us to change properties of one user control based on the properties of another user control. For this task we can use both markup extensions. Let's look at the following example:

```
<Grid Background=
    "{ThemeResource ApplicationPageBackgroundThemeBrush}"
    VerticalAlignment="Center">
```

```
<StackPanel x:Name="LayoutRoot">
    <Image Source="Assets/drone.jpg" Width="400">
        <Image.Projection>
            <PlaneProjection RotationY=
                "{Binding Value, ElementName=slider}">
            </PlaneProjection>
        </Image.Projection>
    </Image>
    <Slider Minimum="0" Maximum="360" Name="slider"
        Width="400" Margin="10"></Slider>
</StackPanel>
</Grid>
```

After running this code, you can see an image and a slider that allows the user to rotate the image around the y-axis. Note that we didn't create any code in C# at all. All dynamic things are only possible using the **Binding** markup extension.

You can see that **Binding** has two parameters:

- **Path:** Allows you to define a property of the source that you are using for the binding. Because Path is the default property, we can declare it implicitly.

- **ElementName:** Allows you to define the name of the element that is the source for the binding.

Let's change our code a little bit:

```
<Grid Background=
    "{ThemeResource ApplicationPageBackgroundThemeBrush}"
    VerticalAlignment="Center">
    <StackPanel x:Name="LayoutRoot">
        <Image Source="Assets/drone.jpg" Width="400">
            <Image.Projection>
                <PlaneProjection x:Name="plainPojection">
                </PlaneProjection>
            </Image.Projection>
        </Image>
        <Slider Minimum="0" Maximum="360" Name="slider"
            Width="400" Margin="10"
                Value="{Binding RotationY,
                ElementName=plainPojection, Mode=TwoWay}">
        </Slider>
    </StackPanel>
</Grid>
```

In the previous code, we used **Binding** to get data from the slider; in this piece of code, we use **Binding** to send data to the **PlaneProjection** object. It's possible because **Binding** can work in two ways. By default, **Binding** uses the OneWay mode, but we easily can change it using the **Mode** property, which can be set to one of the following values:

- **OneTime:** All properties are initialized right after the **Binding** object is created. This mode is useful when we want to present only the current snapshot.

- **OneWay:** With this mode, we can update the target once the source is updated. So we can have an up-to-date interface even if some changes to the object are applied in the code.

- **TwoWay:** With this mode, we can sync between the target and the source both ways.

In the first example, we used **OneWay** binding, and it worked fine because the target was the projection and it was updated every time the source (the slider) was updated. But in the second example, the target is the slider, and we want to update the source (the projection) once the target is updated. So **OneWay** mode doesn't work. Note that if we want to change Value or RotationY from the code, the second example will still work fine, but the first one will not work properly if we change RotationX, because it will not affect Value due to **OneWay** binding.

Let's look at the following example:

```
<Grid Background=
    "{ThemeResource ApplicationPageBackgroundThemeBrush}"
    VerticalAlignment="Center">
    <StackPanel x:Name="LayoutRoot">
        <Image Source="Assets/drone.jpg" Width="400">
            <Image.Projection>
                <PlaneProjection x:Name="plainPojection">
                </PlaneProjection>
            </Image.Projection>
        </Image>
        <Slider Minimum="0" Maximum="360" Name="slider"
            Width="400" Margin="10"
            Value="{Binding RotationY,
            ElementName=plainPojection, Mode=TwoWay}">
        </Slider>
        <TextBox Width="200"
            Text="{Binding RotationY,
            ElementName=plainPojection,Mode=TwoWay}">
```

```
      </TextBox>
   </StackPanel>
</Grid>
```

In this case we added one more control, **TextBox**, and now you can see that the text box and the slider are synchronized because they use the same source—the projection and two-way binding.

You can use **x:Bind** as well, but the syntax is a little bit different:

```
<Grid Background=
    "{ThemeResource ApplicationPageBackgroundThemeBrush}"
    VerticalAlignment="Center">
    <StackPanel x:Name="LayoutRoot">
        <Image Source="Assets/drone.jpg" Width="400">
            <Image.Projection>
                <PlaneProjection x:Name="plainPojection">
                </PlaneProjection>
            </Image.Projection>
        </Image>
        <Slider Minimum="0" Maximum="360" Name="slider"
            Width="400" Margin="10"
            Value="{x:Bind plainPojection.RotationY,
            Mode=TwoWay}">
        </Slider>
        <TextBox Width="200"
                Text=
                "{x:Bind plainPojection.RotationY,
                Mode=TwoWay}">
        </TextBox>
    </StackPanel>
</Grid>
```

The **x:Bind** markup extension uses the same Mode, but by default it uses **OneTime** mode. Additionally, **x:Bind** doesn't have the **ElementName** property, but it's not needed because the compiler knows where to find the object. You should simply use the name of object and the property.

Binding in Code

Because **Binding** works in run time, you can easily make dynamic bindings between user controls and objects in memory or even between different user controls. To implement this, you can use the **Binding** class and assign it the same properties as in XAML using the **Binding** markup extension.

```
protected override void OnNavigatedTo(
```

```
          NavigationEventArgs e)
{
    Binding binding = new Binding();
    binding.ElementName = "slider";
    binding.Path = new PropertyPath("Value");
    binding.Mode = BindingMode.TwoWay;
    BindingOperations.SetBinding(plainPojection,
        PlaneProjection.RotationYProperty, binding);

    base.OnNavigatedTo(e);
}
```

We used the **BindingOperations** class, which accepts a target object, a property, and the **Binding** object as parameters. Note that you can only use **DependencyProperty** as the target. It's important if you want to create your own user control.

Element-to-Object Binding

The most common task related to binding is to bind user controls to objects that are created in the code. Let's create a simple class that can store information about an employee:

```
public class Employee
{
    public string FirstName { get; set; }

    public string LastName { get; set; }

    public string EMail { get; set; }

    public int Age { get; set; }
}
```

This class contains four properties with the **public** access modifier. Obviously, the **Binding** object cannot get access to private or protected properties.

Using the Binding markup extension, define the following XAML, which presents an object of the Employee class:

```
<Grid Background=
    "{ThemeResource ApplicationPageBackgroundThemeBrush}"
    VerticalAlignment="Center"
    HorizontalAlignment="Center">
    <Grid.RowDefinitions>
            <RowDefinition></RowDefinition>
```

```
        <RowDefinition></RowDefinition>
        <RowDefinition></RowDefinition>
        <RowDefinition></RowDefinition>
    </Grid.RowDefinitions>
<Grid.ColumnDefinitions>
    <ColumnDefinition Width="Auto"></ColumnDefinition>
    <ColumnDefinition Width="Auto"></ColumnDefinition>
</Grid.ColumnDefinitions>
<TextBlock Text="First Name:" Grid.Row="0"
    Grid.Column="0" Margin="5" />
<TextBox Text="{Binding FirstName, Mode=TwoWay}"
    Grid.Row="0" Grid.Column="1" />

<TextBlock Text="Last Name:" Grid.Row="1"
    Grid.Column="0" Margin="5"/>
<TextBox Text="{Binding LastName, Mode=TwoWay}"
    Grid.Row="1" Grid.Column="1" />

<TextBlock Text="EMail:" Grid.Row="2"
    Grid.Column="0" />
<TextBox Text="{Binding EMail, Mode=TwoWay}"
    Grid.Row="2" Grid.Column="1" />

<TextBlock Text="Age:" Grid.Row="3" Grid.Column="0" />
<TextBox Text="{Binding Age, Mode=TwoWay}"
    Grid.Row="3" Grid.Column="1" />
</Grid>
```

In the last step, we need to create an object of the Employee class and make it "active" for the context of our form. Let's look at the following code:

```
protected override void OnNavigatedTo(
    NavigationEventArgs e)
{
    Employee emp = new Employee()
    {
        FirstName = "Sergii",
        LastName = "Baidachnyi",
        Age = 37,
        EMail = "sbaydach@microsoft.com"
    };
    this.DataContext = emp;
    base.OnNavigatedTo(e);
}
```

If you run this code, you will see the following form:

141

You can see that all of the data is available for editing, and it happened thanks to this line:

```
this.DataContext = emp;
```

DataContext is a property that is defined in the **FrameworkElement** class and can store a reference to any object. The property itself is nothing special; what is more important is that the **Binding** object will try to check it to find the object with the field that was declared for **Binding** as its parameter. To do so, Binding will start with the **DataContext** property in the target element, and if it's null, Binding will check **DataContext** for containers. In our code we initialized the **DataContext** property for the page, and it automatically initialized **DataContext** for all inner elements. If you want to change **DataContext** of any inner elements, you can simply assign it using other objects.

The following code will work in the same way:

```
<Page
    x:Class="BindingApp.MainPage"
    xmlns="http://schemas.microsoft.com/winfx/2006/
        xaml/presentation"
    xmlns:x="http://schemas.microsoft.com/winfx/2006/xaml"
    xmlns:local="using:BindingApp"
    xmlns:d="http://schemas.microsoft.com/expression/
        blend/2008"
```

```
    xmlns:mc="http://schemas.openxmlformats.org/markup-
compatibility/2006"
    xmlns:code="using:BindingApp.Code"
    mc:Ignorable="d">
    <Page.Resources>
        <code:Employee x:Key="emp" FirstName="Sergii"
LastName="Baidachnyi"
                        Age="37"
EMail="sbaydach@microsoft.com"></code:Employee>
    </Page.Resources>
    <Grid Background="{ThemeResource
        ApplicationPageBackgroundThemeBrush}"
        DataContext="{StaticResource emp}"
        VerticalAlignment="Center"
         HorizontalAlignment="Center">
        <Grid.RowDefinitions>
            <RowDefinition></RowDefinition>
            <RowDefinition></RowDefinition>
            <RowDefinition></RowDefinition>
            <RowDefinition></RowDefinition>
        </Grid.RowDefinitions>
        <Grid.ColumnDefinitions>
            <ColumnDefinition Width="Auto">
            </ColumnDefinition>
            <ColumnDefinition Width="Auto">
            </ColumnDefinition>
        </Grid.ColumnDefinitions>
        <TextBlock Text="First Name:" Grid.Row="0"
            Grid.Column="0" Margin="5" />
        <TextBox Text="{Binding FirstName, Mode=TwoWay}"
            Grid.Row="0" Grid.Column="1" />

        <TextBlock Text="Last Name:" Grid.Row="1"
            Grid.Column="0" Margin="5"/>
        <TextBox Text="{Binding LastName, Mode=TwoWay}"
            Grid.Row="1" Grid.Column="1" />

        <TextBlock Text="EMail:" Grid.Row="2"
            Grid.Column="0" />
        <TextBox Text="{Binding EMail, Mode=TwoWay}"
            Grid.Row="2" Grid.Column="1" />

        <TextBlock Text="Age:" Grid.Row="3"
            Grid.Column="0" />
        <TextBox Text="{Binding Age, Mode=TwoWay}"
```

```
            Grid.Row="3" Grid.Column="1" />
  </Grid>
</Page>
```

You can see that we declared an Employee object directly in the XAML and simply assigned it to **DataContext** of the **Grid** container. In this case we used resources, but XAML allows you to use the **DataContext** element directly to declare an object inside:

```
<Page.DataContext>
    <code:Employee x:Name="emp" FirstName="Sergii"
        LastName="Baidachnyi"
        Age="37"
        EMail="sbaydach@microsoft.com"></code:Employee>
</Page.DataContext>
```

In this case we created an object and assigned it directly to the **DataContext** property of the page. In the XAML declaration of objects, such as these objects based on Employee class, doesn't make any sense, but this approach is very popular when you use the MVVM model. In the case of MVVM, you can simply create a view model and assign it to the context of a page without any C# code in the code-behind class.

Finally, let's look at the following code, which will show the same form:

```
<Page
    x:Class="BindingApp.MainPage"
    xmlns="http://schemas.microsoft.com/winfx/
      2006/xaml/presentation"
    xmlns:x="http://schemas.microsoft.com/winfx/2006/xaml"
    xmlns:local="using:BindingApp"
    xmlns:d="http://schemas.microsoft.com/
      expression/blend/2008"
    xmlns:mc="http://schemas.openxmlformats.org/
      markup-compatibility/2006"
    xmlns:code="using:BindingApp.Code"
    mc:Ignorable="d">
    <Page.Resources>
        <code:Employee x:Key="emp" FirstName="Sergii"
            LastName="Baidachnyi"
            Age="37"
            EMail="sbaydach@microsoft.com"></code:Employee>
    </Page.Resources>
    <Grid Background=
      "{ThemeResource ApplicationPageBackgroundThemeBrush}"
      VerticalAlignment="Center"
```

```
        HorizontalAlignment="Center">
        <Grid.RowDefinitions>
            <RowDefinition></RowDefinition>
            <RowDefinition></RowDefinition>
            <RowDefinition></RowDefinition>
            <RowDefinition></RowDefinition>
        </Grid.RowDefinitions>
        <Grid.ColumnDefinitions>
            <ColumnDefinition Width="Auto">
            </ColumnDefinition>
            <ColumnDefinition Width="Auto">
            </ColumnDefinition>
        </Grid.ColumnDefinitions>
        <TextBlock Text="First Name:" Grid.Row="0"
            Grid.Column="0" Margin="5" />
        <TextBox Text="{Binding FirstName, Mode=TwoWay,
            Source={StaticResource emp}}"
            Grid.Row="0" Grid.Column="1" />

        <TextBlock Text="Last Name:" Grid.Row="1"
            Grid.Column="0" Margin="5"/>
        <TextBox Text="{Binding LastName, Mode=TwoWay,
            Source={StaticResource emp}}"
            Grid.Row="1" Grid.Column="1" />

        <TextBlock Text="EMail:" Grid.Row="2"
            Grid.Column="0" />
        <TextBox Text="{Binding EMail, Mode=TwoWay,
            Source={StaticResource emp}}"
            Grid.Row="2" Grid.Column="1" />

        <TextBlock Text="Age:" Grid.Row="3"
            Grid.Column="0" />
        <TextBox Text="{Binding Age, Mode=TwoWay,
            Source={StaticResource emp}}"
            Grid.Row="3" Grid.Column="1" />
    </Grid>
</Page>
```

You can see that in this case we used the **Source** parameter of the **Binding** object, which allows you to directly assign the context. Usually you will not use it, but this approach is still possible.

Let's spend some time discussing the **x:Bind** markup extension. It has the same syntax for binding, but it doesn't support the **DataContext** property. This is because **DataContext** can be assigned to any reference during run time, but **x:Bind** should know the exact type at compilation. The **Source** property is also not supported for the same reason. To see that it doesn't work, try to compile the following code:

```
<Page
    x:Class="BindingApp.MainPage"
    xmlns="http://schemas.microsoft.com/winfx/2006/
      xaml/presentation"
    xmlns:x="http://schemas.microsoft.com/winfx/2006/xaml"
    xmlns:local="using:BindingApp"
    xmlns:d="http://schemas.microsoft.com/expression/
      blend/2008"
    xmlns:mc="http://schemas.openxmlformats.org/
      markup-compatibility/2006"
    xmlns:code="using:BindingApp.Code"
    mc:Ignorable="d">
    <Page.Resources>
        <code:Employee x:Key="emp" x:Name="emp"
            FirstName="Sergii" LastName="Baidachnyi"
            Age="37"
            EMail="sbaydach@microsoft.com"></code:Employee>
    </Page.Resources>
    <Grid Background=
      "{ThemeResource ApplicationPageBackgroundThemeBrush}"
      DataContext="{StaticResource emp}"
      VerticalAlignment="Center"
      HorizontalAlignment="Center">
      <Grid.RowDefinitions>
          <RowDefinition></RowDefinition>
          <RowDefinition></RowDefinition>
          <RowDefinition></RowDefinition>
          <RowDefinition></RowDefinition>
      </Grid.RowDefinitions>
      <Grid.ColumnDefinitions>
          <ColumnDefinition Width="Auto">
          </ColumnDefinition>
          <ColumnDefinition Width="Auto">
          </ColumnDefinition>
      </Grid.ColumnDefinitions>
      <TextBlock Text="First Name:" Grid.Row="0"
          Grid.Column="0" Margin="5" />
      <TextBox Text="{x:Bind FirstName, Mode=TwoWay}"
          Grid.Row="0" Grid.Column="1" />
```

```
    <TextBlock Text="Last Name:" Grid.Row="1"
        Grid.Column="0" Margin="5"/>
    <TextBox Text="{x:Bind LastName, Mode=TwoWay}"
        Grid.Row="1" Grid.Column="1" />

    <TextBlock Text="EMail:" Grid.Row="2"
        Grid.Column="0" />
    <TextBox Text="{x:Bind EMail, Mode=TwoWay}"
        Grid.Row="2" Grid.Column="1" />

    <TextBlock Text="Age:" Grid.Row="3"
        Grid.Column="0" />
    <TextBox Text="{x:Bind Age, Mode=TwoWay}"
        Grid.Row="3" Grid.Column="1" />
  </Grid>
</Page>
```

You cannot even run it, because the compiler will generate the following error: **Invalid binding path 'FirstName' : Property 'FirstName' can't be found on type 'MainPage'**. With the help of this message, we can predict that instead of **DataContext**, **x:Bind** is looking for all properties of the page. So if you want to use **x:Bind**, you need to declare properties inside your page or use an explicit path. Let's modify our code to use the explicit path:

```
<TextBlock Text="First Name:" Grid.Row="0"
    Grid.Column="0" Margin="5" />
<TextBox Text="{x:Bind emp.FirstName, Mode=TwoWay}"
    Grid.Row="0" Grid.Column="1" />

<TextBlock Text="Last Name:" Grid.Row="1"
    Grid.Column="0" Margin="5"/>
<TextBox Text="{x:Bind emp.LastName, Mode=TwoWay}"
    Grid.Row="1" Grid.Column="1" />

<TextBlock Text="EMail:" Grid.Row="2" Grid.Column="0" />
<TextBox Text="{x:Bind emp.EMail, Mode=TwoWay}"
    Grid.Row="2" Grid.Column="1" />

<TextBlock Text="Age:" Grid.Row="3" Grid.Column="0" />
<TextBox Text="{x:Bind emp.Age, Mode=TwoWay}"
    Grid.Row="3" Grid.Column="1" />
```

Now everything works fine.

Let's extend our example and add one more user control, Button:

147

```xml
<Page
   x:Class="BindingApp.MainPage"
   xmlns="http://schemas.microsoft.com/winfx/2006/
   xaml/presentation"
   xmlns:x="http://schemas.microsoft.com/winfx/2006/xaml"
   xmlns:local="using:BindingApp"
   xmlns:d="http://schemas.microsoft.com/expression/
   blend/2008"
   xmlns:mc="http://schemas.openxmlformats.org/
   markup-compatibility/2006"
   xmlns:code="using:BindingApp.Code"
   mc:Ignorable="d">
   <Page.Resources>
       <code:Employee x:Key="emp" x:Name="emp"
         FirstName="Sergii" LastName="Baidachnyi"
         Age="37"
         EMail="sbaydach@microsoft.com"></code:Employee>
   </Page.Resources>
   <Grid Background=
     "{ThemeResource ApplicationPageBackgroundThemeBrush}"
     DataContext="{StaticResource emp}"
     VerticalAlignment="Center"
     HorizontalAlignment="Center">
     <Grid.RowDefinitions>
         <RowDefinition></RowDefinition>
         <RowDefinition></RowDefinition>
         <RowDefinition></RowDefinition>
         <RowDefinition></RowDefinition>
         <RowDefinition></RowDefinition>
     </Grid.RowDefinitions>
     <Grid.ColumnDefinitions>
         <ColumnDefinition Width="Auto">
         </ColumnDefinition>
         <ColumnDefinition Width="Auto">
         </ColumnDefinition>
       </Grid.ColumnDefinitions>
       <TextBlock Text="First Name:" Grid.Row="0"
           Grid.Column="0" Margin="5" />
       <TextBox Text="{Binding FirstName, Mode=TwoWay}"
           Grid.Row="0" Grid.Column="1" />

       <TextBlock Text="Last Name:" Grid.Row="1"
           Grid.Column="0" Margin="5"/>
       <TextBox Text="{Binding LastName, Mode=TwoWay}"
           Grid.Row="1" Grid.Column="1" />
```

```
        <TextBlock Text="EMail:" Grid.Row="2"
            Grid.Column="0" />
        <TextBox Text="{Binding EMail, Mode=TwoWay}"
            Grid.Row="2" Grid.Column="1" />

        <TextBlock Text="Age:" Grid.Row="3"
            Grid.Column="0" />
        <TextBox Text="{Binding Age, Mode=TwoWay}"
            Grid.Row="3" Grid.Column="1" />
        <Button Content="Regenerate email"
            Grid.Row="4" Grid.ColumnSpan="2"
            HorizontalAlignment="Center" Margin="5"
            Click="Button_Click" />
    </Grid>
</Page>
```

Using the button, I want to change EMail using an event handler for the **Click** event:

```
private void Button_Click(object sender, RoutedEventArgs e)
{
    emp.EMail = "Sergiy.Baydachnyy@microsoft.com";
}
```

If you run this code and click the button, nothing happens. Despite the usage of the TwoWay binding mode, the form doesn't know anything about the changes that we can make in the code.

To fix this problem, we can implement one of the following approaches:

- Inherit our Employee class from the **DependencyObject** class and register all properties there as dependency properties. This approach is good for user controls because all of them have already inherited **DependencyObject**, but it's not a common approach for all other classes. In any case we are going to discuss this question in the chapter about custom user controls;

- You can implement the **INotifyPropertyChanged** interface to notify the **Binding** object about any changes.

We are going to use the second approach. Let's implement it:

```
public class Employee : INotifyPropertyChanged
{
    public event PropertyChangedEventHandler
```

```
        PropertyChanged;
public void OnPropertyChanged(
    PropertyChangedEventArgs e)
{
    if (PropertyChanged != null)
        PropertyChanged(this, e);
}

private string firstName;
private string lastName;
private int age;
private string email;
public string FirstName
{
    get { return firstName; }
    set
    {
        firstName = value;
        OnPropertyChanged(
          new PropertyChangedEventArgs("FirstName"));
    }
}
public string LastName
{
    get { return lastName; }
    set
    {
        lastName = value;
        OnPropertyChanged(
          new PropertyChangedEventArgs("LastName"));
    }
}
public string EMail
{
    get { return email; }
    set
    {
        email = value;
        OnPropertyChanged(
          new PropertyChangedEventArgs("EMail"));
    }
}
public int Age
{
    get { return age; }
```

```
    set
    {
        age = value;
        OnPropertyChanged(
            new PropertyChangedEventArgs("Age"));
    }
    }
}
```

You can see that **INotifyPropertyChanged** declares just the **PropertyChanged** event, and the **Binding** objects can assign their own event handlers to this event. Once the event is fired, the **Binding** objects will update the data on the page. Our main task is to find all the places where it is possible to change the tracked properties and fire the event. Usually we can do so in setters like those implemented in the code above.

Converters

Let's extend our Employee class with the following property:

```
private double salary;
public double Salary
{
    get { return salary; }
    set
    {
        salary = value;
        OnPropertyChanged(
            new PropertyChangedEventArgs("Salary"));
    }
}
```

If we want to display this property, we can add one more row to the Grid and bind this property to a text box. Because the **Binding** object converts Salary to a string, we will see a double representation, but it's not clear in which currency an employee is getting a salary. So we need a way to convert our data to a string representation, which will contain information about the currency. Additionally, because we use **TextBox** and allow the user to edit the Employee fields, we need to implement functionality to convert the string back to the double value. To do all these things possible, we simply need to create a special class, a converter, which should satisfy just one requirement—implement the **IValueConverter** interface.

```
class MoneyConverter : IValueConverter
{
```

```
public object Convert(object value, Type targetType,
    object parameter, string language)
{
    return ((double)value).ToString("C",
        new CultureInfo("uk-UA"));
}

public object ConvertBack(object value,
    Type targetType,
    object parameter, string language)
{
    double result;
    try
    {
        result = double.Parse((string)value,
            NumberStyles.AllowThousands |
            NumberStyles.AllowDecimalPoint |
            NumberStyles.AllowCurrencySymbol);
    }
    catch
    {
        return DependencyProperty.UnsetValue;
    }
    return result;

}
}
```

Look at the code above to see an implementation of the converter. **IValueConverter** requires implementing just two methods. The first method gets an initial value and converts it to the value of the type that accepts the target property. In our case it's string, but it can be any type that makes sense in XAML—for example, **LinearGradientBrush** or a collection of objects. Imagine that I am getting a salary in Ukrainian currency, so I used the ToString method to convert the double value to the Ukrainian currency format. The **ConvertBack** method allows us to get a string and convert it to a double. If something goes wrong, I simply return **DependencyProperty.UnsetValue**, which will prevent us from assigning a wrong value to a double.

To apply the converter, we need to create its object and pass the converter as a parameter to the Binding object:

```
<Page.Resources>
    <code:Employee x:Key="emp" x:Name="emp"
```

```
       FirstName="Sergii" LastName="Baidachnyi"
       Age="37" EMail="sbaydach@microsoft.com"
       Salary="1.15"></code:Employee>
    <code:MoneyConverter x:Key="money">
    </code:MoneyConverter>
</Page.Resources>
. . . . .
<TextBox Text="{Binding Salary, Mode=TwoWay,
    Converter={StaticResource money}}"
         Grid.Row="4" Grid.Column="1" />
```

If you want, you can pass two more parameters: **ConverterParameter** and **ConverterLanguage**. You can see these parameters in the **Convert** method prototype. But in this case, I am not going to use them.

Below you can see the result (the Ukrainian currency hryvnia symbol is applied):

Because we are talking about converters, I want to mention two more properties for **Binding**: **TargetNullValue** and **FallbackValue**. The first one allows you to assign a defined value if the source property is null. The second one allows you to assign a defined value if something goes wrong with the binding (with conversion, for example) and the Binding object has an exception instead of a value.

Let's modify the text box that we created for the salary:

```
<TextBox Text="{Binding Salary, Mode=TwoWay,
    Converter={StaticResource money},
    FallbackValue= {StaticResource exValue},
    TargetNullValue= {StaticResource nullValue} }"
    Grid.Row="4" Grid.Column="1" />
```

Where exValue and nullValue are resource strings:

```
<x:String x:Key="exValue">-1</x:String>
<x:String x:Key="nullValue">0</x:String>
```

To see how to work with these properties, you can change the Convert method of the MoneyConverter class to generate an exception:

```
public object Convert(object value, Type targetType,
    object parameter, string language)
{
    throw new Exception();
    return ((double)value).ToString("C",
        new CultureInfo("uk-UA"));
}
```

You cannot use the converter to test the null value. So just remove the converter and change the Salary property to a nullable value, and simply don't initialize it.

Binding to Collections

We already know how to bind the object properties to simple user-control properties, but it is still not clear how to work with collections, where we have lots of controls, such as **ListView**, **GridView**, **Pivot**, and **FlipView**, that can hold a set of objects at the same time. In fact, when we are talking about controls that work with collections, we have in mind controls that are inherited from the **ItemsControl** class and support several properties, which are important for binding with collections:

- **ItemsSource:** Allows you to define a reference to a collection of objects. To assign **ItemsSource**, we can use the classic binding and x:Bind markup extensions or assign this property in code.

- **ItemTemplate:** With this property, you can use your own template to present data from the current object in the collection.

To test these properties, let's add one more class to our application:

```
class EmployeeViewModel
{
    public List<Employee> Items { get; set; }
```

```
public EmployeeViewModel()
{
    Items = new List<Employee>();
    Items.Add(new Employee()
    {
        FirstName="Sergii",
        LastName="Baidachnyi",
        Age=37,
        EMail="sbaydach@microsoft.com"
    });
    Items.Add(new Employee()
    {
        FirstName = "Viktor",
        LastName = "Baidachnyi",
        Age = 37,
    });
    Items.Add(new Employee()
    {
        FirstName = "Tommy",
        LastName = "Lewis",
        Age = 25,
    });
}
}
```

Thanks to this class, we can prepare all the needed information for the page. In our case, it's just a collection with three elements inside. I used the generic **List** class to store data about employees, but later I will show you why this is not the best choice.

Let's use ListView to present the items from our collection:

```
<Page
    x:Class="BindingApp.MainPage"
    xmlns="http://schemas.microsoft.com/winfx/
    2006/xaml/presentation"
    xmlns:x="http://schemas.microsoft.com/winfx/2006/xaml"
    xmlns:local="using:BindingApp"
    xmlns:d="http://schemas.microsoft.com/expression/
    blend/2008"
    xmlns:mc="http://schemas.openxmlformats.org/
    markup-compatibility/2006"
    xmlns:code="using:BindingApp.Code"
    mc:Ignorable="d">
    <Page.Resources>
```

```
        <code:EmployeeViewModel x:Key="viewModel">
        </code:EmployeeViewModel>
    </Page.Resources>
    <Grid Background=
      "{ThemeResource ApplicationPageBackgroundThemeBrush}"
      DataContext="{StaticResource viewModel}"
      VerticalAlignment="Center"
      HorizontalAlignment="Center">
        <ListView ItemsSource="{Binding Items}"></ListView>
    </Grid>
</Page>
```

You can see that we bind **ItemsSource** to the Items property in the current **DataContext**. I declared an object of EmployeeViewModel in resources to be able to use **x:Bind**.

After running this code, you will see the following data in **ListView**:

BindingApp.Code.Employee

BindingApp.Code.Employee

BindingApp.Code.Employee

This happened because we didn't define any templates, and **ListView** uses the **ToString** method to get data from objects, but **ToString** returns the name of the class by default. So we can start by overriding the **ToString** method in the Employee class:

```
public override string ToString()
{
    return $"{FirstName} {LastName}";
}
```

After running the code once again, we can see the names of the employees.

The **ToString** method is not a very good approach, because it doesn't provide any flexibility in how we display our data, but we can use **ItemTemplate** to declare our own view:

```
<ListView ItemsSource="{Binding Items}">
    <ListView.ItemTemplate>
```

```
    <DataTemplate>
        <Grid>
            <Grid.ColumnDefinitions>
                <ColumnDefinition Width="Auto">
                </ColumnDefinition>
                <ColumnDefinition Width="Auto">
                </ColumnDefinition>
            </Grid.ColumnDefinitions>
            <TextBlock Text="{Binding FirstName}"
            Margin="5">
            </TextBlock>
            <TextBlock Text="{Binding LastName}"
            Margin="5" Grid.Column="1">
            </TextBlock>
        </Grid>
    </DataTemplate>
  </ListView.ItemTemplate>
</ListView>
```

It looks the same, but in this case we control everything and can easily modify the look and feel for the list elements.

We can use **x:Bind** to work with collections as well. Let's have a look at the following code:

```
<Page
    x:Class="BindingApp.MainPage"
    xmlns="http://schemas.microsoft.com/winfx/2006/
    xaml/presentation"
    xmlns:x="http://schemas.microsoft.com/winfx/2006/xaml"
    xmlns:local="using:BindingApp"
    xmlns:d="http://schemas.microsoft.com/expression/
    blend/2008"
    xmlns:mc="http://schemas.openxmlformats.org/
    markup-compatibility/2006"
    xmlns:code="using:BindingApp.Code"
    mc:Ignorable="d">
    <Page.Resources>
        <code:EmployeeViewModel x:Key="viewModel"
        x:Name="viewModel">
        </code:EmployeeViewModel>
    </Page.Resources>
    <Grid Background=
    "{ThemeResource ApplicationPageBackgroundThemeBrush}"
        DataContext="{StaticResource viewModel}"
        VerticalAlignment="Center"
```

```
            HorizontalAlignment="Center">
    <ListView ItemsSource="{x:Bind viewModel.Items}">
        <ListView.ItemTemplate>
            <DataTemplate x:DataType="code:Employee">
                <Grid>
                    <Grid.ColumnDefinitions>
                        <ColumnDefinition Width="Auto">
                        </ColumnDefinition>
                        <ColumnDefinition Width="Auto">
                        </ColumnDefinition>
                    </Grid.ColumnDefinitions>
                    <TextBlock
                        Text="{x:Bind FirstName}"
                        Margin="5"></TextBlock>
                    <TextBlock
                        Text="{x:Bind LastName}"
                        Margin="5" Grid.Column="1">
                    </TextBlock>
                </Grid>
            </DataTemplate>
        </ListView.ItemTemplate>
    </ListView>
    </Grid>
</Page>
```

It's almost the same, but **x:Bind** needs to know the type name that we are using for elements of the collection. So we need to use the **x:DataType** attribute in **DataTemplate**.

If we are using a List collection, we will have the same problem as with the simple objects when we were trying to change some properties in the code. Binding doesn't track changes in the List collection. So in the case of objects, we implement the **INotifyPropertyChanged** interface to provide a way to track property changes. In the case of collections, we need to implement the **INotifyCollectionChanged** interface.

But even having this knowledge, we still face this problem because it is not easy to implement our own collection. That's why the .NET Framework provides a special generic class, **ObservableCollection**, which you can use for the Universal Windows Platform applications as well. Just change **List** to **ObservableCollection**, and the **Binding** object will track all changes dynamically:

```
public ObservableCollection<Employee> Items { get; set; }
```

Chapter 9

Navigation and Windowing

Pages and Navigation

As you can see, when you are developing a page, you are working with an object of the **Page** class. However, the Page class represents the content but not the window itself. If you open Object Browser, you can see that the Page class extends the **UserControl** class. This is a user control that has the **Content** property as the default property. Additionally, the **Page** class contains several methods and properties of its own. Some of these properties, such as **TopAppBar** and **BottomAppBar**, are not very interesting, because they just contain references to the application bars, but all other properties and methods help us to understand what is happening with objects of the **Page** class.

Let us start our investigation with the **Frame** property, which contains a reference to an object of the **Frame** class. Looking at the **Frame** class, you can see that this is the class that is responsible for navigation between different pages in your application. Therefore, the **Page** class helps to create the content, but the **Frame** class supports the infrastructure for working with lots of different pages. It is obvious that an object of the Frame class can present only one page at a time, and if you want to activate a new page, you simply need to call the **Navigate** method of the **Frame** class. This method is overloaded and allows you to pass the type of a page as a mandatory parameter, and additionally you can pass as a parameter an object that can be used by a new page. The third optional parameter allows you to define the transition between the old and new pages if you want to animate the process. So if you have a frame and want it to navigate to a new page, you simply should call the Navigate method:

```
rootFrame.Navigate(typeof(MainPage), e.Arguments);
```

Note that we don't create an object of the **Page** class—we simply pass a type of the new page.

But an object of the **Frame** class is not a window. The window of the application is represented by the **Window** object, which is created by the **Application** object. You can gain access to the object of the Window class using the static **Current** property:

```
var window=Window.Current
```

So initially we have objects of the **Application** and **Window** classes. In turn, the object of the Window class contains the **Content** property as well. If you want to show anything, you need to initialize this property. In fact, you can display a page directly. But the **Page** class doesn't support navigation, and that's why an object of the Frame class is the best candidate to represent the content of the window.

Look at **App.xaml.cs** and find the **OnLaunched** method there:

```
Frame rootFrame = Window.Current.Content as Frame;

if (rootFrame == null)
{
    rootFrame = new Frame();

    rootFrame.NavigationFailed += OnNavigationFailed;

    if (e.PreviousExecutionState ==
        ApplicationExecutionState.Terminated)
    {

    }
    Window.Current.Content = rootFrame;
}

if (rootFrame.Content == null)
{
    rootFrame.Navigate(typeof(MainPage), e.Arguments);
}
Window.Current.Activate();
```

You can see that the template of this method creates a frame and a page according to the scenario that we described above. The **OnLaunched** method is called when a user runs the application using standard approaches (title, icon on taskbar, etc.). The code above checks for the existing frame, and if the frame doesn't exist, it creates a new one and later assigns this frame to the **Content** property of the window. Once the infrastructure is ready, the frame navigates to MainPage, creating and displaying an object of the class. Finally, the current window uses the **Activate** method to appear on the screen.

Since each page contains a reference to its frame, you can easily use this property to navigate from one page to another according to the logic inside.

```
private void Button_Click(object sender, RoutedEventArgs e)
{
    this.Frame.Navigate(typeof(DocumentPage));
}
```

As I mentioned earlier, the **Frame** object creates an instance of the page once you call the **Navigate** method. But by default, **Frame** doesn't store objects of previous pages. So once you navigate to a new page, the previous page is destroyed. You can change this behavior and enable caching for particular pages. Looking at the Page class once again, you can find the **NavigationCacheMode** property. To activate cache mode, you need to assign this property in the constructor of the page or inside the XAML file:

```
<Page
    x:Class="WindowingApp.MainPage"
    xmlns="http://schemas.microsoft.com/winfx/2006/xaml/
    presentation"
    xmlns:x="http://schemas.microsoft.com/winfx/2006/xaml"
    xmlns:local="using:WindowingApp"
    NavigationCacheMode="Enabled">
```

By default, the cache is disabled, but you can change it to **Enabled** or **Required**. If page has **Enabled** cache mode, Frame will try to save it in its own buffer as long as it is possible, but without any special priority. So once a new page is to be stored in the cache, Frame will delete the oldest one. In the case of **Required**, the page will have a set priority and will not be deleted until pages with lower level exist (even newer pages). Using **CacheSize** of **Frame**, you can define the size of the buffer for pages.

Besides the **Navigate** method, the **Frame** class supports several different methods that allow you to use the navigation history to navigate backward and forward without defining a type of a page. You can use the **GoBack** and **GoForward** methods, but before using them, it is better to check whether navigation backward or forward is available. To do this, you can use the **CanGoBack** and **CanGoForward** properties.

```
private void MainPage_BackRequested(object sender,
    BackRequestedEventArgs e)
{
    if (this.Frame.CanGoBack) this.Frame.GoBack();
}
```

Finally, you can find several events that are declared in the **Frame** class. You can use these events to understand whether the navigation has taken place, but, frankly speaking, you will not have to do this very often. It is more important to understand the state of navigation inside a particular page, since the frame doesn't know anything about pages but the page itself should decide which data to load, how to initialize fields, which data should be saved once the user moves to another page, and so on. That's why it is more important to work with methods inside the **Page** class, which already has all the needed infrastructure. So you do not have to create new event handlers and think about where to assign them—just override the existing **OnNavigatedTo**, **OnNavigatedFrom**, and **OnNavigatingFrom** methods. The last you can use to stop navigation if the user wants to save some data, or finish his or her current work. **OnNavigatedFrom** is very useful when some data should be stored before the page is destroyed. You can save the state of the page using this method. Finally, **OnNavigatedTo** is the most popular method because lots of initializations are placed there. Additionally, you can use the parameters of this method to get information about passing a parameter and about the mode of navigation:

```
protected override void OnNavigatedTo(
    NavigationEventArgs e)
{
    var par = e.Parameter;
    var state = e.NavigationMode;

    if (state==NavigationMode.New)
    {

    }

    base.OnNavigatedTo(e);
}
```

Based on the mode of navigation, you can understand what happened with the page earlier and restore its state if needed.

Back Button Is Everywhere

OK. We know how to navigate between pages. Usually you will use content or buttons to navigate to the next page, but what about back functionality? You know that all Windows Phone devices have a hardware or software back button. So when you develop Windows Phone 8.x applications, you need to handle that button. But in the case of Windows 8.x applications, you need to create your own back button from scratch. Of course, Microsoft has published a design guide on how to create and handle the back button in Windows 8.x applications, but the approach is very different compared to Windows Phone.

Starting with Windows 10, developers can use the same approach everywhere. The back button is integrated into Windows 10, and all applications may activate and handle it for their own needs.

If you want to handle the back button in any page, you need to implement the following code:

```
protected async override void OnNavigatedTo(
   NavigationEventArgs e)
{

   SystemNavigationManager.GetForCurrentView().
      AppViewBackButtonVisibility =
         AppViewBackButtonVisibility.Visible;
   SystemNavigationManager.GetForCurrentView().
      BackRequested += MainPage_BackRequested;
   base.OnNavigatedTo(e);

}
```

With these two lines of code, you can activate the back button if it's not available (in the case of a desktop, for example) and apply an event handler for the **BackRequested** event. The **BackRequested** event handler is all you need to handle a software or hardware back button. The simplest implementation can look like this:

```
private void MainPage_BackRequested(object sender,
   BackRequestedEventArgs e)
{

   if (this.Frame.CanGoBack) this.Frame.GoBack();

}
```

Let's see what happens in desktop mode if you run the code above.

You can see that the back button is added to the application title, and users can click it as they would the back button on phone devices.

To see how the back button works in tablet mode (if you don't have a tablet), you need to open the Settings window, navigate to the Tablet mode menu item, and switch Windows to the tablet mode (or click the Notification Hub button and use the shortcut there):

If you resize the Settings window to the minimum size, you can see that the back button is implemented there in the same way.

Once you switch Windows to tablet mode, you can see that the back button is displayed on the taskbar (outside of your interface), but it still works fine.

So the back button is everywhere, and with the help of the Universal Windows Platform, developers can use the same approach to implement the back-button user experience.

Application Life Cycle

In this chapter we will only discuss foreground application life cycle. We already know how to implement navigation between several pages and how to implement back-button functionality, so it is time to see what happens with the application on start-up or on shutdown by the user.

The Universal Windows Platform applications support three states: **NotRunning**, **Running**, and **Suspended**. When your application is not running, it is simply in the **NotRunning** state. Of course, this state is not important and physically doesn't exist when the application is not running. The instance of your application simply doesn't exist. But when the user runs your application, it's possible to find out whether the application had been in the **NotRunning** or **Suspended** state. Once the user runs your application, it goes into the **Running** state. In this state the application is in the foreground and active, but once the user minimizes it or switches to another application, it is moved to the **Suspended** state. This happens because modern devices have enough memory to work with lots of applications at the same time. That's why the system doesn't kill the application as long as there is enough memory; it just moves the application to a Suspended state. This allows the user to activate the application in a second if he or she decides to return to it. So in the **Suspended** state, the applications are "frozen."

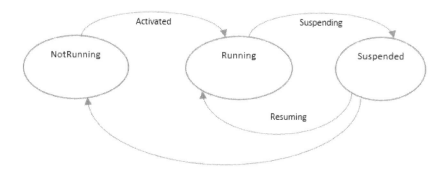

OK. We have the three states, but what is next and how do we use these states in our applications? UWP provides several events that allow you to see what is happening with the application. There are three events: **Activated**, **Resuming**, and **Suspending**. The following image helps you to understand when a particular event fires.

You cannot track any events between the **Suspended** and **NotRunning** states, because your application is destroyed between these two states. But you can handle all other events. Let's start with **Suspending** and **Resuming**, but before testing these events, please make sure that the **Debug Location** toolbar is available. With the help of this toolbar, you can use Visual Studio to send different kinds of events to your application, including **Suspending**.

Otherwise you will not be able to generate the **Suspending** event, because Visual Studio prevents it in debug mode.

Suspending is a very popular event because it is the right time for saving something. You can assign an event handler for this event in the constructor of the **Application** class. A typical implementation looks like this:

```
private void OnSuspending(object sender,
    SuspendingEventArgs e)
{
    var deferral = e.SuspendingOperation.GetDeferral();

    Frame rootFrame = Window.Current.Content as Frame;
    var str=rootFrame.GetNavigationState();
    ApplicationData.Current.LocalSettings.
        Values["navigation"] = str;

    deferral.Complete();
}
```

Because the application doesn't have any details about data on the current page, it is better to use the **Suspending** event handler to save application-related data and navigation history. Once you call the **GetNavigationState** method to return navigation history as a string, **OnNavigatedFrom** will be initiated on the current page. So you can use **OnNavigatedFrom** to save page-related data.

You need to finish the execution of the event handler for the **Suspending** event fast. Usually you have less than five seconds to finish all the work there. But in most cases, the operating system has enough resources to grant them to the **Suspending** event handler. Windows 10 allows you to use the **ExtendedExecutionSession** class to extend the time for running the **Suspending** event handler.

```
private async void OnSuspending(object sender,
    SuspendingEventArgs e)
{
    var deferral = e.SuspendingOperation.GetDeferral();

    ExtendedExecutionSession ext =
        new ExtendedExecutionSession()
    {
        Reason = ExtendedExecutionReason.SavingData
    };
    ext.Revoked += Ext_Revoked;
    var result=await ext.RequestExtensionAsync();
```

```
if (result==ExtendedExecutionResult.Allowed)
{
    //doing something
}


deferral.Complete();
}
```

If the extended session is granted, you can continue to execute your code. Code doesn't have any restrictions, but if the system decides that there are not enough resources, it will send a **Revoke** event, and then you have less than one second to finish all the work.

A few more words about **GetNavigationState**: This method should return a string with the navigation history and parameters that were passed to pages before. That's why it is very important to pass objects to the **Navigate** method, which supports serialization.

To restore the navigation state, you need to call the **SetNavigationState** method. Once you call this method, the **OnNavigatedTo** method will be called in the current page.

The event handler for the **Resuming** event is rarely used. Usually you can use it to update the data if the application was in the **Suspended** state for a long time.

The most interesting event is **Activated**, but you will not be able to find any public event like it. Instead of the **Activated** event, the **Application** class supports several methods that you can override. If the user launches the application using tiles or shortcuts, you can use the **OnLaunched** method to initialize the application. The standard template already contains an implementation of the **OnLaunched** method, but you can extend it. For example, you can use the **LaunchActivatedEventArgs** parameter to understand the previous state of the application. And if the application was **NotRunning** or **ClosedByUser**, you can continue to initialize it as usual. But if the application was terminated by the system, you can restore the latest state that you had saved using the **Suspending** event handler. That's why the template contains the following code:

```
if (e.PreviousExecutionState == ApplicationExecutionState.)
{
    //TODO: Load state from previously suspended application
}
```

But Windows 10 applications can be activated using lots of different contracts.

For example, you can associate your application with a search request to Cortana or declare the ability to work with files that have predefined extensions. In this case, the **OnLaunched** method will not work. To handle the activation of your application by the supported contracts, you need to override the **OnActivated** method.

```
protected override void OnActivated(
    IActivatedEventArgs args)
{
    if (args.Kind==ActivationKind.VoiceCommand)
    {
        //need to create a frame etc...
    }
    base.OnActivated(args);
}
```

Using the **IActivatedEventArgs** parameter, you can understand which contract was used to activate the application, and decide how to initialize the application.

Besides **OnActivated**, the **Application** class contains several other methods for particular contracts: **OnCachedFileUpdaterActivated**, **OnFileActivated**, **OnFileOpenPickerActivated**, **OnFileSavePickerActivated**, **OnSearchActivated**, and **OnShareTargetActivated**. If you implement the contracts above, don't use the **OnActivated** method but use specialized methods only.

Windowing

Windows 10 brings windows back. In Windows 8, developers could only use Windows Runtime to develop full-screen applications. So you didn't have to think about the window title, which can be seen if the user changes the size of the window, and so on. But in Windows 10, the Universal Application Platform allows users to run modern applications as legacy desktop applications. Therefore, applications have titles, icons, minimum size, and many other features that are supported by windowing applications. Let's see which features we can manage from code and how to implement them.

ApplicationView Class

The first class that we will have a look at is **ApplicationView**. An object of this class is associated with a window; it contains lots of important information about the window and allows you to change some things, such as preferred size, minimum size, and full-screen mode. To use this class, you should not create an object directly; instead you need to call the **GetForCurrentView** static method and use a reference that returns this method.

Let's have a look at the methods that you can use with a reference to an **ApplicationView** object:

- **TryResizeView:** This method will try to change the size of the window in run time.

- **TryEnterFullScreenMode:** Very useful method for media applications. You can use this method to switch the application to full screen.

- **ExitFullScreenMode:** Allows you to exit from full-screen mode.

- **SetPreferredMinSize:** Allows you to set the preferred minimum size for the window.

Here is an example of how to call one of these methods:

```
ApplicationView.GetForCurrentView().SetPreferredMinSize(
    new Size(100, 100));
```

Looking at the names of these methods, you can see that developers use words such as "try" and "preferred." This is because the Universal Windows Platform works on many different devices, and some of them may not support windowing. For example, Windows Phone continues to run all applications in full screen, or you can easily switch your desktop to tablet mode and see a modern application in full-screen mode as well. So if a device doesn't support windowing owing to tablet/phone mode, these methods will simply not operate. Of course, some of these methods return a Boolean value, but **SetPreferredMinSize** will not have any effect.

Title Bar

Looking at the **ApplicationView** class, you can find some more properties. Two of them can be very useful if you are going to modify the title bar of the window—the **Title** and **TitleBar** properties. With the former, you can apply any text to the title bar, and the latter property allows you to get access to an object of the **ApplicationViewTitleBar** type, which contains information about colors and font for the title itself and for standard buttons, such as close and maximize.

Let's implement the following code:

```
protected override void OnNavigatedTo(
    NavigationEventArgs e)
{
    ApplicationView.GetForCurrentView().Title =
```

```
    "Custom text";
ApplicationView.GetForCurrentView().TitleBar.
    BackgroundColor = Colors.Yellow;
ApplicationView.GetForCurrentView().TitleBar.
    ForegroundColor = Colors.Green;
ApplicationView.GetForCurrentView().TitleBar.
    ButtonBackgroundColor = Colors.Yellow;
base.OnNavigatedTo(e);
}
```

You can see that our text is added before the application name, which is still there.

But all colors were applied, and you can use these properties to create the style of the title bar for your application according to the style of the content.

If you want to implement something special, the **Title** and **TitleBar** properties will not help, but the Universal Windows Platform supports a way to extend your current view into the title area. Let's implement the following code:

```
<Grid x:Name="myGrid" VerticalAlignment="Top" Margin="5">
    <Grid.RowDefinitions>
        <RowDefinition Height="Auto"></RowDefinition>
        <RowDefinition Height="*"></RowDefinition>
    </Grid.RowDefinitions>
    <StackPanel Orientation="Horizontal" >
        <Ellipse Height="20" Width="20" Fill="Red">
        </Ellipse>
        <TextBlock  Text="Custom content"
            VerticalAlignment="Center"
            Margin="5" Name="txtBox"></TextBlock>
        <Ellipse Height="20" Width="20" Fill="Red">
        </Ellipse>
        <CheckBox Content="with checkbox" Name="chkBox"
            Margin="5"></CheckBox>
    </StackPanel>
    <Grid Grid.Row="1">
        <CheckBox Content="One more checkbox"></CheckBox>
    </Grid>
</Grid>
```

This XAML shows several user controls and graphic primitives—nothing special. Let's see how to bring this XAML to the window title bar. We need to write just one line of code:

```
CoreApplication.GetCurrentView().TitleBar.
  ExtendViewIntoTitleBar = true;
```

This code uses the **ExtendViewIntoTitleBar** property to extend our content into the title-bar area. If you run this code, you can see that the title is gone, but the text block, check box, and two ellipses are in the title area:

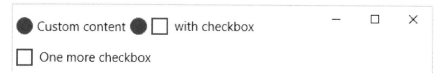

There is a problem: If you try to click on the check box in the title-bar area, it doesn't work. However, the second check box works fine. This happens because the title-bar area is placed over the content to guarantee that users can move the window. But we can change this behavior if we associate the title-bar events with user-control events. Let's see the following code:

```
<Grid x:Name="myGrid" VerticalAlignment="Top">
    <Grid.RowDefinitions>
        <RowDefinition Height="Auto"></RowDefinition>
        <RowDefinition Height="*"></RowDefinition>
    </Grid.RowDefinitions>
    <Rectangle x:Name="titlebar"></Rectangle>
    <StackPanel Orientation="Horizontal" >
        <Ellipse Height="20" Width="20" Fill="Red">
        </Ellipse>
        <TextBlock  Text="Custom content"
            VerticalAlignment="Center"
            Margin="5" Name="txtBox"></TextBlock>
        <Ellipse Height="20" Width="20" Fill="Red">
        </Ellipse>
        <CheckBox Content="with checkbox" Name="chkBox"
            Margin="5"></CheckBox>
    </StackPanel>
    <Grid Grid.Row="1">
        <CheckBox Content="One more checkbox"></CheckBox>
    </Grid>
</Grid>
```

We have added just one control, a rectangle that fills the first line of our Grid, and we placed the **StackPanel** over the rectangle. We can associate the rectangle with the title bar using the following code:

```
Window.Current.SetTitleBar(titlebar);
```

After running this code, you can now see that the check box works, and you can move the window by clicking the title bar outside the stack panel. Because in the title-bar area we have a text element as well, it's better to use the following code instead of the previous one:

```
Window.Current.SetTitleBar(txtBox);
```

Now you are able to move the window by clicking the title bar anywhere outside the check box.

Finally, you should remember two things: your user controls share the title-bar space with standard buttons (close, maximize/minimize), and in the case of full-screen mode, the title is not available. That's why it is important to track the real size of the title bar and its visibility. You can do so by using the **IsVisibleChanged** and **LayoutMetricChanged** events, which are available through **CoreApplication.GetCurrentView().TitleBar**.

How to Handle Window Size Changes

The Universal Windows Platform has only one event that allows you to track any changes in the application window—**SizeChanged**. Anything related to changing the window state generates the **SizeChanged** event: changing its orientation, moving to full screen, and so on. If you assign an event handler to this event, you can use the second parameter, **SizeChangedEventArgs**, which contains two properties: **NewSize** and **PreviousSize**. Using these properties, you can get information about the width and height of the window before and after changes.

The **NewSize** and **PreviousSize** properties don't contain any additional information if the window is in full-screen mode, but you can use **ApplicationView** to get access to this information.

Usually, you will use **SizeChanged** to switch the interface of your application from one state to another using **VisualStateManager**. We are going to discuss this approach in the next chapter.

Working with Additional Views

At the end of this chapter, let's see how to create and manage several windows inside the same application. It's a very cool feature which allows you to open several documents at the same time. For example, you can open several images to select the best, or you can open several text documents to compare them; finally, you simply may not want to close the current document when opening a new one. Windows 10 allows you to implement all these scenarios, and to do this, you need to follow these steps:

- Create a new **CoreApplicationView** object, which represents your new view.

- Using the thread that is associated with the view, initialize it and activate the prepared window.

- Display the already-prepared window as a new stand-alone window, or switch the existing view to it.

The first step is the simplest one. You can create a new application view using the **CreateNewView** method of the **CoreApplication** class:

```
var view = CoreApplication.CreateNewView();
```

Officially, the new view is ready, but it doesn't have any content, and it's not active yet. Usually, to assign new content to the current view, we use **Window. Current**, which returns a reference to the current window. But we cannot do this now, because we will get a reference to the current window, not the new one. That's why we need to implement a method that should be called in a thread associated with the new window. You can create it using the **Dispatcher** property and the **RunAsync** method:

```
var id=0;
await view.Dispatcher.RunAsync(
    CoreDispatcherPriority.Normal, () =>
    {
      var frame = new Frame();
      frame.Navigate(typeof(DocumentPage));
      Window.Current.Content = frame;
      Window.Current.Activate();
      id = ApplicationView.GetApplicationViewIdForWindow(
        view.CoreWindow);
    });
```

You can see that we used Dispatcher to gain access to the right Window object in the new window thread. I used this approach to create a new **Frame**, assign it to the **Content** property of the **Window** object, and activate the window. Note that I used a variable to store the view ID. I will need this ID to show the window, but it's not possible to gain access to it from a different thread.

Finally, I can display the new view as a stand-alone window:

```
var viewShown = await ApplicationViewSwitcher.
```

```
TryShowAsStandaloneAsync(id);
```

If everything is OK, the method returns the true value, and the new window will be displayed over the current window. Just implement a simple interface with a button, and copy all this code to the event handler of the click event for the button.

If you want to switch the current view to the new one, you can simply call the following code:

```
await ApplicationViewSwitcher.SwitchAsync(id);
```

OK, we can create a new window, but it doesn't resolve a problem when a user activates our application by clicking a file when another document is already open in our application. In this case we can utilize the existing code with small changes, and use it in the event handler of any activated event.

Imagine that our application is working with images of different formats. We can associate our application with the most common image extensions to integrate the application with Windows Explorer. To do this, just open the manifest file and add file-type associations:

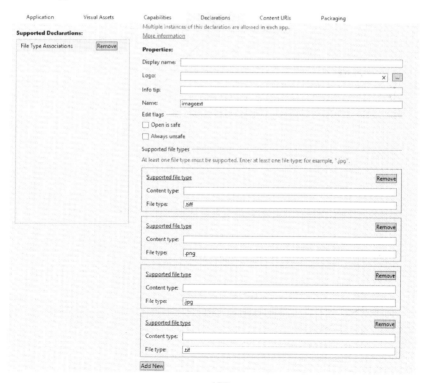

I used several common types here. So if you deploy the application now, you can see that Windows Explorer uses our application in the **Open with** menu item for files with the declared file extensions.

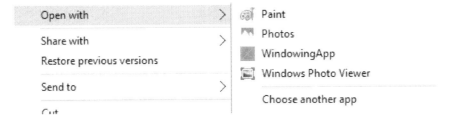

But to work with files, we need to implement the **OnFileActivated** method:

```
protected async override void OnFileActivated(
    FileActivatedEventArgs args)
{
    if (Window.Current.Content != null)
    {
        var view = CoreApplication.CreateNewView();
        var id = 0;
        await view.Dispatcher.RunAsync(
            CoreDispatcherPriority.Normal, () =>
            {
                var frame = new Frame();
                frame.Navigate(typeof(DocumentPage));
                Window.Current.Content = frame;
                Window.Current.Activate();
                id = ApplicationView.
                    GetApplicationViewIdForWindow(
                        view.CoreWindow);
            });
        await ApplicationViewSwitcher.
            TryShowAsStandaloneAsync(id);
    }
    else
    {
        Frame rootFrame = new Frame();
        rootFrame.NavigationFailed += OnNavigationFailed;
        Window.Current.Content = rootFrame;
        rootFrame.Navigate(typeof(DocumentPage));
        Window.Current.Activate();
    }
    base.OnFileActivated(args);
}
```

The method contains two parts. In the first one, we create a new window and show it for our document. This is possible if you have already opened the application and it is active. If the application is not running, we need to use the current window, and we can use it to open the file. Of course, I didn't use the file(s) itself in this application, but you can get access to all files using the parameter args and the **Files** property.

After running this code, we discover that if the application is already open, it will be put on top of all windows, and you will be able to see the new window. This is a very strange behavior, and it's better to fix it. To leave initial window untouched, we need to implement two things:

- Add the following line of code in the beginning of the **OnLaunched** method:

```
ApplicationViewSwitcher.DisableSystemViewActivationPo
licy();
```

- This line will disable the current behavior.

- Change TryShowAsStandaloneAsync to the following line:

```
await args.ViewSwitcher.ShowAsStandaloneAsync(id);
```

You can find the **ViewSwitcher** property by looking at all activation events; it was added specifically to bring a new experience to Windows 10.

Run the application, minimize the main window, and open a new one by selecting a file and opening it. You can see that the main window is still minimized and the new one doesn't affect it.

This page intentionally left blank

Chapter 10

How to Create Adaptive Interfaces

What Do We Already Know about Adaptive Interfaces?

We already know that the Universal Windows Platform allows you to create applications for any Windows 10 device. Additionally, if you are running Windows 10 applications on a PC, you can change the window size of any application or, at least, snap applications to the left and right edges. Therefore, if you create applications for Windows 10, you should use an adaptive interface, an interface that will be adaptable to different screen sizes and different orientations and that will work fine if the user decides to change the window size of your application. Obviously, an adaptive interface changes in run time, and you should be ready to handle these changes to use new layouts, reposition user controls, and present the data in a way that will most satisfy users.

In the previous chapter, we discussed the **SizeChanged** event. Any changes to the application window will generate **SizeChanged**. Even if you decide to change the window size programmatically, the event will be generated. Obviously, **SizeChanged** is the best way to track any changes and rebuild the application view based on these changes.

OK. It's easy to handle **SizeChanged**, but how can we make changes to the application view? In Windows 8 I often used to create several similar panels for different screens and change the **Visibility** properties based on the current screen size. It allowed me to implement **SizeChanged** very quickly, but this approach has lots of disadvantages. In fact, you need to build several different interfaces for different screens. So instead of one form, I developed at least two or three forms, which consumed additional resources. At the same time, this approach requires a lot of memory and CPU ticks because you have to create lots of controls and implement binding to the same set of data several times. Finally, this code is not easy to support. But there was a reason to do it—if you have a complex layout based on Grid(s) and StackPanel(s), it's almost impossible to adapt it to a new screen size. That's why the first and the most important recommendation is to use **new** user controls to create adaptive interfaces. We already discussed these controls in chapter 4: **RelativePanel**, **SplitView**, and **CommandBar**.

The first control allows you to build very complex layouts, but it doesn't use a deep hierarchy inside. You can place all your controls at the same level and simply define their places using attached properties such as **RelativePanel.LeftOf** or **RelativePanel.RightOf**. So it's easy to modify the position of any user control against other controls.

The second control, **SplitView**, allows you to build navigation panels, and thanks to different modes, you can use this control for phones and desktops and easily change the mode in run time.

Starting with Windows 10, **CommandBar** is the same for all devices, and you can easily place any commands and use them even when your application has a lack of space for content.

Therefore, UWP brings new features that allow you to build the same interface for all Windows 10 devices.

In fact, if you want to adapt the interface of your application, you can simply implement the **SizeChanged** event handler and make changes there using new features of the Universal Windows Platform. But what about XAML? We can implement anything in XAML, so there is probably a way to declare all needed changes directly in the XAML code.

Of course, we can avoid lots of code inside the **SizeChanged** event handler, and we can implement mostly all needed changes in XAML. This is possible thanks to **VisualStateManager**.

VisualStateManager

When we discuss user controls, we will spend more time with **VisualStateManager**. In fact, you can find this component if you review any template for common user controls. For example, you can find the following code by reviewing the button template:

```
<VisualStateManager.VisualStateGroups>
    <VisualStateGroup x:Name="CommonStates">
        <VisualState x:Name="Normal">
            <Storyboard>

                . . . . .
            </Storyboard>
        </VisualState>
        <VisualState x:Name="Pressed">
            <Storyboard>

                . . . . .
            </Storyboard>
        </VisualState>
        <VisualState x:Name="Disabled">
            <Storyboard>

                . . . . .
```

```
      </Storyboard>
    </VisualState>
  </VisualStateGroup>
</VisualStateManager.VisualStateGroups>
```

The idea is very simple: any user control can use the **VisualStateManager** component to declare states and groups of states. Each state is a set of animations and setters, which allows you to switch the user control from one state to another. Note that you can do it at once or use long-running animations. You can see that the button has three states and runs some animations when it's disabled or pressed. All states for buttons are located in one group. The controls cannot be at several states in the same group, but you can easily define several groups.

It's not enough to declare different states. There should be code that moves a user control from one state to another. Where to put this code depends on the user control and scenarios that are implemented. For example, there can be different event handlers for pointer events.

OK, user controls can contain some states, but how does this help us? It's easy; you can assign almost any user control its own **VisualStateManager**. For example, you can do it for the main Grid control in the interface of your application and define all needed states and animations there. You can use these animations to hide or show some controls, change the **ItemTemplate** properties, change other controls' properties, and so on. It's easy to declare several states in one group. The group will represent the set of states for different window sizes, and each state will contain animations and setters for a specific resolution. For example, you can use the following template for the main grid:

```
<VisualStateManager.VisualStateGroups>
    <VisualStateGroup>
        <VisualState x:Name="DefaultLayout">
        . . . .
        </VisualState>
        <VisualState x:Name="Layout500">
        . . . .
        </VisualState>
        <VisualState x:Name="Layout1024">
        . . . .
        </VisualState>
    </VisualStateGroup>
</VisualStateManager.VisualStateGroups>
```

Inside each state you can place the **Storyboard** control and define all needed animations. In the code below I used the **ObjectAnimationUsingKeyFrame** animation to change the **Visibility** properties and assign a new **ItemTemplate** value, and so on.

```
<ObjectAnimationUsingKeyFrames
    Storyboard.TargetName="itemListView"
    Storyboard.TargetProperty="Visibility">
    <DiscreteObjectKeyFrame KeyTime="0" Value="Visible"/>
</ObjectAnimationUsingKeyFrames>
<ObjectAnimationUsingKeyFrames
Storyboard.TargetName="itemListView"
    Storyboard.TargetProperty="ItemTemplate">
    <DiscreteObjectKeyFrame KeyTime="0"
        Value="{StaticResource smallItemTemplate}"/>
</ObjectAnimationUsingKeyFrames>
```

Once you have defined all needed visual states, you can implement code that allows you to change the visual state based on the window size. You can do it in the **SizeChanged** event handler using this line of code:

```
VisualStateManager.GoToState(myGrid, "Layout500", true);
```

Setters

Frankly speaking, the approach that allows you to change control properties using animations that run inside visual states is not new. You could use it in Windows 8.x, Windows Phone, and even Silverlight. But in many cases animations are not needed. For example, if you want to change your layout because the user changed the screen orientation, you need to change properties of controls very quickly. So developers usually used **ObjectAnimationUsingKeyFrame** to make all needed changes in zero seconds:

```
<Storyboard>
    <ObjectAnimationUsingKeyFrames
        Storyboard.TargetName="itemListView"
        Storyboard.TargetProperty="Visibility">
        <DiscreteObjectKeyFrame KeyTime="0"
            Value="Visible"/>
    </ObjectAnimationUsingKeyFrames>
</Storyboard>
```

You can see that this approach is not ideal, because it requires the use of several complex objects with many parameters to do a simple thing. That's why a new XAML element called **Setter** can be very useful. For example, you can rewrite the same code using the **Setter** element:

```
<VisualState.Setters>
    <Setter Target="comboBox.Visibility" Value="Collapsed">
    </Setter>
</VisualState.Setters>
```

This is much clearer. Developers need to declare a property's name and a new value in the selected state.

If you want, you can mix Setters and **Storyboard** inside the same state.

Adaptive Triggers

As I mentioned previously, it's not enough to declare all possible states— developers still need to implement code that allows the state to be changed dynamically. For example, if you are going to change the state based on the screen size, you need to implement an event handler for the **SizeChanged** event and use the **GoToState** method of the **VisualStateManager** class. Sometimes it's not clear when a state should be applied. Additionally, if you have several state groups and need to combine several states, you can easily make a mistake. That's why Microsoft implemented an infrastructure for state triggers. It allows you to declare one trigger or a set of triggers inside XAML to understand which state should be applied. So you can declare all needed rules without coding at all.

In the current version of the Universal Windows Platform, Microsoft presented just one trigger, **AdaptiveTrigger**, but you can develop your own triggers as well.

In the following code, you can see the usage of **AdaptiveTrigger**:

```
<VisualState x:Name="Normal">
    <VisualState.Setters>
        <Setter Target="comboBox.Visibility"
            Value="Visible"></Setter>
    </VisualState.Setters>
    <VisualState.StateTriggers>
        <AdaptiveTrigger MinWindowWidth="700">
        </AdaptiveTrigger>
    </VisualState.StateTriggers>
</VisualState>
<VisualState x:Name="Mobile">
    <VisualState.Setters>
        <Setter Target="comboBox.Visibility"
            Value="Collapsed"></Setter>
    </VisualState.Setters>
    <VisualState.StateTriggers>
```

```
        <AdaptiveTrigger MinWindowWidth="0">
        </AdaptiveTrigger>
    </VisualState.StateTriggers>
</VisualState>
```

You can see that **AdaptiveTrigger** has only two parameters: **MinWindowWidth** and **MinWindowHeight**. These parameters allow you to switch the state of the window based on size. In our example, if the width of the window is less than 700 pixels, we will collapse an element called comboBox.

Let's see how to create our own trigger.

It's hard to find an application that is not connected to the Internet. But getting data from the Internet takes some time. Usually I use **ProgressRing** to show that data retrieval is in progress, and I use **VisualStateManager** to show or hide elements based on data availability. Usually I develop three states, **Loading**, **Loaded**, and **Error**. Of course, I need to implement code to change the state of application based on state of the view model. Let's see whether it is possible to implement our own trigger that helps to completely avoid coding in the code-behind class of my page.

First of all, we need to check whether our view-model class is ready for triggers. It's better to implement a property that indicates the current state of our model as well as an event that fires every time the model changes its state. Of course, it's better to implement a base class for all view models in our application. In the next part, we will discuss MVVM patterns and will dive deeply into all these things. But right now we are going to implement a simple class that will contain no data but just the base infrastructure for our triggers:

```
public enum StateEnum
{
    Loading,
    Loaded,
    Error
}
public class StateChangeEventArgs:EventArgs
{
    public StateEnum State { get; set; }
}

public delegate void StateChangedDelegate(object model,
    StateChangeEventArgs args);

public class PageViewModel
```

```
{
    public event StateChangedDelegate StateChanged;

    public void InitModel()
    {
        if (StateChanged != null) StateChanged.Invoke(this,
            new StateChangeEventArgs() {
                State = StateEnum.Loading });
        //load data
        if (StateChanged != null)
            StateChanged.Invoke(this,
                new StateChangeEventArgs() {
                    State = StateEnum.Loaded });
    }
}
```

I have implemented the InitModel method as an example of code where we need to invoke a **StateChanged** event. Usually you will implement this method in your own way and in inherited classes.

Once you have updated the view model, you can create an object inside the page XAML file:

```
<Page.Resources>
    <st:PageViewModel x:Name="model"></st:PageViewModel>
</Page.Resources>
```

It's time to create your own trigger. To do so, you need to create a new class that inherits the **StateTriggerBase** class. Inside the class you can declare any method and properties, but you need to find a place where you will call the **SetActive** method. With this method, you can activate or deactivate your trigger. For example, I implemented the following class:

```
public class DataTrigger: StateTriggerBase
{
    private PageViewModel model;

    public PageViewModel Model
    {
        get
        {
            return model;
        }
        set
        {
            model = value;
```

```
        model.StateChanged += Model_StateChanged;
    }
}

public string StateOfModel { get; set; }

private void Model_StateChanged(object model,
    StateChangeEventArgs args)
{
    SetActive(args.State.ToString().Equals(
        StateOfModel));
}
}
```

You can see that I have two properties in the class that allow us to set a reference to the current view model and define the state that we are going to use to activate the trigger. Once the view model is initialized, we will activate or deactivate the trigger using the event handler for the **StateChanged** event.

Finally, I declared the following states:

```
<VisualState x:Name="Loading">
    <VisualState.Setters>
        <Setter Target="gridView.Visibility"
            Value="Collapsed"></Setter>
        <Setter Target="progress.Visibility"
            Value="Visible"></Setter>
    </VisualState.Setters>
    <VisualState.StateTriggers>
        <st:DataTrigger Model="{StaticResource model}"
            StateOfModel="Loading"></st:DataTrigger>
    </VisualState.StateTriggers>
</VisualState>
<VisualState x:Name="Loaded">
    <VisualState.Setters>
        <Setter Target="gridView.Visibility"
            Value="Visible"></Setter>
        <Setter Target="progress.Visibility"
            Value="Collapsed"></Setter>
    </VisualState.Setters>
    <VisualState.StateTriggers>
        <st:DataTrigger Model="{StaticResource model}"
            StateOfModel="Loaded"></st:DataTrigger>
    </VisualState.StateTriggers>
</VisualState>
```

This is really cool and allows us to make a better implementation of the MVVM pattern.

How to Create Different Views

We already discussed how to create an adaptive interface inside the same view, but in some cases it's not easy to create really universal pages. For example, you can adapt all controls, but you need to remember that phone users usually use just one hand to work with applications. So you need to adapt not only the layout but the user experience as well.

That's why in some cases you might want to create different views for different devices. Let's see how to do this using Visual Studio 2015.

Of course, to start working with additional views, you need to have initial pages. For example, you want to create a new view for the existing MainPage.xaml. To do so, you need to add a new XAML View to your project.

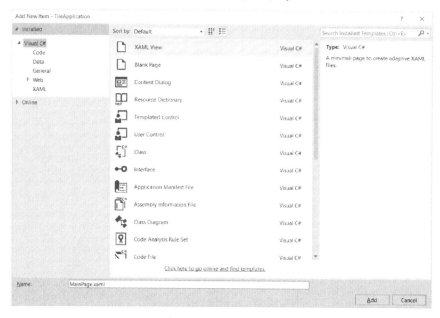

You can see that the XAML View template will create the XAML page only, without the code-behind file. Of course, this is not enough, and to associate a new view with the page by default, you need to select one of these two approaches:

- You can place the view in the same folder with the initial page and call the view using the name of the initial page plus a prefix. I discovered two prefixes right now—**DeviceFamily-Mobile** and **DeviceFamily-Desktop**.

- You can use the same name for the view that has the page by default, but you need to place the view in a special folder—**DeviceFamily-Mobile** or **DeviceFamily-Desktop**.

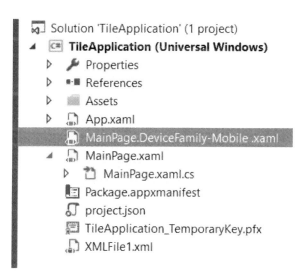

That's all. If you run our application on the phone, and if you have a view under the **DeviceFamily-Mobile** rule, then the view will be applied, but if you didn't implement a new view under **DeviceFamily-Mobile**, then the initial XAML view will be applied. The same is true for the desktop.

It is possible to apply your own views based on custom logic.

First of all, you need to follow the naming rules to associate a new view with the existing code-behind file. To do this, just use the following rule: <initial page name>.<any extension>.xaml. Don't use "DeviceFamily" for your own extensions—this name is reserved by Visual Studio, and you will get a run-time error if you use it. For example, if you create a new view for MainPage.xaml, you can use the name MainPage.Raspberry.xaml.

Once you add a new view to your project, you can see that Visual Studio will generate one more **InitializeComponent** method.

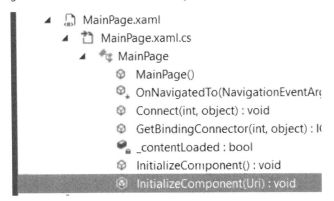

At this step Visual Studio doesn't check anything—it just adds a new method to be used for different device families. Of course, if you use the predefined device family, the **InitializeComponent** method with the parameter will be called automatically, but in the case of your own logic, you can call it directly from your code. Of course, you need to change the existing constructor of the page and call **InitializeComponent** in the following way:

```
this.InitializeComponent(
    new System.Uri("ms-appx:///MainPage.Raspberry.xaml"));
```

Using this approach, you can implement any custom logic in your constructor and apply different views based on different devices, parameters, and so on.

Chapter 11

Tiles and Notifications

Before discussing how to publish applications to the Store, we need to look at one more topic, which is a must-do before doing anything else in the Store. This topic is about tiles, which represent your applications. Additionally, we will discuss Tile and Toast notifications, which provide a unique experience to users, communicating with them even when applications are not running.

You can find several chapters in this book, where we discuss background notifications and notifications that you can send using Windows Notification Service.

Let's start our overview with basic tiles.

Live Tiles

All applications have tiles. Of course, tiles are not very important in desktop mode, but once you use a tablet or phone or switch your device to tablet mode, the tiles allow you to personalize your Start screen, providing information related specifically to you: local news, weather, images, information about unread messages, and so on.

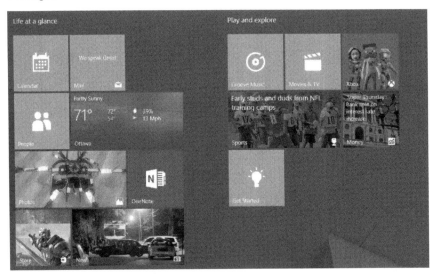

So from a developer's perspective, a tile is something that helps to communicate with users even when the application is closed. And finally, tiles can motivate users to launch the application again and again.

Developers start working with the tiles from the manifest file. Here you can declare which types of tiles will support your application, and you should provide default settings for tiles, such as background, application name, and images.

Applications support up to four types of tiles: small, medium, wide, and large (desktop only), and when editing the manifest, you can simply provide icons for any of these types. Doing this is very boring, and usually it requires you to ask a designer to create all the needed icons for your application. In the manifest you can find all the recommended sizes in pixels, which you can supply to the designer. Of course, if you don't have any designers, this becomes a problem, because tiles represent your application in the Store as well, and personally I never install applications with bad tiles. So invest some time in creating really good tiles. Note that Windows 10 supports a huge set of devices with different form factors, resolutions, and screen sizes. That's why it's better to provide icons for different scale factors. Of course, if you use "scale 100" only, Windows will resize your icons, but since the icons are in pixel format, this can affect the quality of your tiles.

In any case, you should provide a basic set of images for the Start screen, and this is easy to do using the manifest designer. Using the designer, you can provide images for a splash screen and badge logo as well. The first is used when the application is loading, and the second when it is shown on the lock screen, if you support that.

If you are editing the code of the manifest directly, you can find that using the VisualElements tag, you can declare only small and medium tiles. These two types of tiles are a must, but if you want to declare wide and large tiles, you need to use the **DefaultTile** inner element:

193

```
<Applications>
  <Application Id="App" Executable="$targetnametoken$.exe"
    EntryPoint="TileApplication.App">
    <uap:VisualElements DisplayName="TileApplication"
      Square150x150Logo="Assets\Square150x150Logo.png"
      Square44x44Logo="Assets\Square44x44Logo.png"
      Description="TileApplication"
      BackgroundColor="transparent">
      <uap:DefaultTile
        Wide310x150Logo="Assets\Wide310x150Logo.png">
      </uap:DefaultTile>
      <uap:SplashScreen Image="Assets\SplashScreen.png" />
    </uap:VisualElements>
  </Application>
</Applications>
```

All these setup activities are not very interesting for developers; what is really interesting is how to bring tiles alive. So let's switch our context from the manifest designer to the coding practices related to tiles.

When your application is running in the foreground or even the background, you can update the tiles of the application. Officially, any Live tiles may contain several layers: content, a short name, an application icon (44 × 44 pixels), and a badge (a number or a glyph). Of course, for small tiles it never makes sense to change the default behavior, but for all other types, you can easily update any of these layers.

When I presented similar stuff for Windows 8.x developers, I usually started with the **Windows.UI.Notifications** namespace, which contains all classes that allow you to work with tiles and notifications. But in the case of Windows 10, it's better to start with templates owing to the huge changes.

The templates define how your content will be presented, providing fields for filling with text and images. Windows 8.x supports more than forty templates you can use. But in the case of Windows 10, developers should pay attention to adaptive interfaces, which provide lots of ways to present content for different devices, including screen resolutions, screen sizes, and the typical distance between users and devices. But if we create an adaptive interface, it would probably be wise to have adaptive tiles as well. That's why in Windows 10, Microsoft introduced a special adaptive template, which provides better flexibility, works fine in an adaptive environment, and supports all features that were implemented in more than forty legacy templates. So if you are developing a new application for Windows 10, I would recommend using this new adaptive template rather than the old ones.

As before, to start working with the template, you need to work with XML. So first you need to generate an XML document that will contain all needed updates. On a high level, the XML can contain the following elements:

```
<tile>
  <visual>
    <binding template="TileSmall">
      . . . . .
    </binding>
    <binding template="TileMedium">
      . . . . .
    </binding>
    <binding template="TileWide">
      . . . . .
    </binding>
    <binding template="TileLarge">
      . . . . .
    </binding>
  </visual>
</tile>
```

All of the **binding** tags allow you to define the concrete tile, and you can declare all of them or at least one. With the **template** attribute, you can define which tile you are going to update and place all content inside the **binding**. Additionally, the **binding** and **visual** elements can contain the **displayName** attribute. In the case of **visual**, the attribute will be applied to all **binding** elements, but if you place it for **binding**, it will rewrite the display name for the particular tile. The **visual** element supports one more important attribute—**branding**. With this attribute you can define whether you are going to display a small logo and a short name for tiles. Here is an image that shows different looks for different **branding** values:

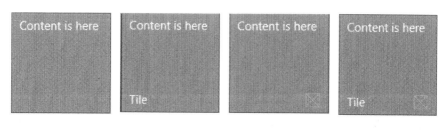

none   **name**   **logo**   **nameAndLogo**

195

You can start testing different values and parameters by running the following code:

```
XmlDocument xml = new XmlDocument();
xml.LoadXml(
    "<tile>" +
    "<visual branding=\"none\">" +
    "<binding template=\"TileMedium\" displayName=" +
    "\"Tile\">" +
    "<text>Content is here</text>" +
    "</binding>" +
    "</visual>" +
    "</tile>"
    );
var updater=Windows.UI.Notifications.
    TileUpdateManager.CreateTileUpdaterForApplication();
TileNotification tile =
    new TileNotification(xml);
updater.Update(tile);
```

It's the same code that works for Windows 8.x, but in this case we are using an adaptive template. In any case, if you want to update tiles, you need to pack all updates into the **XmlDocument** object. You can find the **XmlDocument** class in the **Windows.Data.Xml.Dom** namespace. Simply load your XML there using the **LoadXml** method. Once the tile is ready, we can use two classes to update it: **TileUpdater** and **TileNotification**.

We can use the second one to create an object directly based on our **XmlDocument**. You can add expiration time as well, but if you don't and the user doesn't launch your application, Windows will remove the Tile notification automatically in three days.

We cannot create **TileUpdater** directly, but we can use **CreateTileUpdaterForApplication** of the **TileUpdateManager** class. And finally, once we have **TileUpdater** and **TileNotification** objects, we can simply use them to update the tile(s).

Let's go back to the adaptive template and talk about the type of content that can present tiles.

It's possible to use two types of elements to present some content and two more elements to organize the content inside the tile. To present the content, you can use the **text** and **image** elements, and to organize, **group** and **subgroup**.

Let's start with the **text** element. This element can display any text inside the tile

196

and uses the following attributes:

- **hint-style:** Thanks to styles, you can control font size, color, and weight of text elements. You cannot define your own styles, but you can find lots of predefined styles, including caption, body, base, subtitle, title, subheader, header, titleNumeral, subheaderNumeral, headerNumeral, captionSubtle, bodySubtle, baseSubtle, subtitleSubtle, titleSubtle, titleNumeralSubtle, subheaderSubtle, subheaderNumeralSubtle, headerSubtle, and headerNumeralSubtle.

- **hint-wrap:** By default, text does not wrap, but if you set this attribute to true, it will apply text wrapping to the text.

- **hint-align:** This attribute allows you to align text horizontally. You can use right, left, or center values.

- **hint-maxLines** and **hint-minLines:** Allow you to apply a minimum and maximum amount of lines.

Just modify the XML document by adding one more text element and some attributes:

```
xml.LoadXml(
 "<tile>" +
 "<visual branding=\"none\">" +
 "<binding template=\"TileMedium\" displayName= \"Tile\">"+
 "<text hint-style=\"title\">Content is here</text>" +
 "<text hint-style=\"body\" hint-wrap=\"true\">" +
 "Content is here</text>" +
 "</binding>" +
 "</visual>" +
 "</tile>"
);
```

You can see that the first line is cut off, but for the second one, we used the wrap attribute, so the text wrapped.

One more attribute that can help to align text is **hint-textStacking**. This attribute allows you to align text vertically, but you can apply it to a **binding** element or to a **subgroup** element.

The next element that can present content is **image**. The most important attributes are as follows:

- **placement:** This property supports three values: **inline, background,** and **peek**. In the case of **inline**, you can place an image and text together, and the text will be aligned according to the position of the image. With **background**, you can use an image as a background and place text above the image. In the case of **peek**, the image will use animation to slide up and down.

- **src:** Source of the image.

- **hint-crop:** Allows you to crop the image using a circle—just set this attribute to **circle**.

- **hint-align:** This attribute supports the following values: stretch, left, center, and right. With this you can specify how to place the image within the tile.

- **hint-removeMargin:** By default, an image has 8-pixel margins, but you can remove these by setting this attribute to true.

Extend the previous example by adding an image as the background for the application tile:

```
xml.LoadXml(
 "<tile>" +
 "<visual branding=\"none\">" +
 "<binding template=\"TileMedium\" displayName=\"Tile\">" +
 "<image src=\"Assets/drone.jpg\" " +
 "placement=\"background\""+
 " hint-align=\"stretch\"/>" +
 "<text hint-style=\"title\">Content is here</text>" +
 "<text hint-style=\"body\" hint-wrap=\"true\">" +
 "Content is here</text>" +
 "</binding>" +
 "</visual>" +
 "</tile>"
);
```

You can see the result below:

In this example we used the placement attribute to fill all the space on the tile. Because we are using an image as the background for the tile, we cannot use **hint-removeMargin**—it's not needed for background.

The next two elements that you can use to create adaptive tiles are **group** and **subgroup**.

The first element allows you to either place all of the content that should be displayed on the tile together or not display it at all. It's a very important element for adaptive tiles because you cannot predict all possible sizes for tiles, but you can place several groups inside, and the tile will display as many groups as possible. So if the user uses big tiles on a huge screen, the tile will display several groups, but in the case of a small screen, the same tile will display fewer groups.

Each **group** contains at least one **subgroup**. In fact, a subgroup element allows you to declare columns for the content on the tile. Let's look at the following code:

```
xml.LoadXml(
    "<tile>" +
    "<visual branding=\"none\">" +
    "<binding template = \"TileWide\" displayName = " +
    "\"Tile\">" +
    "<group>"+
    "<subgroup hint-weight=\"1\">" +
    "<text hint-style=\"body\" hint-align =\"center\">" +
    "Team A</text>" +
    "<text hint-style=\"headerNumeral\" hint-align" +
    "=\"center\">0</text>" +
    "</subgroup>"+
    "<subgroup hint-weight=\"1\">" +
    "<text hint-style=\"body\" hint-align =\"center\">" +
    "Team B</text>" +
    "<text hint-style=\"headerNumeral\" hint-align " +
    "=\"center\">2</text>" +
    "</subgroup>" +
    "</group>" +
```

```
"</binding>" +
"</visual>" +
"</tile>"
);
```

This code allows you to prepare information about the current status of a soccer game for the tile.

We defined the width of the columns in the same way as we did for the grid columns. We divided our tile into several parts and specified how many parts are used in each column (in this case, two parts in total with one part for each column).

We already know how to work with the content, title, and icon, but we still have one other element that can be placed on the tile, which is the badge. This element is a number or a glyph that is placed in the bottom-right corner of the tile. Usually you can find this element on tiles of messaging applications, where it displays the number of new or unread messages, but you can add your own meaning to the badge.

Unfortunately, you can not specify a badge using the adaptive-tile template. To change/create a badge, you need to use different classes: **BadgeUpdateManager**, **BadgeNotification**, **BadgeUpdater**, and **BadgeTemplateType**. All these classes are located in the **Windows.UI.Notifications** namespace, and additionally you will need the **Windows.Data.Xml.Dom** namespace to work with the XML document.

As the first step, you should get a template for the badge. Like the template for tiles, this one is an XML document, but you should not create it from scratch. Instead, you should use **BadgeUpdateManager** to get the template:

```
var template=BadgeUpdateManager.
    GetTemplateContent(BadgeTemplateType.BadgeNumber);
```

The **GetTemplateType** method accepts **BadgeTemplateType** as a parameter and can return the template for a number or glyph. In any case, the method will return an **XmlDocument** object, and you can add the number for the badge there:

```
XmlElement element =
   (XmlElement)template.SelectSingleNode("/badge");
element.SetAttribute("value", "5");
```

Finally, we can create an object of the **BadgeNotification** class and update our tile using **BadgeUpdater**:

```
BadgeNotification badge = new BadgeNotification(template);
BadgeUpdateManager.CreateBadgeUpdaterForApplication().
   Update(badge);
```

Running this code, you can see a small number in the bottom-right corner:

I don't know what it might mean for our application, but it works.

Toast Notifications

We already started working with notifications. When we update a tile or a badge, we send a notification to the system using the template, and Windows makes updates. Obviously we can send these notifications not just from a local application. Windows supports several methods to deliver notifications:

- **Local:** We just used this method when sending Tile notifications from the application itself.

- **Scheduled:** You can schedule some notifications, and even if your application is not active, the user can see the scheduled updates.

- **Periodic:** You can ask the system to get updated information from the cloud and update tiles with it.

- **Push:** You can implement integration with Windows Notification Service (WNS), which is located in the cloud. Thanks to WNS, it's possible to send a notification from a server to your application.

We are going to discuss push notifications in part 3 of this book. Right now we will get an overview of the first three types.

We already used local **Badge** and **Tile** notifications, but Windows supports two more types—**Toast** and **Raw**. You can see **Toast** notifications in the Action Center; they look like flyout messages, which the user can click on to navigate to the application. So it's one more way to launch your application, and if your application supports **Toast** notifications, it's one more way to get additional attention on your application. You can use the **Local**, **Scheduled**, and **Push** methods for **Toast**. **Raw** notifications work with the Push method only, so we will discuss it later.

Before discussing how to use the **Scheduled** and **Periodic** notifications, let's spend some time talking about **Toast** notifications.

Windows 10 brings adaptive templates for Toast notifications just as it does for Tile notifications. Toast notifications support several types of elements inside: text, images, actions, and audio. There are no group and subgroup elements, but they are not needed for toasts. As with tiles, you can define toasts using an XML document. In general, you can use the following templates:

```
<toast>
  <visual>
    <binding template="ToastGeneric">
      . . .
    </binding>
  </visual>
  <actions>
    . . .
  </actions>
  <audio src="ms-appx:///..."/>
</toast>
```

Usually you will use the **binding** element, which can contain text and images elements. As with Tile notifications, you can specify text blocks and images using the **text** and **image** elements, but these elements have almost no attributes. The **image** element still has the **src** and **hint-crop** attributes. Additionally, you can use the placement attribute for an image, which supports just two values: **inline** and **appLogoOverride**. The **inline** value allows you to mix text and images inside the notification body, but **appLogoOverride** allows you to use your own image in the logo area instead of a standard one.

Let's see the following example, which allows you to run local Toast notifications:

```
XmlDocument xml = new XmlDocument();
xml.LoadXml(
  "<toast>" +
```

```
"<visual>" +
"<binding template=\"ToastGeneric\">" +
"<text>Football application</text>" +
"<text>Team A - Team B - 2:0</text>" +
"<image src=\"Assets/drone.jpg\" " +
"placement=\"appLogoOverride\" />" +
"</binding >" +
"</visual>" +
"</toast>");
var toastNot =
    ToastNotificationManager.CreateToastNotifier();
ToastNotification toast = new ToastNotification(xml);
toastNot.Show(toast);
```

You can see that we used almost the same classes to send the notification, but we substituted the word "toast" for "tile." Running this code, you will able to see the following message:

If you open the Action Center, you will see the same message there. So if the user misses the message, it's possible to review it later.

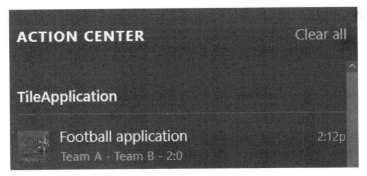

If you close the application and click the message, the application will continue running. So Toast notifications can be used as an additional activation mechanism. To track activation by clicking the Toast notification, you need to implement the **OnActivated** method. We already discussed this method in the previous chapter, but just in case, I want to show the template for this method:

```
protected override void OnActivated(
    IActivatedEventArgs args)
```

```
{
    if (args.Kind == ActivationKind.ToastNotification)
    {
        //doing something
    }
}
```

Of course, there is a way to use a Toast notification to activate a background task (not just foreground), but we will discuss that in the chapter about background tasks.

The next element in the template is the audio. Using this element, you can provide your own sound to be played once the notification arrives.

The last element is **actions**, and it the most interesting element in the template because it supports interaction with a user without the application itself running. This element can contain three different types of controls:

- **input:** This element can represent a text box or combo box depending on the **type** attribute. If the **type** attribute is **text**, then a text box is displayed, but in the case of **selection**, a combo box is presented.

- **selection:** This element allows you to declare an item for the combo box. These elements are located inside the **input** element and support the **id** and **content** attributes.

- **action:** The last element in the list allows you to declare buttons. In general, you can use the **content**, **arguments**, and **imageUri** attributes to place text on the button, image, and passing a parameter to the application logic. This element has an **activationType** attribute as well, which allows you to run some code in the background and not just in the foreground.

OK, now we know how to use Tile and Toast adaptive templates. But if you don't like XML templates and want to avoid them, you can do so with notifications extensions.

Open NuGet package manager and add the **NotificationsExtensions.Win10** package.

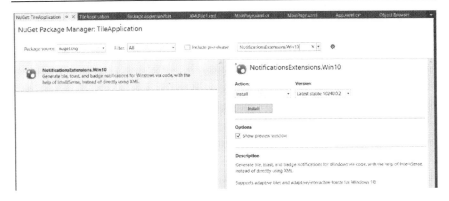

In this package you can find several namespaces, such as **NotificationsExtensions.Badges**, **Tiles**, and **Toasts**, and each of them contains lots of classes. But you will always start with the **ToastContent**, **TileBindingContentAdaptive**, **BadgeNumericNotificationContent**, or **BadgeGlyphNotificationContent** class and continue to build your notifications with other classes. For example, in the code below, we create the same Toast notification as above, but we use **ToastContent** and assign some properties using objects of the **ToastVisual**, **ToastText**, and **ToastAppLogo** classes:

```
ToastContent toastDoc = new ToastContent()
{
    Visual = new ToastVisual()
    {
        TitleText = new ToastText()
        {
            Text = "Football application"
        },
        BodyTextLine1 = new ToastText()
        {
            Text = "Team A - Team B - 2:0"
        },
        AppLogoOverride = new ToastAppLogo()
        {
            Source =
                new ToastImageSource("Assets/drone.jpg")
        }
    }
};

var toastNot =
    ToastNotificationManager.CreateToastNotifier();
ToastNotification toast =
```

```
    new ToastNotification(toastDoc.GetXml());
toastNot.Show(toast);
```

Now we know how to work with the Toast template and how to activate local notifications. It's time to discuss **Scheduled** and **Periodic** notifications.

Scheduled Notifications

With scheduled notifications, you can update application tiles or send notifications to users even when your application is not active. In fact, you can schedule toasts or any changes with tiles in advance when your application is running. Of course, in this case users cannot get up-to-date content, because you need to form the XML document in advance, but it's a good way to keep users' attention.

Frankly speaking, it's very easy to create scheduled notifications. You just need to use the **ScheduledTileNotification** and **ScheduledToastNotification** classes instead of **TileNotification** and **ToastNotification** and use the **AddToSchedule** method instead of **Show** and **Update**.

For example, the code below shows a toast message five times every minute, and it will start doing so one minute after execution:

```
var toastNot =
ToastNotificationManager.CreateToastNotifier();
ScheduledToastNotification toast =
    new ScheduledToastNotification(
        toastDoc.GetXml(), DateTime.Now.AddMinutes(1),
        TimeSpan.FromMinutes(1),5);
toastNot.AddToSchedule(toast);
```

Of course, in some cases you need to remove existing scheduled notifications. To do so, you can use the **GetScheduledToastNotifications** and **RemoveFromSchedule** methods of the **ToastNotifier** class for toasts or **GetScheduledTileNotifications** and **RemoveFromSchedule** of **TileUpdater** for tiles.

Periodic Notifications

Periodic notifications are very interesting because they allow you to get updated information from the server side. But in the case of periodic notifications, you can update tiles and badges only. For Toast notifications, you need to use Windows Notification Service.

To ask Windows to get information from the server, Windows Runtime provides the **StartPeriodicUpdate** method, which you can find in the **TileUpdater** and **BadgeUpdater** classes. This method requires at least two parameters for Uri: information on where to get an updated XML, and an interval that allows you to define the frequency of updates. In general, you can use the following block to start updating the application tile:

```
var updater =
    TileUpdateManager.CreateTileUpdaterForApplication();
updater.StartPeriodicUpdate(
    new Uri("http://toastsbaydachtest.azurewebsites.net
        /ToastHandler.ashx"), PeriodicUpdateRecurrence.Hour);
```

In this case, Windows will request a new XML from the specified URI every hour. Note that the tile will be updated immediately, but if you want to initiate the process at some time, you can use one more parameter for the **StartPeriodicUpdate** method. If you want to stop requests to the server, you can call the **StopPeriodicUpdate** method.

Additionally, the **TileUpdater** class contains the **StartPeriodicUpdateBatch** method, which allows you to pass up to five URIs with different XMLs. Using this method, you can build a queue of tiles that will be shown up to the next update. But you need to enable this feature by calling the **EnableNotificationQueue** method.

To test the approach with periodic notifications, you need to deploy a web service that will return XML. It's the same XML that we used locally. I would recommend using Azure Web Sites and deploying a simple project with a generic handler only. In this case, you will able to concentrate your attention on the XML and not on the web service.

For example, my implementation of the handler looks like this:

```
public void ProcessRequest(HttpContext context)
{
    context.Response.ContentType = "text/plain";
    context.Response.Write(
        "<tile>" +
        "<visual branding=\"none\">" +
        "<binding template = \"TileWide\" displayName =" +
        "\"Tile\">" +
        "<group>" +
        "<subgroup hint-weight=\"1\">" +
        "<text hint-style=\"body\" hint-align " +
        "=\"center\">Team A</text>" +
```

```
            "<text hint-style=\"headerNumeral\" hint-align" +
            "=\"center\">0</text>" +
            "</subgroup>" +
            "<subgroup hint-weight=\"1\">" +
            "<text hint-style=\"body\" hint-align" +
            "=\"center\">Team B</text>" +
            "<text hint-style=\"headerNumeral\" hint-align " +
            "=\"center\">2</text>" +
            "</subgroup>" +
            "</group>" +
            "</binding>" +
            "</visual>" +
            "</tile>"
    );
}
```

And I spent only about five minutes to set up and deploy everything.

In this chapter, we just started discussing tiles and toasts. Later in this book, we will discuss how to work with notifications in the background, Windows Notification Service, and raw notifications.

Chapter 12

How to Publish Applications to the Store

At the end of the first part of the book, I want to take some time to discuss how to publish your applications to the Store. In this chapter I am going to talk about how to create a developer account, what you need to know before publishing, and how to publish your application. But we will return to the topic in chapter 26, where we discuss paid applications, advertising, and other features related to your revenue from the Store.

Create a Publisher Account

Before doing anything, you need to create a developer account, which will allow you to publish applications to the Store. The best way to join the Store is to visit http://dev.microsoft.com. Using this entry point, it's possible to find links to documentation, how-to articles, tools, and so on. And by clicking the Dashboard link, it's easy to join the Store or open an existing account.

Note that you need to create a Live ID to access the dashboard. Using this Live ID, you will be able to associate your application with the Store (download certificates and sign), publish applications, check reports, and so on. You cannot associate two or more Live IDs with the same account and grant some permissions to each of them.

Once you select a Live ID and sign in, you can start the registration process. In the first step, you need to select an account type:

There two types: individual account and company account. The second one will belong to your company, but the first one belongs to you. You can see that there is a difference in price. An individual account costs twenty Canadian dollars while a company account costs ninety-nine. This is one-time payment, but before paying this amount, you can take some time to find a way to avoid any payment at all.

For example, if you are a student, you have access to the DreamSpark.com website, where all students can download Microsoft software for free, and there you can find a way to create a free Store account as well. The same situation applies to MSDN subscribers. Visiting the benefits page of MSDN subscription, you can find a promo code and use it to register for free.

In any case, if you decide to select an individual account, you will probably be able to publish your application in ten minutes, but in the case of a company account, it takes some time until the company verification process is finished.

The account country field is very important. You need to provide the country where you want to make your business and get your money. You will not able to change the country or account type.

In the next step, you need to select the publisher display name and provide contact information. You can select any name for publishing, if it's available, of course:

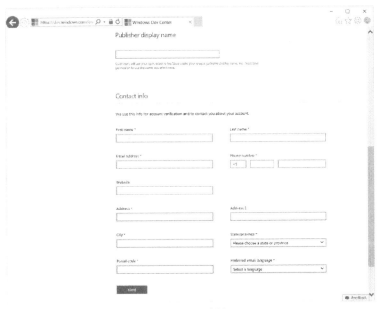

If you register a company account, you will be asked for a company approver:

Company approver

Please provide the following info so we can verify that you are authorized to create and manage this account on behalf of your organization.

First name *

Last name *

Email address *

Phone number *

+1

This information is needed for a third-party agency, which checks whether you have the rights to create the account. Note that in the case of company accounts, you should use corporate e-mails. Once you finish registration, the agency will contact the approver and ask for some documents as well. Usually this process takes three to five days, so you should be patient. Of course, in the case of individual accounts, you do not have to pass any verification process.

In the next step, you need to enter a promo code if you have one from dreamspark.com or MSDN, or you need to provide payment information. And that's all. Once payment is made, you will be redirected to your dashboard and can start publishing the first application.

I am not going to describe the dashboard right now, but later we will discuss some components related to reporting and payments. Just a few words about payment: If you are going to publish your first application and it is not free, you need to set up a payment account. So be ready to fill out two forms: payment account information—you can provide your bank account or PayPal—and tax information.

Get Ready to Publish Your Application

Once your account is created, you can start preparing an application package for publishing. Clicking on the project name and activating the context menu, you can find the **Store** menu item:

Using **Associate App with the Store** and **Create App Packages**, you can reserve a name for your application and sign the package with a certificate associated with your account. The reason why there are two menu items is that some features, such as push notifications and maps, don't work properly with a self-signed local certificate. So if you want to test these features but you are not ready to publish the application yet, you need to select the first menu item. If you want to publish your application, you need to select the second one.

Let's select the **Associate App with the Store** menu item, and you will see a wizard that helps you finish the process:

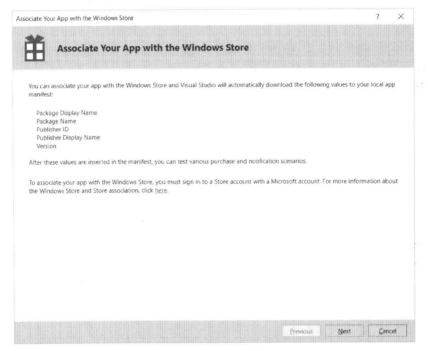

Of course, you need to sign in to the Store, and once you are there, in the next step you need to select or reserve the application name.

If you already reserved the application name using the dashboard or if you have already published a previous version of the application, you can select a name from the list. Note that all names that already have packages are hidden by default. If you are going to publish a new application, you can reserve a new name. This will be the name that will be shown to users, so you need to select wisely, and if the name is already in use, you will not be able to reserve it and will have to select new one.

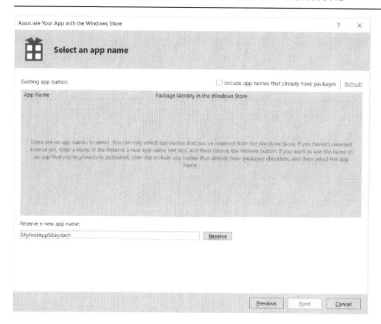

Once you select a name, the wizard will provide information about the association, and the certificate and the application manifest changes will be applied.

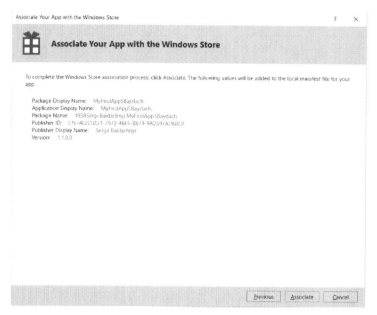

Once you are ready to publish your application, you can select the **Create App Packages** menu item. Pay attention to the first screen of the wizard:

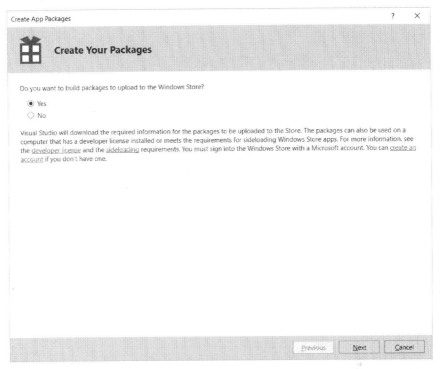

At this step, you can decide which package you want to create, because there is a way to create a package that will not be published to the Store but will be distributed among testers to install on their computers. If you select No in this step, Visual Studio will create a folder with a Power Shell script, the package, and all needed components inside. So if you want to deploy the application to another computer, just copy this folder and run the Power Shell script there. Of course, that computer should be activated for development.

In the next step, you can see the same screen as before that allows you to select the name. So I will simply skip this step.

Finally, you need to select an output directory for the package, version, and supported platforms. Because Windows 10 can be run on different hardware platforms, you can create a package for x86, x64, and even ARM:

215

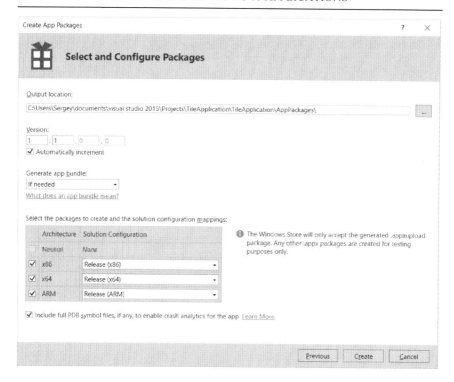

Once you click the Create button, the package is ready. Visual Studio will prepare the **.appxupload** file that you need to deploy to the Store.

Note that Visual Studio uses .NET Native compilation for creating release versions of the application. It's a new approach in Visual Studio 2015 to precompile applications to native code. If you compile the application in debug mode, then the old approach will be used.

And the last step before publishing—you need to verify the package. In this step, you can confirm that your application doesn't use any restricted APIs, has all logos and icons, and declares all capabilities properly. Once you publish the application, Microsoft will use this tool to test your application at the first step, but you can save some time if you find some problems locally. You can run the verification process in the last step of the wizard or run the App Certification Kit application manually:

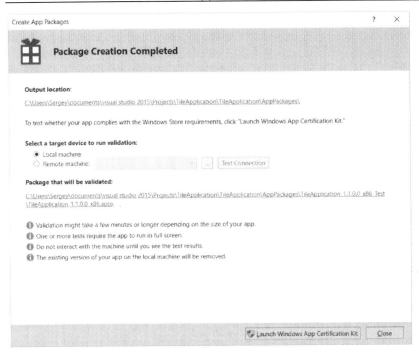

Don't touch your computer until the App Certification Wizard finishes all steps. It will run your application several times and open consoles, and you will not be able to do anything else:

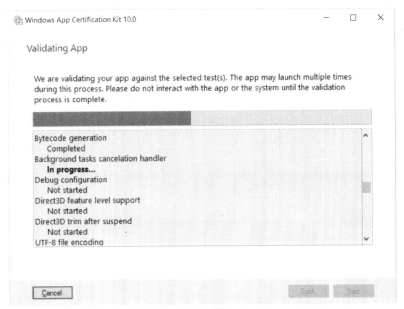

If everything is OK, you will see a message that verification has passed and you can publish your application to the Store. If something went wrong, you need to fix the problem.

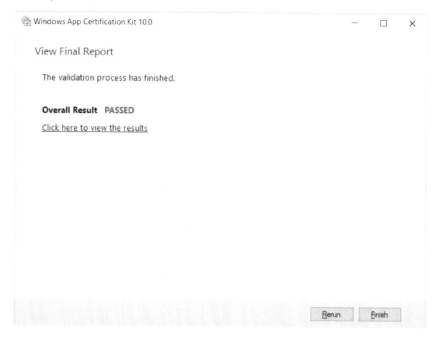

Publishing

Once the package is ready and successfully verified, you can submit it to the Store. To do so, you need to open your dashboard at http://dev.windows.com and select the application from the list.

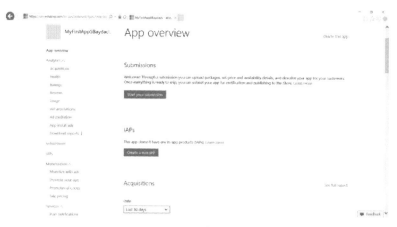

Just click Start your submission, and you will be redirected to the first step:

Submission 1

Delete

Pricing and availability	Not started ○
App properties	Not started ○
Packages	Not started ○
Descriptions	Not started ○
You'll be able to edit your descriptions after you upload packages.	
Notes for certification	Optional ○

Submit to the Store

I will not provide all screenshots, because the wizard has too many options, but let's discuss some of these options.

In the first step, you need to provide information about pricing and availability. You can publish your application as a free application or select a price. You can find lots of free applications in the Store. For example, nobody will pay for an application that allows you to order a taxi, but with that application, the taxi service can increase its number of customers. Some applications can contain advertising and earn revenue from that.

Once you select the price, you can add trial support to your application. Of course, your code should support trial mode as well. We are going to discuss this in the next chapter about the Store.

You can publish your application in 242 markets. By default all markets are selected, but you can click the **Show options** link to select markets that you want and specify a different price for some markets. Of course, if I publish an application for the Canadian market, there is no sense in making it available in all markets.

The next section is the most asked-about by developers—Sales:

Sale pricing

Set limited-time price reductions for your app. Learn more

Note: Sales will only be visible to customers on Windows 10 devices.

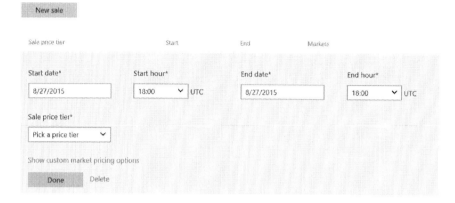

You can specify the sales for your application. They can help advertise the application to more customers. You can add a new sale anytime using a new submission, and you do not have to resubmit all packages.

You can use the next section to organize beta testing or distribute your application among your colleagues. This can be done in the Distribution and visibility section:

Distribution and visibility   Hide options

⦿ Anyone can find your app in the Store

◯ Hide this app in the Store. Customers with a direct link to the app's listing can still download it, except on Windows 8 and Windows 8.1. Learn more

◯ Hide this app in the Store. Only customers with the email addresses you enter below can download it, via a direct link on Windows Phone 8.1 and earlier. Learn more

◯ Hide this app and stop selling Learn more

So you can publish your application to everyone or to people with selected e-mails, or hide the application from the Store search and distribute it only via direct links.

Another new section allows you to decide where your application will be available. You already know that Windows 10 supports lots of different devices, including tablets, laptops, desktops, phones, and Xbox. Right now the Windows 10 Store is available for desktop and mobile devices. But once Microsoft opens the Store for Xbox or HoloLens, your application can be available for new devices as well:

Windows 10 device families   Hide options

Note that customers using a given Windows 10 device can see your app's Store listing only if you have packages which are able to run on that type of device. We recommend leaving all boxes checked unless you have a specific reason to exclude a certain Windows 10 device family.

If you remove a previously-used device family here, customers who already have your app will still be able to use it, and will get any updates you submit. However, no new customers will be able to download it on that type of Windows 10 device. Learn more

☑ Desktop

☑ Mobile

⦿ Let Microsoft decide whether to make this app available to any future device families

○ Require your permission before making this app available to any future device families

Using this section, you can decide whether you want to include your application in new stores automatically or decide yourself.

The next option is for allowing installation of your application using volume licenses online or offline. This installation type is very important for organizations that want to buy a pack of different licenses or have lots of computers without access to the Internet.

Finally, you need to specify a publishing date. You can publish your application automatically once it passes the certification process, or you can select a date or publish the application manually.

In the next step, you need to specify some application properties. In the first section, you need to select a category for your application. Your application will be available in the Store in this selected category.

Note about the Store rating: Read more about each supported rating and note that for some applications, especially for games, you may be asked for rating certificates, which contain information about the rating. In the next section, you can find a list of all possible certificates and the list of countries that accept each of these certificates.

In the next section, you can specify the list of features that are required for your application:

Hardware preferences

Indicate which hardware features are required in order for your app to run properly.
Customers on hardware that doesn't meet your app's requirements will see a warning
before they download your app. Learn more

☐ Touch screen   ☐ Keyboard   ☐ Mouse   ☐ Camera

☐ NFC HCE   ☐ NFC   ☐ Bluetooth LE   ☐ Telephony

For example, I know a game that was not published before, because it required touchscreen features. In Windows 10, customers will see a warning if their devices do not have the declared capabilities but they still want to download or buy the application.

In the last section of this step, Microsoft mixed everything that was not included in its own section: ability to install the application to an SD card, using third-party payment systems, accessibilities, and OneDrive backup.

In the next step of the wizard, you need to upload the packages for all supported platforms. This is the easiest step. Your packages will be analyzed, and you will need to provide a description of your application for each of supported languages.

In the next step, you need to upload lots of images, provide a description and a support e-mail, and so on. Note that if your submission doesn't contain promo images, you will not be able to see your application on the main page of the Store, even if your application is very popular and is of good quality. So try to provide all images with the best quality. And you can easily use Mobile Emulator or Desktop Simulator to make screenshots of your application using different resolutions.

In the last step, you can provide some notes for testers, including everything that helps testers complete the certification process successfully, such as links to agreements with other companies about logo usage, test log-ins, and so on.

Once all steps are passed, you can click the Submit to the Store button to send all filled-out information to Microsoft.

Today Microsoft doesn't take long for certification, and usually you will be able to see the results in several hours. Note that if your application passes the process, it's not always possible to see it in the Store right away. Sometimes Microsoft servers need some time to finish the sync processes.

So now you know how to publish your application.

Part II

Common Features and Extensions

This page intentionally left blank

Chapter 13

Introduction to MVVM

In the book we are not developing complex projects, but in real life you will have lots of different forms, complex business logic, a large number of event handlers, and so on. That is why it is important to select the right approach when you create your application, starting with the design-pattern perspective. When making a decision about what would be the right design pattern, you should remember the following objectives:

- How to share your project with a designer—in this book we do not discuss design guidelines for Windows 10 applications, but there are tons of them. At the same time, developers do not like to spend a lot of time checking usability and thinking about a better place for a particular button, which is very important for touch interfaces. So it's better to share your project with a designer, but you need to do it in a way that allows both of you to work on the project.

- How to create unit tests—many developers like to write unit tests. However, it is not easy if your business logic is mixed with interface code/XAML. So you need to find a way to separate these two things.

- How to reuse your application logic between different forms and even projects.

To achieve these goals, I would recommend using the MVVM (Model-View-ViewModel) pattern. This pattern was introduced with Windows Presentation Foundation and Silverlight ages ago and allows you to create clear code and reliable applications.

The idea is very simple. To follow MVVM, you need to separate your code in three different layers:

- Model: Contains the data as is. Usually you will create classes that reflect your database tables or XML/JSON file structure, but in any case, there is just data.

- View: Just an XAML file. Usually you do not have to create any code in the code-behind page. This approach allows you to work with a designer because you will never touch the XAML.

- ViewModel: You will spend a lot of time working with the ViewModel because it should prepare data for the View. So the code inside the ViewModel should know everything about the Model and View, and if you want to convert some data, combine several fields, calculate something, handle UI events, and so on, all that can be done inside the ViewModel.

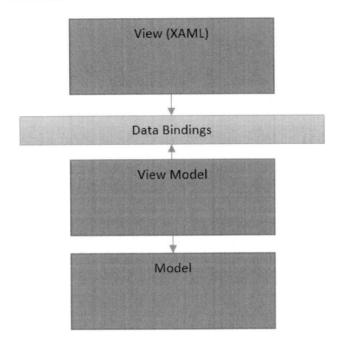

Because the ViewModel knows everything about the Model and can create and initialize the Model itself, you should not build any additional layers between the ViewModel and the Model, but you can create some additional classes that will help to initialize data and update data if needed.

At the same time, ViewModel should not have any specific information about the View. The goal of the ViewModel is to prepare data for the View, but it doesn't need to know controls and their names to initialize data. Instead, the View and the ViewModel use data bindings to send data between them. So you need to create the ViewModel object only and initialize the bindings objects.

Let's create a simple application that allows you to work with news. To do so, we need to start with model and create a class that will contain initial data from a feed, a database, or any other source. You can start with data classes every time because usually the structure is known and well defined.

```
public class NewsItem
{
    public DateTime NewsDate { get; set; }
```

```
public string NewsTitle { get; set; }

public string NewsDescription { get; set; }

public string NewsBody { get; set; }
}
```

This class has nothing special, and we have just those properties that are located in our storage.

To create the ViewModel, it's better to know which fields will be presented in the View. At this stage, you need to have general information about the View, but it's not important where the designer will place the fields and so on.

In our case, we want to show just the date and the title for the news, but we want to show "Today" if a particular piece of news is fresh. So to meet these requirements, we need to implement the following ViewModel:

```
public class NewsItemViewModel
{
    NewsItem Item { get; set; }

    public NewsItemViewModel()
    {
        Item = Helper.GetNewsItem();
    }

    public string Date
    {
        get
        {
            if (DateTime.Today.Day == Item.NewsDate.Day)
                return "Today";
            return String.Format(
                $"{Item.NewsDate:dd.MM.yyyy}");
        }
    }

    public string Title
    {
        get
        {
            return Item.NewsTitle;
        }
        set
```

```
            {
                Item.NewsTitle = value;
            }
        }
    }
}

public class Helper
{
    public static NewsItem GetNewsItem()
    {
        return new NewsItem()
        {
            NewsDate = DateTime.Now.AddDays(-2),
            NewsTitle = "News Item 1",
            NewsBody = "News Body",
            NewsDescription = "News Description"
        };
    }
}
```

You can see that in this code, we have formatted the date and wrapped the title fields that we are going to use in our view. Additionally, we have created a Helper class that initializes our items—you can read data from a file, a database, or from another source.

This code is not ideal, because we are going to use bindings to present our data, but bindings will not work if we change the data inside the ViewModel or even if loading our data takes some time. That's why we need to implement the **INotifyPropertyChanged** interface that we discussed in chapter 8:

```
public class NewsItemViewModel:INotifyPropertyChanged
{
    NewsItem Item { get; set; }

    public NewsItemViewModel()
    {
        Item = Helper.GetNewsItem();
    }

    public string Date
    {
        get
        {
            if (DateTime.Today.Day == Item.NewsDate.Day)
```

```
                return "Today";
            return String.Format(
                $"{Item.NewsDate:dd.MM.yyyy}");
    }
    private set
    {
        Item.NewsDate = Convert.ToDateTime(value);
        RaisePropertyChanged(Date);
    }
}

public string Title
{
    get
    {
        return Item.NewsTitle;
    }
    set
    {
        Item.NewsTitle = value;
        RaisePropertyChanged(Title);
    }
}

public event PropertyChangedEventHandler
    PropertyChanged;

private void RaisePropertyChanged(string propertyName)
{
    PropertyChangedEventHandler handler =
        PropertyChanged;
    if (handler != null)
    {
        handler(this,
            new PropertyChangedEventArgs(propertyName));
    }
}
}
```

Of course, if you want to implement some event handlers, you need to include them in the ViewModel as well. If you have experience with Windows 8.1 or Windows Phone, you know that to implement event handlers, you needed to use the **ICommand** interface. But right now it's not needed, because **x:Bind** supports binding for event handlers as well.

Finally, we can create a simple view:

```
<Page
    x:Class="MVVMProject.MainPage"

xmlns="http://schemas.microsoft.com/winfx/2006/xaml/present
ation"
    xmlns:x="http://schemas.microsoft.com/winfx/2006/xaml"
    xmlns:local="using:MVVMProject"
    xmlns:d="http://schemas.microsoft.com/
        expression/blend/2008"
    xmlns:mc="http://schemas.openxmlformats.org/
        markup-compatibility/2006"
    xmlns:code="using:MVVMProject.Code"
    mc:Ignorable="d">
    <Page.Resources>
        <code:NewsItemViewModel x:Name="viewModel">
        </code:NewsItemViewModel>
    </Page.Resources>

    <Grid Background=
     "{ThemeResource ApplicationPageBackgroundThemeBrush}">
        <StackPanel Orientation="Vertical">
            <TextBlock Text="{x:Bind viewModel.Title}">
            </TextBlock>
            <TextBlock Text="{x:Bind viewModel.Date}">
            </TextBlock>
        </StackPanel>
    </Grid>
</Page>
```

You can see that we have created a NewsItemViewModel object in the XAML document directly and didn't touch the code-behind at all. But in some cases, especially if your data requires a lot of time to load and uses an **async** approach, you can initialize binding in the code-behind as well.

You can simply use the same classes if you want to build a ViewModel class for a list of items View. In this case, you can use **ObservableCollection** and the existing NewsItemViewModel:

```
public class NewsListViewModel
{
    public ObservableCollection<NewsItemViewModel> Items =
        new ObservableCollection<NewsItemViewModel>();
    . . . . .
}
```

This page intentionally left blank

Chapter 14

How to Work with Files and Settings

Working with Files and Folders

The modern application model for Windows applications doesn't allow you to use Win32 API or even .NET Framework classes to get access to all files and folders on the disk. But the Universal Windows Platform implements several scenarios that you can use to get access to files and folders in secure way. In this chapter we will discuss all possible scenarios where you can work with files, including known folders, controls for opening files and folders, the temporary folder, and so on.

Of course, before starting a discussion about existing scenarios, we need to know a basic set of classes. In this chapter we will use three namespaces:

- **Windows.Storage:** Contains classes that allow you to work with files, folders, and application settings.

- **Windows.Storage.Streams:** Classes in this namespace allow you to read and write data to files.

- **Windows.Storage.Pickers:** Contains several user controls that allow you to select files and a folder or a saving location.

Let's start by reviewing the classes in the **Windows.Storage** namespace. This namespace contains lots of classes, but **StorageFolder** and **StorageFile** are the most important. You will use these classes whenever you need to work with folders and files.

It's probably better to start working with files that are in the package of the application. You can open a file using the name of the file or enumerate all files getting access to the folder where the application is deployed.

Let's implement code that will enumerate all folders in the application folder. You can use the **Windows.ApplicationModel.Package** class to get access to the folder:

```
protected async override void OnNavigatedTo(
    NavigationEventArgs e)
{

    var package= Package.Current;
    var folder = package.InstalledLocation;
    var files = await folder.GetFoldersAsync();
    listView.ItemsSource = files;
}
```

In the first line, we get access to an object of the **Package** class. Using the object, you can get access to information about the installation date, installed location, display name, and so on. In our case we need to use the **InstalledLocation** property, which returns **StorageFolder**. That's all that we need, and now we can use the folder object to get access to files, subfolders, and so on. Of course, you cannot modify the **InstalledLocation** folder, but you can open any of its files and subfolders. Below you can find the interface part of the application:

```
<Grid Background=
    "{ThemeResource ApplicationPageBackgroundThemeBrush}">
    <ListView Name="listView" Margin="50">
        <ListView.ItemTemplate>
            <DataTemplate>
                <StackPanel>
                    <TextBlock Text=
                        "{Binding DisplayName}"></TextBlock>
                </StackPanel>
            </DataTemplate>
        </ListView.ItemTemplate>
    </ListView>
</Grid>
```

Let's see how to get access to a package file by name. For example, you might have an XML document in the package that contains some data that you want to read in the application. You can create a simple XML file like this:

```
<Items>
    <Item>Item 1</Item>
    <Item>Item 2</Item>
    <Item>Item 3</Item>
</Items>
```

Just make sure that the file is marked as a content file in the project. To do this, you can open the file properties in Visual Studio and check that **Build Action** is set to **Content**:

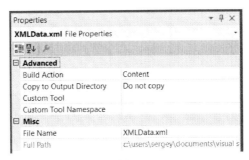

Let's implement the following code instead of the previous one:

```
protected async override void OnNavigatedTo(
    NavigationEventArgs e)
{
    StorageFile file =
        await StorageFile.GetFileFromApplicationUriAsync(
            new Uri("ms-appx:///XMLData.xml"));
    var xml = await XmlDocument.LoadFromFileAsync(file);
    listView.ItemsSource = xml.ChildNodes[0].ChildNodes;
}
```

You can see that we use the **GetFileFromApplicationAsync** method, and to create the **Uri**, we used the **ms-appx:///** prefix. With this prefix, you can get access to any file in the package.

Of course, we need to change the interface code a little bit:

```
<ListView Name="listView" Margin="50">
    <ListView.ItemTemplate>
        <DataTemplate>
            <StackPanel>
                <TextBlock Text="{Binding InnerText}">
                </TextBlock>
            </StackPanel>
        </DataTemplate>
    </ListView.ItemTemplate>
</ListView>
```

In the previous example, we used an opportunity to create an XML document based on an object that implements the **IStorageFile** interface (**StorageFile**, of course), but the **StorageFile** class provides an opportunity to read data from the file directly. For example, we could use the **OpenReadAsync** method to open the stream and read data from it. In the following code, we create a new file and use streams to write a Hello message to it:

```
public async void WriteFile()
{
    StorageFolder current =
        ApplicationData.Current.LocalFolder;
    StorageFile file = await current.CreateFileAsync(
        "hello.txt",
        CreationCollisionOption.ReplaceExisting);
    IRandomAccessStream writeStream =
        await file.OpenAsync(FileAccessMode.ReadWrite);
    IOutputStream outputStream =
```

```
        writeStream.GetOutputStreamAt(0);
    DataWriter dataWriter = new DataWriter(outputStream);
    dataWriter.WriteString("hello");
    await dataWriter.StoreAsync();
    await outputStream.FlushAsync();
}
```

In this code we used the **IRandomAccessStream** interface. It is the base interface for the operations reading/writing content from/to files, and you can see that it's easy to use this interface to get the input or output stream.

But the most important part of this code is in this line:

```
StorageFolder current =
    ApplicationData.Current.LocalFolder;
```

You can see that it uses the **ApplicationData** class, which allows you to get a reference to a folder using the **LocalFolder** property. This folder is a special place that is associated with the application and allows you to store local files there. Let's talk about all possible locations that are available for any application.

Working with Settings and Temporary Data

The Universal Windows Platform doesn't allow you to access all folders and files on the disk. But the application needs a place to store its own files and data. For example, you may need to implement functionality that allows the application to cache some data from the server or simply store some settings that the user has selected. That's why UWP supports three types of storages for your own data:

- **Local storage:** Using this storage, you can use a special folder that is associated with the application to store files and folders. This storage looks like a personal disk for the application.

- **Roaming storage:** This storage is similar to the previous one, but all data will be saved in Microsoft Cloud. Of course, in this case you have limits for storage, but all data will be available for the application on all devices where the application is installed.

- **Temporary storage:** You can use this storage like a temporary directory. The system can remove data there at any time, but it's very useful if you want to have a work space and don't want to think about cleaning up the space.

Let's discuss each of these storage spaces.

Local Storage

With local storage, you can store data using files and folders or a simple dictionary. Of course, it's better to use the dictionary to store simple settings, but in the case of complex data, you can use files.

Below I provide an example of how to access the local folder and create a file. Let's see how to read data from the file:

```
public async void ReadFile()
{
    StorageFolder current =
        ApplicationData.Current.LocalFolder;
    StorageFile sampleFile =
        await current.GetFileAsync("hello.txt");
    IRandomAccessStream readStream =
        await sampleFile.OpenAsync(FileAccessMode.Read);
    IInputStream inputStream =
        readStream.GetInputStreamAt(0);
    DataReader dataReader = new DataReader(inputStream);
    string myString =
        dataReader.ReadString((uint)readStream.Size);
}
```

You can get access to the existing file using Uri as well. In this case you need to use the following prefix to create the Uri: **ms-appdata:///local/**.

If you decide to use the dictionary instead of a file, you need to use the following classes:

- **ApplicationDataContainer:** This is a container that can store data of common value types or data based on **ApplicationDataCompositeValue**. In fact, each application has a container by default, but you can create additional containers if needed.

- **ApplicationDataCompositeValue:** This class allows you to assemble a complex data type based on common value types. With this class you can easily group data.

These two classes are located in the Windows.Storage namespace, and you should not have any problems using them. For example, if you want to access the default container, you can use the following code:

```
ApplicationDataContainer cur=
```

```
ApplicationData.Current.LocalSettings;
```

But if you want to create a new container inside the default one, you can add the following code to your project:

```
ApplicationDataContainer cur =
    ApplicationData.Current.LocalSettings;
ApplicationDataContainer named =
    cur.CreateContainer("myContainer",
        ApplicationDataCreateDisposition.Always);
```

To work with containers, you can simply use a Values collection and an indexer as a way to get access to data by key:

```
cur.Values["myValue"] = 5;
cur.Containers["myContainer"].Values["mySecondValue"] =
    "Hello";
```

Finally, if you want to create a composite value, you can use the following code as a template:

```
ApplicationDataCompositeValue composite =
    new ApplicationDataCompositeValue();
composite["firstVal"] = 1;
composite["secondVal"] = "Hello";
cur.Values["compValue"] = composite;
```

Roaming Storage

If you want to create a setting that will be available to the application on other devices, you can use roaming storage. You can use roaming storage in the same way as local storage. For example, these two lines of code allow you to access the dictionary and the folder in the cloud:

```
ApplicationDataContainer current=
    ApplicationData.Current.RoamingSettings;
StorageFolder fi le=ApplicationData.Current.RoamingFolder;
```

Of course, in the case of roaming storage, you should not use it to store lots of data. You still need to think about Internet bandwidth. To understand existing quotas, you can use the following properties of the ApplicationData class:

- **RoamingStorageQuota:** Contains a number that indicates the amount of space available for the application.

- **RoamingStorageUsage:** Shows the amount of space that the application is using.

Usually you will read data from the cloud once the application is loaded, but if you want, you can track changes in run time. You can use the following code for reference:

```
void InitHandlers()
{
    ApplicationData.Current.DataChanged +=
        DataChangeHandler;
}
void DataChangeHandler(ApplicationData appData, object o)
{
    //update
}
```

Temporary Storage

Finally, if you want to use temporary storage, you can use the following code:

```
StorageFolder folder=
    ApplicationData.Current.TemporaryFolder;
```

Once you get a reference to **StorageFolder**, you can do anything.

File Pickers

In fact, modern applications don't see any files on the disk except their own files, but there is a way to ask the user to provide access to a file or even to a folder. To do so, the Universal Windows Platform contains several classes that allow you to activate the standard dialogs for selecting files/folders and for saving files. Let's look at the following method:

```
public async void SelectFile()
{
    FileOpenPicker openPicker = new FileOpenPicker();
    openPicker.ViewMode = PickerViewMode.Thumbnail;
    openPicker.SuggestedStartLocation =
        PickerLocationId.PicturesLibrary;
    openPicker.FileTypeFilter.Add(".tif");
    StorageFile file =
        await openPicker.PickSingleFileAsync();
}
```

Running this method, you can activate a picker window that allows the user to pick a single file on the disk. To do so, I used the **FileOpenPicker** class and some properties there. For example, I decided to use the **tif** extension by default and navigate the picker to the Pictures library.

If you run this code on desktop, you will see the following window:

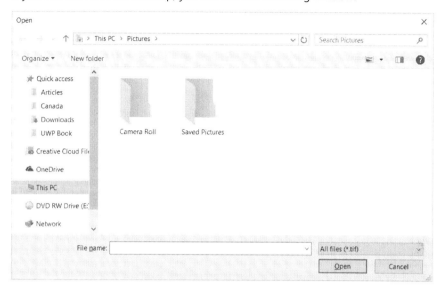

If you want to ask the user to select several files, you can use the same approach but call the **PickMultipleFilesAsync** method.

To select a folder or location for saving, you can use the **FolderPicker** and **SaveFilePicker** classes. Using these classes, you will use the same approach as for **FileOpenPicker**.

Known Folders

Now we know that a modern application can work with files and folders in special folders, or a user can provide access to the application using file pickers. In this section, we will discuss one more way that is supported by modern applications—access to files in common libraries, such as **Pictures**, **Music**, and **Videos**.

Of course, the user should know that the application will have access to the user's libraries, but you should not ask for any permissions or track whether access is granted. Instead, Windows 10 allows you to ask for permissions implicitly using the manifest file. You just need to declare the appropriate capabilities in the manifest, and the user will be able to see all the required permissions prior to the application installation. If the user does not want to install an application that requires access to the **Pictures** library, for example, it's possible to skip installation.

To declare access to the user's libraries, you need to add up to three Capabilities: **Pictures Library**, **Videos Library**, and **Music Library**. Of course, if your application will work with the Pictures library only, you should add just one capability.

Application	Visual Assets	Capabilities	Declarations	Content URIs	Packaging

Use this page to specify system features or devices that your app can use.

Capabilities:

- [ ] All Joyn
- [ ] Blocked Chat Messages
- [ ] Chat Message Access
- [ ] Code Generation
- [ ] Enterprise Authentication
- [x] Internet (Client)
- [ ] Internet (Client & Server)
- [ ] Location
- [ ] Microphone
- [x] Music Library
- [ ] Objects 3D
- [ ] Phone Call
- [x] Pictures Library
- [ ] Private Networks (Client & Server)
- [ ] Proximity
- [ ] Removable Storage
- [ ] Shared User Certificates
- [ ] User Account Information
- [x] Videos Library
- [ ] VOIP Calling
- [ ] Webcam

Description:

Provides the capability to add, change, or delete files in the Pictures Library for the local PC and HomeGroup PCs.

More information

The Universal Windows Platform supports access to the Documents library as well, but you need to ask for special permissions to publish such an application. In fact, this feature is supported for corporate applications only.

Once you have requested permissions in the manifest, you can start working with libraries. Using the next code, we request access to the **Pictures** library and get access to all folders there:

```
var library=
    await StorageLibrary.GetLibraryAsync(
        KnownLibraryId.Pictures);
var folders = library.Folders;
```

Note that we used the **StorageLibrary** class in our code and **KnownLibraryId** enumeration to return a **StorageLibrary** object. With this class, you can get references to all folders in the library, even if they are associated with OneDrive. Looking at other classes, you can find the **KnownFolders** class, which contains some properties and can return the **StorageFolder** directly for **Pictures**, **Videos**, and **Music**. But when using this class, I discovered that it returns a link to the local folder only. So if you want to get all possible folders, you need to use the **StorageLibrary** class.

Of course, when you are working with libraries, Windows will check whether you are working with "known" files only. So in the case of the **Pictures** library, you can work with jpeg, jpg, gif, bmp, and so on.

File-Type Associations

Finally, let's see how to allow the opening of any files using our application directly from Windows Explorer. It's possible if you associate your application with some file extensions. Of course, you need to select just those extensions that are supported by your application. For example, on the screen below, I use the manifest designer to add an association with the **.jpg** extension:

When running the application and using the context menu for any .jpg file, users will see my application among others that support .jpg.

Now, you have to implement some code that will process the file. Usually we need to override the **OnActivated** method, but in the case of file-type associations, the **Application** class supports **OnFileActivated**:

```
protected override void OnFileActivated(
    FileActivatedEventArgs args)
{

    var files=args.Files;
    //create the frame and process the file

}
```

Note that the user can select several files. That's why **FileActivatedEventArgs** contains the collection but not a single **StorageFile**.

Chapter 15

App-to-App Communications

Windows 10 modern applications work inside their own sandboxes, have limited access to the file system, and know nothing about other applications. But the Universal Windows Platform supports several ways to exchange data between applications. In this chapter we will discuss all such ways, starting with simple drag-and-drop functionality and finishing with the publisher cache.

How to Implement Drag-and-Drop Functionality

Starting with Windows 10, you can implement drag-and-drop functionality between UI parts of your application or use external sources/targets, including Win 32 applications.

Let's start with the drag operation. To show how the drag operation works, I simply added an image from the application package to the main page.

```
<Grid Background=
    "{ThemeResource ApplicationPageBackgroundThemeBrush}">
    <Image Source="Assets\drone.jpg" Name="image"
        CanDrag="True" DragStarting="Image_DragStarting"
        Margin="100" VerticalAlignment="Top"
        HorizontalAlignment="Left"></Image>
</Grid>
```

You can see two important attributes that activate the drag operation: **CanDrag** and **DragStarting**. The **CanDrag** attribute is just a flag that enables the feature for all **UIElement** controls, while the **DragStarting** attribute contains the name of the event handler. With this event handler, you can define any content to drag. In my case I implemented the following handler:

```
private async void Image_DragStarting(UIElement sender,
    DragStartingEventArgs args)
{
    List<IStorageItem> files = new List<IStorageItem>();
    StorageFile file =
        await StorageFile.GetFileFromApplicationUriAsync(
            new Uri("ms-appx:///Assets/drone.jpg"));
    files.Add(file);

    args.DragUI.SetContentFromDataPackage();
    args.Data.RequestedOperation =
        DataPackageOperation.Copy;
    args.Data.SetStorageItems(files);
}
```

In this event handler I used the **StorageFile** class to pass my image as a file, and with the Data property of the **DragStartingEventArgs** parameter, I packaged the file in the object of the **DataPackage** class. Usually you need to pass an object of this class to the operating system (OS) so that the OS allows you to select the target application. But in the case of drag functionality, the user selects the target directly. So we just need to prepare the **DataPackage** and that's all.

Additionally, I used two important properties: **DragUI** and **RequestedOperation**. With **RequestedOperation** I can assign the appropriate operation, and the user should not be able to select anything from the system menu—just drag and drop. With **DragUI** I can apply the content that will be shown during the drag operation. If you don't use the **DragUI** property, the user will see the same image with the same width and height as in your application. It's not very handy to drag a huge image, especially if you don't use **RequestedOperation**—the system menu will be behind the image. That's why you can assign other content using **DragUI** or use the **SetContentFromDataPackage** method to ask the API to prepare an appropriate icon for you based on the content in **DataPackage**.

Just run the application and drag and drop the image to the file explorer—the image will be copied to the selected folder.

Let's see how to implement the opposite task—drop functionality. I want to accept several images. So I am going to use **ListView** to show my items.

```
<Grid Background=
    "{ThemeResource ApplicationPageBackgroundThemeBrush}"
    AllowDrop="True" Drop="Grid_Drop"
    DragEnter="Grid_DragEnter">
    <ListView Margin="50" Name="listView">
        <ListView.ItemTemplate>
            <DataTemplate>
                <Grid>
                    <Image Source="{Binding Source}"
                        Width="200" Margin="10"></Image>
                </Grid>
            </DataTemplate>
        </ListView.ItemTemplate>
    </ListView>
</Grid>
```

You can see that I am using **AllowDrop** to activate drop functionality, **DragEnter** to set up the allowed operations (Copy), and **Drop** to get content from **DataPackage** and show it using **ListView**.

To create the item source for images, I created a BitmapItem class:

```
class BitmapItem
{
    public ImageSource Source { get; set; }
}
```

In the next step I implemented a **DragEnter** event handler to notify the system about supported operations.

```
private void Grid_DragEnter(object sender, DragEventArgs e)
{
    e.AcceptedOperation = DataPackageOperation.Copy;
}
```

Finally, I am using **DataPackageView** to get a reference to the content. **DataPackageView** can contain any entities, but I want to work with files only, so I call **GetStorageItemsAsync** to get references to files there and use **BitmapImage** to prepare the image files for **Image** objects.

```
private async void Grid_Drop(object sender,
    DragEventArgs e)
{
    var files=await e.DataView.GetStorageItemsAsync();
    List<BitmapItem> items = new List<BitmapItem>();
    foreach(StorageFile file in files)
    {
        try
        {
            BitmapImage bi = new BitmapImage();
            bi.SetSource(
                await file.OpenAsync(FileAccessMode.Read));
            items.Add(new BitmapItem() { Source = bi });
        }
        catch { }
    }
    listView.ItemsSource = items;
}
```

I am quite lazy, so I decided to avoid any checking—I simply use an empty catch block if the user passes a non-image file.

That's all. You can see that it's easy to implement drag-and-drop functionality, and you can experiment with different content types or implement this functionality inside the same application (drag and drop content from one part of the application to another).

Clipboard

Starting with Windows 10, you can implement clipboard operations not just for desktop but also for all Windows 10 devices.

In the previous section, we used the **DataPackage** class to prepare data for sending to external applications and the **DataPackageView** class to get data that was dragged from an external source. In the case of clipboard, we will use the same approach, but instead of event handlers, we should implement content menus with standard commands.

Let's see how to implement paste functionality. I am going to use the same application that I used in the drag-and-drop section because we can use the same code. I am going to allow the paste feature for images, so I will show images in **ListView**, and I need to implement a simple **MenuFlyout**:

```
<ListView Margin="50" Name="listView"
    RightTapped="listView_RightTapped"
    IsRightTapEnabled="True">
    <ListView.Resources>
        <MenuFlyout x:Name="menuFlyout">
            <MenuFlyout.Items>
                <MenuFlyoutItem Name="pasteItem"
                    Text="Paste" Click="MenuFlyoutItem_Click">
                </MenuFlyoutItem>
            </MenuFlyout.Items>
        </MenuFlyout>
    </ListView.Resources>
    <ListView.ItemTemplate>
        <DataTemplate>
            <Grid>
                <Image Source="{Binding Source}"
                    Width="200" Margin="10"></Image>
            </Grid>
        </DataTemplate>
    </ListView.ItemTemplate>
</ListView>
```

You can see that I declared **MenuFlyout** as a resource of **ListView**. The **MenuFlyout** class doesn't allow you to show the menu automatically. So I allowed right-clicking for my **ListView** and implemented a **RightTapped** event handler in the following way:

```
private async void listView_RightTapped(object sender,
    RightTappedRoutedEventArgs e)
```

```
{
    var format = Clipboard.GetContent().
        Contains("FileDrop");
    pasteItem.IsEnabled = format;
    menuFlyout.ShowAt(listView, e.GetPosition(null));
}
```

To implement a better UX, I check whether any files are available and enable or disable the menu item.

Finally, if the user selects the Paste menu item, I use the Clipboard class to get all available files and prepare them to show in **ListView**:

```
private async void MenuFlyoutItem_Click(object sender,
    RoutedEventArgs e)
{
    var files = await Clipboard.GetContent().
        GetStorageItemsAsync();
    List<BitmapItem> items = new List<BitmapItem>();
    foreach (StorageFile file in files)
    {
        try
        {
            BitmapImage bi = new BitmapImage();
            bi.SetSource(
                await file.OpenAsync(FileAccessMode.Read));
            items.Add(new BitmapItem() { Source = bi });
        }
        catch { }
    }
    listView.ItemsSource = items;
}
```

You can see that we used the same code as in the drag-and-drop section. We changed just the first line of code—we used the Clipboard class to get **DataPackageView**.

You can see that drag-and-drop and clipboard features are better to implement together because you can use the same approach, and these features are now universal.

Data Sharing

Imagine that your application needs to share data using social networks. Of course, you can implement Facebook or Twitter integration, but nobody knows which social networks are used by users of your application, and it's almost impossible to implement integration with all possible networks. Even to implement integration just with Facebook, it takes time.

Windows 10 supports an interesting approach that allows you not to think about possible consumers of your data. You just pass all needed data to the system, and Windows checks whether there are any other applications that can consume these data. For example, if your application shares a link, Windows checks whether any applications registered in the system can receive web links. If such applications are available, Windows gives the user the chance to select any of them. Once the user selects an application, Windows launches it and passes all the data there. So you just need to implement code that passes data that you want to share to Windows.

To share data with Windows, you need to use the **DataTransferManager** class. Usually you will use the **OnNavigatedTo** method to get a reference to the object of this class:

```
dataTransferManager =
    DataTransferManager.GetForCurrentView();
dataTransferManager.DataRequested +=
    DataTransferManager_DataRequested;
```

These two lines of code allow you to get a reference and assign an event handler to the **DataRequested** event. The event will be fired when the application starts sharing data. And using the event handler, you can prepare and send data to Windows.

```
private void DataTransferManager_DataRequested(
    DataTransferManager sender, DataRequestedEventArgs args)
{
    var request = args.Request;
    request.Data.SetWebLink(
        new Uri("http://dev.windows.com"));
    request.Data.Properties.Title = "Dev Center";
    request.Data.Properties.Description =
        "Join dev program!";
}
```

In the code above, I used the **DataRequestEventArgs** parameter to get access to an object that my application will send to Windows. With this object, I can send almost anything: images, links, HTML, text, and so on. In my code I share a link to Dev Center.

Once you have implemented a **DataRequested** event handler, you can activate sharing functionality wherever you want. For example, you can add to your interface a Share button. In the event handler for this button, you simply need to implement a single line of code:

```
DataTransferManager.ShowShareUI();
```

This code will ask Windows to activate an embedded Sharing window, and thanks to the previous event handler, the Sharing window will be able to share the link:

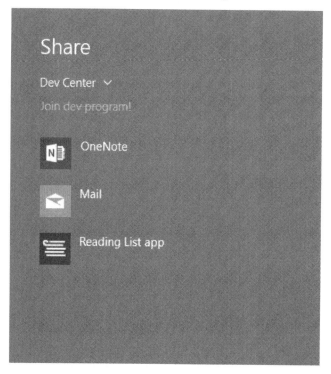

On my PC I have only three applications that can receive links, but I am using a new PC.

Of course, you can accept data that is shared with other applications. To do so, you need to edit the manifest of your application and add a declaration **Share Target**:

You need to provide Windows all data types that you want to use. In the manifest it will look like an extension:

```
<uap:Extension Category="windows.shareTarget">
  <uap:ShareTarget>
    <uap:DataFormat>URI</uap:DataFormat>
  </uap:ShareTarget>
</uap:Extension>
```

Once you have declared the extension, you need to implement code that will be used to activate the application using the Share contract. In the case of sharing functionality, you do not have to use the **OnActivated** method. Instead, the Application class contains an **OnShareTargetActivated** method, and you just need to override it:

```
protected override async void OnShareTargetActivated(
    ShareTargetActivatedEventArgs args)
{
    ShareOperation shareOperation = args.ShareOperation;
    if (shareOperation.Data.Contains(
        StandardDataFormats.WebLink))
    {
        var link =
            await shareOperation.Data.GetWebLinkAsync();
    }
}
```

How to Launch External Applications Based on URL Protocol

In the previous chapter, we discussed file-type associations and how to invoke external applications based on file type. We used the **Launcher** class, and if you

253

check all methods inside the class, you can find that some are not related to files but allow you to do something with URIs. For example, you can run the following code if you want to open the browser and navigate to a website:

```
await Launcher.LaunchUriAsync(
    new Uri("http://dev.windows.com"));
```

We used http in the code above, but the **Launcher** class supports a universal approach and allows you to use any other protocols. For example, in Windows 10, to invoke the Settings window, you can use the **ms-settings** protocol and create a Uri for the **Launcher** class based on it:

```
await Launcher.LaunchUriAsync(new Uri("ms-settings:"));
```

Additionally, you can find embedded protocols for many different tasks:

- **ms-store:**—allows you to activate the Store application and to the selected application

- **mailto:**—launches the default mail client

- **bingmaps:**—launches the Windows Map application

Of course, your application can declare its own protocol and allow you to invoke your application from other applications that are using it. If you want to declare support for one or several protocols, you need to edit the manifest file of your application.

If you use the manifest designer, you need to select the **Protocol** declaration:

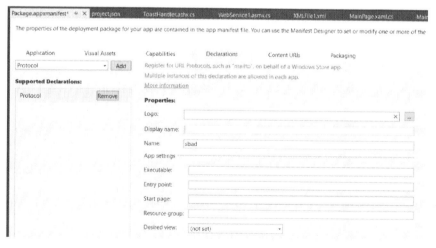

You need to fill in at least **Name**, which contains the name for your protocol that other applications will use to invoke your application.

Once you do this, Visual Studio will add an **Extension** element to the manifest file:

```
<Extensions>
  <uap:Extension Category="windows.protocol">
    <uap:Protocol Name="sbad" />
  </uap:Extension>
</Extensions>
```

You can see that this element has a **Category** attribute that was set to **windows.protocol**. Once the user installs the application, Windows will read this information and associate the application with the protocol.

You can find other associations by visiting **Control Panel** and opening **Set Default Programs** there. Below you can see a screenshot that shows default files and protocols for Microsoft Edge browser:

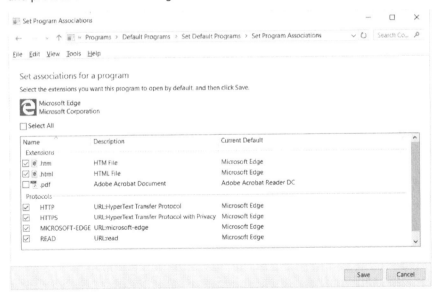

Additionally, you can specify logo and display name fields, which are important for **Set Default Programs** window but don't affect your protocol in general.

Finally, you can specify a **Desired view** that will work for desktop applications only:

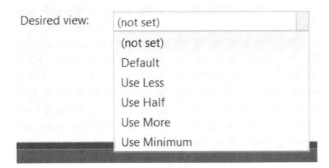

Once the protocol is declared, you need to implement logic that will handle protocol activation using the **OnActivated** method, which we discussed in previous chapters.

```
public partial class App
{
   protected override void OnActivated(
      IActivatedEventArgs args){
      if (args.Kind == ActivationKind.Protocol){
         // doing something
      }
   }
}
```

Let's spend some time discussing the **Launcher** class and its new features in Windows 10.

In Windows 8.x, the **LaunchUriAsync** method didn't allow you to pass anything except a Uri. If you needed to pass some parameters to an external application, you could use the same approach as for http to send parameters using Uri. But if you needed to pass a file as a parameter, you could not do it using **LaunchUriAsync**. The **Launcher** class supported the **LaunchFileAsync** method, but that method supported **StorageFile** as a parameter. So you could not pass several files, and you could not combine both methods (launch an application using Uri and pass the file at the same time). Even to pass a file to a third-party application, you had to register the extensions of accepted files. Additionally, **LaunchUriAsync** and **LaunchFileAsync** didn't allow you to control which application should be launched. If several applications registered the same extension, the user needed to select an application from the list. Finally, there was no way to understand whether an application was launched or how to get some results back.

Let's summarize all the disadvantages that the **Launcher** class had in Windows 8.x:

- Allowed you to pass a Uri or file using two different methods without a way to combine them

- Didn't allow you to pass several files

- System might ask the user to select an application from a list

- No way to know whether an external application was launched

- No way to get a response from an external application

But in the Universal Windows Platform, Microsoft made a huge investment in the **Launcher** class, and today developers can avoid all of these disadvantages. Let's see which changes were implemented.

Look at the following code:

```
LauncherOptions options = new LauncherOptions()
{
    TargetApplicationPackageFamilyName =
        "Microsoft.MicrosoftEdge_8wekyb3d8bbwe"
};
await Launcher.LaunchUriAsync(
    new Uri("http://www.microsoft.com"), options);
```

When running this code, we asked **Launcher** to launch an application that has a defined application-package name. This approach is very useful for corporate systems where you have developed more than one application for customers. Using **LauncherOptions**, you can guarantee that the system will run exactly the application you need from your bunch of applications. Of course, you need to know the application family name, but you can easily find it using the Store:

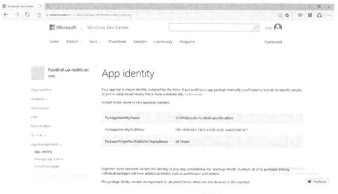

Additionally, you can use the **FindUriSchemeHandlersAsync** method of the **Launcher** class to get information about all packages that accept the selected schema:

```
var res =
    await Launcher.FindUriSchemeHandlersAsync("http");
```

This method returns an array that contains all needed information, including package name:

Watch 1	
Name	Value
🔧 res.Count	1
▲ 🔧 res[0]	{Windows.ApplicationModel.AppInfo}
🔧 AppUserModelId	"Microsoft.MicrosoftEdge_8wekyb3d8bbwe!MicrosoftEdge"
▷ 🔧 DisplayInfo	{Windows.ApplicationModel.AppDisplayInfo}
🔧 Id	"MicrosoftEdge"
🔧 PackageFamilyName	"Microsoft.MicrosoftEdge_8wekyb3d8bbwe"
❌ Native View	To inspect the native object, enable native code debugging.

Of course, if the package doesn't exist in the system, the **LaunchUriAsync** method will return **false**, and you can ask users to install an additional application.

The **Launcher** class contains one more method, **QueryUriSupportAsync**, which allows you to get information if the selected Uri is supported in the system:

```
var res = await Launcher.QueryUriSupportAsync(
    new Uri("http://www.microsoft.com"),
    LaunchQuerySupportType.Uri);
```

This method doesn't return any information about external applications but allows you to check whether you can run an application using a passed **Uri**. And what is more important, this method allows you to check the result using a package family name and even to understand whether an external application can return a response.

I would like to note that you could use the same bunch of methods to open files using external applications: **LaunchFileAsync**, **FindFileHandlersAsync**, and **QueryFileSupportAsync**. Of course, these methods don't resolve the problem with multiple files, but UWP creates an opportunity to use the **LaunchUriAsync** method for passing several files (references) as parameters. Let's see how to implement it.

The idea is to use the **SharedStorageAccessManager** class. With this class you can share files between applications using tokens.

```
var token=SharedStorageAccessManager.AddFile(myfile);
```

Because a token is a string, you can use it as a parameter in **Uri**. So, you do not have to pass any **IStorageFile** objects or anything special—just the same **Uri**. And it is possible to create as many tokens as needed.

An external application can redeem tokens and get access to **IStorageFile** objects:

```
string myFileToken =
    queryStrings.GetFirstValueByName("GpxFile");

if (!string.IsNullOrEmpty(myFileToken))
{
    StorageFile file=
        await SharedStorageAccessManager.
            RedeemTokenForFileAsync(myFileToken));
}
```

Once the token is redeemed, nobody can redeem the token again. But the token may live for fourteen days. So if the application discovers a problem when launching an external application, there is a way to delete the token from the list using the **RemoveFile** method.

Of course, in the case of a file token, it's easy to include tokens in Uri, but you can pass any serializable objects that you want. To do so, you can use the **ValueSet** class, which is a dictionary of serializable objects. Developers can use it to pass tokens as well, but it's possible to pass anything:

```
ValueSet v = new ValueSet();
v.Add("token1", token);
var f = await Launcher.LaunchUriAsync(myUri, options, v);
```

Finally, the Launcher class allows you to launch Uri for results. Imagine an application for making payments. You can use this application as an external method to make payments inside your own application, but you need to get information from an external application on whether the payment was processed and probably some information to check whether the payment was received. In Windows 10 you can implement this using the **LaunchUriForResultsAsync** method. This method has the same parameter list as **LaunchUriAsync**, but it returns a **LaunchUriResult** object instead of **bool**, and you can use this object to see the status and get results on whether the launch succeeded.

```
var result =
    await Windows.System.Launcher.LaunchUriForResultsAsync(
```

```
   myUri, options, inputData);
if (result.Status == LaunchUriStatus.Success)
{
  ValueSet theValues = result.Result;
  //do something here
}
```

Therefore, all Windows 8.x problems with the **Launcher** class are gone, and today you have a great way to communicate between different applications.

Publisher Cache

One other way to communicate between applications of the same publisher is the publisher cache folder. The idea is to create a special folder or folders that are assigned not to applications but to the publisher. So if the publisher creates a bunch of applications and wants to share some data between them, it's possible to use cache folders.

To create a publisher cache folder(s), developers should use the manifest file like this:

```
<Extensions>
  <Extension Category ="windows.publisherCacheFolders">
    <PublisherCacheFolders>
      <Folder Name="myFolder"/>
    </PublisherCacheFolders>
  </Extension>
</Extensions>
```

In this case I have created just one folder, and "created" is the right word because the folder will be created automatically based on the manifest of the application. Note that this folder will be created in a special directory that is associated with the publisher rather than with the application. In my case, the folder looks like C:\Users\Sergey\AppData\Local\Publishers\kj4a6z6kv5v3p\myFolder.

Of course, to start working with this folder (these folders), you just need to get a reference to the **StorageFolder** object, and you can do so using the **ApplicationData** class:

```
var f = ApplicationData.Current.
    GetPublisherCacheFolder("myFolder");
```

Right after you get access to the folder, you can create subfolders, check files inside, and do any available operations as with a simple **StorageFolder** object.

If you want to clear the publisher cache folder, you can do so using the **ClearPublisherCacheFolderAsync** method:

```
ApplicationData.Current.ClearPublisherCacheFolderAsync(
    "myFolder");
```

That's all. You can see that it's easy and it's a good opportunity to share data between applications for enterprise if developers need to implement a bunch of different applications with common settings, temp files, and so on.

This page intentionally left blank

Chapter 16

Application Services and Background Tasks

Background Tasks

In the previous chapters, we discussed foreground applications only. But the Universal Windows Platform allows you to execute some logic in the background when your application is not active. Let's discuss how to create a simple background task and activate it.

First of all, you need to know that if you want to create a background task, you will need to create a separate project that implements it. Because the main idea of background tasks is doing something if the application is not active, you cannot use any methods or classes of the application itself. In fact, you need to create a special component that will be separate from the application. In Visual Studio you just need to add one more project to your solution and select the Windows Runtime Component template:

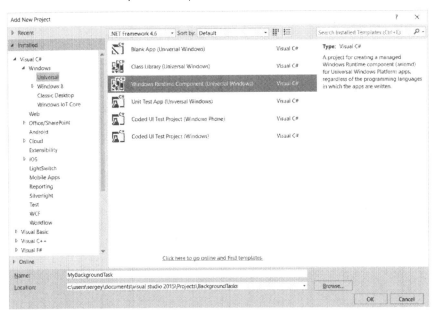

With this template you can create a class that extends Windows Runtime. By default the template contains a class that we can rename and use for our needs.

Of course, Windows cannot use every Windows Runtime component as a background task. And to start your task, Windows requires implementing the **IBackgroundTask** interface. This interface contains just one method, **Run**, and the system will use this method to execute your code right after creating an instance of the task.

264

So in the next step, you need to modify the existing class in the following way:

```
namespace MyBackgroundTask
{
    public sealed class MyTask : IBackgroundTask
    {
        public void Run(
            IBackgroundTaskInstance taskInstance)
        {
            throw new NotImplementedException();
        }
    }
}
```

This step is a must for creating any background task, but before implementing something inside the Run method, we need to know how and when Windows activates background tasks.

The Universal Windows Platform allows you to activate background tasks based on triggers. You can find all possible triggers if you open in Object Browser all classes that implement the **IBackgroundTrigger** interface:

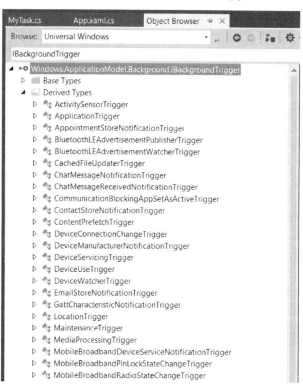

The full list contains thirty-nine classes and allows you to associate your background task with many events. For example, you can execute your code once a push notification arrives or a connection status is changed and even if a time interval has passed.

So in the next step, you need to decode which trigger meets your requirements.

Once you are ready with the trigger, you need to configure your application and let know the system about the available background tasks in the application. To do that, you need to add a **Background Tasks** declaration to the manifest:

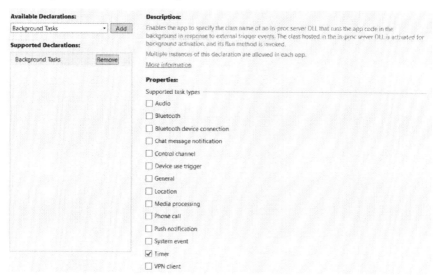

If your application can run several different background tasks, you need to create a declaration for each of them. In the parameters you need to select a type of the task and specify an entry point—the full name of your background task class, including namespaces:

In our example we will create a background task that will be activated with the Time trigger.

OK, it's time to create some code that will register our task in the system. To do so, we will implement a method called RegisterBackgroundTasks and call it when we want.

Before starting any registration activities, you need to request permissions and see whether you can create any background task. You can do so using the **BackgroundExecutionManager** class and the **RequestAccessAsync** method.

```
var status =
    await BackgroundExecutionManager.RequestAccessAsync();
```

Usually this call will not generate any messages, and you will simply get access. But the user can revoke access anytime by visiting the **Privacy** tab in the **Settings** window:

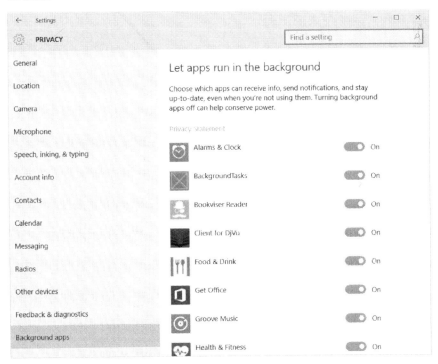

In the next step, you need to start registration by checking whether background tasks are already available. It's a very important practice, and if the background tasks are available, you can delete them or return from the method and pass the registration process. Of course, it depends on the scenario, but I would simply delete all existing background tasks and create new ones. Because the Universal

Windows Platform contains the **BackgroundTaskRegistration** class, we can easily enumerate all tasks that were registered by our application:

```
foreach (var task in BackgroundTaskRegistration.AllTasks)
{
    task.Value.Unregister(true);
}
```

In the next part of our implementation, we need to register the background task itself. But before doing so, you need to add the background task project to the application project using the **Add Reference** window. Once you do so, you can continue to implement the code:

```
var timeTrigger = new TimeTrigger(15, true);
var backgroundBuilder = new BackgroundTaskBuilder();
backgroundBuilder.Name = "timerTask";
backgroundBuilder.TaskEntryPoint = typeof(MyTask).FullName;
backgroundBuilder.SetTrigger(timeTrigger);
backgroundBuilder.Register();
```

In the code above, we used **TimeTrigger** to create a trigger that will activate our background task in fifteen minutes. You cannot define an interval less than fifteen minutes for the time trigger. The second parameter in the constructor of the time trigger allows you to define whether the task will be activated just once or repeatedly. In our case we will activate the task just once.

We can register the task with the **BackgroundTaskBuilder** class. Using an instance of the class, you can specify the name of the task, the Windows Runtime component name, and the trigger. After calling the **Register** method, we finish the registration process. So below you can find the full version of our method:

```
public async void RegisterBackgroundTasks()
{
    var status =
     await BackgroundExecutionManager.RequestAccessAsync();

    if (status == BackgroundAccessStatus.Denied)
        throw new Exception("Access is denied");

    foreach (var task in
        BackgroundTaskRegistration.AllTasks)
    {
        task.Value.Unregister(true);
    }
```

```
    var timeTrigger = new TimeTrigger(15, true);
    var backgroundBuilder = new BackgroundTaskBuilder();
    backgroundBuilder.Name = "timerTask";
    backgroundBuilder.TaskEntryPoint =
        typeof(MyTask).FullName;
    backgroundBuilder.SetTrigger(timeTrigger);
    backgroundBuilder.Register();
}
```

The **BackgroundBuilder** class has one more important method, called AddCondition. With this method you can ask to run the task if certain conditions are applied. For example, you can run the task if the user is available:

```
backgroundBuilder.AddCondition(
    new SystemCondition(SystemConditionType.UserPresent));
```

But we still haven't implemented any code for the background task. I am going to show a Toast notification only. So we can use the following code:

```
public void Run(IBackgroundTaskInstance taskInstance)
{
    XmlDocument xml = new XmlDocument();
    xml.LoadXml(
      "<toast>" +
      "<visual>" +
      "<binding template=\"ToastGeneric\">" +
      "<text>Football application</text>" +
      "<text>The second period will start shortly</text>" +
      "</binding>" +
      "</visual>" +
      "</toast>");
    var toastNot =
        ToastNotificationManager.CreateToastNotifier();
    ToastNotification toast = new ToastNotification(xml);
    toastNot.Show(toast);
}
```

Right now you can build the solution and launch the application. Note that you should not wait fifteen minutes to test the task. If you are running the application in debug mode, you can fire all available tasks using the Debug Location toolbar:

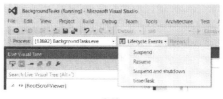

In our example we used synchronous calls only in the task implementation, but if you need to call some **async** methods from the Run method, you need to work with deferral, and I would recommend using the following template:

```
BackgroundTaskDeferral _deferral;
public async void Run(IBackgroundTaskInstance taskInstance)
{
    _deferral = taskInstance.GetDeferral();

    //doing async tasks

    _deferral.Complete();
}
```

If you don't use deferral in the case of **async** calls, the system may finish your task before you get a return from the method.

Application Services

In the next part of the chapter, I am going to talk about one more way to establish communication between different applications—Application Services. Implementing Application Services, Microsoft combines two ideas, such as background tasks and web services, making it possible to use background tasks as services for other applications on the same PC.

I prefer to think about this feature as something for enterprise companies, which use lots of different applications for different tasks, and I know many scenarios when common tasks can be moved to separate background tasks and published for other applications. For example, the IT department of a bank can develop an application for offline work that can reserve some contract IDs in advance and share these IDs with other applications on the same PC, collect information about their usage, and sync data from its own interface. At the same time, the bank can ask vendors to develop other applications that will not communicate with the bank's server directly but will use the bank's application as a way to get contract IDs and send data for sync. Additionally, Application Services can be used for standard Windows applications, but I have less faith in public applications with Application Services inside. In any case, let's see how to implement Application Services, and then we will see how developers decide to use it.

I am going to implement two applications. The first one will have a background task as a service, and it will get information about the user from the second application and return a new contract ID. The second app will work as a consumer of the service. I am not going to implement any interface—just code that shows Application Services feature.

Note that Application Services can be implemented inside a standard Universal Windows Platform application. So even if you don't need a user interface and only want to create some services, you need to create a standard UWP application. To activate an application service, users should not launch your application, but you still need to implement a main screen of your application, just in case. So to start implementing and testing Application Services, you need to create two blank UWP projects.

Right after you create the two projects, you can start with the project that will host the service. Let's start with a background task and declare the following class:

```
class ContractIDService : IBackgroundTask
{
    public void Run(IBackgroundTaskInstance taskInstance)
    {
        throw new NotImplementedException();
    }
}
```

It's a typical template for a background task, but to make it the service, we need to make some changes inside the manifest file of the application:

```
<Application Id="App"
. . . . .
 <Extensions>
  <uap:Extension Category="windows.appService"
     EntryPoint="AppService.ContractIDService">
   <uap:AppService Name="GetContractIDService"/>
  </uap:Extension>
 </Extensions>
</Application>
```

We used the name of the class (including the namespace) as an entry point for the service, and using the **AppService** element, we declared the name of the service that should be used in the client application. You can select any name.

OK. Let's start implementing the ContractIDService class. First of all, we need to implement the Run method:

```
private static BackgroundTaskDeferral taskDeferal;

public void Run(IBackgroundTaskInstance taskInstance)
```

```
{
    taskDeferal = taskInstance.GetDeferral();

    var appService = taskInstance.TriggerDetails as
        AppServiceTriggerDetails;
    if (appService.Name== "GetContractIDService")
    {
        appService.AppServiceConnection.RequestReceived +=
            AppServiceConnection_RequestReceived;
    }
    else
    {
        taskDeferal.Complete();
    }
}
```

This code just creates a deferral object and checks the service name. If you don't create a deferral in this method, it finishes the work, and the service will be destroyed. Additionally, you can have several services with the same entry point, so it's better to check the name. To get data, we need to assign an event handler for the **RequestReceived** event, as we did in our code.

Let's see a sample implementation of the **RequestReceived** event handler:

```
private async void AppServiceConnection_RequestReceived(
    AppServiceConnection sender,
    AppServiceRequestReceivedEventArgs args)
{
    var messageDeferal = args.GetDeferral();
    var message = args.Request.Message;
    string name = message["Name"].ToString();

    ValueSet returnMessage = new ValueSet();
    returnMessage.Add("contractID",
        $"{Guid.NewGuid().ToString()}{name}");
    var responseStatus=
        await args.Request.SendResponseAsync(returnMessage);

    messageDeferal.Complete();
    taskDeferal.Complete();
}
```

Of course, this is a fake implementation, and in real life your application will open storage to get a new ID and save the incoming data. Additionally, you can check permissions and implement many different things, but you can use this template as a starting point.

You can see that our event handler was declared with the **async** keyword, and we get one more deferral to guarantee that all available calls will be finished and an incoming message will not be destroyed. Using Message properties, we can easily access the object of the **ValueSet** class. We will use this class to pack data. With this dictionary you can pack any serializable objects, and **ValueSet** is used by many UWP classes, such as **Launcher**. Additionally, we use the same class to create storage for outgoing data and use the **SendResponseAsync** method to send data back to the client.

Note that I ask the deferral from the **Run** method to leave the process. It means that the next time the client sends the data to the same service, the system will create it once again and call the **Run** method. So if you know that you will use the service from time to time, you can leave the deferral alive and simply implement a dispose command for it. If you do this, developers can optimize performance of their client applications:

```
private async void AppServiceConnection_RequestReceived(
    AppServiceConnection sender,
    AppServiceRequestReceivedEventArgs args)
{
    var messageDeferal = args.GetDeferral();
    var message = args.Request.Message;
    string command = message["Command"].ToString();

    switch (command)
    {
        case "getID":
            string name = message["Name"].ToString();

            ValueSet returnMessage = new ValueSet();
            returnMessage.Add("contractID",
                $"{Guid.NewGuid().ToString()}{name}");
            var responseStatus =
                await args.Request.SendResponseAsync(
                    returnMessage);

            messageDeferal.Complete();
            break;
        case "exit":
            taskDeferal.Complete();
            break;
```

```
        }
}
```

In the next step we need to implement the client application. Let's look at the following code:

```
AppServiceConnection app = new AppServiceConnection();
app.AppServiceName = "GetContractIDService";
app.PackageFamilyName = "ad5ff53a-7ccc-4f70-b0c2-
6b909bba77a0_kj4a6z6kv5v3p";

AppServiceConnectionStatus status = await app.OpenAsync();

if (status == AppServiceConnectionStatus.Success)
{
    ValueSet message = new ValueSet();
    message.Add("command", "getID");
    message.Add("Name", "Sergii");
    AppServiceResponse response =
        await app.SendMessageAsync(message);
    if (response.Status ==
        AppServiceResponseStatus.Success)
    {
        //doing something
    }
}
```

We simply create an **AppServiceConnection** object and make a connection to the service using the **OpenAsync** method. Note that you need to know the package family name property. You can get it from the Store if you have already published your application, but for testing purposes, you can use one of two approaches:

- When you deploy your service, Visual Studio prints something like this to the output window: Deployment complete (113ms). Full package name: "ad5ff53a-7ccc-4f70-b0c2-6b909bba77a0_1.0.0.0_x86__kj4a6z6k v5v3p". Just remove the version and platform from this message (_1.0.0.0_x86_), and you will get your package family name.

- You can use this string to get the package family name directly in your application:

```
string name = Package.Current.Id.FamilyName;
```

Just use a breakpoint and get the name in debug mode.

Once you make a connection, you can use it to send a message using the **SendMessageAsync** method.

Note that the **AppServiceConnection** class has the **RequestReceived** event. So your application can receive requests from the service as well. Using these classes, you can establish two-way communication.

Finally, if you need to debug the service, I would recommend using the **Do not launch but debug my code when it starts** feature. It allows you to see what happens when the client activates your service.

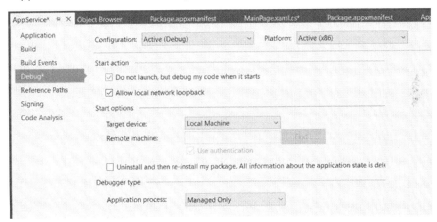

This page intentionally left blank

Chapter 17

Networking

Network Information

Let's start this chapter with classes that allow you to get information about the network status. All of these classes are located in the **Windows.Networking.Connectivity** namespace. You can find more than twenty classes there, but the most important are **NetworkInformation** and **ConnectionProfile**. Using these classes you easily can get the current network status. To do so, you just need to use the **GetInternetConnectionProfile** static method, which you can find in the **NetworkInformation** class, and with that you can get a reference to a **ConnectionProfile** object:

```
var connectionProfile =
NetworkInformation.GetInternetConnectionProfile();
var connectionProfileInfo = new StringBuilder(
    $"ProfileName : {connectionProfile.ProfileName}\n");
switch (connectionProfile.GetNetworkConnectivityLevel())
{
    case NetworkConnectivityLevel.None:
        connectionProfileInfo.AppendLine(
            "Connectivity Level : None");
        break;
    case NetworkConnectivityLevel.LocalAccess:
        connectionProfileInfo.AppendLine(
            "Connectivity Level : Local Access");
        break;
    case
NetworkConnectivityLevel.ConstrainedInternetAccess:
        connectionProfileInfo.AppendLine(
        "Connectivity Level : Constrained Internet Access");
        break;
    case NetworkConnectivityLevel.InternetAccess:
        connectionProfileInfo.AppendLine(
            "Connectivity Level :Internet Access");
        break;
}
var connectionCost =
    connectionProfile.GetConnectionCost();
switch (connectionCost.NetworkCostType)
{
    case NetworkCostType.Unrestricted:
        connectionProfileInfo.AppendLine(
            "Cost: Unrestricted");
        break;
    case NetworkCostType.Fixed:
```

```
            connectionProfileInfo.AppendLine("Cost: Fixed");
            break;
    case NetworkCostType.Variable:
            connectionProfileInfo.AppendLine("Cost: Variable");
            break;
    case NetworkCostType.Unknown:
            connectionProfileInfo.AppendLine("Cost: Unknown");
            break;
    default:
            connectionProfileInfo.AppendLine("Cost: Error");
            break;
}
connectionProfileInfo.AppendLine(
    $"Roaming: {connectionCost.Roaming}");
connectionProfileInfo.AppendLine(
    $"Over Data Limit: {connectionCost.OverDataLimit}");
connectionProfileInfo.AppendLine(
    $"Approaching Data Limit :
    {connectionCost.ApproachingDataLimit}");
```

You can place this code in the **OnNavigatedTo** method and use a breakpoint to check the information in connectionProfileInfo:

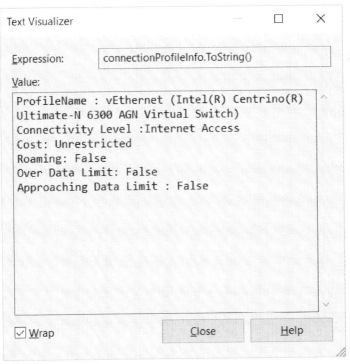

Additionally, using **ConnectionProfile**, we can get information about the amount of received and sent data. To do so, you can use the **GetLocalUsage** method and read all information using the **DataUsage** class.

Therefore, there you have everything you need in your applications.

Working with Data

Once you know the status of the network connection, you can start working with data on the Internet. The Universal Windows Platform provides several classes. The simplest is **HttpClient**, which you can find in the **Windows.Web.Http** namespace. Compared to **HttpWebRequest/HttpWebResponse** from the .NET Framework, this class is based on a new **async/await** approach, and you will see that here you do not have to use any specific delegates, event handlers, and so on. So to request content using a Uri, you can use the following code:

```
HttpClient client = new HttpClient();
string s=await client.GetStringAsync(
    new Uri("http://www.microsoft.com"));
```

So in most cases, if you want to read JSON or XML data, you will use this simple code and work with string objects once the method returns data. But if you want to send more-complex data, including custom headers, you can use the **PostAsync**, **PutAsync**, or **SendRequestAsync** methods. All these methods allow you to pass an object that implements the **IHttpContent** interface. So you can choose between different types of content.

Of course, **HttpClient** works fine if a user is still on the same page and is just waiting for data. But in some cases, if you want to download or upload lots of data, **HttpClient** doesn't work. I am not sure whether the user have to wait for several minutes on the same page while a file is downloading. In fact, the user can even switch to other applications. So if you want to download or upload a large amount of content, it's better to use the **BackgroundDownloader** and **BackgroundUploader** classes, which can work in the background. These classes are located in the **Windows.Networking.BackgroundTransfer** namespace, and you can use them directly from the foreground part of the application. So you do not have to create any special tasks, libraries, and so on. Let's look at the following example:

```
DownloadOperation download = null;
try
{
    Uri source = new Uri(serverAddressFile);
```

```
StorageFile destinationFile =
    await KnownFolders.PicturesLibrary.CreateFileAsync(
    "Image.jpg",
    CreationCollisionOption.GenerateUniqueName);
BackgroundDownloader downloader =
    new BackgroundDownloader();
download = downloader.CreateDownload(
    source, destinationFile);
Progress<DownloadOperation> progressCallback =
    new Progress<DownloadOperation>(DownloadProgress);
await download.StartAsync().AsTask(
    progressCallback);}
catch (Exception ex)
{

}
```

Here we have started to download a file from a server to save it on the local disk. You can see that to start downloading a file, you simply need to create a **BackgroundDownloader** object and call the **CreateDownload** method there. Once the **DownloadOperation** object is created, we can start the process and pass the reference to an event handler to receive update about the status.

Note that this code works fine, but if the user closes the page or the application itself, we need to implement additional code that gets active downloads and updates the UI according to that information. To do so, we simply can use the **GetCurrentDownloadsAsync** static method of the **BackgroundDownloader** class.

How to Work with RSS Feeds

One more useful namespace is **Windows.Web.Syndication**. With this namespace you can simplify your work with RSS feeds. This namespace supports RSS 2.0 and Atom 1.0.

To start working with a feed, you need to use the **SyndicationClient** class, which allows you to download the feed and get a reference to the **SyndicationFeed** object that contains feed data:

```
SyndicationClient client = new SyndicationClient();
SyndicationFeed currentFeed =
    await client.RetrieveFeedAsync(uri);
```

Additionally, you can use the **BypassCacheOnRetrieve** property to avoid any problems with cached data.

Once data is loaded, we can use the Items property to get access to each record:

```
foreach (var item in currentFeed.Items)
{
    string title = item.Title != null ? item.Title.Text :
        "(no title)";
    string link = string.Empty;
    if (item.Links.Count > 0)
    {
        link = item.Links[0].Uri.AbsoluteUri;
    }
    string content = "(no content)";
    if (item.Content != null)
    {
        content = item.Content.Text;
    }
    else if (item.Summary != null)
    {
        content = item.Summary.Text;
    }
}
```

So you can see that these classes don't take much time to use.

Using the WebAuthenticationBroker Class

Modern applications often don't use their own authentication system but allow the user to sign in using Facebook, Live ID, or other accounts. Usually the authentication process is based on an OAuth mechanism and requires you to use WebView to open an external page for authentication, handle navigation for the WebView, and provide your own logic based on the status and the current page. You can handle all these things from scratch, but UWP supports a special class, **WebAuthenticationBroker**, that simplifies your work. With this class you can use OAuth or Open ID, and all that you need to do is call the **AuthenticateAsync** static method and handle the result.

The following code shows you how to use Facebook to authenticate users in your application. In the first stage, we need to prepare URIs that use Facebook. You can find all these URIs by visiting the Facebook page for developers:

```
private static string FACEBOOK_DATA_LINK =
    "https://graph.facebook.com/me?access_token=";
private static string FACEBOOK_URI =
    "https://www.facebook.com/dialog/oauth";
private static string FACEBOOK_REDIRECT_URI =
```

```
    "https://www.facebook.com/connect/login_success.html";
private static string CLIENT_ID = "…";
private static string CLIENT_SECRET_KEY = "…";
private static string RESPONSE_TYPE = "token";
private static string TOKEN_PATTERN =string.Format(
    "{0}#access_token={1}&expires_in={2}",
    FACEBOOK_REDIRECT_URI, "(?<access_token>.+)",
    "(?<expires_in>.+)");
```

To get a client ID and a secret key, you need to register your application on the Facebook page for developers and copy the values from there. Once all strings are ready, you can implement the authentication code itself:

```
try
{
    var requestUri =
        new Uri(string.Format(
"{0}?client_id={1}&redirect_uri={2}&response_type={3}&displ
ay=popup&scope=publish_stream&client_secret={4}&scope=publi
sh_stream,user_photos,user_location,offline_access",
        FACEBOOK_URI, CLIENT_ID, FACEBOOK_REDIRECT_URI,
        RESPONSE_TYPE, CLIENT_SECRET_KEY),
        UriKind.RelativeOrAbsolute);
    var callbackUri = new Uri(FACEBOOK_REDIRECT_URI,
    UriKind.RelativeOrAbsolute);
    var auth =
        await WebAuthenticationBroker.AuthenticateAsync
            (WebAuthenticationOptions.None, requestUri,
            callbackUri);
    switch (auth.ResponseStatus)
    {
        case WebAuthenticationStatus.ErrorHttp:
            break;
        case WebAuthenticationStatus.Success:
            var match = Regex.Match(
                auth.ResponseData, TOKEN_PATTERN);
            var access_token =
                match.Groups["access_token"].Value;
            var expires_in =
                match.Groups["expires_in"].Value;
            break;
        case WebAuthenticationStatus.UserCancel:
            break;
        default:
            break;
```

```
      }
}
catch(Exception ex)
{
    throw ex;
}
```

Running this code, you can see the following Windows, which allow you to pass authentication using a Facebook account:

Of course, your application will not be able to access the log-in and password, but in the case of success, you will get a unique token that you can associate with your user. Using the token, you can get access to the requested user's data.

Note that in the case of Facebook, you need to specify the application type. Facebook supports Windows applications, but if you still don't know the application ID from the Store, you can modify the Client OAuth Settings to avoid any security problems during application testing:

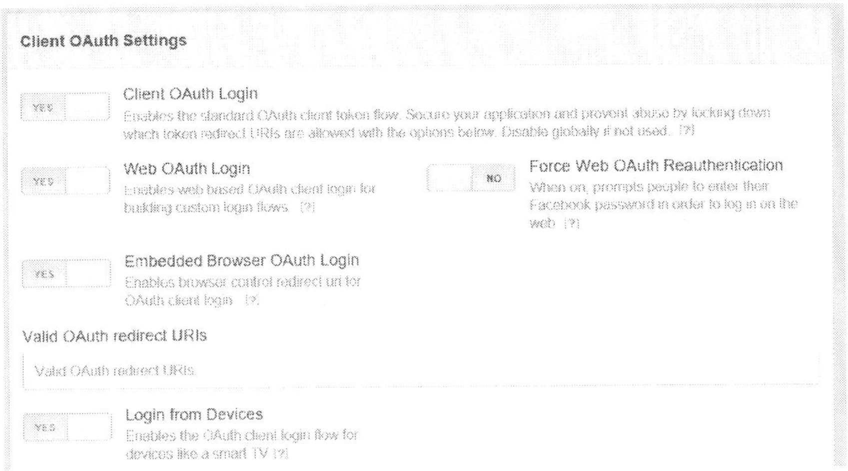

Client OAuth Settings

YES   Client OAuth Login
Enables the standard OAuth client token flow. Secure your application and prevent abuse by locking down which token redirect URIs are allowed with the options below. Disable globally if not used. [?]

YES   Web OAuth Login
Enables web based OAuth client login for building custom login flows. [?]

NO   Force Web OAuth Reauthentication
When on, prompts people to enter their Facebook password in order to log in on the web. [?]

YES   Embedded Browser OAuth Login
Enables browser control redirect uri for OAuth client login. [?]

Valid OAuth redirect URIs

Valid OAuth redirect URIs

YES   Login from Devices
Enables the OAuth client login flow for devices like a smart TV [?]

This page intentionally left blank

Chapter 18

Audio and Video

Media Controls

MediaElement

The simplest way to display video on the screen is to place on the page a **MediaElement** control. This control is a base for all other players that can play audio and video. To play something, you simply need to place a **MediaElement** control on your page and provide a path to the video or audio file. For example, this code allows you to play a video where I am catching a salmon:

```
<Grid Background=
   "{ThemeResource ApplicationPageBackgroundThemeBrush}">
   <MediaElement Source="Assets/salmon.mp4">
   </MediaElement>
</Grid>
```

So it's just one line of code, and I can watch myself using all available space in the application window:

Of course, it's a very basic code, and in reality **MediaElement** contains lots of methods, events, and properties. In this section we will discuss some of them. I think that it is better to start with supported formats and video sources.

When I was writing my book about Windows 8, there was a way to include all supported formats in the book. Today it's not so easy, because it depends on the container and the version of Windows (desktop, IoT, mobile, Xbox). That's why you simply need to know that Windows supports Windows Media Video, including Windows Media Video with Advanced profile, and MPEG file formats, including H.265. Additionally, you will not have any problems with adaptive streaming. Of course, if you need more details, you can visit MSDN and find several spreadsheets there.

Talking about possible sources, we should note that in our example, we used a file that was embedded in the application, but you can refer **MediaElement** to any file in the application's local storage or using a URI that supports **http**, **https**, and **mms**. And you can use the Source property to apply a source in XAML or C#, but **MediaElement** has a **SetSource** method as well that allows you to pass an **IRandomAccessStream** reference. This approach is better if you are working with **StorageFile** objects.

Let's talk about basic properties, events, and methods of **MediaElement**. In addition to the Source property, MediaElement has the following basic properties:

- **AutoPlay:** Allows you to play video/audio automatically once **Source** is provided. This property is set to true by default.

- **IsMuted:** With this property you can mute audio. Usually you will use this property if you implement mute-button functionality.

- **Volume:** Allows you to set or get volume.

- **Balance:** If the user has stereo speakers, this property allows you to set the ratio of volume for them.

- **Position:** Allows you to get or set the current position of the playing fragment. Sometimes this property is not available. For example, in the case of live streaming, you cannot change the position, but looking at the next property, you can understand whether you can work with **Position** in the current context.

- **CanSeek:** Allows you to see whether you can work with the **Position** property.

- **CanPause:** Usually if you cannot seek, you cannot pause either, but in some cases it's possible (as with advertisements). That's why **MediaElement** contains a separate **CanPause** property.

- **CurrentState:** Allows you to understand the current state of the MediaElement and contains a value from the **MediaElementState** enumeration type: **Buffering**, **Opening**, **Playing**, **Closed**, **Paused**, and **Stopped**.

- **DownloadProgress:** Returns the percentage of download completed.

- **DownloadProgressOffset:** Contains an offset that is a starting point for the downloading fragment. Usually this property is not 0 if the user changes the position inside the media element to content that is not downloaded yet.

- **Markers:** Contains a collection of markers. We will discuss markers in detail later in this chapter.

- **NaturalDuration:** Returns total duration of the media.

- **NaturalVideoWidth:** Returns video width.

- **NaturalVideoHeight:** Returns video height.

So as you can see, there are lots of properties of **MediaElement**. But in the case of methods, the most popular are **Play** and **Pause**.

Finally, **MediaElement** supports lots of events:

- **BufferingProgressChanged:** Fires when a new media fragment is buffered.

- **CurrentStateChanged:** Occurs when the Position property is changed.

- **DownloadProgressChanged:** Fires when a new fragment is downloaded from the server.

- **MarkerReached:** Occurs when a marker is reached.

- **MediaEnded:** Fires when **MediaElement** finishes playing media.

- **MediaFailed:** Occurs if something happened with the source.

- **MediaOpened:** Occurs when the media source is found and validated.

Let's implement a simple interface that will use some of these properties and events. Of course, I am not going to create a beautiful interface, and in real life also you do not create your own media interface very often, but it allows us to understand **MediaElement** better:

```
<StackPanel HorizontalAlignment="Left">
  <MediaElement Name="myMedia" Height="300"
   Source="Assets/salmon.mp4" Margin="5" AutoPlay="False"
   MediaOpened="myMedia_MediaOpened"
   MediaEnded="myMedia_MediaEnded" />
  <StackPanel Orientation="Horizontal">
    <TextBlock Name="durationText" Text="Duration: " \
     Margin="5" />
    <TextBlock Text=
     "{Binding Position.TotalSeconds,
      ElementName=myMedia,
      Mode=OneWay}" Margin="5" />
    <TextBlock Text="/" Margin="5" />
    <TextBlock Text="" Name="secondsText" Margin="5" />
  </StackPanel>
  <StackPanel Orientation="Horizontal">
    <Button Content="Play" Name="playButton"
     Margin="5" Width="100" IsEnabled="False"
     Click="playButton_Click" />
    <Button Content="Pause" Name="pauseButton"
     IsEnabled="False" Margin="5" Width="100"
     Click="pauseButton_Click" />
    <Button Content="Stop" Name="stopButton" Margin="5"
     Width="100" IsEnabled="False"
     Click="stopButton_Click" />
    <CheckBox Content="Mute" Margin="5" IsEnabled="False"
     Name="muteBox" IsChecked="{Binding IsMuted,
     ElementName=myMedia, Mode=TwoWay}" />
  </StackPanel>
  <StackPanel Orientation="Horizontal" >
    <TextBlock Text="Volume:" Margin="5" />
    <Slider Name="volumeSlider" Minimum="0" Maximum="1"
     Width="200" IsEnabled="False" StepFrequency="0.1"
     Value="{Binding Volume, ElementName=myMedia,
     Mode=TwoWay}" />
  </StackPanel>
</StackPanel>
```

Of course, you need to implement an event handler to make it work:

```
private void myMedia_MediaOpened(object sender,
   RoutedEventArgs e)
{
```

291

```
        volumeSlider.IsEnabled = true;
        playButton.IsEnabled = true;
        stopButton.IsEnabled = true;
        muteBox.IsEnabled = true;
        secondsText.Text = myMedia.NaturalDuration.TimeSpan.
            TotalSeconds.ToString();
}
private void playButton_Click(object sender,
    RoutedEventArgs e)
{

    playButton.IsEnabled = false;
    pauseButton.IsEnabled = true;
    myMedia.Play();
}
private void pauseButton_Click(object sender,
    RoutedEventArgs e)
{

    pauseButton.IsEnabled = false;
    playButton.IsEnabled = true;
    myMedia.Pause();
}
private void stopButton_Click(object sender,
    RoutedEventArgs e)
{

    pauseButton.IsEnabled = false;
    playButton.IsEnabled = true;
    myMedia.Stop();
}
private void myMedia_MediaEnded(object sender,
    RoutedEventArgs e)
{

    pauseButton.IsEnabled = false;
    playButton.IsEnabled = true;
}
```

Finally, running this code, you can see something like this:

So it's not very hard to implement a media player with basic functionality. You will spend much more time designing an interface for your media player.

Let's discuss one more feature of media element—markers.

Markers allow you to identify special points on the media timeline, and you can use them in many media scenarios. For example, you can use markers to create educational content, where the user can see some tests or animations if a marker is reached. You can use markers to apply subtitles.

In the following example, I am going to use markers to show some text associated with my video. The XAML code is here:

```
<StackPanel>
    <MediaElement Width="400" Height="300" Name="myMedia"
    Source="Assets/salmon.mp4"
    MediaOpened="myMedia_MediaOpened"
    MarkerReached="myMedia_MarkerReached" />
    <TextBlock Text="" HorizontalAlignment="Center"
    Name="subtitleText" FontSize="16" FontWeight="Bold" />
</StackPanel>
```

And the code:

```
public sealed partial class MainPage : Page
{
    Subtitle[] subtitles = new Subtitle[3];
    public MainPage()
    {
```

```
        InitializeComponent();
        Subtitle s = new Subtitle();
        s.text = "Lots of people in the water";
        s.time = new TimeSpan(0, 0, 0);
        subtitles[0] = s;
        s = new Subtitle();
        s.text = "Something strange. Is it a shark?";
        s.time = new TimeSpan(0, 0, 15);
        subtitles[1] = s;
        s = new Subtitle();
        s.text =
            "No. It's a pink salmon. 10... no, 20 lb!";
        s.time = new TimeSpan(0, 0, 20);
        subtitles[2] = s;
    }
    private void myMedia_MediaOpened(object sender,
        RoutedEventArgs e)
    {
        TimelineMarker t;
        foreach (Subtitle s in subtitles)
        {
            t = new TimelineMarker();
            t.Time = s.time;
            t.Text = s.text;
            myMedia.Markers.Add(t);
        }
    }
    private void myMedia_MarkerReached(object sender,
        TimelineMarkerRoutedEventArgs e)
    {
        subtitleText.Text = e.Marker.Text;
    }
}

class Subtitle
{
    public TimeSpan time;
    public String text;
}
```

Running this application, you can see the video and subtitles:

AudioAndVideo — □ ✕

No. It's a pink salmon. 10... no, 20 lb!

Of course, using today's **MediaElement** control, you don't have to implement captions from scratch, and below we will show how to use existing features and formats.

Though the existing **MediaElement** control is not new, it still has a number of new features brought by Windows 10. I have developed lots of applications that work with video, and I know about the disadvantages of media controls in Windows 8.x:

- Problem with adaptive streaming: To start working with adaptive streaming, you needed to use external libraries such as Player Framework (http://playerframework.codeplex.com/) and Smooth Streaming SDK, because Windows 8.x SDK doesn't support embedded features for adaptive streaming. Even if you use these libraries, you will get support for Smooth Streaming only.

- No support of existing formats for closed captions: Windows 8.x SDK doesn't support closed captions at all. SMPTE-TT and TTML were introduced in Player Framework SDK only.

- No way to change the template for existing media-player control: Windows 8.x supports **SystemMediaTransportControls**, but there was a sufficient variety of ways to change something. So you had to design your own player from scratch or use an existing player from Player Framework with less ability to change anything there.

Let's see how Microsoft fixed all these disadvantages in the Universal Windows Platform.

Adaptive Streaming

HTTP Live Streaming (HLS), Dynamic Adaptive Streaming over HTTP (DASH), and Microsoft Smooth Streaming are the most popular technologies for adaptive streaming. The new **MediaElement** control supports all of them.

If you want to test how it works, it's better to use an Azure account (you can use trial) and create a Media Service instance. Media Service supports dynamic packaging, so you can upload your video and encode it using one of the profiles that are ready for adaptive streaming.

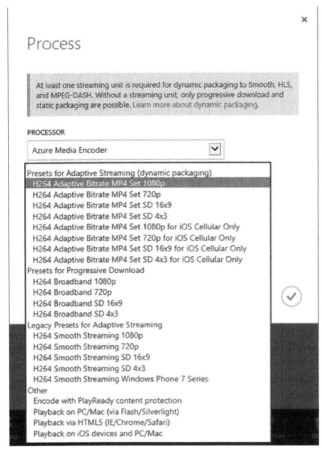

Note that you need to create at least one streaming unit. Once the video is encoded, thanks to dynamic packaging, you can stream it using any format that I mentioned previously (HLS, DASH, Smooth).

Let's see how to work with DASH. To do so, you just need to add **MediaElement** to the XAML page:

```
<MediaElement Name="media"
    AreTransportControlsEnabled="True" />
```

To create an adaptive media source, you can use the **AdaptiveMediaSource** class, like this:

```
AdaptiveMediaSourceCreationResult result =
    await AdaptiveMediaSource.CreateFromUriAsync(
    new Uri("http://testadaptive.streaming.mediaservices.
    windows.net/e1f03724-c228-4f86-9570-
    7321f1767fc5/Module%202.1_H264_4500kbps
    _AAC_und_ch2_128kbps.ism/Manifest(format=mpd
    -time-csf)",
    UriKind.Absolute));
if (result.Status ==
    AdaptiveMediaSourceCreationStatus.Success)
{
    var astream = result.MediaSource;
    media.SetMediaStreamSource(astream);
}
```

My video works fine, and thanks to **MediaTransportControls**, I have a great interface for my media player:

297

Captions

If you want to add closed captions, it's easy to do with new controls as well. Just use the following code to associate a TTM file with an existing adaptive stream:

```
AdaptiveMediaSourceCreationResult result =
   await AdaptiveMediaSource.CreateFromUriAsync(
      new Uri("http://testadaptive.streaming.mediaservices.
      windows.net/e1f03724-c228-4f86-9570-
      7321f1767fc5/Module%202.1_H264_4500kbps_
      AAC_und_ch2_128kbps.ism/Manifest(format
      =mpd-time-csf)",
      UriKind.Absolute));
if (result.Status ==
   AdaptiveMediaSourceCreationStatus.Success)
{

   var astream = result.MediaSource;
   var ttmSource = TimedTextSource.CreateFromUri(
      new Uri("ms-appx:///assets/captions.ttm"));
   var mediaSource=MediaSource.
      CreateFromAdaptiveMediaSource(astream);
   mediaSource.ExternalTimedTextSources.Add(ttmSource);

   var mediaElement = new MediaPlaybackItem(mediaSource);

   media.SetPlaybackSource(mediaElement);
}
```

You can see that we use the **TimedTextSource** class to create the source based on a file with captions. To associate the captions with the media source, we used the **MediaSource** class and the **MediaPlaybackItem** class to prepare the source for **MediaElement**.

Template for Media

Starting with Windows 10, the **MediaTransportControls** class has its own states and a template according to the modern design. It allows you to change anything there by modifying the existing XAML template. So you do not have to create buttons from scratch, implement logic, and so on. There are three ways to get an existing template for **MediaTransportControl**: visit MSDN, find the generic.xaml file on your computer, or use Blend.

Because I am writing this text before the release of Windows 10 SDK, there is no information on MSDN, but I hope that you can find it right after the release.

You can find the generic.xaml file using the following path: C:\Program Files (x86)\Windows Kits\10\DesignTime\CommonConfiguration\Neutral\UAP\10.0.10240.0\Generic. Just open generic.xaml and find the template for **MediaTransportControls**.

Finally, you can extract the template using the Blend tool. I would like recommend this way because it's an easy way not only for creating a copy of the template but for modifying it as well. To extract a template for **MediaTransportControls**, you need to create a new project (or open an existing one) in Blend and add **MediaTransportControls** to a page. Using the context menu, select Edit Template→Edit a Copy menu item.

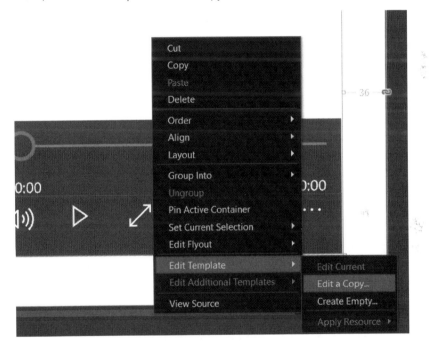

Blend will allow you to select a location and name for the new style. So select it and click OK.

299

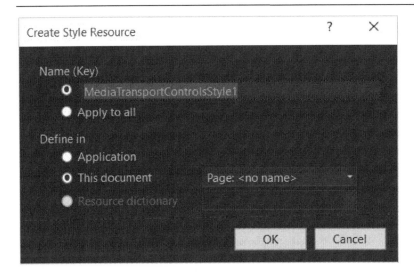

Right after this you can open the XAML and modify the new template there, or use the powerful editor in Blend to see and modify everything there.

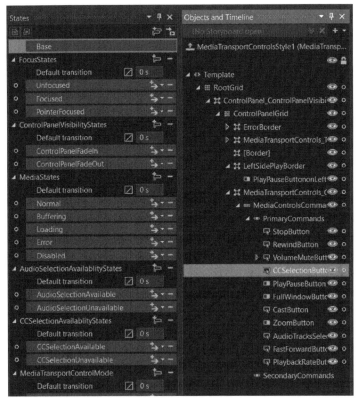

Media Casting

Media casting is a very important functionality that is quite easy to implement, but lots of developers forget about it when implementing their own media players. Last month I installed and immediately deleted three players because they didn't support media casting to my Xbox. Media casting is a special feature of Windows 10 that allows you to stream media content to an external device. Almost all modern TVs, consoles, and media players support protocols such as UPnP that allow you to send media to them using your computer. For example, I like looking at some technical content on my computer, but if I can, I stream the content to my Xbox to watch it on a bigger screen. How do you implement media casting in your applications?

First of all, you need to make sure that your PC allows you to send media files to remote devices. On my Windows 10 Enterprise machine, this option was turned off, and it was not clear why I could not find any devices. So you need to visit **Media streaming options** and check whether everything is OK.

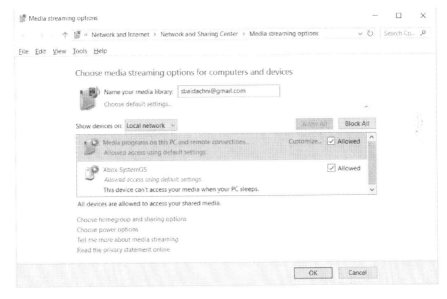

To start streaming your media, in some cases you should not do anything. For example, if you decided to use the media transport control that we discussed earlier, media casting is available by default.

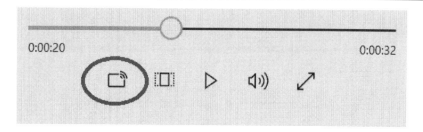

Clicking the **Cast to Device** button, you can see a dialog that contains a list of available devices. Just select a device and start streaming your media:

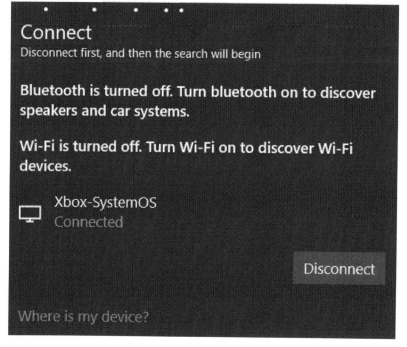

In my case I have an Xbox One system where I need to launch Xbox Video or Media Player, and all other things Xbox will do automatically.

Of course, if you have decided to create your own interface, you can do that as well. The Universal Windows Platform proposes a **Windows.Media.Casting** namespace that contains lots of classes such as **CastingDevice**, **CastingConnection**, **CastingSource**, **CastingDevicePicker**, and so on. You can use all these classes to implement your own media interface and even your own picker for media devices.

We will not create our own device picker, but let's see how to use an existing picker—**CastingDevicePicker**. Just add a button to the page where **MediaElement** is located and implement the following event handler for the **Click** event there:

```
private void Button_Click(object sender, RoutedEventArgs e)
{
    CastingDevicePicker picker = new CastingDevicePicker();
    picker.CastingDeviceSelected +=
        Picker_CastingDeviceSelected;
    picker.Show(new Rect(x,y,100,100));
}
```

We simply created an object of the **CastingDevicePicker** class and used the **Show** method there. With this method you can display the standard casting-device picker near the edge of the provided rectangle. This picker is good enough and supports two events that can fire if a device is selected or a dialog is dismissed. In my case I decided to implement an event handler for the **CastingDeviceSelected** event if the user selects a device:

```
private async void Picker_CastingDeviceSelected(
    CastingDevicePicker sender,
    CastingDeviceSelectedEventArgs args)
{
    await Dispatcher.RunAsync(
        Windows.UI.Core.CoreDispatcherPriority.Normal,
        async () =>
        {
            CastingConnection connection =
                args.SelectedCastingDevice.
                    CreateCastingConnection();

            await connection.RequestStartCastingAsync(
                myMedia.GetAsCastingSource());

            myMedia.Position = TimeSpan.FromSeconds(0);
        });
}
```

You can see that it's not a very complex event handler. You simply need to run your code in the interface thread. Using the selected device, you need to create a connection and request casting. Additionally, I have changed the position of my video to 0 to start casting from the beginning.

Media Editing and Transcoding

The Universal Windows Platform supports two more useful namespaces that allow you to edit and transcode media. You can find all needed classes if you check **Windows.Media.Editing** and **Windows.Media.Transcoding**.

In the case of transcoding, the most important classes are **MediaTranscoder**, which supports encoding media files from one format to another, and **MediaEncodingProfile** from the **Windows.Media.MediaProperties** namespace, which supports several predefined profiles for encoding. Therefore, if you want to encode a file or data from a stream, you need to create a profile and use **MediaTranscoder** to encode.

To create a profile, we can use the following code:

```
var profile = MediaEncodingProfile.CreateMp4(
    VideoEncodingQuality.HD1080p);
```

Or you can create a new profile based on existing media files using the **CreateFromFileAsync** or **CreateFromStreamAsync** methods. Alternatively, you can use the constructor of **MediaEncodingProfile** and initialize all needed properties to create your own profile from scratch.

Once the profile is created, you need to create an object of the **MediaTranscoder** class and call **PrepareFileTranscodeAsync** (or **PrepareStreamTranscodeAsync**) to pass the incoming file, the result file, and the profile. If the result of calling this method returns **CanTranscode**, you simply can call the **TranscodeAsync** method.

Thanks to the **Progress** and **Completed** events, you can determine the progress and whether the process is completed.

In the case of editing, you can use the **MediaClip** and **MediaComposition** classes from the **Windows.Media.Editing** namespace. The first class represents a media clip and supports trimming features, and the second one represents a collection of clips from which the final media file will be generated.

Chapter 19

Camera API

Using CameraCaptureUI Dialog

The Universal Windows Platform supports several ways to integrate your applications with a camera. You can use an API to get access to a video stream, create your own interfaces to work with the camera, or use embedded controls to simplify your code. In this chapter I am going to discuss all available methods. So let's start with the simplest way—the **CameraCaptureUI** dialog window.

Let's implement a simple interface that contains a button and an **Image** control. I am going to use the button to invoke the **CameraCaptureUI** dialog to take a picture and will show the picture in my application using the **Image** control.

```
<Grid Background="{ThemeResource
ApplicationPageBackgroundThemeBrush}">
    <StackPanel Orientation="Vertical">
        <Button Content="Take a Picture"
            Click="Button_Click" />
        <Image Name="photo" Height="400" Width="400">
        </Image>
    </StackPanel>
</Grid>
```

In the code below, you can see that once the user clicks the button, the **CameraCaptureUI** dialog will be invoked.

```
private async void TakePicture()
{
    CameraCaptureUI camera = new CameraCaptureUI();
    camera.PhotoSettings.Format =
        CameraCaptureUIPhotoFormat.Png;
    camera.PhotoSettings.MaxResolution =
        CameraCaptureUIMaxPhotoResolution.HighestAvailable;
    StorageFile file =
        await camera.CaptureFileAsync(
            CameraCaptureUIMode.Photo);
    if (file != null)
    {
        BitmapImage btn = new BitmapImage();
        btn.SetSource(await file.OpenAsync(
            FileAccessMode.Read));
        photo.Source = btn;
    }
}
private void Button_Click(object sender, RoutedEventArgs e)
{
```

```
TakePicture();
}
```

In fact, **CameraCaptureUI** supports not just photos but videos as well. And depending on whether you select photos or videos, you can modify the **PhotoSettings** or **VideoSettings** property. In our case we needed to use **PhotoSettings**, and the most popular settings here are **Format** and **MaxResolution**.

Once we are finished with settings, we can invoke **CaptureFileAsync**, which activates Windows embedded dialog window. Note that you should not declare any specific capabilities in the manifest, because you don't have direct access to camera, and the user can cancel the dialog at any time. That's why you need to check whether the dialog returns an image. If the returned object of the **StorageFile** class is not null, you can save it in the application folder, show it on the screen, or access the pixel array.

To present the image, we used the **BitmapImage** class, but if you want to use **SoftwareBitmap**, you can modify the code in the following way:

```
if (file != null)
{
    IRandomAccessStream stream = await
        file.OpenAsync(FileAccessMode.Read);
    BitmapDecoder decoder =
        await BitmapDecoder.CreateAsync(stream);
    SoftwareBitmap sBitmap =
        await decoder.GetSoftwareBitmapAsync();

    SoftwareBitmapSource bitmapSource =
        new SoftwareBitmapSource();
    await bitmapSource.SetBitmapAsync(sBitmap);

    photo.Source = bitmapSource;
}
```

But this code doesn't work, and if you debug it, you can see the following message:

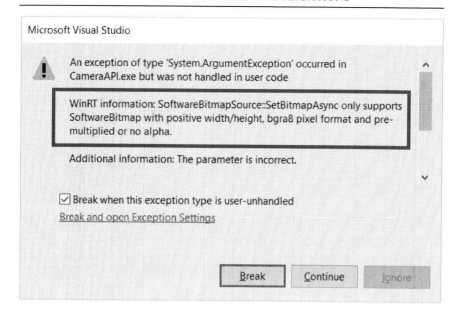

So the problem is in the format, and we need to add a couple of lines of code to convert the existing **SoftwareBitmap** to the right one. Let's see how we can finalize our code:

```
if (file != null)
{
    IRandomAccessStream stream =
        await file.OpenAsync(FileAccessMode.Read);
    BitmapDecoder decoder =
        await BitmapDecoder.CreateAsync(stream);
    SoftwareBitmap sBitmap =
        await decoder.GetSoftwareBitmapAsync();

    var sBitmapConverted = SoftwareBitmap.Convert(sBitmap,
        BitmapPixelFormat.Bgra8,
        BitmapAlphaMode.Premultiplied);

    SoftwareBitmapSource bitmapSource =
        new SoftwareBitmapSource();
    await bitmapSource.SetBitmapAsync(sBitmapConverted);

    photo.Source = bitmapSource;
}
```

If you run this code and click the **Take a Picture** button, you can see the dialog, but right after that you can see the cropping window:

This window is good if you want to ask the user to update a profile photo or something like that. But in some cases this default behavior is not needed. It's easy to change it using **PhotoSettings** and the **AllowCropping** property—just set it to false to disable the cropping functionality.

Let's modify our interface to get videos instead of images:

```
<Grid Background=
    "{ThemeResource ApplicationPageBackgroundThemeBrush}">
    <StackPanel Orientation="Vertical">
      <Button Content="Take a Video"
      Click="Button_Click" />
      <MediaElement x:Name="video"
      Width="320" Height="240"
      AreTransportControlsEnabled="True"/>
    </StackPanel>
</Grid>
```

I have changed the **Image** control to the **MediaElement** to present video. So there are not too many changes to the interface. But we need to rewrite our logic a little bit more:

```
private async void TakePicture()
{
    CameraCaptureUI camera = new CameraCaptureUI();
    camera.VideoSettings.Format =
        CameraCaptureUIVideoFormat.Wmv;
    camera.VideoSettings.MaxResolution =
        CameraCaptureUIMaxVideoResolution.HighestAvailable;
    StorageFile file =
        await camera.CaptureFileAsync(
            CameraCaptureUIMode.Video);
    if (file != null)
    {
        IRandomAccessStream stream =
            await file.OpenAsync(FileAccessMode.Read);
        video.SetSource(stream, "");
    }
}
private void Button_Click(object sender, RoutedEventArgs e)
{
    TakePicture();
}
```

You can see that the idea is the same, and if you run the application, Windows will show a dialog that allows you to record the video:

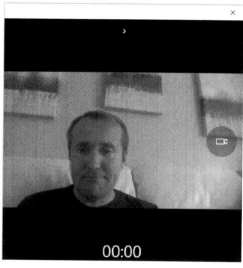

And preview it before sending it to the application:

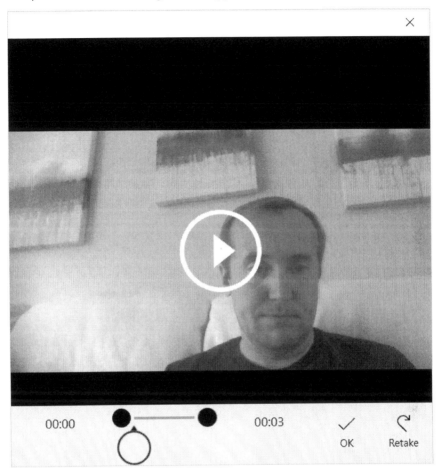

Media Capture API

Now we know how to get photos and videos using embedded dialogs for the camera, but if you want to create your own API, you need to use a different approach—Media Capture API. Let's look at the classes there and see how to use them.

Since we are going to get direct access to the camera, the first step is changing the manifest. You can open the manifest in design mode and activate the **Microphone** and **Webcam** capabilities:

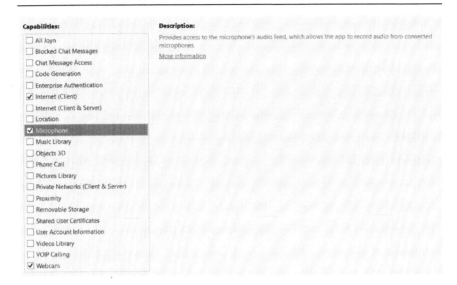

Media Capture API contains lots of different classes, but the most important one is the **MediaCapture** class. With this class you can create an object that can access video and audio streams. So our first task is to prepare a **MediaCapture** object. We can do so using the following code:

```
private async void VideoPreview()
{
    var devices =
        await DeviceInformation.FindAllAsync(
            DeviceClass.VideoCapture);
    var device = devices.FirstOrDefault();
    if (device==null)
    {
        throw new Exception("No camera device");
    }

    var media = new MediaCapture();

    var settings =
        new MediaCaptureInitializationSettings();
    settings.StreamingCaptureMode =
        StreamingCaptureMode.Video;
    settings.VideoDeviceId = devices[0].Id;

    try
    {
        await media.InitializeAsync(settings);
```

```
    }
    catch(Exception ex)
    {
        throw new Exception("Access denied", ex);
    }
    capturePreview.Source = media;
    await media.StartPreviewAsync();
}
```

Before starting to capture any video or audio, we need to make sure that there is a device available. We can do so using the **DeviceInformation** class. It allows you to find many different types of devices, but we need **VideoCapture** and/or **AudioCapture** devices only. Of course, the user can have several cameras or microphones, so usually you will need to create an interface that allows users to select a preferred device. Additionally, you can select a device whose **IsDefault** property is set to **true**. But in our case we just select the first device in the list. Of course, we need to check whether there are any devices available.

In addition to the **IsDefault** property, the **DeviceInformation** class has an **EnclosureLocation** property that helps you to select a video device based on its placement. For example, you can find out whether the camera is on the back panel or on the front of the device.

```
if (device.EnclosureLocation.Panel==
    Windows.Devices.Enumeration.Panel.Back)
{
    //doing something
}
```

Once we select a camera, we can start working with the **MediaCapture** class. There are three separate tasks: creating an object of the class, creating an object that contains settings, and initializing the **MediaCapture** object using the created settings. Of course, the first task is very simple. To prepare the settings, UWP supports the **MediaCaptureInitializationSettings** class, which allows you to initialize the capture mode and device ID. In the last step, we need to call the **InitializeAsync** method of the **MediaCapture** class. This is critical because if the user revokes permissions for your application, it will throw an exception. So we need to call this method in a **try** block and be ready to handle the exception in the right way.

That's all; we are ready to start recording. You can do that using **StartRecordToStreamAsync** and **StartRecordToStorageFileAsync**, but usually the user wants to see a preview of the video before starting to record something.

Of course, the preview should not take up too many GPU resources (especially for HD cameras). To get a preview, UWP supports a special class, **CaptureElement**. You can place this control anywhere and use it for a preview:

```
<Grid Background=
   "{ThemeResource ApplicationPageBackgroundThemeBrush}">
   <CaptureElement Name="capturePreview"
       Stretch="UniformToFill"></CaptureElement>
</Grid>
```

Once the control is placed, we can initialize it and start previewing using these two lines of code:

```
capturePreview.Source = media;
await media.StartPreviewAsync();
```

But as soon as the user clicks the record button, you can start recording.

Of course, it's easy to create a **MediaCapture** object. You will spend much more time creating a user interface for your application, and you should handle lots of different situations. For example, right after you create the object of the **MediaCapture** class, it's better to handle a **RecordLimitationExceeded** event that allows you to avoid problems with memory and video timing. Once the limits are reached, you need to stop recording and notify the user.

Chapter 20

Speech Recognition and Cortana

Frankly speaking, I am not sure whether it's a good idea to talk to your computer, but it depends on the situation. Of course, if you are going to move a mouse cursor using your voice, it's probably not a very good idea, but what about IoT devices? In some cases, you already use your voice for managing some devices, such as a GPS navigator. In the case of GPS, you use voice in both directions. It's not easy to check your way, especially if you are in traffic, but modern GPS systems can notify you about directions, the right lanes, and road conditions using text-to-speech technologies. In a similar way, it's not easy to type in a new address, but it's easy to say it. So speech engines can be very useful in some cases, and I understand Microsoft presenters who like to start their presentations with Cortana because things like Cortana allow us to introduce new user experiences and open doors for developers.

Let's see how to use a speech-recognition engine for UWP applications. I am going to discuss text-to-speech classes as well as speech-recognition classes, and finally new Cortana features.

Text to Speech

To transform your text to speech, you can use the **SpeechSynthesizer** class from the **Windows.Media.SpeechSynthesis** namespace. In the simplest case, you can use the following code:

```
private async void TalkSomething(string text)
{
    SpeechSynthesizer synthesizer =
        new SpeechSynthesizer();

    SpeechSynthesisStream synthesisStream =
        await synthesizer.SynthesizeTextToStreamAsync(text);

    media.AutoPlay = true;
    media.SetSource(
        synthesisStream, synthesisStream.ContentType);
    media.Play();
}
```

In the first two lines, we create a **SpeechSynthesizer** object and use the **SynthesizeTextToStreamAsync** method to get a reference to the stream, which should contain an audio output. To play the audio in our application, we can use **MediaElement**, which you can place anywhere on your page. This code is very simple, and you should not ask for any permissions or anything else of the kind. But if you are going to use a text-to-speech service in a more advanced way, you need to spend more time. For example, this code doesn't answer questions like, what is the language? or how should complex text be pronounced?

Let's start with the language. Because your application can use only the installed languages, you cannot assume that the user's computer is able to speak Russian or Spanish. So if you are going to use a language other than English, it's better to check whether the language is available. If you are using English, it's better to check that the default language is English because in some cases that's not true. To do so, you can use the following static properties of the **SpeechSynthesizer** class:

- **DefaultVoice:** Provides information about the default voice that your application will use if you don't set up a different one.

- **AllVoices:** Allows you to get access to a list of all voices in the system. You can use LINQ or indexer to find the right voice.

Note that if you are looking for a particular language, you can find several voices because a voice is not just a language. For example, I have two default voices in my system; both of them are English, but the first one is male while the second one is female. The **DefaultVoices** and **AllVoices** properties allow you to work with **VoiceInformation** objects that contain all needed information, such as Language, DisplayName, and Gender.

So if you want to check the language, you can use the following code:

```
var list = from a in SpeechSynthesizer.AllVoices
           where a.Language.Contains("en")
           select a;

if (list.Count() > 0)
{
    synthesizer.Voice = list.Last();
}
```

If you look at the **SpeechSynthesizer** methods, you can find that there are two methods, **SynthesizeTextToStreamAsync** and **SynthesizeSsmlToStreamAsync**. The second method allows you to implement more-complex text-to-speech scenarios. It supports speech synthesis markup language (SSML), which allows you to make more-complex sentences and manage their pronunciation. Of course, SSML is a text format that is based on XML, so you can easily create your own or modify an existing one.

Let's look at some SSML elements:

- **speak:** Root element for SSML, which allows you to set up the default language as well.

- **audio:** Allows you to include an audio file in the speech. It allows you to include some effects, music, and so on.

- **break:** You can declare a pause using this element. It has attributes such as **duration** and **strength**.

- **p** or **s:** Allows you to define a paragraph that has its own language. With this element you can use different (supported) languages in the speech.

- **prosody:** Allows you to set up volume.

- **voice:** Allows you to select one of the predefined voices based on attributes such as gender.

Here is an example of a short SSML file that combines English and Russian sentences:

```
<speak version="1.0"
       xmlns="http://www.w3.org/2001/10/synthesis"
       xml:lang="ru-RU">
  <s xml:lang="ru">
    Чтобы сказать добрый день по английски, произнесите</s>
  <s xml:lang="en">Good morning</s>
</speak>
```

If you are going to create SSML in Visual Studio, you need to use an XML template and define the **speak** element, and Visual Studio will start to support the IntelliSense system.

To use an SSML file, you need download it as a string and pass it to the **SynthesizeSsmlToStreamAsync** method.

Speech Recognition

We already know how to transform text to speech, so it's time to talk about the opposite task.

The Universal Application Platform supports the **Windows.Media.SpeechRecognition** namespace and several ways to recognize your speech. You can predefine your own grammar, use the existing one, or use grammar for web search. In any case, you will use the **SpeechRecognizer** class. Let's see how to use this class in different scenarios.

Like the **SpeechSynthesizer** class, **SpeechRecognizer** has some static properties that allow you to understand available languages for recognition. The first property is **SystemSpeechLanguage**, which shows the system language, which should be the default language as well. The next properties, **SupportedTopicLanguages** and **SupportedGrammarLanguages**, are not very clear, because in the case of text-to-speech classes, we have just one property for all supported languages, but **SpeechRecognizer** allows you to recognize your speech locally or use several dictionaries online. That's why **SpeechRecognizer** has two properties: **SupportedGrammarLanguages** for general offline tasks and **SupportedTopicLanguages** for online grammars.

Let's start by checking out how to use **SpeechRecognizer** objects in several ways. First of all, you need to declare the capability in the manifest of your application, which will allow you to use the recognizer. UWP doesn't have any special capabilities there, so you just need to declare microphone capability. So usually, your manifest will look like this:

```
<Capabilities>
  <Capability Name="internetClient" />
  <DeviceCapability Name="microphone" />
</Capabilities>
```

You also need to implement additional actions to make sure that the user grants permissions to your application. To do this, you can implement the following code:

```
bool permissionGained =
    await AudioCapturePermissions.
        RequestMicrophonePermission();
```

```
if (!permissionGained)
{
    //ask user to modify settings
}
```

In Windows 10 the user can disable microphone permissions for the selected applications or for all applications at once. You can easily find the window that allows you to do it (Settings→Privacy→Microphone).

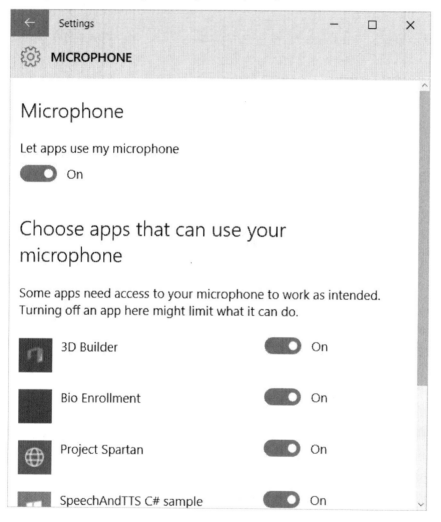

If everything is OK with permissions, you can start executing some methods that implement speech-recognition logic.

Based on your scenario, you can implement the following approaches for speech recognition:

- **Predefined grammars:** In this case the recognizer uses online grammars, so you do not have to create your own. There are two opportunities: you can use general grammar or grammar that is based on the most popular web-search queries. Using the first grammar, you will be able to recognize any text, but the second one is optimized for search.

- **Programmatic list constraints:** This approach allows you to create a list of strings with particular words or phrases that the user can use when speaking. It's better to use this approach when your application has a predefined list of commands.

- **SRGS grammar:** With SRGS language you can create an XML document with grammar inside. It allows you to create more-flexible applications without hard-coded grammar inside.

No matter what approach you have selected, you need to implement the following steps:

- Create an object of the **SpeechRecognizer** class. This is the simplest step and doesn't require any special knowledge.

- Prepare your dictionary. To do so, you need to create an object of a class that implements **ISpeechRecognitionConstraint**. There are four constraint classes, but in this post I am going to talk about three of them: **SpeechRecognitionGrammarFileConstraint**, **SpeechRecognitionListConstraint**, and **SpeechRecognitionTopicConstraint**. The first one allows you to create a grammar based on a file. You can just create a StorageFile object and pass it as the parameter. The second one allows you to use a programmatic list as your grammar, and the last one supports predefined grammars.

- Once you create a constraint (or constraints), you can add it to the Constraints collection of the **SpeechRecognizer** object and call the **CompileConstraintsAsync** method to finish all preparations. If you don't have any errors in your constraints, the method will return a Success status, and you can move forward.

- In the next step, you can start recognition, and here there are several options as well: you can start recognition of your commands using the **RecognizeAsync** method of the **SpeechRecognizer** object, or you can use the **ContinuousRecognitionSession** property and call the **StartAsync** method. The first method allows you to recognize short commands and uses predefined settings while the second one is adopted for the continuous recognition of free-dictation text. Using the **StartAsync** method, you need to use event handlers for the **ContinuousRecognitionSession.Completed** and **ContinuousRecognitionSession.ResultGenerated** events.

Additionally, you can use the set of methods that allows you to utilize built-in dialog panels for speech recognition—just use the **RecognizeWithUIAsync** method.

If you want to find some examples of speech recognition, I would recommend using https://github.com/Microsoft/Windows-universal-samples. You can find speech and text-to-speech examples there. Next time I am going to cover more interesting topics related to Cortana.

Cortana

Windows 10 supports different scenarios of using Cortana with your applications. As before, you can integrate some commands into Cortana that will help users launch your application and pass it some parameters. But today's Cortana is not just a speech-recognition engine but a helper, a decision maker, and a system that supports dialogs with users. That's why UWP has brought some new features that allow users to use your application as a knowledge base that runs in the background and provides answers to their questions. So in the first part of this section, we will discuss how to implement simple commands with Cortana, and in the second part, we will discuss how to use your application in the background to work with Cortana.

Before doing something with Cortana, you need to check whether Cortana is activated on your device. To do so, you can click the Search window and navigate to Settings.

Cortana is still not available in many regions. So if you are living in a nonsupported region, you can simply change the location of your computer to the United States, and right after you restart the device, Cortana should be available.

Once Cortana is available on your device, you can start developing applications that have Cortana-related features.

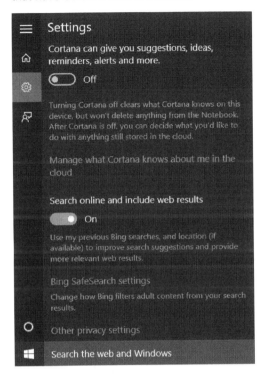

To add new commands to the Cortana database, you need to create an XML file that contains commands based on Voice Command Definition (VCD). A VCD file is a simple XML file that should contain the standard XML declaration:

```
<?xml version="1.0" encoding="utf-8"?>
```

and can contain the following main elements:

- **VoiceCommands:** This is the root element.

- **CommandSet:** This element describes the command set for a specific language and can contain commands.

- **Command:** Describes a command itself. You will use the Name attribute to assign the command name, but the command itself you will describe with the following elements.

- **Example:** Example of phrases that users can say.

- **ListenFor:** Contains words or phrases that Cortana should recognize.

- **Feedback:** Specify a text that will be displayed and read back if the command is recognized.

- **PhraseList:** With this element you can define a list of words or phrases that can be associated with the command. Users can say any of them to activate the command.

Let's look at the following code:

```xml
<?xml version="1.0" encoding="utf-8" ?>
<VoiceCommands
xmlns="http://schemas.microsoft.com/voicecommands/1.2">
  <CommandSet xml:lang="en-us">
    <CommandPrefix> Cinema Application, </CommandPrefix>
    <Example> Find show times to Terminator </Example>

    <Command Name="showtimesCommand">
      <Example> find show times to Terminator  </Example>
      <ListenFor> find show times to {film} </ListenFor>
      <Feedback> Finding show times to {film} </Feedback>
      <Navigate/>
    </Command>

    <PhraseList Label="film">
      <Item> Mission Impossible </Item>
      <Item> No escape </Item>
      <Item> Terminator </Item>
    </PhraseList>
  </CommandSet>
</VoiceCommands>
```

This XML contains just one command for American English and allows you to activate your application using the Cinema name and the **Find show times to** command.

To activate this command, your application should be run at least once:

```
var storageFile =
    await StorageFile.GetFileFromApplicationUriAsync(
        new Uri("ms-appx:///VoiceCommands.xml"));
await VoiceCommandDefinitionManager.
    InstallCommandDefinitionsFromStorageFileAsync(
        storageFile);
```

In this case I created a **StorageFile** object based on our XML file and used the **VoiceCommandDefinitionManager** class to make the registration.

If everything is OK, you can run the application to register the VCD file, and right after that you can use Cortana to run the application:

Of course, the application will not work, because we need to handle activation using voice command. In this case, you can use the **OnActivated** method and check the activation kind:

```
protected override void OnActivated(IActivatedEventArgs e)
{
    if (e.Kind == ActivationKind.VoiceCommand)
    {
        var vArgs = e as VoiceCommandActivatedEventArgs;
        var command=vArgs.Result.Text;
        //activate the application
    }
}
```

So you need to create a frame, parse parameters, and navigate the frame to the needed page.

Of course, you will need to update the phrase list from time to time. For example, in the case of cinemas, you need to update the full film list on weekly basis. To do so, you can use the following code:

```
VoiceCommandDefinition commandSet;

if (VoiceCommandDefinitionManager.
    InstalledCommandDefinitions.TryGetValue(
        "CinemaApp_en-us", out commandSet))
{
    await commandSet.SetPhraseListAsync(
      "film", new string[] {"film 1", "film 2", "film 3"});
}
```

Here CinemaApp_en-us is the name of the **CommandSet**. We didn't provide it in the original file, but if you want to change phrases dynamically, you need to use the **Name** attribute.

OK. We know how to use Cortana to launch our applications, but Cortana is a personal assistant, and if the user wants to implement a simple task in your application, there is no sense in launching the application in the foreground—just ask Cortana to do whatever is needed. To achieve this, UWP allows your applications to communicate with Cortana using background tasks.

The idea is simple: you can use application services as a source of data to Cortana. I will not describe how to add an application service, because you can find all the information in chapter 16, but I want to show you what you need to do to activate the feature.

First of all, you need to modify the VCD file by adding the **VoiceCommandService** element:

```
<Command Name="showTripToDestination">
  <Example> find show times to Terminator  </Example>
  <ListenFor> find show times to {film} </ListenFor>
  <Feedback> Finding show times to {film} </Feedback>
  <VoiceCommandService Target="CinemaCommandService"/>
</Command>
```

Note that the **VoiceCommandService** element was included in the 1.2 VCD specification. Lots of examples on MSDN refer to 1.1.

In this example, CinemaCommandService is the service name that you used in the manifest when declaring the application service.

Implement the application service in the following way:

```
public sealed class CinemaCommandService : IBackgroundTask
{
    private BackgroundTaskDeferral deferral;
```

326

```
VoiceCommandServiceConnection voiceConnection;

public async void Run(
    IBackgroundTaskInstance taskInstance)
{
    deferral = taskInstance.GetDeferral();

    var triggerDetails =
      taskInstance.TriggerDetails as
        AppServiceTriggerDetails;

    try
    {
        voiceConnection =
          VoiceCommandServiceConnection.
            FromAppServiceTriggerDetails(
            triggerDetails);

        voiceConnection.VoiceCommandCompleted +=
        (obj, arg) => {
          if (deferral != null) deferral.Complete(); };

        VoiceCommand voiceCommand =
          await voiceConnection.GetVoiceCommandAsync();

        switch (voiceCommand.CommandName)
        {
            case "showtimesCommand":
                {
                    var film =
                      voiceCommand.
                        Properties["film"][0];
                    SendResponse(film);
                    break;
                }
            default:
                var userMessage =
                    new VoiceCommandUserMessage();
                userMessage.SpokenMessage =
                    "Launching Cinema Application";

                var response = VoiceCommandResponse.
                    CreateResponse(userMessage);

                await voiceConnection.
```

```
                         RequestAppLaunchAsync(response);
                break;
        }
    }
    finally
    {
        if (deferral != null)
        {
            deferral.Complete();
        }
    }
}

private async void SendResponse(string film)
{
    var userMessage = new VoiceCommandUserMessage();
    userMessage.DisplayMessage =
      "Show times for "+film;
    userMessage.SpokenMessage = "Show times for today";

    var tileList = new List<VoiceCommandContentTile>();

    var tile = new VoiceCommandContentTile();
    tile.ContentTileType =
      VoiceCommandContentTileType.TitleWithText;

    tile.AppLaunchArgument =
      string.Format("film={0},type=IMAX", film);
    tile.Title = "IMax";
    tile.TextLine1 = "03:00pm, 05:00pm, 09:30pm";
    tileList.Add(tile);

    var tile2 = new VoiceCommandContentTile();
    tile2.ContentTileType =
      VoiceCommandContentTileType.TitleWithText;

    tile2.AppLaunchArgument =
      string.Format("film={0},type=DBOX", film);
    tile2.Title = "DBox";
    tile2.TextLine1 = "03:10pm, 05:20pm, 09:30pm";
    tileList.Add(tile2);

    var response =
      VoiceCommandResponse.CreateResponse(
        userMessage, tileList);
```

```
response.AppLaunchArgument =
  string.Format("film={0}",film);

await voiceConnection.ReportSuccessAsync(response);
  }
}
```

This code is quite long, but in fact it's not very complex. In the first step, we need to get a reference to the VoiceCommandServiceConnection object to get information about the command and send results back.

Right after that, we need to check the command name that we used in VCD file, and if the command name is found, we can prepare a response based on it.

To generate the response, I used the **VoiceCommandUserMessage** and **VoiceCommandContentTile** classes to create a title and a list of messages inside the response. These classes have very simple properties, and you will find that you can show messages that contain texts and images. Clicking on each message, the user can invoke the application and, thanks to the parameters, navigate to the page that matches the message.

To activate our component, we need to run the application.

Asking Cortana about a film, you can see the following message:

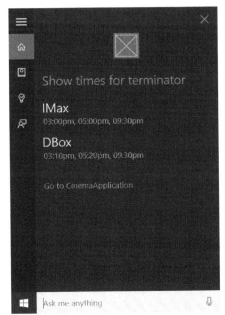

This page intentionally left blank

Chapter 21

Maps

In this chapter I am going to talk about the use of maps in Universal Windows Platform applications. The best way to start is to answer the question that developers have asked me many times: When will offline maps be available for Windows applications?

Starting with Windows 10, offline maps are available, not just for phones but for desktops, laptops, tablets, and so on. Users can visit the Settings window and download all needed maps there. Once the maps are downloaded, the existing map control will use them by default.

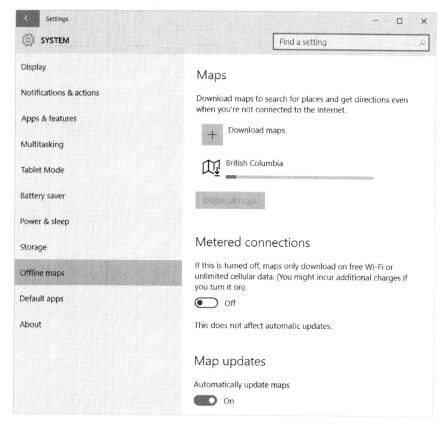

It's really cool because I can use my Windows 10 devices anywhere to find addresses, directions, and so on, and you can access all these things directly from your application.

But offline maps are not the only feature of new Windows 10 maps. Let's look at other features there:

- **Unified platform:** Starting with Windows 10, you do not have to use several services such as Here or Bing Maps for different tasks (or different services on different devices). All services are available under the same umbrella and can be used for any UWP applications.

- **Adaptive interface:** The existing Maps application works fine on all devices. You can use touch, pen, or mouse as well as different screen sizes. The same can be said about **MapControl**, which is available for developers.

- **2-D view with business and traffic information:** Existing maps support all common features for 2-D maps, such as different views and traffic information, and provide information about business locations and transit.

- **Location:** The existing Maps application allows you to find and display the user location. Using the Windows.Devices.Geolocation API, you can find the user location in your application to provide a better user experience and implement lots of different tasks.

- **External elements:** Developers can place their own icons, rectangles, polygons, and even XAML controls on maps. This allows you to customize existing maps and extends the number of possible scenarios.

- **Geofence:** The Geofencing API allows you to notify the application if the user arrives at a defined area.

- **Routing:** Developers can use Maps services that can calculate the route to the selected destination using different ways to get there (driving, walking).

- **StreetSide:** New functionality that allows you to get images of the selected area to display inside the interface. It's very useful if the user wants to know what the selected area looks like.

- **3-D views:** One more new functionality that is available for developers starting with Windows 10: now you can show maps not just in 2-D but in 3-D view modes. If 3-D view is available for the selected area, you can implement the same set of features as in the standard Maps application.

It's time to talk about how to use maps in your applications. You have two ways: you can redirect user requests to the existing Maps application, or you can integrate maps directly into your application.

If you are going to utilize the existing Maps application, you can redirect the user to it using the **Launcher** class. This class contains the **LaunchUriAsync** static method, which allows you to open an external application using information from Uri. For example, if you use "http://" in your Uri, then **Launcher** will open the web browser, but in the case of Maps, you need to start your Uri with **bingmaps:**. You also need to pass some parameters using your Uri. You can find the full list of possible parameters using https://msdn.microsoft.com/en-us/library/windows/apps/xaml/jj635237.aspx. For example, this code will open the Maps application, move the center to North Vancouver, and zoom the map to level 14:

```
await Launcher.LaunchUriAsync(new Uri(
    "bingmaps:?lvl=14&rpt=adr.North%20Vancouver%20BC"));
```

To start working with maps in your application, you need to get an access key by visiting Maps Dev Center (https://www.bingmapsportal.com/). You can select a trial key or basic key based on your needs. When Windows 10 is released, you will be able to find Universal Application in the list of possible applications, but right now there is still no information about Windows 10. In any case, you cannot publish Windows 10 applications right now, so you can use maps without the key. It works fine, but you will see a message that **MapServiceToken** is not specified and you cannot publish your application without **MapServiceToken**.

Once Windows 10 is available, you can create a basic key for your universal application using the portal:

Create key

Application name *

MyFirstW10Application

Application URL

Enter application URL

Key type *
What's This

Trial

Application type *

Public Windows App (8.x and earlier)

Enter the characters you see *

jD%3f

jD%3f   ×

Create

To start working with maps in your application, you need to use three namespaces—**Windows.UI.Xaml.Controls.Maps**, **Geolocation**, and **Maps**—and one control, **MapControl**. The first namespace contains **MapControl** itself and several classes that allow you to place something on maps, set up the camera and styles, and prepare the street view. The second namespace allows you to get the user location and contains the Geofencing API as well. And the last one supports several utility classes that allow you to find a location by address, calculate a route, and so on.

Because **MapControl** is not in a default XAML namespace, you need to add a new namespace to the XAML file:

```
xmlns:maps="using:Windows.UI.Xaml.Controls.Maps"
```

And you are ready to use **MapControl**:

```
<maps:MapControl MapServiceToken="..."/>
```

Now you know how to add maps to your application, so it's time to look at some tasks there.

Let's start with basic functionality, such as how to center a map, zoom in, and so on. Let's have a look at the following code:

```
maps.ZoomLevel = 14;
maps.Center = (
    await MapLocationFinder.FindLocationsAsync(
        "North Vancouver, BC", null)).Locations[0].Point;
```

In this code we use a reference to **MapControl** to assign two properties, **ZoomLevel** and **Center**. Of course, in the case of **ZoomLevel**, you do not have to do anything specific, but if you want to center your map based on the address, you need to use map services, in this case **MapLocationFinder**. In my example I used the **FindLocationsAsync** method and assigned the first location from the list to the **Center** property.

To apply 3-D view to the maps, you simply need to use the **Style** attribute. It's somewhat confusing because the Style attribute exists for all UI controls and can have different meanings.

```
<maps:MapControl Name="maps" Style="Aerial3D"/>
```

Of course, in the case of 3-D view, it's better to change the default angle for the map camera. You can do so using a static method of the **MapScene** class called **CreateFromLocationAndRadius**. With this method you can create a scene using the radius (meters), zoom level, and radius (degrees). Once you have a **MapScene** object, you need to use the **TrySetSceneAsync** method to apply the scene:

```
await maps.TrySetSceneAsync(
    MapScene.CreateFromLocationAndRadius((
        await MapLocationFinder.FindLocationsAsync(
            "Vancouver Downtown, BC",
            null)).Locations[0].Point,500,90,60));
```

If you run my code, you will see the center of Vancouver in 3-D:

So applying the 3-D view is easy. The same works for StreetView functionality. If you want to use the street view, you need just two lines of code:

```
StreetsidePanorama panorama=
    await StreetsidePanorama.FindNearbyAsync((
        await MapLocationFinder.FindLocationsAsync(
            "Vancouver Downtown, BC", null)).Locations[0].Point);
maps.CustomExperience = new StreetsideExperience(panorama);
```

If you run this code, you can see something like this:

Of course, the existing maps show lots of different information, but if you integrate maps with your application, you probably want to add your own objects to maps.

The simplest objects that you can add to maps are **MapIcon**, **MapPolygon**, and **MapPolyline**. For example, if you want to add an icon to the maps, you can run the following code:

```
MapIcon mapIcon = new MapIcon();
mapIcon.Location = maps.Center;
mapIcon.NormalizedAnchorPoint = new Point(0.5, 1.0);
mapIcon.Image = RandomAccessStreamReference.CreateFromUri(
    new Uri("ms-appx:///Assets/weather.png"));
mapIcon.ZIndex = 0;
maps.MapElements.Add(mapIcon);
```

You can use this code to place weather icons in the area, points of interest, and so on.

Additionally, you can add XAML controls to the maps. In this case you need to use the **Children** collection instead of **MapElements** as before. But it's not enough to add an XAML UI control; you need to place the control in the right position on the maps. To do so, you can use the **SetLocation** method of the

MapControl class. This method has two parameters: a reference to the added UI control and a location.

You can see that the current version of **MapControl** is very powerful and supports lots of features. It's even possible to write a separate book just about this control. If you want to know more, the best starting point for you is the Bing portal for developers (http://www.bing.com/dev/). The portal contains lots of examples and information on how to use Bing maps from JavaScript or in applications for alternative platforms.

Chapter 22

Inking

One more powerful control in the Universal Windows Platform is **InkCanvas**. With this control you can enable inking anywhere in your application, and you can use not just a stylus but fingers and a mouse as well. So thanks to this feature, you can bring inking functionality to any device based on Windows 10.

To enable inking, you need to start with an **InkCanvas** element and place it inside any container, such as **StackPanel**, **Grid**, and so on. Like other UI controls based on **FrameworkElement**, **InkCanvas** contains a bunch of properties, but in the simplest case, you do not have to declare anything:

```
<Grid Background=
  "{ThemeResource ApplicationPageBackgroundThemeBrush}">
    <InkCanvas Name="ink"></InkCanvas>
</Grid>
```

In this case **InkCanvas** will fill all space inside the container, and you can start making your notes or painting something. Note that by default, **InkCanvas** accepts input from the stylus (pen) only. So if you want to use fingers or a mouse, you need to implement the following code:

```
ink.InkPresenter.InputDeviceTypes =
    CoreInputDeviceTypes.Mouse|CoreInputDeviceTypes.Touch;
```

In this code we are using the second important object—**InkPresenter**. **InkCanvas** is a control that contains just one inking property, a reference to **InkPresenter**, but **InkPresenter** contains all information about input methods and lots of different settings, including a collection of strokes. You cannot create **InkPresenter** directly, but you can get the reference to an object of this class using the **InkPresenter** property of **InkCanvas**. **InkCanvas** doesn't contain any other properties or methods related to inking. But we still have something to discuss about **InkCanvas**, and the most important question is how to enable inking anywhere, because usually you need to enable inking for images, videos, and text rather than inside a blank container. Let's add several controls to the container and see what happens.

```
<Grid Background=
    "{ThemeResource ApplicationPageBackgroundThemeBrush}">
    <InkCanvas Name="ink"></InkCanvas>
    <StackPanel>
        <TextBlock Text="Hello. Here is some text."
            Margin="20"></TextBlock>
        <Button Content="Click me" Margin="20"></Button>
    </StackPanel>
</Grid>
```

If you run this code, you will see that all controls work fine, and you can make notes.

In our example we placed **InkCanvas** behind other controls, but if you swap **StackPanel** and **InkCanvas**, you can see that **InkCanvas** is placed above **StackPanel** while controls like Button don't work at all. You can resolve this with the help of the **Canvas.ZIndex** property.

```
<Grid Background=
    "{ThemeResource ApplicationPageBackgroundThemeBrush}">
    <StackPanel Canvas.ZIndex="1">
        <TextBlock Text="Hello. Here is some text."
            Margin="20"></TextBlock>
        <Button Content="Click me" Margin="20"></Button>
    </StackPanel>
    <InkCanvas Name="ink" ></InkCanvas>
</Grid>
```

Let's talk about the settings of **InkPresenter** and how to create different effects. You simply need to create an object of this class and set different properties such as Color, PenTip, Size, and so on.

```
InkDrawingAttributes attr = new InkDrawingAttributes();
attr.Color = Colors.Red;
attr.IgnorePressure = true;
```

```
attr.PenTip = PenTipShape.Circle;
attr.Size = new Size(4, 10);
attr.PenTipTransform = Matrix3x2.CreateRotation(
    (float)(70 * Math.PI / 180));
ink.InkPresenter.UpdateDefaultDrawingAttributes(attr);
```

The code above shows how to use **InkDrawingAttributes**. To update attributes, you need to call **UpdateDefaultDrawingAttributes** and pass the **InkDrawingAttributes** object there. In the code above I used the **PenTipTransform** property as well. This is a very interesting property that allows you to apply a transformation to the pen shape and get a more natural look for strokes using different stroke heights based on the direction of the pen (moving direction/angle).

You can check out the image above, where I tried to paint the symbol *f*, and you can see that the image contains strokes with different height values. In fact, I used the same settings, but this effect was applied thanks to **PenTipTransform**.

Finally, you can paint anything, but how can you erase if you do something wrong? To do this, you need to change the mode of **InkPresenter**:

```
ink.InkPresenter.InputProcessingConfiguration.Mode =
    InkInputProcessingMode.Erasing;
```

The next important class that is related to inking is **InkStroke**. Anything that you paint on **InkCanvas** consists of **InkStroke**. To get access to functionality around **InkStroke** objects, you can use the **StrokeContainer** property of **InkPresenter**. With this property you can save existing strokes to a file, add new strokes, access selected strokes, and so on. So if you want to implement any functionality around strokes, then **StrokeContainer** is your friend. The most popular methods are **LoadAsync** and **SaveAsync**.

Lots of applications require recognition functionality as well. To recognize text based on handwriting, you can use the **InkRecognizerContainer** class. The simplest way you can use this class is the following:

```
InkRecognizerContainer container = new
InkRecognizerContainer();
var result=await
container.RecognizeAsync(ink.InkPresenter.StrokeContainer,
   InkRecognitionTarget.All);
string s=result[0].GetTextCandidates()[0];
```

This code will use a default recognizer and convert the first text candidate from the list to the text. Of course, this is not enough for more complicated scenarios. For example, I spent ten years at school to train my handwriting for Russian and Ukrainian but not for English. So when I am trying to write something in English, the right result is usually in the second or third place in the list of text candidates. Additionally, I can have several recognizers on my computer.

So it's better to allow selection of the right recognizer. You can simply use **SetDefaultRecognizer** and **GetRecognizers** of the **InkRecognizerContainer** object to do it. In the case of nonnative English writers, I am not sure that you need to present the full list of possible results. It's better to ask users to set up the recognizer using system settings. For example, I can set up the default recognizer to adapt to my writing style if I select "Write each character separately":

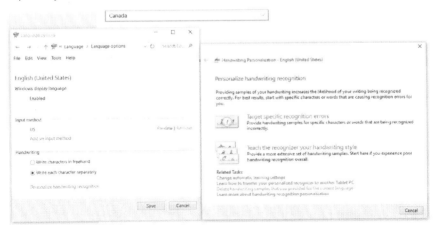

At the end of the section, I want to draw your attention to the Ink Toolbar control. It's not a default UWP control, and you need to install this control separately by visiting https://visualstudiogallery.msdn.microsoft.com.

Once you install the control, it will be available in the Extension tab of the Add Reference dialog (close and open Visual Studio after installation), and it's ready to use. You just need to add the reference to the library:

```
xmlns:ink="using:Microsoft.Labs.InkToolbarControl"
```

Find a place for the control and make a reference to the existing **InkCanvas**:

```
<InkCanvas Name="ink" ></InkCanvas>
<ink:InkToolbar TargetInkCanvas="{x:Bind ink}"
    VerticalAlignment="Top"
    HorizontalAlignment="Right"></ink:InkToolbar>
```

Below you can see the control itself, which generates our code:

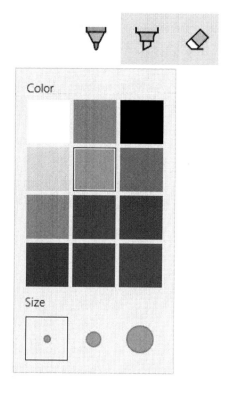

Chapter 23

Sensor API

Modern devices have lots of different sensors that allow you to get information about the device orientation, to track any movements of the device, to understand whether there are any objects in front of the device, to track the amount of light, and so on. Of course, some devices have fewer sensors, but some of them have lots of sensors. And it's really hard to divide all devices into separate groups because today you can find lots of hybrid devices on the market. For example, any phone, tablet, or two-in-one PC can track orientation—this is a huge category of devices that covers almost everything. Small devices like phones have proximity sensors, but at the same time, the biggest Windows 10 device, Surface Hub, has a proximity sensor as well. That's why when you work with any sensor, you should check whether the sensor exists and returns any data, and you should implement the interface of your application in a way that allows it to work even without needed sensors.

Let's look at the list of sensors that are supported by Windows 10:

- **Light sensor:** This sensor allows you to determine the amount of light around the sensor. Using this number, you can change the UI parameters of your application. For example, if you develop a book reader, you can change the contrast based on the amount of light.

- **Accelerometer:** With this sensor, you can find g-force values along the x-, y-, and z-axis. It's a very common and popular sensor that developers like to use in their games—by changing the angle of a device, the user can accelerate objects in a game.

- **Proximity sensor:** Using a proximity sensor, you can determine whether any objects are in front of the sensor and the distance to the objects. For example, in phones the sensor is used to determine whether the user is speaking. Additionally, you can use this sensor to work with the UI even without touching it.

- **Activity sensor:** With this sensor you can indicate the current status of the device. There is a choice between several predefined statuses, such as biking, running, in vehicle, and so on. Usually developers use this sensor in fitness applications. Windows 10 allows you to collect and store information from this sensor for up to thirty days.

- **Magnetometer:** This sensor returns the magnetic field's strength. You probably will not use the sensor directly, but Compass, Inclinometer, and Orientation sensor data are based on Magnetometer data.

- **Compass:** Thanks to the magnetometer and gyrometer, Windows 10 allows you to get compass data. It supports True North as well as Magnetic North mode.

- **Orientation sensor:** Windows 10 supports two orientation sensors: **SimpleOrientationSensor** and **OrientationSensor**. The first one allows you to determine whether the device is in horizontal or vertical orientation and whether the face of the device is up or down. The second one provides detailed information that describes the position of the device in 3-D space with a very high accuracy.

- **Pedometer:** One more sensor that is very popular in fitness applications. It allows you to calculate the number of steps that are made by the user.

- **Barometer:** Allows you to calculate the atmospheric pressure and predict the weather. It's probably a good idea to develop your own weather application using this sensor because local weather sites have been promising rain in Vancouver for the last three days, but it is still sunny.

- **Altimeter:** Allows you to track the altitude of a device. You can try to use it in fitness applications or to build your own aircraft on Windows 10.

- **Gyrometer:** This sensor allows you to measure angular velocities along the x-, y-, and z-axis. You can use it in games or in hardware solutions.

- **Inclinometer:** Allows you to identify angles of tilt with respect to gravity. This sensor is very useful in development, but you can use it to build your own drone based on Windows 10 or even to determine the orientation of a device.

After reading the descriptions of these sensors, you can see that they can implement lots of different tasks. So to create a really cool application, you should know how to work with them. Let's have a closer look at some of them.

First of all, to use any classes that can work with sensors, you need to look at the **Windows.Devices.Sensors** namespace because all that you need can be found there. You can find all classes, and it is really easy to identify which class is related to which sensor. Looking at the classes, you can see that there is not any specific base class. But lots of sensors contain similar properties, events, and methods, such as **MinimumReportInterval**, **ReportInterval**, **ReadingChanged**,

GetDefault, and **GetCurrentReading**. The first two properties allow you to get the minimum report interval that a sensor supports and set a preferable report interval to measure the data you want. The **ReadingChanged** event fires if new data or a new batch of data is available; usually you will use this event if you want to receive data as soon as it is available. Thanks to the **GetDefault** method, you can get a reference to the current sensor of the selected type. Finally, if you need to read data just once, you can use the **GetCurrentReading** method, which will return the latest data.

For example, in the case of the barometer sensor, you can use the following code:

```
protected override void OnNavigatedTo(
    NavigationEventArgs e)
{
    barometer = Barometer.GetDefault();
    if (barometer==null)
    {
        Debug.WriteLine("Barometer is not found");
    }
    double curData = barometer.GetCurrentReading().
        StationPressureInHectopascals;
    Debug.WriteLine($"The current pressure is: {curData}");
    barometer.ReadingChanged += Barometer_ReadingChanged;
}

private void Barometer_ReadingChanged(Barometer sender,
    BarometerReadingChangedEventArgs args)
{
    Debug.WriteLine($"The new pressure is:
        {args.Reading.StationPressureInHectopascals}");
}
```

Note that **BarometerReading** and other reading data can be set to null if something happened with the sensor (especially if you have an external sensor), so it's better to check also whether that value equals null.

Talking about external sensors such as pedometer, proximity, and activity, it's better to implement some code that will check sensor availability in run time. To do so, we can use the **DeviceWatcher** class.

```
DeviceWatcher watcher;
Pedometer pedometer;

protected override void OnNavigatedTo(
    NavigationEventArgs e) {
```

```
watcher = DeviceInformation.CreateWatcher(
    Pedometer.GetDeviceSelector());
watcher.Added += Watcher_Added;
watcher.Start();
}

private async void Watcher_Added(DeviceWatcher sender,
    DeviceInformation args){
    pedometer = await Pedometer.FromIdAsync(args.Id);
}
```

Note that in most cases, you should do not have to do anything special before using a sensor, but in the case of some sensors such as pedometer and activity, you need to declare a special device capability in the manifest:

```
<Capabilities>
    <DeviceCapability Name="activity" />
</Capabilities>
```

This is not very critical data, but the user should know that you are going to collect some information.

If you decide to use sensors in your application, you need to test them. This is the most common problem that I have on my devices, because usually I have fewer sensors on a developer machine. So in most cases, you will need to buy a device with useful sensors, and you can use Remote Debugging to test your application. In the case of the light sensor, magnetometer, and accelerometer, you can try to use a Windows Phone emulator. The latest version has a special tool for emulating the accelerometer, and you can at least get data from the light sensor, magnetometer, and gyroscope:

Looking at the **Windows.ApplicationModel.Background** namespace, you can find a special trigger that allows you to execute your code if the activity sensor returns new data:

```
ActivitySensorTrigger tr = new ActivitySensorTrigger(5000);
tr.SubscribedActivities.Add(ActivityType.Biking);
tr.SubscribedActivities.Add(ActivityType.Running);
```

It can be very useful if you integrate your fitness application with Toast notifications.

Finally, if you have some custom sensors and universal drivers for them, you can use these sensors as well. To do so, you need to declare the device capability, where you need to use the interface ID of your sensor:

```
<Capabilities>
  <DeviceCapability Name="sensors.custom">
    <Device Id="any">
      <Function Type=
        "interfaceId:4025A865-638C-43AA-A688-98580961EEAE"/>
    </Device>
  </DeviceCapability>
</Capabilities>
```

And right after that, you can use the **CustomSensor** class to get a reference to the sensor and start reading data:

```
customSensor = await CustomSensor.FromIdAsync(
    customSensorDevice.Id);
if (customSensor != null)
{
    CustomSensorReading reading =
        customSensor.GetCurrentReading();
    if (reading.Properties.ContainsKey(myKey))
    {
        //doing something
    }
}
```

Chapter 24

Platform Extensions

The Universal Windows Platform allows you to build universal applications for all devices that run Windows 10. All the topics that we discussed before were around classes that work fine for desktops, laptops, tablets, phones, and so on, but what about device-specific features? For example, Raspberry Pi has a set of pins that are not available for phone and tablets; you can use desktops and laptops to print something directly from your application, but this functionality is not available for phones; lots of phones support vibration, which is very uncommon for laptops; and so on.

Windows Runtimes for Windows 8.1 and Windows Phone 8.1 have lots of differences. Before, you would normally need to create different views for desktop and phones and resolve problems in logic using preprocessor directives. Of course, this approach was not good, as you needed to duplicate lots of code and support several projects for different devices, even using Universal Application templates.

To avoid these problems and create a real universal platform, Microsoft decided to change this approach and introduced platform extensions. In fact, platform extensions are a set of contracts that are still not implemented for all platforms owing to different reasons. The existing extensions look like external libraries, but there is one important difference—you should not create a separate project or recompile your application for one more platform if you add an extension, because checking the available contracts is done in run time and you can still run the same binaries on any Windows 10 device.

Of course, if some contracts are not found, then any usage of nonexisting contracts will generate exceptions. So you can identify all places where noncommon contacts are used and process possible exceptions. This approach is not good, because you don't have any chance to tune the user interface before an exception happens, but UWP supports a set of APIs that allows you to check the availability of particular contracts in advance.

Let's look at existing extensions and get an overview of the APIs.

Before using any of the available extensions, you need to include them in your project using the Add Reference dialog and open the Extensions tab. Today you can find the three most important extensions there: mobile extension, desktop extension, and IoT extension:

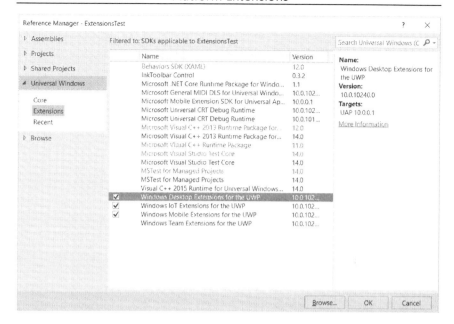

Of course, you might see more extensions soon. For example, Microsoft might publish some extensions for Xbox and HoloLens.

If you want to see all contracts that were included in the extension, you can open the manifest file for the selected extension and check all contracts there. For example, you can find the IoT extension manifest using the following folder: C:\Program Files (x86)\Windows Kits\10\Extension SDKs\WindowsIoT\10.0.10240.0. The manifest looks like this:

```xml
<?xml version="1.0" encoding="utf-8"?>
<FileList TargetPlatform="UAP"
   TargetPlatformMinVersion="10.0.0.1"
   TargetPlatformVersion="10.0.10240.0" SDKType="Platform"
   DisplayName="Windows IoT Extensions for the UWP"
   AppliesTo="WindowsAppContainer" MinVSVersion="14.0"
   ProductFamilyName="Windows.IoT"
   SupportsMultipleVersion="Error"
   TargetFramework=".NETCore, version=v4.5.3;"
   SupportPrefer32Bit="True"
   MoreInfo="http://www.microsoft.com/en-us/server-
   cloud/internet-of-things.aspx">
      <ContainedApiContracts>
         <ApiContract
         name="Windows.Devices.DevicesLowLevelContract"
         version="1.0.0.0"/>
```

```
      <ApiContract
      name="Windows.System.SystemManagementContract"
      version="1.0.0.0"/>
   </ContainedApiContracts>
</FileList>
```

So right now there are only two contracts, and you can find all classes there using Object Browser in Visual Studio by looking at **Windows.Devices.DevicesLowLevelContract** and **Windows.System.SystemManagementContract**.

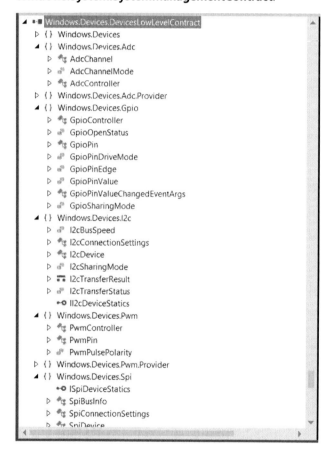

You can see that in the case of Internet of Things, we have several classes that allow us to work with GPIO, I2C, and SPI and even provide infrastructure for PWM and analog input. I think that people who don't have any experience with microcontrollers haven't even seen any of these terms before. But if you have experience with Raspberry, Arduino, or any other board, you will find lots of useful classes in this extension.

If you are interested in the IoT extension, you can open chapter 35, where we discuss all Internet of Things–related questions.

In the manifest for the mobile extension, you can find a few more contracts. For example, you can see contracts that allow you to work with virtual smart cards or phone calls.

But the separation of noncommon contracts between different extensions is conditional. For example, it's possible to have tablets that allow you to make phone calls or to use a phone like a small computer that is connected to a dock station with a monitor, printer, and so on. Finally, Microsoft can implement some noncommon contracts for all devices. So it's just logical separation, and you should not rely on it. All that you need to do is to check whether the selected contract is available on the device, and you need to check it in run time. The best way to do so is by using the **ApiInformation** class.

ApiInformation is located in the **Windows.Foundation.Metadata** namespace and contains several static methods, such as **IsApiContractPresent**, **IsEventPresent**, and **IsMethodPresent**.

So if you want to check whether GPIO is available, you can use the following code:

```
if (ApiInformation.IsApiContractPresent(
    "Windows.Devices.DevicesLowLevelContract", 1))
{
    //doing something with GPIO
}
```

Note that **IsApiContractPresent** requires two parameters. The second one is the major version (you can use the minor version as well, which is the third parameter). This parameter is needed because Microsoft can update some contracts and you can target specific version(s).

The code above doesn't mean that you need to create hundreds of **if** blocks if you include one or several contracts. It's better to create a custom trigger based on this information and implement several visual states.

This page intentionally left blank

Chapter 25

How to Publish Web Applications to the Store

In this chapter we will discuss how to make your websites/applications available to Store users. Of course, Visual Studio 2015 supports JavaScript/HTML 5 projects, and Microsoft guys, including me, like to show how to copy and paste existing HTML/JavaScript and recompile it as a Windows 10 application. But in fact, it's not so easy, and you can find some problems with this approach:

Not all web applications are built on pure JavaScript/HTML. For example, I like ASP.NET, and there is no way to copy/paste an ASP.NET application to a Windows 10 project in Visual Studio. Lots of other developers like PHP, JSP, and even Node.js.

Even if I port my web application to Windows 10, I will have two separate projects: the web application and the Windows 10 application. If I continue to invest many resources to grow my web application, I will need to invest the same amount of resources into the Windows 10 application. If I don't have enough time and money, my Windows 10 application will probably die soon.

Taking into account the problems above, let's discuss some ways to publish an existing web application to the Store without porting it at all. I am going to start our overview with the simple **WebView** user control and then finish the chapter with project Westminster.

WebView

Starting with Windows 8, Microsoft introduced the **WebView** user control for developers, which allows you to navigate to external web content using a URI. At that time this control didn't even work as a standard XAML control, and developers needed to do a rain dance for it to run properly. But starting with Windows 8.1, the **WebView** control was updated, and now it's inherited from **FrameworkElement** and supports lots of XAML features, such as opacity and transformation.

Of course, in Windows 8.1, the **WebView** user control was based on Internet Explorer, and it supports almost all features of IE, excluding plug-ins. But since Windows 10, Microsoft has rewritten the **WebView** control, and now it is based on the new browser from Microsoft—**Microsoft Edge**. This is good news because Microsoft Edge supports lots of new HTML 5 features and has better performance of JavaScript for modern web applications. Additionally, Microsoft has promised to update Microsoft Edge more frequently than Internet Explorer, and these updates will be available for the **WebView** control at the same time. Let's see how to use **WebView** in your applications.

You can add a WebView user control to a page as you would any other XAML control. For example, this code adds WebView and navigates to dev.windows.com:

```
<Grid>
    <WebView Source="http://dev.windows.com"></WebView>
</Grid>
```

After running this page, you can see a fully functional web application:

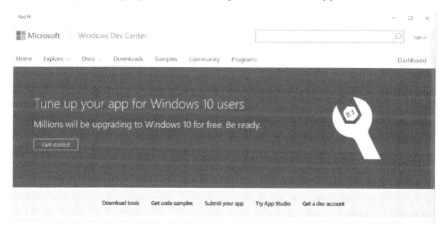

So in the worst case, you can publish an application to the Store that will navigate to your web application. But in this case, the application will not have any Windows 10 features. So in the case of **WebView**, it's better to inject some online content to a real Store application.

If you want to navigate **WebView** from C# code, you can use the **Navigate** method.

```
webView.Navigate(new Uri("http://www.microsoft.com"));
```

Note that starting with Windows 8.1, the **WebView** control can navigate to external as well as in-package content. To do navigation you need to use special prefixes for **Uri**, and this prefix will be added automatically to all relative URIs inside your document.

```
<WebView Source="ms-appx-web:///html/index.html"
    Name="webView"></WebView>
```

This code navigates the **WebView** user control to page index.html in the local package. Just create an html subfolder in your project using Visual Studio and place index.html there with any content inside.

I don't remember any cases in my practice when I needed to navigate **WebView** to any local page in the package, but I have used the **ms-appdata:///local** prefix several times.

```
<WebView Source="ms-appdata:///local/html/index.html"
    Name="webView"></WebView>
```

This code navigates **WebView** to the same page in the html folder, but the page and the folder are located inside the local storage of the application. So you can easily use this approach for offline scenarios. For example, I know a partner that publishes magazines in HTML format and distributes them as zip archives. The archive contains all scripts, images, and HTML files, and all that you need to do is to present it using **WebView**. So I have developed an application that allows a user to download all issues that the user likes. Once issues are downloaded, the user can read them in offline mode. For content in local storage, you can use the same rules: the prefix will be applied to all the relative content. So you do not have to do anything special but just unpack the archive to local storage and navigate **WebView** to the main page of the issue.

Besides the Navigate method, WebView contains three more important methods that can help you to present HTML content:

- **NavigateToString:** Allows you to use the content of a string variable as HTML content. This method is very popular for news applications when external content from RSS is received in HTML format.

- **NavigateWithHttpRequestMessage:** This method allows you to send a POST request to a server. This method is important when the server asks you to send authentication data.

- **NavigateToLocalStreamUri:** This method allows you to use your own URI resolver for local content.

Let's talk about **NavigateToLocalStreamUri** in more detail. Earlier I told about an example with a magazine where the publisher sent a zip archive with new issues to users. Of course, you can unpack issues to a local folder, but in some cases you will not want to do this. For example, the publisher may ask you to store encrypted content only, to preventing copying and pasting the content from the local disk. In this case you can leave the content in the archive and implement a special URI resolver. Once you pass a Uri to **NavigateToLocalStreamUri**, it will pass the URI to your resolver and will be waiting for the back stream with content to present. If you have any links to dependent content inside the web page, the same rules will be applied. For our partner we implemented a resolver based on the following template:

```
public sealed class StreamUriWinRTResolver :
    IUriToStreamResolver
{
    private string magazineID;

    public StreamUriWinRTResolver(string magazineID)
    {
        this.magazineID = magazineID;
    }

    public IAsyncOperation<IInputStream>
        UriToStreamAsync(Uri uri)
    {
        lock (this)
        {
            if (uri == null)
            {
                throw new Exception();
            }
            string path = uri.AbsolutePath;

            return GetContent(path).AsAsyncOperation();
        }
    }

    private async Task<IInputStream> GetContent(
        string path)
    {
        //get content from archive
    }
}
```

You can see that the resolver implements the **IUriToStreamResolver** interface. There is the **UriToStreamAsync** method, which takes a Uri as a parameter and returns a stream with the content. To use this resolver, you need to implement the following code:

```
Uri url = webView.BuildLocalStreamUri(id, "index.html");
StreamUriWinRTResolver myResolver =
    new StreamUriWinRTResolver(id);
webView.NavigateToLocalStreamUri(url, myResolver);
```

In the first line of this code, we used **BuildLocalStreamUri**, which helps to create a Uri in the right format, pointing to local content. Right after that we create the resolver and pass the Uri and the resolver to the **NavigateToLocalStreamUri** method.

In addition to the navigate methods, **WebView** has some methods and properties that can help you to implement a better interface for navigation between pages. For example, you can use the **CanGoForward** and **CanGoBack** properties to understand whether there is a way to enable buttons in the interface of your application to navigate back and forward. To perform actual navigation, you can use methods such as **GoBack**, **GoForward**, **Refresh**, and **Stop**.

The **WebView** user control contains some useful events as well.

I know some websites where developers like to open a new window when the user clicks any link inside. For example, if you develop a search system, it's better to open a new window/tab when a user clicks a link from a result set, because the user might want to open several links. But **WebView** doesn't support several tabs. Once the user clicks a link that requires a new window, **WebView** redirects this link to Microsoft Edge and opens it there. It's not good to lose contact with the application and navigate the user to another one. So in Windows 8.1 I liked to parse all HTML content to remove all **target** attributes that lead to opening new windows. But in Windows 10, **WebView** has a good event called **NewWindowRequested**. If you want to avoid opening the content in a new window, you can implement an event handler like this:

```
private void webView_NewWindowRequested(WebView sender,
    WebViewNewWindowRequestedEventArgs args)
{
    webView.Navigate(args.Uri);
    args.Handled = true;
}
```

In this example I simply navigate **WebView** to new content instead of opening a new window in an external application. Of course, in real life you need to implement a more complex algorithm, but the idea will be the same.

Three more events are **NavigationStarting**, **NavigationFailed**, and **NavigationCompleted**. Thanks to these events, you can do anything with navigation in your application.

Starting with Windows 10, **WebView** supports a special constructor that allows you to run **WebView** in a non-UI thread. Right now you can make it by creating **WebView** dynamically in your code.

```
WebView wv =
    new WebView(WebViewExecutionMode.SeparateThread);
grid.Children.Add(wv);
wv.Navigate(new Uri("http://www.microsoft.com"));
```

OK. Now we know how to present web content using the **WebView** control. Let's see which features **WebView** has for integration of external web content and XAML applications.

First of all, external web content may define a special interface for your XAML application. It can be any set of JavaScript methods, which you can invoke from C# code using the **InvokeScriptAsync** method. Let's test this approach and create an empty web application in Visual Studio and add a simple page:

```
<!DOCTYPE html>
<html>
<head>
    <title></title>
        <meta charset="utf-8" />
    <script>
        function f()
        {
            document.body.innerText =
                "Hello from Windows Runtime";
        }
    </script>
</head>
<body></body>
</html>
```

This page contains one function only, which is not called by default. Just run this application locally and copy the web URL from browser. Use this URL to create the following **WebView**:

```
<WebView Name="wv"
    NavigationCompleted="Wv_NavigationCompleted"
    Source="http://localhost:10289/"></WebView>
```

Once WebView downloads the content, it will fire the NavigationCompleted method, where we call our JavaScript:

```
private async void Wv_NavigationCompleted(WebView sender,
```

```
    WebViewNavigationCompletedEventArgs args)
{

    await wv.InvokeScriptAsync("f", null);
}
```

If you don't have any special JavaScript API, you can inject some JavaScript code using the **eval** JavaScript function and **InvokeScriptAsync**. It allows you to extend the functionality of a web page using dynamically generated scripts directly from C# code.

You can invoke C# code from JavaScript as well. Using the Universal Windows Platform, you have two ways to implement it.

First of all, you can use **window.external.notify** to send notifications to **WebView**, and using a **ScriptNotify** event handler, you can process a passing string and decide what you are going to do with it in C#. Let's modify the page in our web application in the following way:

```
<!DOCTYPE html>
<html>
<head>
    <title></title>
        <meta charset="utf-8" />
    <script>
        function f()
        {
            window.external.notify(
                "Hello from JavaScript");
        }
    </script>
</head>
<body onload="javascript:f()">
    Web page content
</body>
</html>
```

This code sends a notification to the external application (to **WebView**) once the body is loaded. To test whether **WebView** receives the message, I propose implementing the following XAML code:

```
<Grid Background=
    "{ThemeResource ApplicationPageBackgroundThemeBrush}">
    <Grid.RowDefinitions>
        <RowDefinition Height="Auto"></RowDefinition>
        <RowDefinition></RowDefinition>
    </Grid.RowDefinitions>
```

```
<TextBlock Text="" Name="myText" Margin="10">
</TextBlock>
<WebView x:Name="webView" Grid.Row="1"
    ScriptNotify="webView_ScriptNotify">
</WebView>
</Grid>
```

I am going to use **TextBlock** to show the received message, and I have assigned a **ScriptNotify** event handler to handle the event. The implemented code is very simple:

```
protected override void OnNavigatedTo(
    NavigationEventArgs e)
{
    webView.Navigate(new
        Uri("http://localhost:1877/index.html"));
    base.OnNavigatedTo(e);
}

private void webView_ScriptNotify(object sender,
    NotifyEventArgs e)
{
    myText.Text = e.Value;
}
```

But if you run this code, the text block will not display anything. The problem is in the default security settings—external web pages cannot send any notifications to **WebView** or use any Windows Runtime objects. So you need to add all trusted pages to the manifest file of the application. You can do this with the help of the Visual Studio 2015 manifest designer—just open the Content URIs tab and add the URI of the web page.

You need to use an **include** rule for the page to list, and it's sufficient to have the **Allow for web only** setting. If you want to edit the manifest using an XML editor, you need to add the following lines of code to the **Application** element:

```
<uap:ApplicationContentUriRules>
  <uap:Rule Match="http://localhost:1877/index.html"
      Type="include"
      WindowsRuntimeAccess="allowForWebOnly" />
</uap:ApplicationContentUriRules>
```

If you run the Windows application once again, the text block should display the message.

Note that you should not use any security settings for JavaScript from the application package or from local or temporary storage.

Starting with Windows 10, **WebView** supports passing Windows Runtime objects to JavaScript code. So you can prepare a special object with lots of utility methods inside. JavaScript will able to activate some Windows 10 features using these methods. To activate this feature, you need to create a separate Windows Runtime object. If you create a class inside your application directly, you will not be able to use it. So use Visual Studio 2015 to implement a Windows Runtime component and add a reference to it from the application. My object is very simple, but it's enough to make a demo:

```
[AllowForWeb()]
public sealed class W10Util
{
    public string getData()
    {
        return "Hello from W10";
    }
}
```

To use an object of the class, you need to apply the **AllowForWeb** attribute to the class as shown above. The class is ready, so let's implement the following code in our application:

```
W10Util w10obj=new W10Util();
protected override void OnNavigatedTo(
    NavigationEventArgs e)
{
    webView.AddWebAllowedObject("w10obj", w10obj);
    webView.Navigate(
        new Uri("http://localhost:1877/index.html"));
    base.OnNavigatedTo(e);
}
```

In the code above, we created an object of the W10Util class and passed the object to WebView using AddWebAllowedObject. This method uses two parameters: name, which you can use in JavaScript, and a reference to the object.

Finally, in JavaScript we can use the passed object as any other object:

```
function f()
{
    if (window.w10obj!==undefined)
        document.body.innerText=w10obj.getData();
    else
        document.body.innerText="Object is not found";
}
```

Therefore, you can use **WebView** not just for displaying web content but for communicating between C# and JavaScript as well. Of course, this approach works fine for those scenarios when you develop your application in C# and want to inject some web content. But starting with Windows 10, you can grant the web application full access to Windows Runtime. This is possible thanks to project Westminster. Let's see how to use this approach.

Project Westminster

WebView allows you to use Windows Runtime components inside external web pages, but it requires you to create some wrappers, and, frankly speaking, **WebView** is not a necessary layer if you want to make your web application available in the Store and don't want to affect the existing publishing workflow. That's why during the Build 2015 conference, Microsoft introduced several bridges that allow you to bring native applications from other platforms to the Windows 10 Store. One of these bridges is project Westminster. Thanks to this, you can publish existing web applications to the Store without any redevelopment at all. Of course, it was possible before. For example, you can place a simple **WebView** in your application and just navigate it to the main page of your site. However, applications like this lack Windows features owing to limited access to Windows Runtime. But project Westminster allows you to get full access to Windows Runtime without any wrappers and any proxy controls such as **WebView**. So you can continue to work with your website on the server side and implement all the needed code there. At the same time the user will have access to the latest version of your web application all the time.

Unfortunately, right now project Westminster works for JavaScript Windows applications only. But in some cases you can edit the manifest only.

Let's create a new JavaScript Windows application. Once the application is created, you need to make some changes in the manifest file.

First of all, you need to point the start page to the main page of your web application:

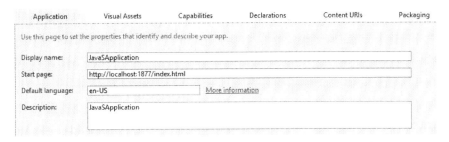

Right now the application will start using the remote page on the site. But it's not enough, and we need to resolve the same security issues as for **WebView**. So open the Content URIs tab and add the URL of the web page:

In this case, I selected the **All** setting for WinRT access to be able to work with Windows Runtime components directly without wrappers. In the case of **Allow for web only**, you can work with injected objects only.

Once we have added all pages (we can use * for the selected domain as well) to the manifest file, we can publish the application (don't forget to apply icons). All Windows 10–related features will be implemented on the server side in JavaScript. For example, the following web page will generate a Toast notification if it's running as a part of a Windows 10 application. If it's running from the browser, it will have different behavior:

```
<!DOCTYPE html>
<html>
<head>
    <title></title>
        <meta charset="utf-8" />
    <script>
        function f()
```

```
          {
        if (typeof Windows !== 'undefined' &&
            typeof Windows.UI !== 'undefined' &&
            typeof Windows.UI.Notifications !==
                'undefined') {
            var notifications=Windows.UI.Notifications;
            toast = notifications.
                ToastTemplateType.toastText01;
            toastContent = notifications.
                ToastNotificationManager.
                getTemplateContent(toast);
            toastText = toastContent.
                getElementsByTagName('text');
            toastText[0].appendChild(
                toastContent.createTextNode(
                    'Message from JavaScript'));

            var toastNotification =
                new notifications.
                ToastNotification(toastContent);

            notifications.ToastNotificationManager.
                createToastNotifier().
                show(toastNotification);
        }
        else {
            document.body.innerText =
                "I am running in a browser";
        }
    }
    </script>
</head>
<body onload="javascript:f()">
    Web page content
</body>
</html>
```

Once you start developing the web application, you will need to debug the JavaScript code to make sure that everything works fine. But if you want to debug Windows 10–related code, you will not be able to run the web application in debug mode directly, because the web application should be started from Windows 10 client. But Visual Studio 2015 can help you. Just open/create a solution that contains the Windows 10 project and the web application project and set up all needed breakpoints inside JavaScript. Using Project properties, you need to open the Web tab and select: **Don't open a page. Wait for a request from an external application**. This option allows you to initiate the debugger once the page is loaded inside the Windows 10 application:

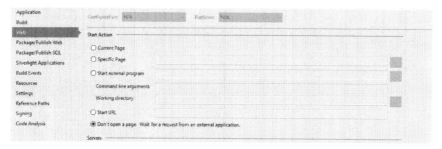

In the next step, make the Windows 10 application a **Startup project** and start debugging. Visual Studio will navigate you to the web application once the breakpoint is reached.

Of course, if you decide to have some local JavaScript pages in your Windows 10 application, you can definitely create them. So project Westminster allows you to publish not pure hosted applications but hybrid applications as well.

In summary, you can see that Windows 10 creates lots of opportunities for web developers. You can easily integrate any web application with Windows 10 applications and even publish it as a hosted application without any coding on the client side. All the obstacles are gone.

Chapter 26

How to Make Money in the Store

In chapter 12 we discussed how to publish your first application to the Store. But once you know how to develop Windows 10 applications, you will start thinking about how to make money with your applications in the Store. Because the Store provides lots of different opportunities, I decided to divide all applications into two separate groups: paid applications and free applications. Looking at each group, you will find the best methods for monetizing your applications.

Paid Applications

The simplest way to try to earn money from the Store is to publish several paid applications. But this way is not effective, and in some cases you can publish a hundred paid applications to the Store and get nothing. It's because people don't like to buy a black box, and if you didn't sell the previous version of your application and don't have a huge customer base, nobody will buy your application. That's why you need to think about additional activities from your side to engage as many people as possible. I am not going to discuss advertising campaigns or how to work with companies that can generate traffic. It's very hard to recommend something, and we will discuss the Store opportunities only from technical perspective.

Twins

I know that lots of people at Microsoft don't like this approach, but in some cases it works fine. The idea is simple: you can publish paid and free versions of your application as separate entities. Just type the keyword "Lite" in the Store, and you will find lots of applications that are published using this model. Usually, developers publish a free version with limited functionality; this version shows the main features and promotes the paid one. Of course, you can combine several approaches. For example, you can publish a full-featured free version but with advertising or in-app purchases.

The main reason why developers publish two separate applications is their belief that people do not like to install paid applications even with a trial mode. Additionally, some people think that users will browse the free category only and simply will not find your application. It's not completely true, and the Store contains more than a hundred thousand applications now. So usually people will use search, and your application will be included even if it's paid. At this stage it's important to use this opportunity and show the best icons and graphics and a clear description and provide trial support. But if you decide to publish two separate versions, you can do so, and there is nothing to discuss from technical prospective. All that you need to do is implement code that will promote the paid version of your application. To do so, you can show different types of messages, flyouts, and so on. But in the end you need to provide a way for the user to navigate to the paid version and purchase it. To do so, you can use the **Launcher** class:

```
Launcher.LaunchUriAsync(
    new Uri("ms-windows-store://pdp/?ProductId=<your id>"));
```

Trial Mode

This is probably the best way to encourage people to install your paid application. Visiting the dashboard, you will find that you can select two types of trials: trial never expires and *n*-day trial.

Free trial

No free trial
Trial never expires
1 day
7 days
15 days
30 days

In the first case, the user can use your application in trial mode as much as he or she wants. Usually, you will use this mode to limit the number of features in your application, but once a user buys the application, you need to handle this event and provide full functionality. In the case of business applications, you can disable some menu items, and in the case of games, you can provide access to some levels only.

In the case of time-based trials, developers usually provide full functionality, but the application will work only a limited number of days.

Note that in the case of a time-based trial, it's easy to enable it. In general, you can do nothing and just select the number of days. Windows will watch your application, and once the trial is expired, the user will not be able to start the application. Instead Windows will provide a message to encourage people to purchase your application. In the case of a feature-based trial, you will need to implement all code that checks the current licensing model, so you need to decide in advance what model to select.

Once you select the model, you can start implementing code that will enable some features and disable advertising messages if the user buys the application. To do so, you can use the **LicenseInformation** class, which contains information about whether the application is in trial and whether the trial mode is still active. The **LicenseInformation** class doesn't contain any public constructors, but you can get an object of the class using the **CurrentApp** class from the **Windows.Applicationmodel.Store** namespace:

```
var license = CurrentApp.LicenseInformation;
```

Using the received reference, you can check whether the application is in trial mode, whether the trial mode is still active (for a time-based period), and what the expiration date is. So in general, if you want to disable some features or show some advertising screens, you can use the following code:

```
if (license.IsTrial)
{
   //disable some features or ask a user to buy the
   //application
}
```

The code looks trivial, but there is a problem: the **CurrentApp** class will not work properly if your application is not in the Store. So you cannot test the application properly. To fix the problem, you can use a special class, **CurrentAppSimulator**, that allows you to provide the same information as the **CurrentApp** class, but you can provide settings for the class yourself. While your application is in development, you can use **CurrentAppSimulator**, but once you want to publish the application to the Store, you need to remove the word "Simulator."

Of course, the class itself doesn't make any sense without the ability to provide your own settings. You can do this by creating a WindowsStoreProxy.xml file and placing all settings there. Thanks to Microsoft, you do not have to create this file from scratch. Once you use CurrentAppSimulator, the file will be created automatically. Usually you can find it in the following folder:

```
C:\Users\<username>\AppData\Local\Packages\<appid>\LocalSta
te\Microsoft\Windows Store\ApiData
```

If you open this file, you can find similar XML:

```
<?xml version="1.0" encoding="utf-16" ?>
<CurrentApp>
```

```xml
<ListingInformation>
    <App>
        <AppId>00000000-0000-0000-0000-000000000000
        </AppId>
        <LinkUri>
            http://apps.microsoft.com/webpdp/app/
            00000000-0000-0000-0000-000000000000
        </LinkUri>
        <CurrentMarket>en-US</CurrentMarket>
        <AgeRating>3</AgeRating>
        <MarketData xml:lang="en-us">
            <Name>AppName</Name>
            <Description>AppDescription</Description>
            <Price>1.00</Price>
            <CurrencySymbol>$</CurrencySymbol>
            <CurrencyCode>USD</CurrencyCode>
        </MarketData>
    </App>
    <Product ProductId="1" LicenseDuration="0"
        ProductType="Durable">
        <MarketData xml:lang="en-us">
            <Name>Product1Name</Name>
            <Price>1.00</Price>
            <CurrencySymbol>$</CurrencySymbol>
            <CurrencyCode>USD</CurrencyCode>
        </MarketData>
    </Product>
    <Product ProductId="2" LicenseDuration="0"
        ProductType="Consumable">
        <MarketData xml:lang="en-us">
            <Name>Product2Name</Name>
            <Price>1.00</Price>
            <CurrencySymbol>$</CurrencySymbol>
            <CurrencyCode>USD</CurrencyCode>
        </MarketData>
    </Product>
</ListingInformation>
<LicenseInformation>
    <App>
        <IsActive>true</IsActive>
        <IsTrial>true</IsTrial>
    </App>
    <Product ProductId="1">
        <IsActive>true</IsActive>
    </Product>
```

```
  </LicenseInformation>
  <ConsumableInformation>
      <Product ProductId="2" TransactionId=
        "00000000-0000-0000-0000-000000000000"
        Status="Active" />
  </ConsumableInformation>
</CurrentApp>
```

You can see that all the needed information is contained in the **LicenseInformation** element, and you can start your experiments there. The other parts are useful if you want to implement in-app purchase in your application.

In some cases, developers want to know whether the licensing status has changed. Sometimes you may need to change some configuration settings or even may want to enable all needed features on the fly. To do so, you can handle the **LicenseChanged** event, and once the handler is fired, you need to update licensing information and implement your own logic. Frankly speaking, I don't see lots of applications that implement this event handler.

Finally, if the user decides to buy your application, you can use the **CurrentApp** class instead of a Launcher. Just call **RequestAppPurchaseAsync**, and Windows will do everything else for you.

Sale!

Since Windows 10, the Store has supported several important features that allow you to promote your applications using the Store. One of these features is sales. With sales you can change the application price for a limited period of time. For example, you can have a special promo for holidays or launch a special promo campaign.

To create a new sale, you simply need to create a new submission for your application, but you do not have to upload the same package or do anything else—just visit the Pricing and availability tab and create a new sale:

You can see that you can select the start and end date and a price and even select different prices for different markets.

Of course, there is nothing to do from a developer's perspective, but it's a very important feature, and I simply could not skip it.

Promo Codes

Starting with Windows 10, Microsoft added an ability to request promo codes for your applications. It's very useful if you want to distribute a link to your application to mass media, provide access to your application as a prize, and so on. To order promo codes for your application, you simply need to open the Monetization tab on the dashboard and select the Promotional codes tab:

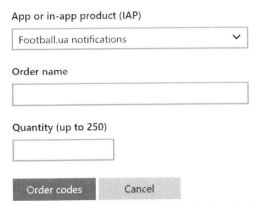

Free Applications

Of course, you can use free applications as a way to promote your paid applications, as we discussed earlier. But there are opportunities to make money even with free applications. The main ways are in-app advertising and in-app purchases. Let's look at these opportunities.

Advertising

Lots of free applications contain advertising. In this case, users can download your application for free, but you can make money thanks to ads.

But before doing anything with ads in your application, you need to select a provider that supports Universal Windows Applications, provides ads, and allows you to earn revenue. Traditionally you can use Microsoft Ads, but there are lots of different providers on the market. Since Windows 8.x and Windows Phone were introduced, you can find SDKs for AdDuplex, Smaato, and so on. Not all these companies have updated their SDK to Windows 10, but I have found at least AdDuplex has done so. In any case, once you have access to the SDK, you can start injecting ad controls into your application. But there is one problem: different providers support a different set of markets, and additionally, it's very hard to predict whose ads will work better. That's why Microsoft recommends using an ad mediator, which allows you to select all supported ad networks and configure the usage of each network using the dashboard.

To start working with the ad mediator, you need to install a special extension for Visual Studio. You can find it here: https://visualstudiogallery.msdn. microsoft.com/401703a0-263e-4949-8f0f-73830 5d6ef4b. Once the extension is installed, you can find a new control in the toolbox called **AdMediatorControl**. It's better to drag and drop this control to your form to allow Visual Studio to fill in all needed properties and add references to libraries.

If you do everything right, Visual Studio will add a line similar to this one:

```
<Universal:AdMediatorControl x:Name="AdMediator_3699BC"
    Height="250"
    Id="AdMediator-Id-61C6D7FC-A97C-421B-9FAE-9388E7A75DD8"
    Width="300"/>
```

It's time to set up the mediator and create a configuration file for it. You can do so with the **Connected Service** window. Just invoke the context menu in Solution Explorer and use the **Add** menu item to select **Connected Service**. Visual Studio will run the wizard. Select Ad Mediator:

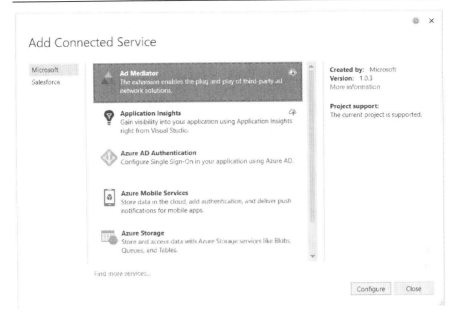

In the next step, select all ad providers that you want and click Add:

Once you click Add, Visual Studio will create a configuration file.

Looking at the image above, you can see that there is Microsoft Advertising only. Yes, when I was writing the book, Ad Mediator supported Microsoft Ads for UWP only, but I hope that we will see some changes soon. For example, an AdDuplex control exists for UWP, but you cannot find it in the extension. Developers probably need some time to update the extension.

Looking at the control, you can find some events that allow you to handle any errors related to the control. Additionally, you can set up the width and height of the control based on the selected banner type. But in general, you can try to deploy the application to the Store. Microsoft has implemented integration between Ad Mediator and the Store. So once you upload the package, you will be able to find all settings.

Note that to modify the advertising rate for selected providers and markets, you do not have to create a new submission—just open the dashboard and use the Monetize tab to edit all parameters.

In-App Purchases

The last thing that we will discuss here is in-app purchase. Using this feature, you can sell additional instruments or digital items directly from your application. You can find lots of games that sell new levels, internal money to buy upgrades, and many other things. That's why if we are talking about in-app purchases, we need to divide them into two separate groups: standard in-app purchases and consumable ones. In the case of standard, you can buy permanent things such as new levels or access to additional features, but in the case of consumable in-app purchases, you can buy gold, coins, and other things that you can spend in the application and buy again and again.

Windows 10 supports both in-app purchases, and there are two steps that you need to take.

In the first step, you need to create all products that you are going to sell through the in-app engine. To do so, you can visit the IAPs tab and create a new product:

Once you create the product, you need to fill in all parameters. The most important is the Properties tab, which contains basic information about in-app purchase type, content type, and keyword:

As we discussed earlier, you need to select between consumable and durable in-app purchases. The Store supports temporary durable products as well.

Once you create all products in the Store, you can start to implement your code around in-app purchase functionality.

To implement functionality around durable products, you can use the same **LicenseInformation** class, but in this case, you need to use the **ProductLicenses** collection:

```
var license = CurrentApp.LicenseInformation;
if (!license.ProductLicenses["coins10"].IsActive)
{
    try
    {
        await CurrentApp.RequestProductPurchaseAsync(
        "coins10", false);
    }
    catch (Exception)
    {

    }
}
else
{

}
```

Of course, to test your application, you can use **CurrentAppSimulator** as before. Inside **ListingInformation** in **WindowsStoreProxy.xml**, you can define a list of products using the **Product** element:

```
<Product ProductId="2" LicenseDuration="0"
ProductType="Consumable">
    <MarketData xml:lang="en-us">
        <Name>Product2Name</Name>
        <Price>1.00</Price>
        <CurrencySymbol>$</CurrencySymbol>
        <CurrencyCode>USD</CurrencyCode>
    </MarketData>
</Product>
```

To emulate products that the user has already bought, you can use the **LicenseInformation** element and the **Product** element inside:

```
<Product ProductId="1">
    <IsActive>true</IsActive>
</Product>
```

In the case of consumable items, you can use the same code, but the user will not be able to buy this item again until your application notifies the Store about fulfillment:

```
var result = await CurrentApp.
  ReportConsumableFulfillmentAsync(
    "coins10", transactionId);
```

You can get the transaction ID using the result of a RequestProductPurchaseAsync method call.

To emulate transactions and consumable items, **WindowsStoreProxy.xml** supports one more element—**ConsumableInformation:**

```
<ConsumableInformation>
    <Product ProductId="2"
      TransactionId="00000000-0000-0000-0000-000000000000"
      Status="Active" />
</ConsumableInformation>
```

Part III

Advanced Features

This page intentionally left blank

Chapter 27

Windows Notification Service

In chapter 11 we discussed local notifications like Toast and Tile notifications. There are lots of scenarios where local notifications work fine, but in some cases we need something more. For example, if you want to notify users about the status of a soccer game, it's not possible to use local notifications, because your application cannot look into the future to download all results locally once the user launches it. Of course, if your application is in the foreground, it's possible to check your services from time to time, looking for updates, but if the user closes your application, you can do nothing. That's why Windows allows you to get external notifications and provides the infrastructure for that.

Of course, when talking about external notifications for a device, we need to assume that the device is connected to the Internet. At the same time, messages should be delivered in a secure manner, using the same format and without using too much bandwidth (this is especially important for mobile devices). That's why you cannot implement a service that will deliver messages to a particular device. Instead you need to use a special service that is a part of Windows infrastructure—Windows Notification Service (WNS).

In fact, WNS looks like a gateway that supports communications between your service and application instances.

If you want to implement functionality that uses WNS, it's better to start with a Windows 10 application itself. In the first step, an instance of a particular application should initiate the registration process (1, 2). It's not a complex process; your application just needs to send WNS a message that it wants to get messages. You can implement this using a couple lines of code:

```
PushNotificationChannel channel = null;

try
{
    channel = await PushNotificationChannelManager.
        CreatePushNotificationChannelForApplicationAsync();
}

catch (Exception ex)
{
    // Could not create a channel.
}
```

You can see that we used the **PushNotificationChannelManager** class, which allows you to register the instance and returns a special object, namely the push-notification channel. This is a special Uri that contains all needed information about how to send a notification to the application. So because the object (URI) is returned to the application itself, the application can decide how to share the URI.

Therefore, in the next step, you need to provide the URI to the external service (3). Usually, it will be your own service that needs to send a notification to all active clients. You can implement anything there because the service should not use any special technology. You can use any database to store URIs and any related information, and when you need to send a message, you can select just those URIs that satisfy your requirements. In some cases, you need to send a message to a particular device only, but in others you will need to send the message to all subscribers. But in any case, if you want to send the message to all subscribers in your database, you need to do so one by one. Of course, this can affect server traffic, and in the case of many subscribers, you should be able to manage the number of servers and maintain a message queue. But all these problems can be resolved thanks to Microsoft Azure, which we are going to discuss in the next chapter.

When your service wants to send a message, it will use the URI that is provided by the application instance. Of course, this URI should be used to send the message using WNS but not to the application directly (4). Your service will connect to WNS and provide the URI and the message, and WNS will finish the process (5).

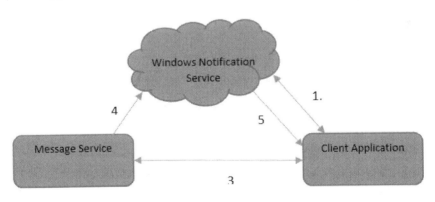

The most complex task in the process is sending a message from the service to WNS. To guarantee that URIs will not be intercepted, WNS requires additional authentication from the service. The authentication is based on OAuth 2.0 and requires a special application ID and a secret key. Therefore, to implement the service, you need to start with the authentication process. But before that, you need to find where to get the ID and the key.

You can get the ID and the key during the publication process only. So to test notifications, you need to request a name for the application in the Store and associate the application itself with the Store. WNS will not provide the proper URI to the application until you perform the association.

Once you finish the association, you can open the Services→Push notifications tab in the dashboard:

Push notifications

Windows Push Notification Services (WNS) and Microsoft Azure Mobile Services

The Windows Push Notification Services (WNS) enables you to send toast, tile, badge, and raw updates from your own cloud service. Learn more

If you have an existing WNS solution or need to update your current client secret, visit the Live Services site

You can also use Microsoft Azure Mobile Services to send push notifications, authenticate and manage app users, and store app data in the cloud. Sign in to your Microsoft Azure account or sign up now to add services to up to ten apps for free.

Click the Live Services site to navigate to the page where you can find the ID and the key:

Football.ua notifications

The next step is a little bit complicated. Once you have the ID and the key, you need to use **https://login.live.com/accesstoken.srf** to pass the authentication process using OAuth 2.0 protocol. Of course, the code depends on the technology that you select, but it's not very hard to find an example.

Using OAuth 2.0, you will get an authentication token. Once you have the token, the authentication process is finished, and you can send the message. To do so, you can use the URI that initially was provided to the client and generate a POST message using the authentication token to form a header in the right format:

```
Authorization: Bearer
EgAaAQMAAAAEgAAACoAAPzCGedIbQb9vRfPF2Lxy3K//QZB79mLTgK
X-WNS-RequestForStatus: true
X-WNS-Type: wns/toast
Content-Type: text/xml
Host: db3.notify.windows.com
Content-Length: 196
```

For the content, you can use an XML document with the same format as for local notifications.

Frankly speaking, I don't think that it's wise to implement your own server that uses WNS to send notifications, because Microsoft Azure can do it for you and it will not be as expensive as your local services, traffic, and so on. That's why in this chapter we have discussed just the idea. You can find a detailed description of how to implement enterprise-ready notification systems in the next chapter.

This page intentionally left blank

Chapter 28

Sending Notifications Using Azure

Microsoft Azure provides lots of different services, and most of them you can use to make your applications more powerful. Because this book is not about Azure, we cannot cover all features of the Azure SDK and all available services, but I think that we can discuss at least one service and extend the previous chapter about Windows Notification Service.

To get more information about Azure, you can visit http://azure.microsoft.com to find an overview of all services and also create a trial account. Note that to use the material from this chapter, you will need to create a trial account as well.

"Native Development" Scenario

I started to learn Microsoft Azure beginning with the first announcement at the Build conference in 2008, but I had my first real experience with it only in 2010. At that time, Microsoft started to push a stable version of the platform to clients, and we got several requests from our partners for technical support. During that time, I worked with the biggest Ukrainian media holding and helped to deploy several applications for Windows Phone 7, one of them related to Microsoft Push Notification Service (MPNS, the Windows Notification Service for UWP).

The client owned the biggest soccer portal in Ukraine, and their technical staff wanted to implement a service that could notify all subscribers (primary WP and iOS) of the portal about changes during live soccer games worldwide. Of course, it was not hard to implement a simple Windows Phone application that provided the latest news and received Toast notifications. But we expected several complex problems from the server side. The biggest problems were about the hardware resources and Internet capacity. The portal had hundreds of thousands of visitors during any game, and it was hard to find more servers as well as to guarantee an acceptable quality of the Internet channel for sending messages from the MPNS server to all subscribers at the same time. That is why we decided to move the server side of the service to Azure.

In 2010 Microsoft had already introduced Cloud services (Web and Worker roles), Storage services (Tables, Blobs, and Queue), and SQL Azure. We used all of them. Let's look the schema below, where I show the solution in more detail.

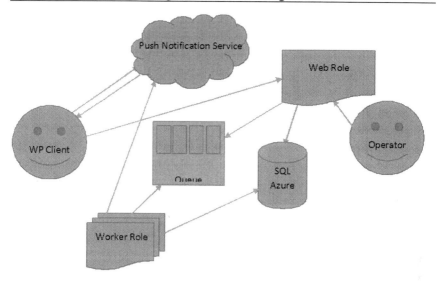

First, we implemented a Web service (Web role) that was able to store data from Windows Phone devices about notification channel URIs. The unique URI is generated by MPNS for the specific device, and it can be used to send notifications to this device. So if you have a hundred devices, you should have a hundred URIs to send the message to each of them. To store information about URIs and users, we used SQL Azure.

In the second step, we created a Web service (it was a Web role but we could use the existing Web role from the previous step) that allowed the application to receive messages from an operator (a human on the client side or something else). The messages contained information about the game status that had to be sent to subscribers. Of course, we could not use this Web service to deliver these messages to our subscribers, because it could take significant amount of time (up to several hours, in the case of a big number of subscribers) and we needed to send a response to the operator as soon as possible. That is why the Web service stored new messages to Queue in Azure Storage. This structure was adopted to simultaneously access messages inside, and it works very well if you use several instances of Worker role for processing the messages.

At the last step, we created a Worker role that was used for sending the messages to the subscribers. We were able to monitor the queue and increase or decrease the number of instances of Worker role based on the number of games, the number of subscribers, and the number of messages in Queue.

The proposed solution is stable and flexible, but there are some disadvantages. At first sight, the solution is quite complex, and you need to know several Azure features to implement it. From the other side, you should be aware of the price of separate services such as Cloud, Storage, and SQL Azure. These disadvantages could discourage many developers from implementing a simple and common solution, such as sending notifications to clients' applications. But it was just a background for "native development" on Azure. Since that time Microsoft has released several good solutions-in-a-box such as Azure Mobile Services and Mobile Apps Service, which contain a Notification Hub component. Let's look this component in details.

Introduction to Notification Hub

Notification Hub allows us to work without knowledge of the details that are going on in the background. We do not have to be aware of SQL Azure, Worker roles, Queues, and client platform, and we still can use the Web role to manage authentication, format messages, and so on.

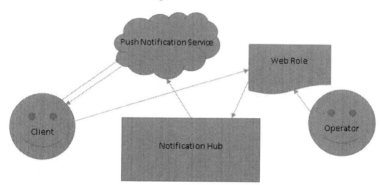

In the simplest scenario, we just need Notification Hub, which provides interfaces for sending messages via operator applications as well as for updating the notification channel from client devices.

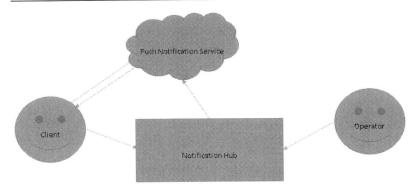

We just need to create a new Notification Hub service inside the Azure account and configure it, and the service will allow you to subscribe an unlimited number of devices and send messages to them. Additionally, Notification Hub supports different types of client platforms such as Windows, iOS, Android, and so on. In other words, Notification Hub is a black box that allows us to implement client applications and "operator" applications only. Notification Hub is a ready-to-use common scenario that was prepared by Microsoft.

Here are some features that could be interesting for developers:

- **Platform agnostic:** A developer can configure the Notification Hub to send notifications to most clients on the market, such as Windows 8, Windows Phone, iOS, Android, Kindle, and so on. At the same time there is an API that supports these platforms to register a device of any type.

- **Tag support:** A developer can send a message to a subset of all subscribers using tags. For example, a user can subscribe to news related to local soccer games only.

- **Template support:** You can personalize messages and localize them using templates. For example, the operator can send just one message with localized parameters, and the Notification Hub will resend it based on different templates for different devices. Some of these devices will receive a message with text in Ukrainian while others will get their message in English.

- **Device-registration management:** You can integrate the code into the registration pipeline to preauthorize clients before registration. This is very important in the case of paid services.

- **Scheduled notifications:** Yes, you can schedule notifications for a specific time.

You should now be able to understand the purpose of Notification Hub. I am planning to show some features of Notification Hub in the next section.

Creating a Simple Notification Hub

Previously I gave a short overview of Notification Hub, but the last section was mostly about some benefits of Notification Hub in comparison with the "native" solution, rather than its features. Now, I am planning to bring your attention to a step-by-step guideline that will show you how to use Notification Hub and will provide many more details about its particular features.

First of all, we should understand that Microsoft has prepared several boxed solutions for common mobile scenarios, which are called Azure Mobile Services and Mobile Apps. However, Notification Hub is NOT one of them. This service does not require Mobile Services or Mobile Apps, and we can create it using the App Services tab.

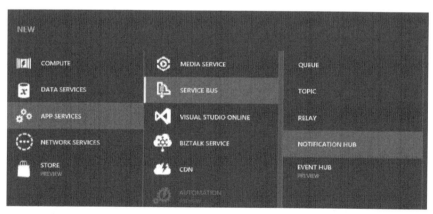

However, there are several additional opportunities if we associate Notification Hub with Mobile Services or Mobile Apps service. That is why I suggest starting with Mobile Services, and if we create them first, Notification Hub will be created automatically for us.

If you want to use Mobile Apps, you can do almost the same thing, but in the case of Mobile Services, you need to use the old management portal at https://manage.windowsazure.com, and in the case of Mobile Apps, you need to use the new portal at https://portal.azure.com.

So let's start working with Mobile Services:

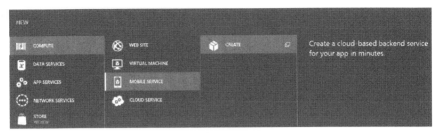

This step is very simple. You should select the name (URL), SQL database, and region. The Backend field helps you to select the right technology for back-end coding, and you have a choice between .NET (C# of course) and JavaScript options. I do not like JavaScript very much, but I would recommend it for Notification Hub scenarios because you will not create much code owing to the limited number of such scenarios. Basically, there is only one scenario, and it is related to the registration process of new devices. Additionally, it is easy to deploy a JavaScript registration script because the Azure dashboard has special options and a JavaScript editor, which should make your deployment process pretty simple. In any case, I am planning to show JavaScript and C# usage in the next section. Therefore, you can pick either of these two languages.

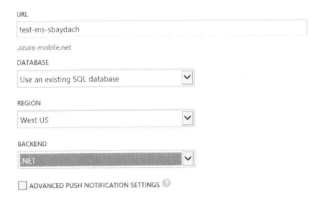

If you click OK, you will have your Mobile Service as well as Notification Hub inside or one to two minutes (in the case of Mobile Apps, you need to create Notification Hub by visiting Settings in the new portal). There are several ways to open the Hub dashboard. Personally, I like the Mobile Services tab because it allows you to edit the JavaScript registration script and to change permissions for the registration endpoints. These permissions allow you to set up additional security rules for endpoints, which will be used to register new devices. There are the following options:

- **Everyone:** All devices will be able to pass the registration process. It's OK for many scenarios because the registration activity itself will not allow the application to receive any notifications with the wrong certificate (or client secret and package SID in the case of Windows 8).

- **Anybody with application key:** This option allows devices that have sent the application key in their requests to pass the registration process. Note that this method will not guarantee any type of security for apps, because in most cases developers store an application key inside their applications, so the key can be stolen very easily. If you want to add security features, you should implement the authentication mechanism inside your app.

- **Only Authenticated Users:** Users are required to authenticate via one of the supported authentication providers, such as Facebook, Twitter, Google, Microsoft Account, and Azure Active Directory.

- **Only Script and Admins:** Only a script with the master key and the admin (via Management Portal) will be able to use the service.

Note that you will not see the registration endpoints section if you select .NET as the back-end technology. If you use C#, you will be able to set permissions in the WebApiConfig.cs file.

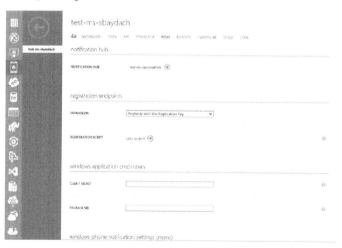

We just discussed the security options, and we mentioned the application key and the master key. They can be found on the Mobile Service dashboard, and you can easily regenerate these keys in case of leaks.

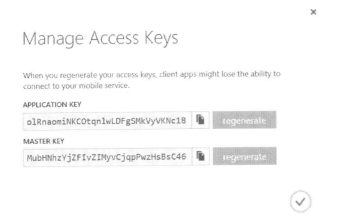

Of course, you should be aware of Media Services security options just in case you decide to use Media Services client libraries, but you can work with Notification Hub to avoid Media Services. It does not depend on whether your Notification Hub is integrated with Media Services in your subscription.

If you want to work with Notification Hub directly, you can forget about the application and the master keys, but you will need to apply the policies of Notification Hub. To understand these policies, let's go to the Notification Hub dashboard (Configure tab). You can find there several access policies, and you can modify them or create new ones. We should use these policies to directly connect Notification Hub. Additionally, there are two keys for each policy, which should be used for connection strings. You can find all the connection strings on the Dashboard page of Notification Hub. You can select one of them based on the existing permissions. Of course, if you need a connection string for client devices that will listen to notifications only, you can use the DefaultListenAccessSignature connection string. If you create a back-end service that will send notifications, you can use a connection string with Send permission, and so on.

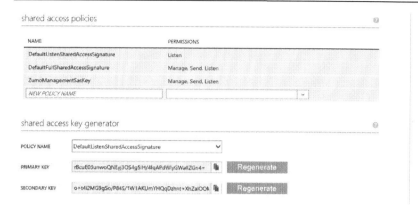

OK, I think that we can create a simple application that is able to receive our notifications. To do so, I selected Windows Phone application (Silverlight) because this type of application doesn't require Store registration, but it requires you to turn on the **Enable unauthenticated push notifications** check box on the Configure tab. It will let us send up to five hundred messages without a certificate, and this number is enough for testing.

Let's open Visual Studio and create a Windows Phone (Silverlight) application. It will use an old type of notification service, unlike Windows Runtime applications, but it will not require a certificate as mentioned above.

We will try to communicate with Notification Hub both directly and via Mobile Service. I will start with the direct method. To do this, you should use the NuGet tool to add the **WindowsAzure.Messaging.Managed** assembly, which will help you to send data to our hub, because I don't want to create JSON code and work with the **WebRequest** and **WebResponse** classes.

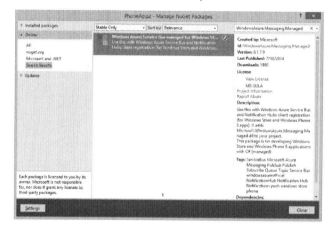

Now we are ready to add some code. Open the App.xaml.cs file and change the Application_Launching method in the following way:

```
private async void Application_Launching(object sender,
    LaunchingEventArgs e){
    var channel = HttpNotificationChannel.Find(
        "MyPushChannel2");
    if (channel == null)      {
        channel = new HttpNotificationChannel(
            "MyPushChannel2");
        channel.Open();
        channel.BindToShellToast();
    }

    channel.ChannelUriUpdated +=
        new EventHandler<NotificationChannelUriEventArgs>
        (async (o, args) =>      {
        var hub = new NotificationHub(
            "test-ms-sbaydachhub",
            "<connection string>");
        await hub.RegisterNativeAsync(
            args.ChannelUri.ToString());

    });
}
```

This code will allow you to receive the notification channel from the MPNS and update the channel in our Notification Hub. That's all. You can run the application on your phone and try to send a message. To send a message, you can use the Debug tab in the Azure Management Portal.

settings

PLATFORMS	Windows Phone ∨	
RANDOM BROADCAST	ON OFF	
SEND TO TAG		

body

```
1  <?xml version="1.0" encoding="utf-8"?>
2  <wp:Notification xmlns:wp="WPNotification">
3  <wp:Toast>
4  <wp:Text1>NotificationHub</wp:Text1>
5  <wp:Text2>Test message</wp:Text2>
6  </wp:Toast>
```

If you want to use Mobile Services to register your device for notifications, you need to add the Azure Mobile Service package to your project and change Application_Launching in the following way:

```
private async void Application_Launching(object sender,
    LaunchingEventArgs e)
{
    var channel = HttpNotificationChannel.
        Find("MyPushChannel2");
    if (channel == null)
    {
        channel = new HttpNotificationChannel(
            "MyPushChannel2");
        channel.Open();
        channel.BindToShellToast();
    }

    channel.ChannelUriUpdated +=
        new EventHandler<NotificationChannelUriEventArgs>(
        async (o, args) =>
        {

            MobileServiceClient MobileService =
                new MobileServiceClient(
                "https://test-ms-sbaydach.azure-mobile.net/"
            );
            await MobileService.GetPush().
                RegisterNativeAsync(
                    channel.ChannelUri.ToString());
        });
}
```

Note that this code doesn't use connection strings from Notification Hub, but it will not work if you don't set the Everyone permission to the registration pipeline (or put an application key as the second parameter of the MobileServiceClient constructor).

Mobile Service API vs. Notification Hub API

In the previous section, we got basic knowledge about Notification Hub and described some methods that will help us communicate with it. And now it's time to build a simple Windows Runtime application and a simple front-end application for sending notifications.

I am not going to make something virtual. So I will try to reproduce the application that I mentioned in the section about Notification Hub versus native development. It will be a universal application that will show the latest information about soccer games and will allow users to receive notifications "from the field."

But before we start writing some code, we should select a method to communicate with Notification Hub. As I showed in the previous section, we are able to communicate with Notification Hub directly, or we can use the Mobile Service infrastructure. These ways are similar, but in our case we need to store the archive of messages in Azure because the application should show old messages as well. That's why we need to create a table for messages on the Azure side. Additionally, we need to create a service that will help to update the table. We also must think about security. Therefore, if we use Notification Hub directly, we still need to implement many things, but if we use Mobile Services, it can help us, and we will avoid additional work. The most important feature of Mobile Services is an infrastructure for data management. Thanks to Mobile Services, we have a simple way to create tables, manage data inside, and write our own business logic that will work as a trigger for operations such as inserting, deleting, and so on. Additionally, the Mobile Service infrastructure supports some security mechanisms.

Note that the Mobile Service API doesn't allow you to send notifications outside the Mobile Services infrastructure. That's why tables and triggers are the most important part of the story. In fact, our back end will work with a table—it will just send new data to insert into the table—but a trigger will help to broadcast our notifications to the registered devices.

Tables

Therefore, we should start our development with tables. In our case, we will need just one table to store our messages. To create this table, you can use Azure Management Portal, and you will need to set Name and permissions for available actions such as insert, delete, update, and select. Because we will modify data in the table from our back end only, and we are planning to show our archive to all clients without special permissions, we may configure our table to use Application Key for Update, Delete, and Insert actions and use the Everyone permission for the Select action.

When you click OK, your table will be ready for your data. However, we have not created any columns yet. If you open the Columns tab, you will find several precreated columns.

notificationdata

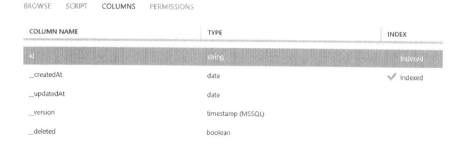

We can create more columns using the Add Column button, but we don't need to, because all tables have dynamic schema by default.

Dynamic schema is available for Media Services with a JavaScript back end and allows you to create all needed columns based on data received in JSon format. So if you send data that requires new columns, they will be created on the fly, and there is a recommendation to disable the dynamic mode in the production mode. Since we are using JavaScript, we will finish with the table and move our attention to the business logic.

How to Send Notifications from the Server

Business logic is very simple. Let's open the Insert trigger for our table and modify the initial code in the following way:

```
function insert(item, user, request)
{
    request.execute(
    {
        success: function()
        {
            push.mpns.sendToast(null,
            {
                text1:item.text
            },
            {
                success: function (pushResponse) {
                    console.log(
                        "Sent push:", pushResponse);
                }
            });

            request.respond();
        }}
    );
}
```

In this code we kept the execute method of the request object, but we added a parameter. It's an anonymous method that helps to send our notifications. To do this, we are using a **push** object, which includes several properties such as **mpns**, **wns**, **awns**, and **gcm**. These properties contain references to the objects that can help to send notifications to different notification servers from Microsoft, Google, and Apple. Because we already have some code for the Windows Phone (Silverlight) application, I decided to use an mpns object, but I will show wns as well in the next topic.

The **sendToast** method is very simple, and it allows us to send a message to a particular device that broadcasts our message. We are using broadcasting in our example. That is why we use a null value as the first parameter. If the method returns success, we will put a record about it in the Mobile Service log. The log is a very important feature when we are using JavaScript because it allows us to find mistakes in the code. For example, I made several mistakes, and the log showed these errors to me.

test-ms-sbaydach

| | DASHBOARD | DATA | API | SCHEDULER | PUSH | IDENTITY | CONFIGURE | SCALE | LOGS |

LEVEL	MESSAGE	SOURCE	TIME STAMP
Information	Sent push: { isSuccessful: true, statusCode:...	NotificationData/insert	Mon Sep 22 2014, 9:04:36 PM
Error	Error in script '/table/NotificationData.inse...	NotificationData/insert	Mon Sep 22 2014, 8:58:12 PM
Error	Error in callback for table 'NotificationData...	NotificationData/insert	Mon Sep 22 2014, 8:56:48 PM
Error	Error in script '/table/NotificationData.inse...	NotificationData/insert	Mon Sep 22 2014, 8:55:48 PM
Error	Error in callback for table 'NotificationData...	NotificationData/insert	Mon Sep 22 2014, 8:52:23 PM
Error	Error in callback for table 'NotificationData...	NotificationData/insert	Mon Sep 22 2014, 8:51:45 PM

"Operator" application

Right now, we are ready to create code that will send messages to the client. Of course, I cannot share partner code inside the ASP.NET portal. So I created a simple console application.

```
static void Main(string[] args)
{
    MobileServiceClient MobileService =
        new MobileServiceClient(
        "https://test-ms-sbaydach.azure-mobile.net/",
        "<application key>");
    IMobileServiceTable<NotificationData> messageTable =
        MobileService.GetTable<NotificationData>();
```

```
messageTable.InsertAsync(new NotificationData()
    { Text = "My first notification" }).Wait();
}
```

That is all. Now we can create a more advanced application for Windows Runtime.

Windows Notification Service and Windows Runtime

It's time to start developing a real application, one with a user-friendly interface that will implement several types of notifications and will be ready for the Store. I don't have experience in Android and iOS development, so I will develop just a UWP application, and I will publish it to the Microsoft Store.

In the previous section, we developed a Windows Phone (Silverlight) application without a specific interface, and we used Microsoft Push Notification Service (MPNS) in the anonymous mode, which is good for testing only. Now we are going to use Windows Notification Service (WNS), which is supported by UWP.

Before we start coding, we should configure Windows Application Credentials in our Mobile Service (Push tab), but this requires Store registration. So if you don't have a Store account yet, it's the right time to create one.

If you have an account in the Store, you should go to the dashboard and try to submit a new Windows Store application (I know that we haven't developed it yet). During the submission process, you will reserve the application name and provide selling details. But we need the next step, which will generate the client secret key for our application. Let's click the Live Service site link.

Push notifications

Windows Push Notification Services (WNS) and Microsoft Azure Mobile Services

The Windows Push Notification Services (WNS) enables you to send toast, tile, badge, and raw updates from your own cloud service. Learn more

If you have an existing WNS solution or need to update your current client secret, visit the Live Services site

You can also use Microsoft Azure Mobile Services to send push notifications, authenticate and manage app users, and store app data in the cloud. Sign in to your Microsoft Azure account or sign up now to add services to up to ten apps for free.

You will be redirected to the App Settings page, where you can find the package SID, client ID, and client secret.

Football.ua notifications

This information is required to send notifications to registered devices. So copy these keys and put them in the Identity tab of Media Services.

Once you set up Mobile Services and create an application name in the Store, you may download all needed information to your Visual Studio project as well. If you forget to do this, you will not be able to test your applications, because they will not be able to receive notifications owing to the wrong package identity. To do this, you may use the context menu for each of our projects.

Server Side for Windows Runtime Application

We finished configuring Media Services, but to enable server-side messages to registered devices, we need to modify our Insert trigger. In the previous section, we implemented a simple JavaScript trigger, which was able to send notifications through MPNS. Let's substitute MPNS with WNS. Additionally, I am going to add more notifications types, such as raw and Tile notifications. Raw notifications allow users to receive notifications when an application is active. They allow the content of the application to be updated in real time. Tile notifications are used for application Tile updates.

Below you can find code that allows sending Toast notifications; Tile notifications we will add later.

```
function insert(item, user, request)
{
    request.execute(
    {
        success: function()
```

```
{
        push.wns.sendToastText02(null,
        {
            text1:"Football.ua",
            text2:item.text
        },
        {
            success: function (pushResponse)
            {
                console.log("Sent push:",
                    pushResponse);
            }
        });

        request.respond();
    }
}
);
}
```

When we used MPNS, we called just the sendToast method, but Windows 8.1 and Windows Phone 8.1 allow different presentations of Toast and Tile notifications. In this application, I decided to use the ToastText02 template, which will show text1 as the title of the notification (single line) and text2 as the body of the notification (two lines on the screen).

Interface of Our Application

We will start with the code that requests a notification channel for our device and sends the channel to our Mobile Services. Because you need to do this every time the application launches, we will use the App.xaml.cs file.

To create a notification channel, we will use the **PushNotificationChannel** and **PushNotificationChannelManager** classes. MSDN says that we should store our notification channel after each request and compare the new channel to the old one to avoid sending a duplicate to our server side. However, I decided to avoid this practice. We will get the notification channel for our application on every launch event, and we will send it to Mobile Services at once. We should understand that there might be a problem with the Internet, so we will check possible exceptions related to it, and in the case of an exception, we will continue to launch our application without any notifications. This type of behavior is justified because we will upload old data in the next stage. So we will have a chance to notify a user about a problem with the network. In any case, we cannot use the notification channel as a guaranteed way for delivering our messages.

I propose the following method for receiving a notification channel and for registering it in Mobile Services:

```
private async void CreateNotificationChannel()
{
    try
    {
        PushNotificationChannel channel;

        channel = await PushNotificationChannelManager.
        CreatePushNotificationChannelForApplicationAsync();

        MobileServiceClient mobileService =
        new MobileServiceClient(
        "https://test-ms-sbaydach.azure-mobile.net/");

        await mobileService.GetPush().
        RegisterNativeAsync(channel.Uri);
    }
    catch
    {

    }
}
```

Note that we don't use the application key on the client side. So you need to modify the permission for the registration script accordingly.

registration endpoints

PERMISSION	Everyone ▼

Right now, we can put the method call at the beginning of the OnLaunched event handler, and it will allow us to receive Toast notifications at once.

It's time to implement the business logic of our application. Since data classes are not related to a specific interface, I am going to use the shared project to create all needed classes. Let's create a Code folder there and the DataClasses.cs code file inside. We will create two classes.

One of these classes should describe our data table in Azure Mobile Service. We need to use the table and column names to avoid using attributes or any other mapping approaches. So our class may look like this:

```
public class NotificationData
{
    public string id { get; set; }
    public string text { get; set; }
    public DateTime __createdAt { get; set; }
}
```

The second class is a utility class. I am going to use it as a class for loading our data from Azure Mobile. So we can use the following code:

```
public class DataClass
{
    public static async
        Task<ICollection<NotificationData>> LoadData()
    {
        MobileServiceClient client =
            new MobileServiceClient(
            "https://test-ms-sbaidachni.azure-mobile.net/");
        var table=client.GetTable<NotificationData>();
        var query = (from item in table
                        orderby item.__createdAt descending
                        select item).Take(100);
        var items = await query.ToCollectionAsync();

        return items;
    }
}
```

Because we allowed everyone to get data from Azure Mobile, we don't use any keys there. But I am going to download just a hundred records from our database. Later you can add one more method with incremental downloading. You can use the Skip(n) method to skip already-downloaded records: .Skip(n).Take(100).

Since we have already implemented all business logic and our application allows us to receive notifications, we may finalize the work by brushing up the interface of our application.

I decided to use the GridView control to show all messages. We need to disable all "selection" and "click" functionality and show messages and dates. Let's review my code:

411

```xml
<Page.BottomAppBar>
    <CommandBar>
        <AppBarButton Label="Refresh" Icon="Refresh"
        Click="AppBarButton_Click">
        </AppBarButton>
    </CommandBar>
</Page.BottomAppBar>


<Grid Background=
 "{ThemeResource ApplicationPageBackgroundThemeBrush}">
    <Grid.RowDefinitions>
        <RowDefinition Height="Auto"></RowDefinition>
        <RowDefinition Height="*"></RowDefinition>
    </Grid.RowDefinitions>
    <Image Source="Assets/football.png" Height="36"
     HorizontalAlignment="Left" Margin="120,30,0,10">
    </Image>
    <GridView Name="myGrid" Grid.Row="1"
     Padding="120,40,100,80" SelectionMode="None"
     Visibility="Collapsed">
        <GridView.ItemTemplate>
            <DataTemplate>
                <Grid Width="450"
                  HorizontalAlignment="Left" Height="100"
                  Background="Gray" >
                    <Grid.RowDefinitions>
                        <RowDefinition Height="Auto">
                        </RowDefinition>
                        <RowDefinition Height="*">
                        </RowDefinition>
                    </Grid.RowDefinitions>
                    <TextBlock Text="{Binding __createdAt}"
                     Style="{StaticResource
                     CaptionTextBlockStyle}"
                     Foreground="Green" Margin="5">
                    </TextBlock>
                    <TextBlock Text="{Binding text}"
                     Grid.Row="1" Style="{StaticResource
                     BodyTextBlockStyle}"
                     TextWrapping="Wrap" Margin="5">
                    </TextBlock>
                </Grid>
            </DataTemplate>
        </GridView.ItemTemplate>
    </GridView>
```

```xml
<ProgressRing Name="progressBox" IsActive="True"
 HorizontalAlignment="Center"
 VerticalAlignment="Center" Width="100" Height="100"
 Grid.Row="1" Visibility="Visible"></ProgressRing>
<TextBlock Name="errorBox" TextWrapping="Wrap"
 Text="Try again" Visibility="Collapsed"
 HorizontalAlignment="Center"
 VerticalAlignment="Center" TextAlignment="Center"
 Grid.Row="1"
 Style="{StaticResource HeaderTextBlockStyle}">
</TextBlock>

<VisualStateManager.VisualStateGroups>
    <VisualStateGroup x:Name="Common">
        <VisualState x:Name="Loading">
            <Storyboard>
                <ObjectAnimationUsingKeyFrames
                Storyboard.TargetName="errorBox"
                Storyboard.TargetProperty="Visibility">
                    <DiscreteObjectKeyFrame
                    Value="Collapsed"
                    KeyTime="0">
                    </DiscreteObjectKeyFrame>
                </ObjectAnimationUsingKeyFrames>
                <ObjectAnimationUsingKeyFrames
                Storyboard.TargetName="progressBox"
                Storyboard.TargetProperty="Visibility">
                    <DiscreteObjectKeyFrame
                    Value="Visible" KeyTime="0">
                    </DiscreteObjectKeyFrame>
                </ObjectAnimationUsingKeyFrames>
                <ObjectAnimationUsingKeyFrames
                Storyboard.TargetName="myGrid"
                Storyboard.TargetProperty="Visibility">
                    <DiscreteObjectKeyFrame
                    Value="Collapsed" KeyTime="0">
                    </DiscreteObjectKeyFrame>
                </ObjectAnimationUsingKeyFrames>
            </Storyboard>
        </VisualState>
        <VisualState x:Name="Loaded">
            <Storyboard>
                <ObjectAnimationUsingKeyFrames
                Storyboard.TargetName="errorBox"
                Storyboard.TargetProperty="Visibility">
```

```
                    <DiscreteObjectKeyFrame
                     Value="Collapsed" KeyTime="0">
                    </DiscreteObjectKeyFrame>
                </ObjectAnimationUsingKeyFrames>
                <ObjectAnimationUsingKeyFrames
                Storyboard.TargetName="progressBox"
                Storyboard.TargetProperty="Visibility">
                    <DiscreteObjectKeyFrame
                     Value="Collapsed" KeyTime="0">
                    </DiscreteObjectKeyFrame>
                </ObjectAnimationUsingKeyFrames>
                <ObjectAnimationUsingKeyFrames
                Storyboard.TargetName="myGrid"
                Storyboard.TargetProperty="Visibility">
                    <DiscreteObjectKeyFrame
                     Value="Visible" KeyTime="0">
                    </DiscreteObjectKeyFrame>
                </ObjectAnimationUsingKeyFrames>
            </Storyboard>
        </VisualState>
        <VisualState x:Name="Error">
            <Storyboard>
                <ObjectAnimationUsingKeyFrames
                Storyboard.TargetName="errorBox"
                Storyboard.TargetProperty="Visibility">
                    <DiscreteObjectKeyFrame
                     Value="Visible" KeyTime="0">
                    </DiscreteObjectKeyFrame>
                </ObjectAnimationUsingKeyFrames>
                <ObjectAnimationUsingKeyFrames
                Storyboard.TargetName="progressBox"
                Storyboard.TargetProperty="Visibility">
                    <DiscreteObjectKeyFrame
                     Value="Collapsed" KeyTime="0">
                    </DiscreteObjectKeyFrame>
                </ObjectAnimationUsingKeyFrames>
                <ObjectAnimationUsingKeyFrames
                Storyboard.TargetName="myGrid"
                Storyboard.TargetProperty="Visibility">
                    <DiscreteObjectKeyFrame
                     Value="Collapsed" KeyTime="0">
                    </DiscreteObjectKeyFrame>
                </ObjectAnimationUsingKeyFrames>
            </Storyboard>
        </VisualState>
```

```
        </VisualStateGroup>
    </VisualStateManager.VisualStateGroups>
</Grid>
```

I know that it's longer than you imagined, but it allows me to demonstrate different parts of the interface based on different events in our application. We can divide this code into three parts.

In the first part, we declared the application-bar control with the refresh button. I am going to use this button to allow a user to update the interface in case he or she opened the application some time ago and it is still in memory.

In the second part, I declared a Grid layout and some controls, such as GridView, Image, and several text boxes with different messages. We are going to show GridView or messages based on the situation.

In the last part, I declared the VisualStateManager control, which allows you to declare several custom states there. We will have three states:

- Loading: Data is loading from Azure Mobile Services.

- Loaded: Data is loaded and ready to show.

- Error: We have a problem with the Internet connection.

Depending on the state, we are going to hide and show certain parts of our interface.

Finally, we need to implement code that will set the state of our interface. It will use our utility class to download data. I propose using the following code inside MainPage.xaml.cs:

```
protected override void OnNavigatedTo(NavigationEventArgs e)
{
    base.OnNavigatedTo(e);
    LoadData();
}

private void AppBarButton_Click(object sender,
    RoutedEventArgs e)
{
    LoadData();
}

private async void LoadData()
{
```

```
try
{
    VisualStateManager.GoToState(this,
        "Loading", false);
    var items = await DataClass.LoadData();
    myGrid.ItemsSource = items;
    VisualStateManager.GoToState(this,
        "Loaded", false);
}
catch(Exception ex)
{
    VisualStateManager.GoToState(this, "Error", false);
}
}
```

It's probably better to use triggers and setters, but I implemented this code before Windows 10 was released. But you can change it as you want.

The most important method here is LoadData. We use this method to move the interface to the right state, and it allows us to download and bind the data as well.

We have now developed an application that allows us to get notifications about soccer games using Windows Notification Service and can show the latest messages as well.

FOOTBALL.UA

.NET Back End

Previously we used a JavaScript back end to handle the insert operation. Thanks to that, I was able to send broadcast notifications to all subscribers. In this example, we had a small amount of code, and using JavaScript was reasonable despite my love for .NET. But in many projects, your code might be more complex, so you might want to use Visual Studio and C# to develop it. Therefore, I want to show you how to use Visual Studio to build our back end.

First of all, to use C# in the back end, you must select .NET as the back-end technology in the new Mobile Service dialog.

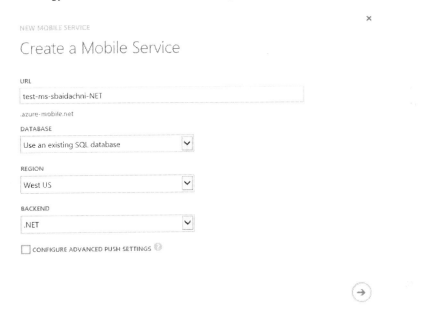

You may use Visual Studio as well as create a Mobile Service, but I like the management panel. I simply got used to using the management panel over the past several years.

Now we are ready to use Visual Studio. In the first step, we will create a project based on the Azure Mobile Service template. You need to provide the name of your project/solution.

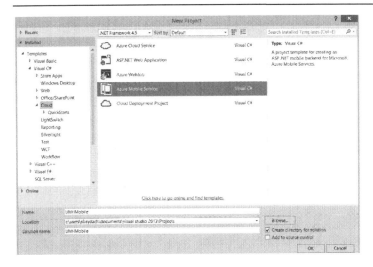

In the second step, you need to select some options. You should switch off the **Host in the cloud** check box. If you forget to do so, Visual Studio will propose creating a new Mobile Service.

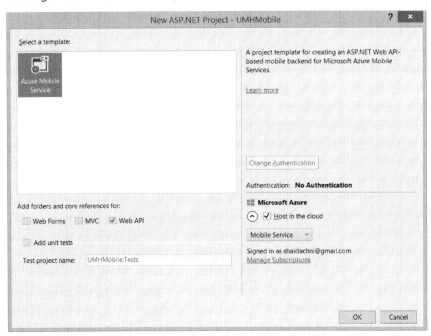

Once you click OK, Visual Studio will create a project for you. It contains several ready-to-use classes such as TodoItem, TodoItemController, and so on. You can use this code to deploy the TodoItem table to Azure Mobile Service.

I am not going to remove the autocreated code, but I would prefer my own names for table and columns. So I will change TodoItem to NotificationData. You can use refactoring tools to change the class name. Additionally, I will remove the **Complete** property and change **Text** to **text** property using **JsonProperty** attribute.

```
public class NotificationData : EntityData
{
    [JsonProperty("text")]
    public string Text { get; set; }
}
```

Because Entity Framework and Web API already have all the needed infrastructure for our service, we will concentrate our attention on the following questions:

- how to broadcast notifications from our code,

- how to set permissions for operations with the tables, and

- how to create your own code that handles the registration of new devices.

The simplest question is about sending notifications. You need to open the TodoItemController.cs file and modify the PostTodoItem method in the following way:

```
public async Task<IHttpActionResult> PostTodoItem(
    NotificationData item)
{
    NotificationData current = await InsertAsync(item);

    WindowsPushMessage message = new WindowsPushMessage();

    message.XmlPayload =
      @"<?xml version=""1.0"" encoding=""utf-8""?>" +
      @"<toast><visual><binding template=""ToastText02"">" +
      @"<text id=""1"">football.ua</text>" +
      @"<text id=""2"">" + item.Text + @"</text>" +
      @"</binding></visual></toast>";
    try
    {
```

```
        var result = await Services.Push.SendAsync(message);
        Services.Log.Info(result.State.ToString());
    }
    catch (System.Exception ex)
    {
        Services.Log.Error(ex.Message, null,
          "Push.SendAsync Error");
    }

    return CreatedAtRoute("Tables", new {
        id = current.Id }, current);
}
```

You can see that we have used two classes. **WindowsPushMessages** allows you to create a toast message, and **ApiServices** (Service instance) allows you to send the message and add information to the log. As in the case of JavaScript, we used the ToastText02 template, which contains a title and message. So we have the same code but in C#.

Let's talk about permissions. In the case of JavaScript, we used the Azure Management panel to set permissions, but in the case of C#, we need to use attributes. You need to use the AuthorizeLevel attribute to set the right permissions for methods in the Controller class.

```
[AuthorizeLevel(AuthorizationLevel.Application)]
public async Task<IHttpActionResult>
PostTodoItem(NotificationData item)
[AuthorizeLevel(AuthorizationLevel.Anonymous)]
public IQueryable<NotificationData> GetAllTodoItems()
```

Of course, this approach will work only for table operations, but in the case of JavaScript, you can set the authorization level using the Azure management panel. In the case of C#, you may set it in the WebApiConfig.cs file. Just add the following line of code to the Register method:

```
options.PushAuthorization = AuthorizationLevel.Anonymous;
```

In our example, we didn't change the registration pipeline, but if you want to do so, you can implement an INotificationHandler interface.

```
{
    public System.Threading.Tasks.Task Register(
        ApiServices services, HttpRequestContext context,
        NotificationRegistration registration)
    {
        throw new NotImplementedException();
```

```
}

public System.Threading.Tasks.Task Unregister(
    ApiServices services, HttpRequestContext context,
    string deviceId)
{
    throw new NotImplementedException();
}
}
```

The implementation of the interface will be picked up automatically, and you may run your own code.

Finally, to test our solution, we need to deploy it. To do so, just select the Publish menu item from the context menu and set up all needed parameters:

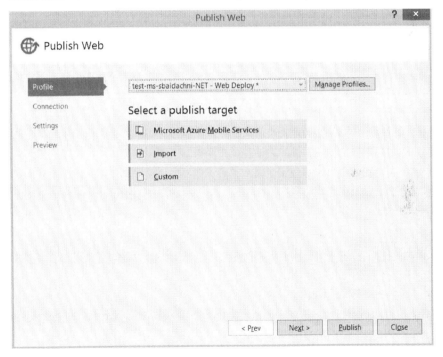

To simplify this process, you can download the Publishing profile from the dashboard of the already-created service:

mobile service endpoint status PREVIEW

You have not configured mobile service endpoint monitoring.

CONFIGURE MOBILE SERVICE ENDPOINT MONITORING →

quick glance

Other Mobile Services Features

I have described a very simple application, but what about other features of Azure Mobile Services? Frankly speaking, I used about half of all its features. Therefore, I will describe the rest of the features for you to have a complete view of the topic.

Tags

This feature is related to Push Notification Hub, but Azure Mobile Services encapsulates it as well. The idea is very simple—use special tags to target the right groups of users. For example, if you create a news site, you can create a tag for each group of news, and the user might select just the groups that are interesting to him or her. I don't like politics so much, but somebody else might not like sports news, and so on.

Of course, to implement this approach, you need to have a way to select tags during the user registration process, and you should have a method to broadcast messages only for the selected tags. There is good news—the Mobile Service API supports tags. For example, to make a registration using some tags, you can use the following code:

```
await mobileService.GetPush().RegisterNativeAsync(
    channel.Uri,
    new List<string>() {"sport", "movies", "Canada" });
```

In this example, three tags will be associated with the user registration.

To send a message to all users with the tag "movies," you can use the following code (C#):

```
await Services.Push.SendAsync(message, "movies");
```

Note that the methods that we use to send messages to users usually allow you to pass a tag expression. A tag expression can be used for passing expressions based on tags, using logical operators such as &&, ||, and !: **"(tagA && !tagB)"**.

Templates

Templates are one more way to create personalized messages for users. For example, to send a message from C# to Windows users, you may use the following code:

```
WindowsPushMessage message = new WindowsPushMessage();

message.XmlPayload =
    @"<?xml version=""1.0"" encoding=""utf-8""?>" +
    @"<toast><visual><binding template=""ToastText02"">" +
    @"<text id=""1"">football.ua</text>" +
    @"<text id=""2"">" + item.Text + @"</text>" +
    @"</binding></visual></toast>";
```

And if you form a message in this way, all your users will see the same message. However, in some cases you might want to pass parameters to your message based on user preferences. For example, if your application supports several languages, you might want to send localized messages; if your application provides data like mileage or temperature, you might want to use the measurement system that is familiar to users; and so on.

Templates allow us to use parameters in XML or JSon messages (based on the platform), which we usually form on the server side. In the case of templates, your server side should not form a message from scratch. Instead, the client application should register a message template, including parameters, and the name of the template. The server side will send just the parameter to the selected templates.

For example, if you create Windows application, your client can use the following code to register a template:

```
string xmlTemplate =
    @"<?xml version=""1.0"" encoding=""utf-8""?>" +
    @"<toast><visual><binding template=""ToastText02"">" +
    @"<text id=""1"">football.ua</text>" +
    @"<text id=""2"">$(ru_message)</text>" +
    @"</binding></visual></toast>";

await mobileService.GetPush().RegisterTemplateAsync(
    channel.Uri, xmlTemplate, "langTemplate");
```

In this case, the client application registers a template with the langTemplate name and with the parameter ru_message. The second device might use the en_message parameter instead of ru_message, and so on. It's needed to get a message in the native language of the device's user. So all devices will have the same template but with different parameters.

In the next step, the server side should form a message that will contain the template name and all parameters. This allows Notification Hub to create unique messages for all devices based on the registered templates and parameters. To prepare a server-side message, you can use predefined classes. For example, if you use C#, you can use the following code:

```
TemplatePushMessage mess = new TemplatePushMessage();

mess.Add("ru_message", "Сообщение");
mess.Add("en_message", "Message");

await Services.Push.SendAsync(mess);
```

Notification Hub will look at every registered template and send a message if the template contains one of these parameters.

Jobs

Some applications, such as Facebook for Windows Phone, send many notifications during a predefined time period. For example, usually at eleven o'clock at night, I get messages about upcoming birthdays of my friends. Of course, it's a good idea to have something on the Azure side that can send notifications according to a schedule. Azure Mobile Services support this feature.

With Azure Mobile Services, you can schedule any code. You may set up a single time frame or create a complex schedule. You can use the Azure Management panel if you are going to create JavaScript code, or Visual Studio if you are going to create C# code.

In the case of JavaScript, it's easy to create something using the Scheduler tab. Note that there is a way to create a job that will run on demand:

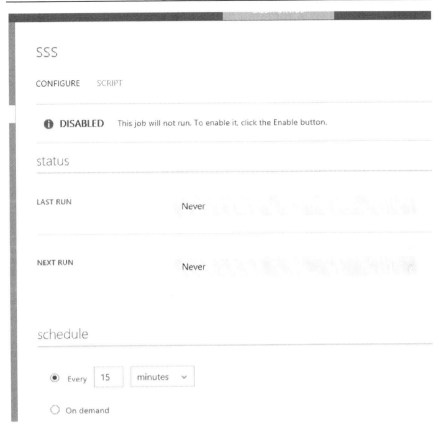

JavaScript code may have access to all objects that we used before, including a **push** object.

In the case of C#, you need to work with Visual Studio, as we did in the previous section, and you should create a class that is derived from the **ScheduledJob** class. The **ExecuteAsync** method will allow you to create any code inside.

Custom API

One more interesting thing in Azure Mobile Services is the ability to create a custom API. You can create a set of JavaScript server-side functions using the management panel:

hhh

SCRIPT   PERMISSIONS

```
 1  exports.post = function(request, response) {
 2      // Use "request.service" to access features of your mobile service, e.g.:
 3      //   var tables = request.service.tables;
 4      //   var push = request.service.push;
 5
 6      response.send(statusCodes.OK, { message : 'Hello World!' });
 7  };
 8
 9  exports.get = function(request, response) {
10      response.send(statusCodes.OK, { message : 'Hello World!' });
11  };
```

In the case of Visual Studio, you need to create a class that is derived from **ApiController**.

Because your code will be called using a standard HTTP protocol, you may use one of the following methods: GET, POST, PUT, PATCH, DELETE.

Chapter 29

How to Build Your Own User Controls

The Universal Windows Platform proposes lots of different user controls, but you don't have any specific limitations if you want to create one of your own. In fact, if you are thinking about creating your own control, there are three opportunities:

- You can create a new control based on an existing one, where you can change a template and its behavior a little bit. It's possible thanks to templates, where you can redesign the control and implement your own visual-state manager.

- You can combine several controls and add some specific methods and behavior to simplify your work with the same group of controls that you are using on many pages. For example, you can create a log-in control that will contain text boxes, buttons, and text blocks.

- It's possible to create fully new control from scratch.

In this chapter we will discuss how to create each of these types of user controls.

Templates

As we discussed earlier, almost all controls support the **Template** property. This property is introduced in the **Control** class and allows you to store an XAML representation of the control.

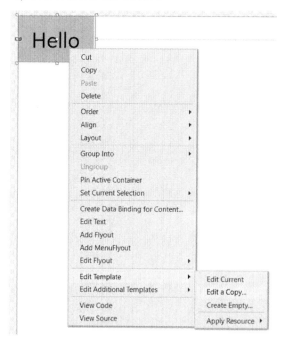

If you want to change the look of a control, it's better to start with a copy of the existing template. You can easily create one using Visual Studio 2015. Just place an instance of the control on a page and use the context menu to create a copy of the template (see above).

Once you select a location for the template, Visual Studio will include the XAML template in your project, and you can start editing it.

Note that the template includes not just assignment for the **Template** property but lots of setters to assign default properties of the control. But the **Template** property is the most interesting one because it contains a representation of the control itself and allows you to change not just the basic view but visual states as well. Let's see a short overview of the control template for Button:

```
<ControlTemplate TargetType="Button">
    <Grid x:Name="RootGrid"
        Background="{TemplateBinding Background}">
        <VisualStateManager.VisualStateGroups>
            <VisualStateGroup x:Name="CommonStates">
                <VisualState x:Name="Normal">
                    <Storyboard>
                    . . . . .
                    </Storyboard>
                </VisualState>
                <VisualState x:Name="PointerOver">
                    <Storyboard>
                    . . . . .
                    </Storyboard>
                </VisualState>
                <VisualState x:Name="Pressed">
                    <Storyboard>
                    . . . . .
                    </Storyboard>
                </VisualState>
                <VisualState x:Name="Disabled">
                    <Storyboard>
                    . . . . .
                    </Storyboard>
                </VisualState>
            </VisualStateGroup>
        </VisualStateManager.VisualStateGroups>
        <ContentPresenter x:Name="ContentPresenter"
            BorderBrush="{TemplateBinding BorderBrush}"
            . . . . . />
    </Grid>
```

```
</ControlTemplate>
```

I have removed all animations and some properties to have easy-to-read code. And you can see that in terms of XAML representation, the Button control is a Grid with a **ContentPresenter** control inside. And that's all. Of course, buttons support lots of states, and you can review all these states using the control template, but if you want to create your own button, you can simply modify an existing template or create a new one from scratch.

In some cases your representations will require additional properties. You can look at **AppBarButton** as an example:

```
<ControlTemplate TargetType="AppBarButton">
    <Grid x:Name="Root" Background=
        "{TemplateBinding Background}" >
        <VisualStateManager.VisualStateGroups>
            <VisualStateGroup
             x:Name="ApplicationViewStates">
                <VisualState x:Name="FullSize"/>
                <VisualState x:Name="Compact">
                    <Storyboard>
                    </Storyboard>
                </VisualState>
                <VisualState x:Name="Overflow">
                    <Storyboard>
                    </Storyboard>
                </VisualState>
            </VisualStateGroup>
            <VisualStateGroup x:Name="CommonStates">
                <VisualState x:Name="Normal">
                    <Storyboard>
                    </Storyboard>
                </VisualState>
                <VisualState x:Name="PointerOver">
                    <Storyboard>
                    </Storyboard>
                </VisualState>
                <VisualState x:Name="Pressed">
                    <Storyboard>
                    </Storyboard>
                </VisualState>
                <VisualState x:Name="Disabled">
                    <Storyboard>
                    </Storyboard>
                </VisualState>
```

```
        </VisualStateGroup>
      </VisualStateManager.VisualStateGroups>
      <StackPanel x:Name="ContentRoot" >
        <ContentPresenter x:Name="Content" />
        <TextBlock x:Name="TextLabel"  />
      </StackPanel>
      <TextBlock x:Name="OverflowTextLabel" />
    </Grid>
</ControlTemplate>
```

Looking at the template, you can see that Microsoft fully redesigned the button. But this new button requires new properties (at least an Icon) that should satisfy the new template. That's why Microsoft implemented a new class, **AppBarButton**, that extends the **Button** class and contains additional logic inside.

Note that templates use a special markup extension called **TemplateBinding**. It's a sort of binding that allows you to make references to control properties. So developers can use styles or change control properties dynamically to modify the look of the control.

User Controls

The second set of controls is controls that you can create based on the **UserControl** class. **UserControl** is inherited from **Control** and has one addition only—the **Content** property. Consequently, you can use **UserControl** as a container that includes elements such as **Grid**, **StackPanel**, and so on. So the idea is very simple: if you need to combine several controls and reuse them in your application, just put all of them inside **UserControl**, using any of the common containers. Of course, we need a way to place a user control in a separate file and add business logic in the code-behind file as well. And there is a way: Visual Studio provides all needed templates and supports designer mode, code-behind features, and other things for user controls.

To start developing a composite control, you need to add a new item based on the User Control template:

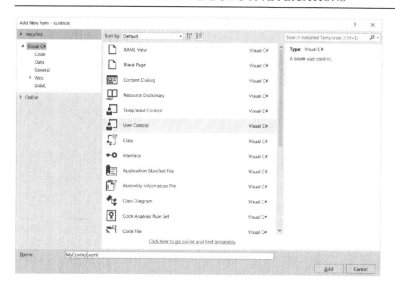

Once you click OK, Visual Studio will create an XAML file and a code-behind file:

  ◢ 🔲 MyControl.xaml

    ▷ 📄 MyControl.xaml.cs

Now you can work with the control as with a page. So you can start with a container, place any controls inside, and implement event handlers. There is only one difference: usually pages don't have a public API, but in the case of composite controls, you need to assume that your controls will be placed on a page, and you need to provide a basic set of methods and properties to set up the properties of the control and its behavior and probably to handle some events.

Once the control is ready, you can use it. The easiest way to do so is to rebuild your application, and you will find your control on the toolbox:

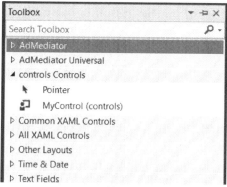

Just drag and drop it on a page, and Visual Studio will create a namespace for you.

Templated Controls

Finally, you can create a completely new control from scratch. To do this, it's better to start with the Templated Control template:

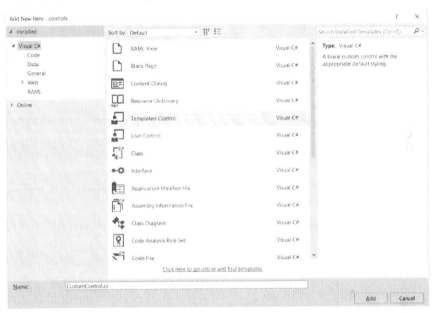

You can see that Visual Studio will create a class that contains a few lines of codes:

```
public sealed class CustomControl : Control
{
    public CustomControl()
    {
        this.DefaultStyleKey = typeof(CustomControl);
    }
}
```

But this is enough to start, because this class is inherited from Control and has the Template property, which allows you to provide presentation for the control. Thanks to **DefaultStyleKey**, we can specify that the control uses an implicit style, and if you check Solution Explorer, you will find one more file—generic.xaml. It's a simple resource file that you can use as a starting point for the user interface of your control:

```
<ResourceDictionary

xmlns="http://schemas.microsoft.com/winfx/2006/xaml/present
ation"
    xmlns:x="http://schemas.microsoft.com/winfx/2006/xaml"
    xmlns:local="using:controls">

    <Style TargetType="local:CustomControl" >
        <Setter Property="Template">
            <Setter.Value>
                <ControlTemplate
                    TargetType="local:CustomControl">
                    <Border
                        Background=
                        "{TemplateBinding Background}"
                        BorderBrush=
                        "{TemplateBinding BorderBrush}"
                        BorderThickness=
                        "{TemplateBinding BorderThickness}">
                    </Border>
                </ControlTemplate>
            </Setter.Value>
        </Setter>
    </Style>
</ResourceDictionary>
```

By default this file contains the **Border** element only, but even now you can place this control on a page, assign some basic properties, and see it:

```
<local:CustomControl Height="100" BorderThickness="3"
    BorderBrush="Red"/>
```

So in the next steps, you need to do the following:

- Create a user interface for your control in XAML, including states.

- Implement the logic of the control.

- Implement public methods and events.

- Implement properties.

In the case of properties, it's better to work with dependency properties. Using this approach, you can work with properties in XAML. Below you can find an example of a dependency-property implementation:

```
public string Label
{
    get { return GetValue(LabelProperty).ToString(); }
    set { SetValue(LabelProperty, value); }
}

public static readonly DependencyProperty LabelProperty =
    DependencyProperty.Register(
        "Label",
        typeof(string),
        typeof(CustomControl),
        new PropertyMetadata(
            false,
            new PropertyChangedCallback(OnLabelChanged)
        )
    );
```

Of course, this is not everything that you need to know about user controls. For example, we didn't discuss attributes, property editors, or many other things. But it should be enough to start developing your first user control.

This page intentionally left blank

Chapter 30

Testing and Debugging

In this chapter I describe all the information about Visual Studio 2015 and tools for Windows 10 applications development that I didn't get to in the previous chapters. We will discuss emulators, debugging tools, and some new XAML features that you may find useful.

Emulators and Simulators

First of all, I want to start with emulators and simulators. In my case, these things are very important because I am used to developing on my desktop without a touch monitor and many other features that you can find when using modern tablets and phones. At the same time, it's better to test your interface using different screen sizes, orientations, and resolutions. Of course, you can buy several different devices and use them to deploy and test your application, but that's quite expensive, and it's inconvenient to use several devices at the same time. Therefore, the standard toolbar is your friend:

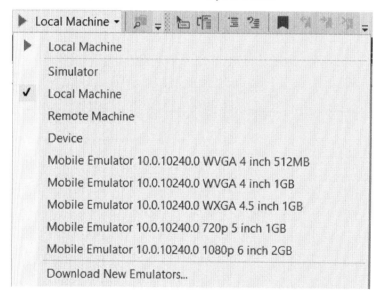

By default Visual Studio runs your applications on your local machine, but you can easily switch this behavior by selecting the simulator, a device, a remote machine, or a mobile emulator.

Using the simulator, you will continue to install and run your application on your local machine, but Visual Studio will run a tool that allows you to interact with your desktop using lots of different instruments:

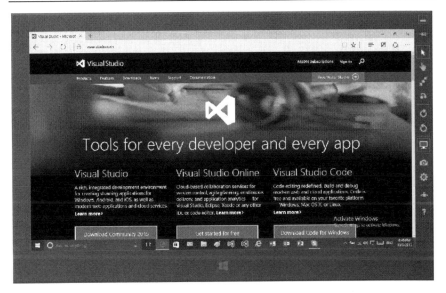

On the right panel of the simulator, you can find the following tools:

- Touch tools: Using these tools, you can emulate basic touch or gestures such as zooming and rotation. Of course, if you are developing an application that requires more-complex gestures, these tools will not help, but in most cases they're good enough.

- Orientation tools: Allows you to change the orientation of the simulator. So using the tools, you can see how your application works in landscape mode.

- Resolution selector: Using this tool, you can easily emulate different resolutions and even DPIs, which is important to check resources as well as the interface.

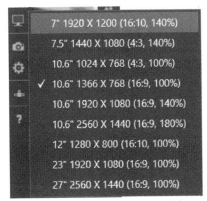

439

- Copy-screenshot tool: You will use this tool all the time once you are ready to publish your application to the Store—just run the application and take some screenshots at the required resolutions.

- Network tool: You can emulate different conditions for the network connection. You can use this tool to check how your application works in case of any problem with the network or if access to the Internet is limited.

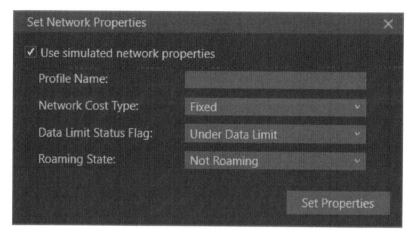

Note that if you develop Windows 10 applications on Windows 8.x, you will not be able to run the simulator.

Unlike the simulator, the emulator is a tool that runs a virtual machine with a real image of an operating system. Consequently, you can run emulators even on Windows 8.x machines. But the emulator works with Windows 10 Mobile SKU only, so you will not be able to run Windows 10 Desktop SKU, but in some cases it's enough, especially if you develop on a Windows 10 machine.

The emulator has the same touch and orientation tools, but it doesn't support changing the resolution on the fly. Instead you can run different virtual machines that emulate different phones. The emulator supports several additional tools. You can find emulations for the accelerometer, location tool, several sensors such as light and magnetometer, NFC, SD card, and notifications. So the emulator contains lots of tools, and you can test your applications even without real phones.

Live Visual Tree in Visual Studio

Live Visual Tree is available for Store and WPF applications, including Store applications for Windows 8.x.

Live Visual Tree allows you to observe an XAML visual tree in run time, review properties of elements, and even change properties in run time to see how changes will affect the interface without restarting application itself. There are lots of scenarios when you need to use a tool like this, and I have already adapted this tool for the following tasks:

- If you have a huge number of visual states in your interface, it's really hard to understand whether a state has not been fired. Thanks to Live Visual Tree, you can check properties of all controls and see what happens by applying changes to these properties—check whether a state is applied and what the result looks like.

- Visual designer in Visual Studio works fine, but if you have lots of bindings, you can use Live Visual Tree to change something in run time

441

and see how it affects the design of the running application with active bindings and data.

- Live Visual Tree allows you to visualize the layout to show alignments and space for UI elements. It allows you to find mistakes that you cannot find in design mode owing to the absence of real data.

- Checking the number of elements in each container, you can find a potential problem with performance.

- Live Visual Tree allows you to check the XAML tree not just for your applications—you can easily attach the debugger to any running XAML application and see an XAML visual tree there and apply any changes in the same way.

To open the Live Visual Tree window for your application, you need to run your application in debug mode, and you can find Live Visual Tree using the Debug→Windows menu item. The second window that is associated with the Live Visual Tree is Live Property Explorer. With Live Visual Tree, you can navigate between XAML elements, and using Live Property Explorer, you can check, change, and create properties.

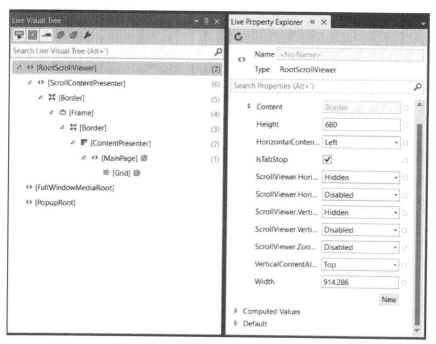

You can see that Live Visual Tree provides information about the number of XAML elements inside each container. Note that you can see elements from the XAML visual tree only. So Live Visual Tree contains visible elements only, and if the interface changes from one state to another, you can see that Live Visual Tree changes in run time.

Live Property Explorer shows default values for properties, values that were inherited from other controls, and local values of control properties. Of course, you can modify local values only. If a value was assigned to a property previously, you can modify it, but you can add any other available properties and assign values to these properties as well.

In the Live Visual Tree window, you will find two useful buttons. The first one allows you to select any element in the running application to find it in the XAML tree. It's very useful when you want to locate the place of a button and other controls that have a tap event handler. The second one allows you to visualize the layout. Once you select an element, you will be able to see the layout.

As I mentioned earlier, you can attach Visual Studio to any existing XAML window. For example, you can run the settings window and select Attach to Process in the Debug menu of Visual Studio 2015. In the Attach to Process dialog, select SystemSettings process, and you will be able to see the structure of the window. You can even change current settings and check the layout of the window.

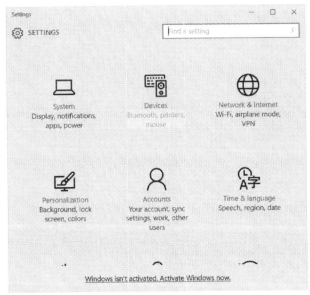

So Live Visual Tree is a very powerful tool that can help make your application better.

Profiling and Debugging Tools in Visual Studio 2015

Let's talk about other tools that allow you to tune your application on the Universal Windows Platform.

But before starting, just make sure that you switch on **Enable Diagnostic Tools while debugging** and **PerfTip while debugging** in the Debugging options. These tools should be enabled by default, but it's better to know how to disable/enable them:

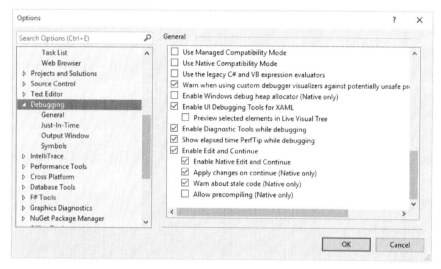

OK, let's talk about particular features. I would like to start with performance tips. Thanks to this feature, you can use breakpoints and debug mode to exactly see how much time has elapsed since the last breakpoint:

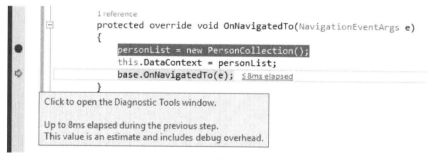

If you want to see this information for each line in your code, you simply need to use the debugger to go through the code step by step. But if you need to know the elapsed time for any of the blocks, then you just need to set two breakpoints at the beginning and end of the block. So using the performance tips, you can easily locate problems with performance.

You can see that Visual Studio displays this information as tips, and you can easily click these tips to navigate to the Diagnostic Tools window, which is the second important tool you can use, along with the performance tips:

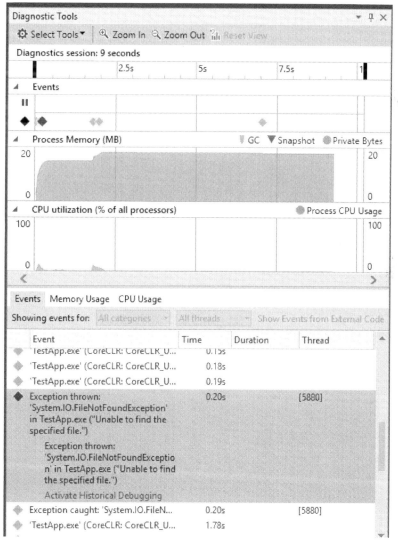

Diagnostic Tools contains three sections. The first one shows events such as information about exceptions, even if an exception is caught; messages from the output window that are generated by the Debug class; and IntelliTrace events related to threads, assemblies, and so on. The next two sections show CPU utilization and the usage of memory at run time, but you can easily pause the debugger and select any time frame to check events and memory and CPU usage.

Additionally, you can take a snapshot of memory anytime during debugging of the application and check the number of references for each object, amount of memory, and so on.

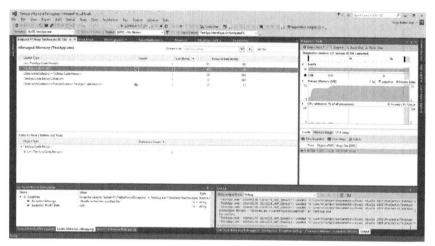

You can find the next set of tools if you execute the **Start diagnostic tools without debugging** command.

These tools allow you to collect information during run time. Because these tools collect all information not in the **debug** mode, this data is better quality, but you cannot check it in real time. Instead, the tools collect information about the application until you stop them.

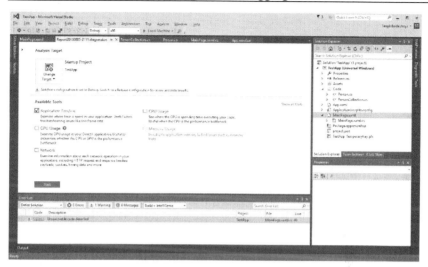

Once they are stopped, a report about the collected metrics is generated, and you can analyze the data using the dashboard.

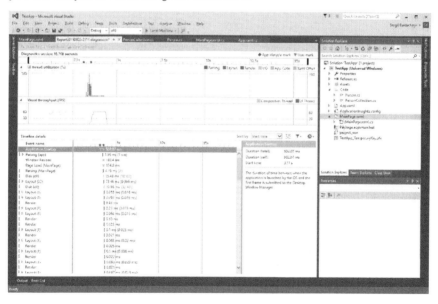

I would like to recommend Application Timeline among all tools. With this tool, you can find problems with rendering and review the most critical parts of your application.

XAML Tools in Visual Studio 2015

Visual Studio is the best editor ever. So it's very hard to implement something new that can excite me, but the developers of Visual Studio 2015 did, and now I want to talk about several features related to the XAML editor.

The first feature is the peek window. This feature can be used not just in the XAML editor, but in the case of XAML, it's really valuable because it allows you to do a lot of things that were not possible before. This feature allows you to inject dependent code directly into the current editing window.

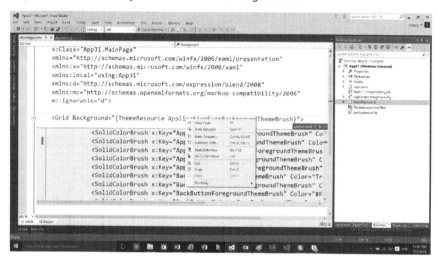

Thanks to that, I can easily check styles even in **generic.xaml**, review definitions of controls, modify event handlers, and so on. And I do not have to close my primary window to do so.

You can call the peek window using the context menu, or you can find this window using some features of Visual Studio 2015. For example, Visual Studio 2015 contains an updated template editor. If you want to create a new template for any control, you can use the context menu and select Edit Template→Edit a Copy:

If you use Application resources or Resource Dictionary, Visual Studio redirects you to the appropriate file. But in the case of Visual Studio 2015, you continue to work with a new template using the same window, editing the template in the designer and checking and modifying code using the peek window.

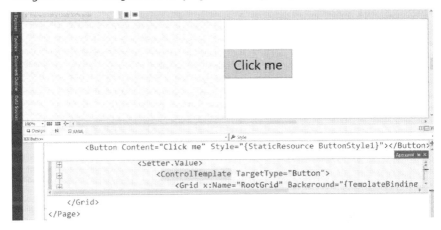

Visual Studio 2015 applies a color border to the visual editor in template-editor mode.

One more feature of the XAML editor is its ability to add named regions in the XAML code as in C#. You can use the following syntax to create a marked region inside your XAML:

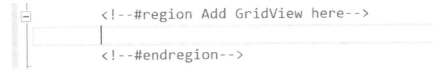

As in C#, you can collapse it:

You can use this feature in many ways: mark the existing code for some reason or create templates for future work.

I have shown you three new features in the XAML editor: peek window, updated template editor, and marked XAML blocks. Let's use these features to make coding smoother.

This page intentionally left blank

Chapter 31

Win2D: How to Use Graphics without Deep DirectX Knowledge

Direct2D is a great technology, but using it requires some DirectX knowledge. Sure, DirectX is cool, but lots of developers who build business applications have never used DirectX in their entire life. That's why many of them ask about Direct2D features as a separate Windows Runtime API, ready for nongame developers. Win2D is just that.

Win2D is a C++ and C# Windows Runtime API with GPU-optimized 2-D graphics for Windows 8.x/Windows 10 XAML applications.

The best way to start working with Win2D is to visit the Win2D Team Blog (http://blogs.msdn.com/b/win2d/), where you can find links to the documentation, sample code, source code (Win2D is an open-source project), and so on. However, the best way to learn is to practice, so let's develop an application using this API.

First things first—let's install Win2D. Since Win2D is an open-source project and is not a part of the Universal Windows Platform by default, you will need to use the NuGet package manager to add the latest version of Win2D libraries (**use Win2D.uwp**).

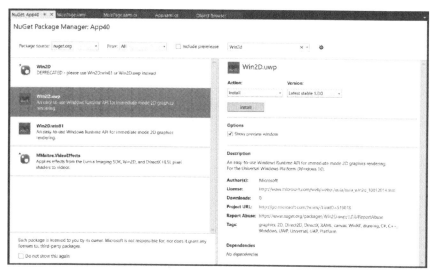

NuGet will add a reference to the **Microsoft.Graphics.Canvas** assembly, which contains all Win2D classes. Open this assembly, and find all namespaces and classes.

452

▲ ▪·▪ Microsoft.Graphics.Canvas
  ▷ { } Microsoft.Graphics.Canvas
  ▷ { } Microsoft.Graphics.Canvas.Brushes
  ▷ { } Microsoft.Graphics.Canvas.Effects
  ▷ { } Microsoft.Graphics.Canvas.Geometry
  ▷ { } Microsoft.Graphics.Canvas.Text
  ▷ { } Microsoft.Graphics.Canvas.UI
  ▲ { } Microsoft.Graphics.Canvas.UI.Xaml
    ▷ ⚙ CanvasAnimatedControl
    ▷ ⚙ CanvasAnimatedDrawEventArgs
    ▷ ⚙ CanvasAnimatedUpdateEventArgs
    ▷ ⚙ CanvasControl
    ▷ ⚙ CanvasDrawEventArgs
    ▷ ⚙ CanvasImageSource
    ▷ ⚙ CanvasSwapChainPanel
    •○ ICanvasAnimatedControl

The **Microsoft.Graphics.Canvas.UI.Xaml** namespace contains XAML controls. You can see that there are two classes based on **UserControl**: **CanvasAnimatedControl** and **CanvasControl**. Additionally, there is the **CanvasSwapChainPanel** class, which is derived from the **Grid** class.

To start working with those controls, you need to add the **Microsoft.Graphics.Canvas.UI.Xaml** namespace to your XAML file:

```
xmlns:canvas="using:Microsoft.Graphics.Canvas.UI.Xaml"
```

Then you can use the controls in your application. We will start with the simplest one, **CanvasControl**.

```
<canvas:CanvasControl
   Draw="CanvasControl_Draw"></canvas:CanvasControl>
```

CanvasControl creates a drawing board, but we also need some mechanisms to implement drawing algorithms. For that, **CanvasControl** has two important events: **Draw** and **CreateResources**. Let's start with the **Draw** event. Look at the code below:

```
int i = 0;
private void CanvasControl_Draw(
   Microsoft.Graphics.Canvas.UI.Xaml.CanvasControl sender,
   Microsoft.Graphics.Canvas.UI.Xaml.CanvasDrawEventArgs
   args)
{
```

```
i++;
CanvasTextFormat format = new CanvasTextFormat()
{
    FontSize = 96, FontWeight = FontWeights.Bold
};
args.DrawingSession.DrawText($"Hello {i}",
    200, 100, Colors.Green, format);
}
```

In this event handler, we used the **DrawText** method to print text. There are many methods inside the **CanvasDrawingSession** class, and they all are relatively easy to use. Note that I injected an integer variable into the output string. Thanks to this variable, we can see when our event handler actually works. Just run the application and try to work with the window for some time. You will see that the **Draw** event fires when Windows has to redraw the application window. Anytime you change window size or position, the counter increments by one, but if you don't touch the window at all, the counter will not update.

The second important event for **CanvasControl** is the **CreateResources** event. The application creates a **CanvasTextFormat** object each time the **Draw** event handler is invoked. Our object is rather simple, but in real-life scenarios, developers create many objects before they can start drawing. Even more, developers should guarantee that all objects are created before the event handler is invoked. There are two ways to initialize those objects: assign a **Draw** event handler dynamically (right after initialization methods) or use a **CreateResources** event handler. The second method is more straightforward and implements some asynchronous programming functionality.

Let's modify our XAML page:

```
<canvas:CanvasControl Draw="CanvasControl_Draw"
    CreateResources="CanvasControl_CreateResources">
</canvas:CanvasControl>
```

And the code behind that:

```
CanvasLinearGradientBrush brush;
CanvasTextFormat format;
private void CanvasControl_CreateResources(
    Microsoft.Graphics.Canvas.UI.Xaml.CanvasControl sender,
    Microsoft.Graphics.Canvas.
        UI.CanvasCreateResourcesEventArgs args)
{
    brush = new CanvasLinearGradientBrush(
        sender, Colors.Red, Colors.Green);
    brush.StartPoint = new Vector2(50, 50);
    brush.EndPoint = new Vector2(300, 300);
    format = new CanvasTextFormat()
    {
        FontSize = 96, FontWeight = FontWeights.Bold
    };
}

int i = 0;
private void CanvasControl_Draw(
    Microsoft.Graphics.Canvas.UI.Xaml.CanvasControl sender,
    Microsoft.Graphics.Canvas.UI.Xaml.
        CanvasDrawEventArgs args)
{
    i++;
    args.DrawingSession.DrawText($"Hello {i}", 50, 50,
        brush, format);
}
```

I just used the CanvasControl_CreateResources method to make a brush for my text.

By using a **CreateResource** event handler, you guarantee that the **Draw** event will not be fired before the event handler is completed.

App40   —   □   ✕

Hello 47

In the previous example, we used a synchronous event handler for the **CreateResource** method, but even for simple image-loading actions, you need to call asynchronous APIs. If you are an advanced C# developer, you may think of adding the keyword **async** before the event handler signature. This approach will not work for a **CreateResources** event handler. Instead of the keyword **async**, you should use the following:

```
CanvasImageBrush brush;
CanvasTextFormat format;
private void CanvasControl_CreateResources(
    Microsoft.Graphics.Canvas.UI.Xaml.CanvasControl sender,
    Microsoft.Graphics.Canvas.UI.
      CanvasCreateResourcesEventArgs args)
{
    args.TrackAsyncAction(
        CreateResources(sender).AsAsyncAction());
}

async Task CreateResources(
    Microsoft.Graphics.Canvas.UI.Xaml.CanvasControl sender)
{
    brush = new CanvasImageBrush(sender);
    brush.Image= await CanvasBitmap.LoadAsync(
      sender, "Assets/drone.jpg");

    format = new CanvasTextFormat()
```

```
    { FontSize = 96, FontWeight = FontWeights.Bold };
}

int i = 0;
private void CanvasControl_Draw(
    Microsoft.Graphics.Canvas.UI.Xaml.CanvasControl sender,
    Microsoft.Graphics.Canvas.UI.Xaml.
        CanvasDrawEventArgs args)
{
    i++;
    args.DrawingSession.DrawText($"Hello {i}", 50, 50,
        brush, format);
}
```

We used a parameter of the event handler to call the **TrackAsyncAction** method, and this method can get the **async** method as an argument.

You can draw static content with **CanvasControl**, and for many scenarios it works fine. For example, you can use this control to apply visual effects to images; you can create graphs or high-performance text-rendering applications. But you cannot use **CanvasControl** for developing simple 2-D games or similar applications that require dynamic content. For those, Win2D provides another control: **CanvasAnimatedControl**.

We can start with the same code, with slight modifications:

```
<canvas:CanvasAnimatedControl
    Draw="CanvasAnimatedControl_Draw"
    CreateResources="CanvasAnimatedControl_CreateResources">
</canvas:CanvasAnimatedControl>
```

```
CanvasImageBrush brush;
CanvasTextFormat format;
async Task CreateResources(
    Microsoft.Graphics.Canvas.UI.Xaml.CanvasAnimatedControl
        sender)
{
    brush = new CanvasImageBrush(sender);
    brush.Image= await CanvasBitmap.LoadAsync(
        sender, "Assets/drone.jpg");

    format = new CanvasTextFormat()
    { FontSize = 96, FontWeight = FontWeights.Bold };
}
```

```
int i = 0;
private void CanvasAnimatedControl_Draw(
   Microsoft.Graphics.Canvas.UI.Xaml.ICanvasAnimatedControl
      sender, Microsoft.Graphics.Canvas.UI.Xaml.
      CanvasAnimatedDrawEventArgs args)
{
   i++;
   args.DrawingSession.DrawText($"Hello {i}", 50, 50,
      brush, format);
}

private void CanvasAnimatedControl_CreateResources(
   Microsoft.Graphics.Canvas.UI.Xaml.CanvasAnimatedControl
      sender, Microsoft.Graphics.Canvas.UI.
      CanvasCreateResourcesEventArgs args)
{
   args.TrackAsyncAction(
      CreateResources(sender).AsAsyncAction());
}
```

You can see the same text, but the counter now will increase a lot faster compared to the previous version (every 16.6 milliseconds, or sixty times per second). **CanvasAnimatedControl** is better to create a large number of dynamic objects that are flying, firing, jumping, and so on. Of course, it's not enough to have just the **Draw** method, because in real games, you need to guarantee timing and have the same speed on all devices. Thus, a game loop is more complicated than a simple Draw method. But developers of Win2D thought of that and provided more events and useful properties in the **CanvasAnimatedControl** class.

Let's review those properties and events by slightly modifying the previous **Draw** event handler:

```
private void CanvasAnimatedControl_Draw(
   Microsoft.Graphics.Canvas.UI.Xaml.
      ICanvasAnimatedControl sender,
   Microsoft.Graphics.Canvas.UI.Xaml.
      CanvasAnimatedDrawEventArgs args)
{
   i++;
   args.DrawingSession.DrawText($"Hello {i}", 50, 50,
      brush, format);
   sender.Paused = true;
}
```

458

We now used the **Paused** property to pause our game loop. If you don't touch the application, the counter will remain unchanged, but once you resize the window, the counter will increment very fast. It happens because in pause mode, the **Draw** method is called when Windows needs to redraw the window. It is more effective to use a **Draw** event handler only for drawing. If you need to change data in the game loop, then it is better to use an **Update** event. The **Update** event handler will be called before the **Draw** method, and in the case of pause, the **Update** event handler will be frozen.

```
private void CanvasAnimatedControl_Update(
    Microsoft.Graphics.Canvas.UI.Xaml.
        ICanvasAnimatedControl sender,
    Microsoft.Graphics.Canvas.UI.Xaml.
        CanvasAnimatedUpdateEventArgs args)
{
    i++;
}
```

In general, the **Draw** and **Update** event handlers should be called every 16.6 milliseconds, but if you have a slow device and the running time frame is greater, an **Update** call may be passed. So you can see several **Draw** calls before an **Update** call. It provides for the same speed of the game on all devices but can create problems with the drawing operations. It may not happen too often, but in some cases you can decrease the elapsed time for each step (for example, thirty frames per second). You can easily do it using the **TargetElapsedTime** property.

Additionally, you can use events like **GameLoopStarting** and **GameLoopStopped**. These events fire before and after the game loop and can be used for scene initialization and for destroying all objects from memory respectively.

Note that all event handlers fire in a separate gaming loop. So any actions there will not block the interface thread. Developers should think about how to pass the data to the gaming thread from the interface thread, and the best way is to call the RunOnGameLoopThreadAsync method from the interface thread:

```
await myCanvas.RunOnGameLoopThreadAsync(()=>
    {/*call something here*/});
```

The last control in the **Microsoft.Graphics.Canvas.UI.Xaml** namespace is **CanvasSwapChainPanel**. If you know something about game development, you should have heard about swap chains. The main idea is to have two or more buffers (pages) for your game. The first page you would use for presenting an updated scene on the screen while updating the second one behind the scene. You should not use the **CanvasSwapChainPanel** class or **CanvasSwapChain** with **CanvasAnimatedControl**, because the latter uses swap chains internally. But if you want to implement your own **CanvasAnimatedControl** or a similar control, you can use both classes.

```
var swapChain = new CanvasSwapChain(
    device, width, height, dpi);
swapChainPanel.SwapChain = swapChain;
//draw
swapChain.Present();
```

By now we have some knowledge about drawing objects and the differences between the controls. It is a perfect time to talk about other useful classes, and I am going to start with image effects.

Image effects is the fastest-growing category in Win2D: just several days ago Microsoft team added ten more effects and some classes to create our own custom effects. In any case, the Win2D API already contains over fifty effects, and you definitely can find some useful filters there. Here is an example of applying two effects to the same image:

```
GrayscaleEffect effect;
GaussianBlurEffect blurEffect;
async Task CreateResources(
    CanvasControl sender)
{
    effect = new GrayscaleEffect();
    var bitmap=await CanvasBitmap.LoadAsync(
        sender, "Assets/drone.jpg");
    effect.Source = bitmap;

    blurEffect = new GaussianBlurEffect();
    blurEffect.BlurAmount = 5;
    blurEffect.Source = effect;
}

private void myCanvas_Draw(CanvasControl sender,
    CanvasDrawEventArgs args)
{
    args.DrawingSession.DrawImage(blurEffect);
}

private void myCanvas_CreateResources(CanvasControl sender,
    CanvasCreateResourcesEventArgs args)
```

```
{
    args.TrackAsyncAction(
        CreateResources(sender).AsAsyncAction());
}
```

In this example I used the blur and grayscale filters inside of the **CreateResources** event handler.

If you need to use the same effect for the same image, you can simply apply this effect in advance and reuse it later. But in many cases you will need to build more-complex objects that should contain not just the effect but some other drawing. For that you can use the **CanvasCommandList** class to prepare and preserve your object for future use. Let's change the example above:

```
GrayscaleEffect effect;
GaussianBlurEffect blurEffect;
CanvasCommandList cl;
async Task CreateResources(CanvasControl sender)
{
    cl = new CanvasCommandList(sender);
    using (CanvasDrawingSession clds =
        cl.CreateDrawingSession())
    {
        effect = new GrayscaleEffect();
        var bitmap = await CanvasBitmap.LoadAsync(
            sender, "Assets/drone.jpg");
        effect.Source = bitmap;

        blurEffect = new GaussianBlurEffect();
        blurEffect.BlurAmount = 5;
```

```
        blurEffect.Source = effect;

        clds.DrawImage(blurEffect);
    }
}

private void myCanvas_Draw(CanvasControl sender,
    CanvasDrawEventArgs args)
{
    args.DrawingSession.DrawImage(cl);
}

private void myCanvas_CreateResources(CanvasControl sender,
    CanvasCreateResourcesEventArgs args)
{
    args.TrackAsyncAction(
        CreateResources(sender).AsAsyncAction());
}
```

In this example we created our own **CanvasDrawingSession** and used it to draw objects and apply filters. Immediately after that, we destroyed **CanvasDrawingSession** and preserved **CanvasCommandList** for future use (making a global reference to it). With this approach you can create all complex objects in advance and later draw them as images.

When we discussed image effects, I did not mention geometry and text, but you can apply effects to these entities as well. You will need the **CanvasRenderTarget** class to convert vector data to pixels:

```
private void myCanvas_Draw(CanvasControl sender,
    CanvasDrawEventArgs args)
{
    var myBitmap = new CanvasRenderTarget(sender,
        300, 300);
    using (var ds = myBitmap.CreateDrawingSession())
    {
        ds.DrawText("Hello", 0, 0, Colors.Green,
            new CanvasTextFormat()
            {FontSize=96, FontWeight=FontWeights.Bold });
    }

    var blur = new GaussianBlurEffect
    {
        BlurAmount = 10,
        Source = myBitmap
```

```
    };
    args.DrawingSession.DrawImage(blur);
}
```

Running this code, you will see the following window:

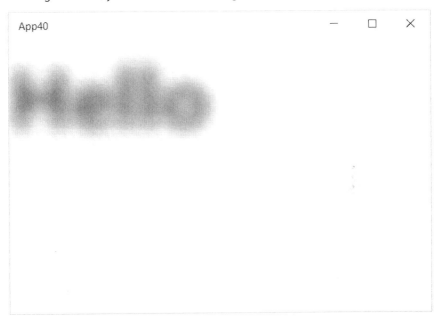

Do you think this is enough for a first look at Win2D? I think so too. I have not covered a lot of classes that work outside XAML or allow you to work with images pixel by pixel, but I hope they will be easy to understand using Win2D documentation.

This page intentionally left blank

Chapter 32

Composition API

When you are working with XAML user controls, you do everything in the Framework layer. In the case of modern applications for Windows 10, it is a Universal Windows Platform layer. But before sending all data to the graphic-device layer to display the content pixel by pixel, the operating system needs to build a Visual layer. The Visual layer is responsible for rendering, executing animations, layering of all components, and so on. When I say "the operating system needs to build," I mean that there is a special object, which we can call a compositor, that allows the application to get all the different components and compose them in the Visual layer.

It was not very important previously, because developers didn't have access to the Visual layer. In the case of an XAML application, you could work with XAML controls only, but if you needed something special, you could work with DirectX directly. But in the Universal Windows Platform, the first preview version of the Composition API was published, and thanks to the Composition API, you can get access to the Visual layer.

Note that the Composition API is in preview mode only. Right now you cannot use it to publish applications to the Store. First of all, Microsoft developers want to get feedback about this API. But if you have already started to think about absolutely new, rich user controls, you definitely should look at the Composition API.

With the help of the Composition API, you can create UWP applications that don't contain XAML at all. But it's not very interesting in the context of this book, so I will show you how to use Composition API together with XAML user controls.

Since the API is in preview, it requires additional capabilities to execute an event on the developer's computer. So to start working with the Composition API, you need to make some changes in the manifest file. Add the following namespace to the root element of the manifest (Package):

```
xmlns:rescap="http://schemas.microsoft.com/appx/manifest/
    foundation/windows10/restrictedcapabilities"
```

Restricted capabilities are not declared in standard schemas, so this step is important. Once you add the namespace, you can add capabilities that grant access to the Composition API:

```
<Capabilities>
  <Capability Name="internetClient" />
  <rescap:Capability Name="previewUiComposition"/>
</Capabilities>
```

Let's start working with the most common classes. All Composition API classes can be found in the **Windows.UI.Composition** namespace, and you don't have to add any special packages to use them, because the Composition API is included in the core of the Universal Windows Platform. That's why all the code will run fine on any device with Windows 10, including phones.

Looking at the **Windows.UI.Composition** namespace, you can find lots of classes. But, as I mentioned earlier, it should be a compositor and classes that represent objects in the Visual layer as well as the layer itself. It's easy to find these classes. The first one is the **Compositor** class, which allows you to create different objects and has a reference to the graphic device. The base class for different visual objects is **Visual**, which contains lots of properties such as **Opacity, Scale, RotationAngle**, and so on. All these properties allow you to define the position of the visual object and different types of transformations. But you cannot create an object of the **Visual** class directly. It's just a base class that defines common properties but doesn't represent any objects itself. So let's see whether there are any classes that are inherited from **Visual**:

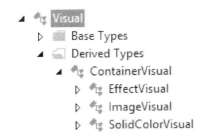

The next class is **ContainerVisual**, and you can create an object of this class using methods in **Compositor**. In fact, **ContainerVisual** is a class that can combine any other visual objects. This class itself doesn't contain anything new except the **Children** property, which points to a collection. Using this property, you can add any number of visuals and combine them together. So to start doing anything, we need to find a way to get a reference to this object.

Finally, **ContainerVisual** has three derived classes: **EffectVisual, ImageVisual**, and **SolidColorVisual**. All these classes represent the simplest visual objects. Once we have a reference to **ContainerVisual**, we can create any of these objects and add them to the collection.

Using the **ElementCompositionPreview** class, we can get **ContainerVisual** for any user control. It's obvious, since each XAML element is represented by a **Visual** object in the Visual layer, that the best way to integrate the Composition

API and XAML is to use the existing **Visual** object.

Therefore, if you have a **Grid** on your page called myGrid, you can get a reference to **ContainerVisual** using the following code:

```
visual = ElementCompositionPreview.
   GetContainerVisual(myGrid) as ContainerVisual;
```

And because **ContainerVisual** has a reference to **Compositor**, it's easy to start doing something. Look at the following code:

```
visual = ElementCompositionPreview.
   GetContainerVisual(myGrid) as ContainerVisual;
comp = visual.Compositor;

SolidColorVisual background =
   comp.CreateSolidColorVisual();
background.Size = new System.Numerics.Vector2(100, 100);
background.Color = Colors.Red;
visual.Children.InsertAtBottom(background);
```

In this code we created an object of **SolidColorVisual** and added it to **ContainerVisual**, which is related to the myGrid object. Running this code, you can see a red rectangle that is 100 by 100 pixels.

Let's try to create an image visual. This is not very hard either, but you need to use more properties to tune the image. The code is below:

```
visual = ElementCompositionPreview.
   GetContainerVisual(myGrid) as ContainerVisual;
comp = visual.Compositor;

CompositionImage profilePic =
   comp.DefaultGraphicsDevice.CreateImageFromUri(
     new Uri("ms-appx:///Assets/drone.jpg"));

ImageVisual profilePicVisual = comp.CreateImageVisual();
profilePicVisual.Image = profilePic;
profilePicVisual.Stretch =
   CompositionStretch.UniformToFill;
profilePicVisual.Size =
   new System.Numerics.Vector2(100,100);
profilePicVisual.Offset =
   new System.Numerics.Vector3(100,100,0);

visual.Children.InsertAtTop(profilePicVisual);
```

Because an image can be a source for different tasks, **ImageVisual** doesn't contain the image itself. It contains just properties related to the image (how to present it) and a reference to **CompositionImage** (**ICompositionSurface**), which is the image source. To create **CompositionImage**, we used the reference to the default graphic device and **CreateImage** from the Uri method.

Note that we used the **InsertAtTop** method, but in the previous example we used **InsertAtBottom**. In our case it's not important which method to use, but by using different methods, you can place a new visual element exactly where you need inside the collection.

OK. Now we know how to add images and color rectangles to the visual container, but the power of the Composition API is in its effect and animation systems. Let's discuss the effect system.

We already know that to add some effects, we can use the **EffectVisual** class and create objects of this class using **Compositor**. But **EffectVisual** is just a representation of a visual element; it doesn't contain any methods that allow you to create and apply any effects. Instead, it contains an **Effect** reference, and you need to prepare an effect in advance and apply it using this reference. So let's look at the **Compositor** class and find out how to create the effect itself. Because any effect requires a description, there is no sense in creating all effects from scratch, especially if you want to apply the same effect to several elements. That's why the **Compositor** class contains a method that allows you to create a factory instead of a particular effect, and with the help of the factory, you can reproduce the effect as many times as you want.

Therefore, the process is very conventional: create a factory based on a description, use the factory to make a **CompositionEffect** object, and assign this object to the **Effect** property of **EffectVisual**. But there is a problem: where to get an effect description. The Composition API doesn't provide its own effect description, because other subsystems of UWP have already implemented lots of effects. The Composition API uses Win2D to utilize effect descriptions from there. At the end of June 2015, the Composition API supported the following effects: ArithmeticComposite, Blend, Saturation, and Composite. But you need to check the latest version of the API to see whether more effects are supported. Nonetheless, even these four effects have lots of parameters that allow you to implement a huge number of combinations.

So to apply an effect, you need to use the NuGet package manager and install the Win2D.UWP package. In the following example, I use the Saturation effect.

Note how this code uses **CompositionEffectSourceParameter** to create a parameter that you can fill in right after the factory generates a new **CompositionEffect** object.

```
visual = ElementCompositionPreview.
   GetContainerVisual(myGrid) as ContainerVisual;
comp = visual.Compositor;

var rectangle=comp.CreateSolidColorVisual();
rectangle.Color = Colors.Green;
rectangle.Size= new System.Numerics.Vector2(320, 220);
rectangle.Offset= new System.Numerics.Vector3(90, 90, 0);

visual.Children.InsertAtTop(rectangle);

CompositionImage profilePic =
   comp.DefaultGraphicsDevice.CreateImageFromUri(
      new Uri("ms-appx:///Assets/drone.jpg"));

SaturationEffect saturationEffect = new SaturationEffect();
saturationEffect.Saturation = 0;
saturationEffect.Source = new
CompositionEffectSourceParameter("image");
saturationEffect.Name = "saturationW2D";

CompositionEffectFactory effectFactory =
comp.CreateEffectFactory(saturationEffect);

CompositionEffect eff = effectFactory.CreateEffect();
eff.SetSourceParameter("image", profilePic);

EffectVisual saturationVisual = comp.CreateEffectVisual();
saturationVisual.Effect = eff;
saturationVisual.Size =
   new System.Numerics.Vector2(300, 200);
saturationVisual.Offset =
   new System.Numerics.Vector3(10, 10, 0);
rectangle.Children.InsertAtBottom(saturationVisual);
```

In this example I used a **SolidColorVisual** object as a container for **EffectVisual** to create a border and be able to apply animations to the border and image at the same time. Upon running this code, you can see a black-and-white image on the screen.

Finally, let's discuss the animation system that is supported by the Composition API.

Composition API supports two animation types: **KeyFrameAnimation** and **ExpressionAnimation**, but the first one is the base class for four more significant classes that work with scalar values and vectors:

- CompositionAnimation
  - Base Types
  - Derived Types
    - ExpressionAnimation
    - KeyFrameAnimation
      - ScalarKeyFrameAnimation
      - Vector2KeyFrameAnimation
      - Vector3KeyFrameAnimation
      - Vector4KeyFrameAnimation

Each of these types can be created with the help of the **Compositor** object. We already used standard XAML key-frame animations, but expression animation is more interesting, and it is something new. Let's start with a simple key-frame animation. In the code below, you can see how to animate the angle of a visual object:

```
var keyframe = comp.CreateScalarKeyFrameAnimation();

keyframe.InsertKeyFrame(1.0f, angle);
keyframe.Duration = TimeSpan.FromMilliseconds(1000);

animator=visual.ConnectAnimation(
    "RotationAngle", keyframe);
animator.Start();
```

In this code we created a simple **KeyFrameAnimation** object and applied it to an object of the **Visual** class using the **ConnectAnimation** method, which returns **CompositionPropertyAnimator**. The latter starts the animation and assigns its own event handler, which will run once the animation is finished.

Look at the similar code, which uses an expression key frame instead of the standard one:

```
var keyframe = comp.CreateScalarKeyFrameAnimation();

keyframe.InsertExpressionKeyFrame(1.0f,
    "visualObj.RotationAngle+initial");
keyframe.Duration = TimeSpan.FromMilliseconds(2000);
keyframe.SetReferenceParameter("visualObj", rectangle);
keyframe.SetScalarParameter("initial", 1.0f);

animator=visual.ConnectAnimation(
    "RotationAngle", keyframe);
animator.Start();
```

After running this code, you can see that the animator uses an up-to-date **RotationAngle** all the time. So the rectangle will keep rotating for two seconds. Of course, you can create more-complex expressions based on different objects.

Below I want to provide the full version of the code that rotates our image in an infinite loop:

```
Compositor comp;
ContainerVisual visual;
SolidColorVisual rectangle;
CompositionPropertyAnimator animator;
float angle = 1;

protected override void OnNavigatedTo(
```

```
    NavigationEventArgs e)
{

    visual = ElementCompositionPreview.GetContainerVisual(
        myGrid)
        as ContainerVisual;
    comp = visual.Compositor;

    rectangle = comp.CreateSolidColorVisual();
    rectangle.Color = Colors.Green;
    rectangle.Size = new System.Numerics.Vector2(320, 220);
    rectangle.Offset = new System.Numerics.Vector3(
        190, 190, 0);
    rectangle.RotationAngle = 45;

    visual.Children.InsertAtTop(rectangle);

    CompositionImage profilePic =
        comp.DefaultGraphicsDevice.CreateImageFromUri(
            new Uri("ms-appx:///Assets/drone.jpg"));

    SaturationEffect saturationEffect =
        new SaturationEffect();
    saturationEffect.Saturation = 0;
    saturationEffect.Source =
        new CompositionEffectSourceParameter("image");
    saturationEffect.Name = "saturationW2D";

    CompositionEffectFactory effectFactory =
        comp.CreateEffectFactory(saturationEffect);

    CompositionEffect factory =
        effectFactory.CreateEffect();
    factory.SetSourceParameter("image", profilePic);

    EffectVisual saturationVisual =
        comp.CreateEffectVisual();
    saturationVisual.Effect = factory;
    saturationVisual.Size =
        new System.Numerics.Vector2(300, 200);
    saturationVisual.Offset =
        new System.Numerics.Vector3(10, 10, 0);
    rectangle.Children.InsertAtBottom(saturationVisual);

    ApplyAnimation(rectangle,angle);
```

```
        base.OnNavigatedTo(e);
}


private void ApplyAnimation(
    ContainerVisual visual, float angle)
{

    if (animator!=null)
    {
        animator.Dispose();
        animator = null;
    }

    var keyframe = comp.CreateScalarKeyFrameAnimation();

    keyframe.InsertExpressionKeyFrame(
        1.0f, "visualObj.RotationAngle+initial");
    keyframe.Duration = TimeSpan.FromMilliseconds(4000);
    keyframe.SetReferenceParameter("visualObj", rectangle);
    keyframe.SetScalarParameter("initial", angle);

    animator=visual.ConnectAnimation(
        "RotationAngle", keyframe);
    animator.AnimationEnded += Animator_AnimationEnded;
    animator.Start();
}


private void Animator_AnimationEnded(
    CompositionPropertyAnimator sender,
    AnimationEndedEventArgs args)
{

    sender.AnimationEnded -= Animator_AnimationEnded;
    angle = -angle;
    ApplyAnimation(rectangle, angle);
}
```

In this code we used the **AnimationEnded** event to start the animation in the reverse way. So the rectangle will rotate in opposite directions.

If you want to know more about the Composition API, you can follow the composition team on Twitter at @wincomposition.

Chapter 33

How to Use Blend

Overview to Blend

As a developer, I can create a complex Windows 10 application very fast, but the most important problem is the user experience. From a developer's prospective, I can present data and implement business logic, but I know nothing about the right design and usability. That's why it's so important to engage a designer, who can create a better interface, icons, images, and so on. Thanks to MVVM, you can share your XAML code with the designer as well and concentrate your attention on the C# code while both of you continue to work on the same forms together. But there is a problem: designers don't like Visual Studio. That's why Microsoft supports one more tool that is installed together with Visual Studio—Blend for Visual Studio.

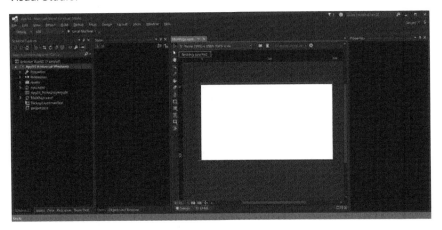

Microsoft Blend is a separate tool that allows you to edit XAML interfaces and can be very useful for designers and developers who want to edit the XAML interface using lots of designer features. Using Microsoft Blend, you can continue to work with the same solution format, and you can even use Blend to create a new project and open it in Visual Studio later. You have probably already noticed that by visiting the **View** menu in Visual Studio, you can find the **Design in Blend** menu item, while by visiting the **View** menu in Blend, you can find the **Edit in Visual Studio** menu item. So you can easily switch the context between the two editors. But Microsoft Blend is powerful enough to allow you to run and debug your applications directly in Blend.

In any case, the best scenarios for Blend are

- generating XAML pages using graphical primitives and controls,

- creating animations and transformations,

- working with templates, and

- creating adaptive triggers.

When creating a new project in Blend, you will discover that Blend supports not just UWP projects but Silverlight, WPF, and Windows 8.x/Windows Phone 8.x projects. So anything where XAML is used can be created in Blend, and the UI can be edited there, too.

Microsoft Blend has lots of features, and I want to show several of them. Let's see how to edit an animation, work with templates, and create state triggers in Blend. These tasks are very important, and usually it's not easy to do all these things using Visual Studio, but it's easy with Blend.

How to Create Animations in Blend

I propose creating an empty interface and placing an ellipse or another element there. Let's animate this element in Blend.

To create animations in Visual Studio, you need to create a Storyboard object and place all needed animations there along with passing lots of parameters and editing the XAML directly. Using Blend, we will do all these things in design mode. Just open the **Objects and Timeline** window and create a new Storyboard using the menu:

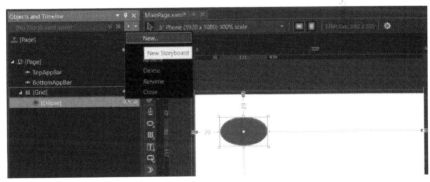

Visual Studio will ask you to provide a name for the storyboard:

477

And you will see that Blend switches the storyboard to record mode:

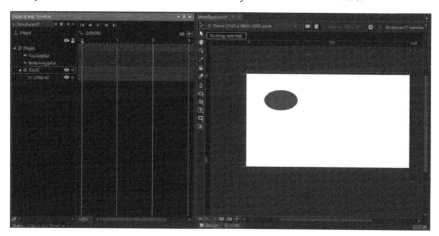

In this mode you can select any interface elements and apply animations to them one by one using drag and drop. Just select any control and property, move the timeline pointer several seconds forward, and change the property. You can change the position, color, or anything that you can animate:

Blend will create animations, and you can select them to edit easing functions or other parameters. Play the final storyboard by clicking the Play button, and see the result.

If you play with the Objects and Timeline window for some time, you will find that this feature is very powerful, and it's easy to use even if you don't design interfaces in Blend—just copy the created animations to the right place in your project.

States and State Triggers and Blend

To see the new features, just create a new project in Blend and select **MainPage.xaml** in **Solution Explorer**. Once you do this, the **Objects and Timeline** window will show the structure of the page. Usually, when we create visual states, we work with a main container such as Grid. So to create several visual states, it's better to select the root **Grid** element in the **Object and Timeline** and **States** windows to start editing visual states.

Blend allows you to edit visual states without coding at all. With the help of the States window, you can create as many states as needed, and once you select a state, Blend switches the editor to the **Record** mode (Ctrl+R). In this mode you can change the properties of any user controls, and all these changes will be included in the selected state automatically. So I propose creating just one state using the Add State button in the States window and selecting the main grid to change some properties. For example, you can change **Opacity** and **Visibility** using the **Properties** window.

If you open the XAML document, you can find the following code there:

```
<VisualState x:Name="Normal">
    <VisualState.Setters>
        <Setter Target="grid.(UIElement.Opacity)"
```

```
        Value="0.5"/>
      <Setter Target="grid.(UIElement.Visibility)"
      Value="Collapsed"/>
   </VisualState.Setters>
</VisualState>
```

So you can see that the Blend editor is fully integrated with the new approach that the Universal Windows Platform implements thanks to Setter elements.

If you want to use the old approach or animate your properties from one state to another, you can continue to use the timeline, and Blend will use animation instead of setters.

One more feature of the Universal Windows Platform is state triggers, which allow you to move the interface from one state to another without coding at all. UWP supports just **AdaptiveTrigger**, but you can create your own triggers. Let's see how to use triggers in Blend.

I propose adding a class to the project that will have just one property, but this class should be inherited from **StateTriggerBase**:

```
class MyTrigger: StateTriggerBase
{
    public int State { get; set; }
}
```

Of course, this class doesn't make any sense because it does not have any logic inside, but it's enough to show it in Blend. Just recompile the application because Blend will look at the assemblies.

Let's try to apply the created trigger to one of the states using the States window. Note that this window contains a new button called edit adaptive triggers:

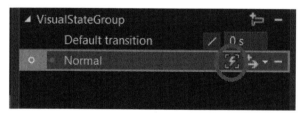

Just click the button for any state, and Blend will show a dialog, which allows you to select available triggers for the project:

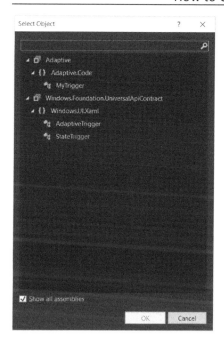

Just select our trigger, and Blend will allow you to initialize all public properties (we have just one):

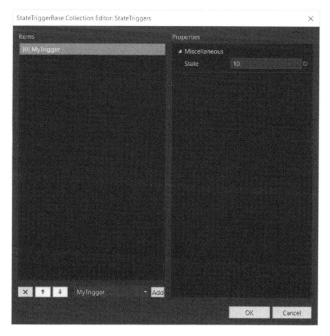

Enter any value and click OK. Blend will generate the following code:

```
<VisualState.StateTriggers>
    <Code:MyTrigger State="10"/>
</VisualState.StateTriggers>
```

Therefore, if you want to create a real adaptive interface and need to create lots of states and use many triggers, Microsoft Blend is the best tool for that.

Chapter 34

Internet of Things

Overview of Microboards

The Internet of Things is a very hot topic today. Everybody wants to create his or her own device, connect it to the Internet, and implement his or her own software to enable new scenarios that are possible thanks to the availability of microcontrollers. You can find microcontrollers inside TV sets, fridges, and media players, and they help us to build automation systems and create new wearable devices.

It's really hard to give an overview of microcontrollers because you can find lots of them on the market. And if you want to create your own device, you can invest fifteen dollars or a little bit more and create your own robot, drone, or home automation system.

Arduino

This is a very popular open-source prototyping platform that is based on an ATMega chip and supports all common needs such as digital input, analog input, I2C, SPI, and other important things. Arduino boards are pretty cheap. You can buy an Arduino Uno board for thirty to thirty-five dollars, or you can create your own board for fifteen dollars. But Arduino is not just a board that you can find on http://arduino.cc but an IDE to build software for Arduino, and it's a great community.

By visiting the Arduino website, you can download and install Arduino IDE to Windows, Mac, or Linux, and if you open the community forums, you can find an answer to any question. Using Arduino, you can easily understand how to connect external sensors and components to the board and how to start developing something around the IoT.

Let's get an overview of the most important parts of the board for developers. We will discuss Arduino Uno only because it's easy to use without any additional components.

Arduino Uno contains two sets of pins, which allow us to control inputs and outputs. The first set of pins are digital pins. We can use this set to send outputs and receive inputs. You can use these pins for outputs in on/off mode. So the output voltage may be 0 V or 5 V.

We have thirteen pins for digital input/output. But you can see that some of these pins have a special mark: ~. This shows that we may use these pins to send signals (outputs) in pulse mode. It allows us to emulate a rheostat effect, when we have a way to send just *n* percent of current per unit of time. You can use this effect to regulate the brightness of LEDs or the temperature in your apartment, and so on. Usually this set of pins are called PWM (pulse-width modulation) pins.

The second set of pins (A0–A5) is used for input only. But in this case it should be analog input, such as data from thermometers, potentiometers, variable resistors, and so on.

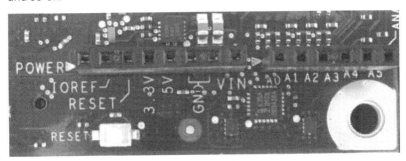

This set of pins is important when we receive data that describes more than two states. You can use these pins in more advanced projects.

Finally, you can find some more pins, such as POWER, 5V, GND, and so on. Some of these pins are used to control the board, some pins (such as 5V and VIN) are used as a source of current, and GND pins are used for the ground.

So now we have some knowledge about the pins, and it's time to look at the development tools for Arduino.

To install the Arduino IDE, you simply need to visit https://www.arduino.cc/en/Main/ Software and download the installer. Right after Arduino tools are installed, you can connect your Arduino Uno board to your computer using USB and run the Arduino IDE.

If everything is OK, your Arduino board will be detected, and you can use the Tools menu item to set up the right COM post and board type. It should be initialized to the right value by default, but in case of any problems, you can do it manually.

The simplest way to test your Arduino board is to run a Blink sketch. To do so, you need to go to the File→Examples→Basic menu items and select Blink. Arduino IDE will open ready-to-deploy code that will use digital pin 13 to send on/off signals:

Of course, you don't have anything connected to your digital pin 13, but this pin is linked to the board LED. So if you run this example, you can find a blinking LED on the board.

Look at the **setup** and **loop** functions in our code. There is just one call from the **setup** function—the pinMode method, which informs our board that we will work with pin number 13 in output mode. The **loop** method contains four lines of code, but the most important call there is the **digitalWrite** call. This function allows two parameters, number of pin and state. The LOW state shows that we should have a voltage of 0 V, and HIGH 5 V.

Let's use the existing code in the template but try to use an external LED. To do this, we need the following components:

- LED: Usually an LED consumes voltage around 1.7 V.

- Resistor: To resist our voltage, we need a 330 Ω resistor.

- Breadboard: Usually you will use this stuff to create a prototype of your final board, and it's good for testing and investigations. You can buy this one separately or find it in many kits.

- Two wires.

Finally, I created this:

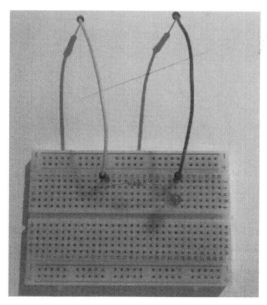

To understand how it works, you need some information about the breadboard. You can see that our breadboard has several lines that are marked by numbers (from 1 to 30). The pins in each of these lines are connected. I used a yellow wire to connect the pin on my board to the pin in line 12 on my breadboard. So when I switch my digital pin to HIGH, the current will be in line 12. The resistor connects lines 12 and 21. It's time to connect our LED—put the longer lead (anode) to the same line (21) and put the shorter lead (cathode) to line 23. Connect the blue wire with the same line (23).

Run our code once again, and you will see the external LED blinking.

Arduino and Visual Studio

If you like Visual Studio as much as I do, you can use it for Arduino development as well. To do so, visit http://www.visualmicro.com/ and download the Visual Micro plug-in for Visual Studio.

This plug-in exists in two versions: free and paid. The paid version promises a better debugger and many additional features. But if you just started working with Arduino, you can use the free version, which extends Visual Studio and supports IntelliSense, basic debugging, settings, samples, and so on. Of course, it's not perfect, but I was excited to use many cool features for free. And if you are going to develop lots of Arduino applications, you can spend twenty-nine dollars and get all the paid features on your development machine.

So to install the plug-in, you need to install the Arduino IDE first. Visual Micro supports Arduino 1.6.3 at this time, but it's changing quickly, so check the latest version installation guide to find the right Arduino IDE version. Once you install the Arduino IDE, you can install the Visual Micro plug-in for Visual Studio, but check the version of your Visual Studio because Visual Micro doesn't support Express versions, though you may use the Community Edition, which is free as well.

When you launch Visual Studio for the first time after installation of the plug-in, you will see a window that asks to set up an Arduino IDE directory and prompts you to buy the plug-in. The Arduino IDE directory is needed to have the same storage place for your sketches.

I don't know why, but to start a new project in Visual Studio, you need to select not **New→Project** but **New→Sketch Project**. It took me thirty seconds to find where I could create a project, but it's not a very big problem.

So once you create a project, you are ready to start coding. Visual Studio has several combo boxes that allow you to select the Arduino SDK version, the type of your boards, and the port that you are using to connect to your board. Additionally, there is an access to examples, a property window, and many other tools that you can find in the Tools→Visual Micro menu item.

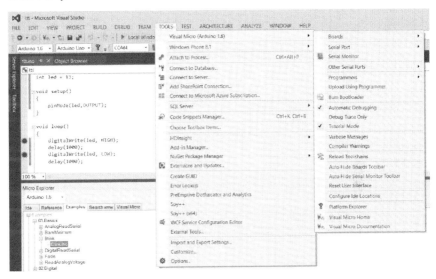

I found that Visual Micro can be very useful and really help me to develop using my favorite tool. And if you are developing not just Arduino code but some services and external applications, you can do this inside the single solution.

Netduino

The next microboard is Netduino. You can find several models at http://www.netduino.com/hardware/. I would recommend Netduino 3 with Wi-Fi, which is the most advanced board there.

In any case, all Netduino boards are based on the .NET Micro Framework, which is an open-source platform developed for low-memory devices with limited amount of resources. In fact, the .NET Micro Framework can be run on devices with sixty-four kilobytes of memory, which is very important for cheap and really small devices. The .NET Micro Framework has a very interesting story. It was probably announced too early, about nine years ago, and since that time the .NET Micro Framework has supported many different microcontrollers. Today, the most popular microcontrollers are Netduino and Gadgeteer. And Netduino is Arduino compatible. It's very important right now because it's easy to find many different things for Arduino.

In my case I have a Netduino Plus 2 board and develop some small projects there. And of course, if you have a board, you will need to install some stuff to your computer such as the .NET Micro Framework SDK, tools for Visual Studio, and a board-specific SDK. In the case of Netduino Plus 2, I would recommend the following steps:

- Update Netduino firmware—when I bought the board, I found that it had a version of .NET MF older than 4.3. But if you have an older version of firmware on your board, you will not be able to use the latest version of the SDKs. You can find information on how to update the firmware in the Arduino forum.

- Install the .NET Micro Framework SDKs and tools for Visual Studio.

- Install the Netduino SDK.

In any case, before you download something, check for the latest versions of the SDKs and firmware.

Once you install all needed software, you can use a USB-to-micro-USB cable to connect the board to the PC. You can use this cable to provide power to the Netduino board. Using Visual Studio, you can create an application based on special templates for Netduino boards, and you can start using C# and many classes from the .NET Micro Framework and Arduino. Visual Studio supports not just deployment of applications to Netduino but debugging and IntelliSense as well. So your developer experience should feel like the usual Windows platform experience. It's really cool.

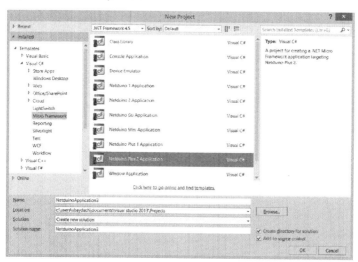

Raspberry Pi 2

The rest of the discussion in this chapter will be around the Raspberry Pi 2 board.

Raspberry Pi 2 is not an Arduino-compatible board; it's completely different. Usually you will use Arduino and Netduino for basic projects or for basic components of more-complex projects because these boards are very limited compared to real computers. But Raspberry Pi 2 contains all common attributes of real computers: GPU, HDMI port, audio support, four USB ports, network socket, powerful processor, and so on. But what is more important, you can install Windows 10 on Raspberry.

So in the next sections, we will see how to use our knowledge of the Universal Windows Platform to build Windows 10 applications on Raspberry.

How to Create Schemas

At the end of this section, I would recommend using a free, open-source application called Fritzing. If you create some projects, you will need a tool that allows you to create schemas, and you can do this with Fritzing.

This application was developed by University of Applied Sciences in Potsdam, Germany. You can download the tool here: http://fritzing.org. It contains links to different versions of operating systems such as Windows, Linux, and OS X.

It's easy to identify the required components, put them on a breadboard, and understand whether your circuit is completed. Just drag and drop the needed components from the parts section to the breadboard, and connect them to make a route.

I tried to create a schema for the previous example, and you can see the result below:

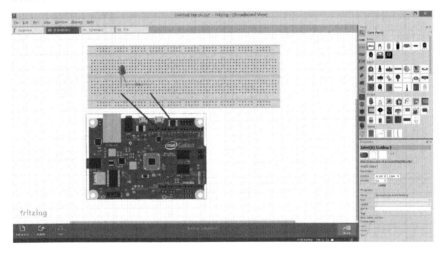

If you are not able to find some components here, you can search on the Internet.

Windows 10 IoT Core

As we mentioned in chapter 1, Microsoft supports different SKUs for Windows. One of these SKUs is Windows IoT Core, which you can install on your IoT devices for free.

To start, you can visit https://dev.windows.com/en-US/iot and download the build and setup instructions there. You can see that all installation files are open to the public, and you simply need to click the link to start downloading the image.

Before installing Windows 10 on Raspberry, note the following:

- You need to use microSD card level 10. I overlooked that requirement and was quite upset when found that my Raspberry was not even trying to start. When I checked manual once again, I checked my SD and found that it has level 4! So I changed it, and everything started working fine.

- The first start requires a lot of time to finish everything. So you need to be patient.

- You need to connect your Raspberry to a local network to deploy applications there from your Windows 10 machine. So prepare the network cable and router or use a Wi-Fi adapter.

- If everything is OK, you will see a Raspberry image and important information such as device name and IP address on the screen. So your device is ready, and it's time to establish a connection between your PC and Raspberry. To do this, you can visit http://ms-iot.github.io/content/en-US/win10/samples/PowerShell.htm to set up a connection using PowerShell.

Once you connect to your Raspberry, you can change its password and device name, run some configuration cmdlets, and so on. Note that Raspberry supports two modes: headed and headless (with and without GUI).

Right after you establish a connection between your PC and Raspberry, you can try to develop something. Thanks to Visual Studio, it's very easy to develop, deploy, and debug solutions on Raspberry. Raspberry runs Remote Debugger by default, so you should not perform any additional configuration.

To start, you need to select a language. You can select between Node.js, Python, and standard languages for universal applications such as C#. Of course, I decided to use C#, but you an easily install Python or Node.js tools from the

Connect site. So to start, you need to create a simple universal application, change the platform to ARM, and select Remote Machine for deploying and debugging.

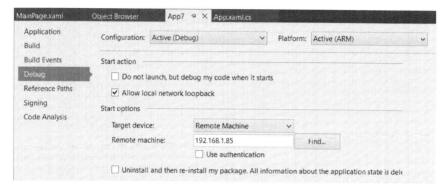

Finally, I developed and deployed my first application for Raspberry.

IoT Extensions

If you have already installed Windows 10 on Raspberry, it's time to discuss how to use pins and I2C. Of course, if you are going to deploy an application that doesn't work with GPIO, you don't have to do anything special—you need to create the same universal application as for desktop or phone using C# or other languages and deploy it using the ARM platform selection directly from Visual Studio. But GPIO is a device-specific feature, and it makes no sense to include it in the common library. So if you are going to use some IoT-specific features, you need to add IoT extension to your project.

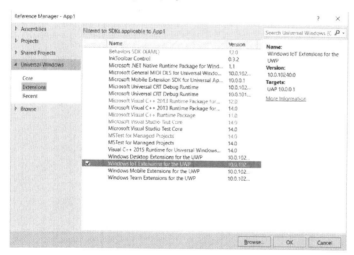

This extension declares just two contracts: Windows.Devices.DevicesLowLevelContract and Windows.System.SystemManagementContract. It's easy to find these declarations if you go to the following folder: C:\Program Files (x86)\Windows Kits\10\Extension SDKs\WindowsIoT\10.0.10240.0 and check SDKManifest.xaml. SystemManagement doesn't contain anything special—just classes that help to shut down the device and change the time zone. But **DevicesLowLevelContract** contains many important classes. Let's look at the Raspberry and see what we can achieve with these classes.

3.3V PWR	1		2	5V PWR
I2C1 SDA	3		4	5V PWR
I2C1 SCL	5		6	GND
Reserved	7		8	Reserved
GND	9		10	Reserved
SPI1 CS0	11		12	GPIO 18
GPIO 27	13		14	GND
GPIO 22	15		16	GPIO 23
3.3V PWR	17		18	GPIO 24
SPI0 MOSI	19		20	GND
SPI0 MISO	21		22	GPIO 25
SPI0 SCLK	23		24	SPI0 CS0
GND	25		26	SPI0 CS1
GPIO 0	27		28	GPIO 1
GPIO 5	29		30	GND
GPIO 6	31		32	GPIO 12
GPIO 13	33		34	GND
SPI1 MISO	35		36	GPIO 16
GPIO 26	37		38	SPI1 MOSI
GND	39		40	SPI1 SCLK

In the case of GPIO, you can use the yellow pins to send signals to sensors or receive data from them. On Raspberry, all pins generate 3.3 V of voltage. Pink pins support SPI protocol, and you can connect up to two devices/sensors (probably three but I never tried this). Finally, blue pins allow you to use an I2C hub, which supports more than a hundred devices/sensors. Of course, GND pins are for ground and have four power pins (two 5 V pins and two 3.3 V pins).

Let's start with GPIO. You can find necessary classes (and enumeration types) in the **Windows.Devices.Gpio** namespace, and they allow developers to control GPIO pins on the board. The first class there is **GpioController**, which allows you to get access to a controller and get a reference to the needed pins. If you are going to use GPIO, you need to start by calling the **GetDefault** method, which returns a reference to the current GPIO controller (if one exists):

```
var controller=GpioController.GetDefault();
```

If you are going to write really universal code, you need to check whether the controller is null. If it is, your device doesn't have a GPIO (desktop, phone, and so on). It's very useful because starting with Windows 10, we have a universal platform, and you can run the same binary anywhere.

Once you have access to a controller, you can try to get references to pins. The **OpenPin** method allows you to get a reference to a pin and lock it exclusively or leave it in shared mode. Of course, this method doesn't help you to set up the pin but just returns a reference to a **GpioPin** object. There is a similar thing for **GpioController**—you need to check whether the returned reference is not null, because other processes can lock the pin for their own purposes.

```
var pin = controller.OpenPin(0);

if (pin == null)
{
        return;
}
```

The **OpenPin** method should get the number of the pin, and you should use the same numbers as in the image above. Finally, if you got access to the pin, you can try to work with it. There are three important methods: **SetDriveMode**, **Read**, and **Write**. With the first one, you can set up the pin as an input or output pin. The **Read** and **Write** methods allow you to send or receive a signal.

More interesting classes are located in the **Windows.Devices.I2C** and **Windows.Devices.SPI** namespaces.

I bought a MPU6050 sensor that provides data from the gyroscope and accelerometer and is very useful for people who would like to build their own drones and helicopters. You can find many different boards in the market

This sensor doesn't require soldering, and it contains a 5V-to-3.3V convertor (the 6050 chip uses 3.3 V), which allows you to use power from ESC or other boards with 5 V power pins.

MPU 6050 uses an I2C hub to communicate. So to get the sensor ready to work, you need to connect the 5V and GND pins on the Raspberry to VCC and GND on the sensor. Additionally, you need to connect the SDA and SCL pins. This sensor doesn't have any LEDs, and it's not easy to understand whether everything is OK. So the simplest way to check whether it works is to start developing something.

You can find all needed classes in the **Windows.Devices.I2c** namespace. The first one is **I2cDevice**. Each device that you connect using the I2C hub should be associated with an object of the **I2cDevice** class, and with this object developers can communicate with the device. The most common methods are **Read** and **Write**, which work with an array of bytes to receive or send data. But in many cases you need to send data to the device to ask something and get a response. To avoid calling two methods, the **I2cDevice** class supports the **WriteRead** method. This method has two parameters as arrays of bytes. The first array contains the data that you are going to send to device and the second one is a buffer for data from the device.

Thanks to **I2cDevice**, it's easy to communicate with devices, but to get a reference to the **I2cDevice** object, you need to accomplish several tasks.

First of all, you need to get a reference to the I2C device on the board (not your sensor but existing I2C pins). Microsoft uses the same approach as for all other devices such as Bluetooth, Wi-Fi, and so on. You need to use a friendly name to create a query string for the device and try to find the device on the board. The **GetdeviceSelector** method of the **I2cDevice** class allows you to create the query string, and you should use an **I2C1**-friendly name there. To find information about the existing device, you should use the FindAllAsync method of the **DeviceInformation** class. This method returns information about the available I2C device, and you can use this information to create the I2cDevice object. In the next step, you need to create a connection string for your sensor. It's easy to do using the I2cConnectionString class by passing the address of the sensor to the constructor of the class. Once you have information about the I2C on your board and a connection string for an external device/sensor, you can create an **I2cDevice** object using the **FromIdAsync** method.

So for my MPU 6050, I created the following code:

```
class MPU6050
{
    //I2C address
    private const byte MPUAddress = 0xD2>>1;

    private I2cDevice mpu5060device;

    public async Task BeginAsync()
    {
        string advanced_query_syntax =
            I2cDevice.GetDeviceSelector("I2C1");
        DeviceInformationCollection dic =
            await DeviceInformation.FindAllAsync(
                advanced_query_syntax);
        string deviceId = dic[0].Id;

        I2cConnectionSettings mpu_connection =
            new I2cConnectionSettings(MPUAddress);
        mpu_connection.BusSpeed = I2cBusSpeed.FastMode;
        mpu_connection.SharingMode = I2cSharingMode.Shared;

        mpu5060device =
            await I2cDevice.FromIdAsync(
                deviceId, mpu_connection);

        mpuInit();
    }
}
```

The mpuInit method sends initial values to the sensor, and I will describe it below.

The MPUAddress should be 0xD2 according to the documentation, but we need to take just seven bits of this value, so I moved the value one bit to the right.

Once we have an **I2cDevice** object, we can start working with the device. It's not so easy, because MPU 6050 has lots of registers, and you need to understand most of them. Additionally, you need to initialize the sensor to get values using the needed scale range and so on. Let's look at several registers:

- 0x6B: Power management. It's possible to set up different settings related to power mode, but the most important bit is bit number seven. With this bit you can set the sensor to an initial state.

- 0x3B–0x40: Accelerometer data. There are six bytes that contain data for the x-, y-, and z-axis. Because two bytes are required to present the data per each axis, there are six bytes (not three). So to get the result, you need to use the first byte as the high byte of a short (int16) and the second one as the low byte.

- 0x41–0x42: Two bytes that represent temperature—high and low byte.

- 0x43–0x48: Six bytes for gyroscope data (as for the accelerometer).

So you can use the mpuInit method to set up the initial state of the sensor. For example, you can reset the sensor using the following command:

```
mpu5060device.Write(new byte[] { 0x6B, 0x80 });
```

To measure something, you can use the **WriteRead** method. I don't want to create a lot of code in this chapter, so I will show you how to measure temperature only. You can use the following code:

```
byte mpuRegRead(byte regAddr)
{
    byte[] data=new byte[1];

    mpu5060device.WriteRead(new byte[] { regAddr },data);

    return data[0];
}
public double mpuGetTemperature()
{
    double temperature;
    short calc = 0;
    byte []data = new byte[2];
    data[0] = mpuRegRead(MPU_REG_TEMP_OUT_H);//0x41
    data[1] = mpuRegRead(MPU_REG_TEMP_OUT_L);//0x42
```

```
calc = (short)((data[0] << 8) | data[1]);

temperature = (calc / 340.0) + 36.53;
return temperature;
}
```

Analog and PWM on Raspberry

Compared to Arduino, Raspberry Pi 2 doesn't have analog pins or even PWM pins (just one that doesn't supported by Windows 10). If you check the IoT extension for the Universal Windows Platform, you will discover three sets of classes: I2C, SPI, and GPIO. The last one allows you to use Raspberry GPIO for sending/receiving high or low voltage only. So if you want to create a drone or a cool robot based on Raspberry Pi 2 and powered by Windows 10, you need to answer the following questions:

- How to read analog signals

- How to emulate PWM

- How to read digital signals from various digital sensors (if these signals are not LOW or HIGH)

I have discovered several ways to answer these questions. The first way is using external convertors. In the case of analog input, I would recommend using convertors from Microchip Technology, and there is a great selection of different chips: MCP3002, MCP3008, MCP3208, and so on. I bought MCP3008 because it supports up to eight channels and represents analog data in ten-bit format. Because Arduino and Netduino use the same format (from 0 to 1024), I am used to using ten bits.

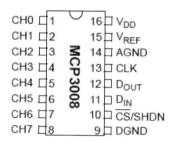

MCP3008 works based on an SPI bus, so we should use an SPI bus on Raspberry. To do so, I connected the CLK leg of the chip to the SPI0 CSLK pin (19), the D(out) leg to the SPI0 MISO pin (21), the D(in) leg to SPI0 MOSI (23), and CS/SHDN to

500

SPI0 CS0 (24). The V(dd) and V(ref) legs I connected to the power, and DGND to the ground.

I have an analog photoresistor sensor only. So I used just channel 0 and connected the signal leg of the sensor to CH0.

Below you can find my code, which you can copy and paste to the MainPage.xaml.cs of your universal application. I didn't create an interface and just used the Debug class to print sensor data to the output window:

```
byte[] readBuffer = new byte[3];
byte[] writeBuffer = new byte[3] { 0x06, 0x00, 0x00 };

private SpiDevice spi;

private DispatcherTimer timer;

private void Timer_Tick(object sender, object e)
{
    spi.TransferFullDuplex(writeBuffer, readBuffer);
    int result = readBuffer[1] & 0x07;
    result <<= 8;
    result += readBuffer[2];
    result >>= 1;
    Debug.WriteLine(result.ToString());
}
```

```csharp
protected async override void OnNavigatedTo(
    NavigationEventArgs e)
{
    await StartSPI();
    this.timer = new DispatcherTimer();
    this.timer.Interval = TimeSpan.FromMilliseconds(500);
    this.timer.Tick += Timer_Tick;
    this.timer.Start();
    base.OnNavigatedTo(e);
}

private async Task StartSPI()
{
    try
    {
        var settings = new SpiConnectionSettings(0);
        settings.ClockFrequency = 5000000;
        settings.Mode = SpiMode.Mode0;

        string spiAqs =
            SpiDevice.GetDeviceSelector("SPI0");
        var deviceInfo =
            await DeviceInformation.FindAllAsync(spiAqs);
        spi = await SpiDevice.FromIdAsync(
            deviceInfo[0].Id, settings);
    }
    catch (Exception ex)
    {
        throw new Exception(
            "SPI Initialization Failed", ex);
    }
}
```

The second way is much more radical—I decided to build an Arduino shield for Raspberry Pi 2. With that you can get PWM, analog, and digital inputs.

Of course, the Raspberry Pi and Arduino boards have different form factors, and the Arduino board cannot be stacked on Raspberry, so I decided to build my own Arduino from scratch as a shield for Raspberry.

Visiting http://www.bc-robotics.com/, which is physically located in Vancouver Island, I bought the following things:

- Raspberry Proto Strip Board

- Stacking header

- ATMega 328P-PU with bootloader (you can buy it without the bootloader, but you need another Arduino to flash the bootloader there)

- 16 MHz crystal

- Some 22 pF capacitors, 0.1 uF capacitors, and one 10 uF capacitor

Additionally, you need to make sure that you have different resistors (at least 10 kΩ and 220 Ω), at least one LED, a button, and a serial-to-USB converter. In the case of the converter, you need to make sure that it has a DTR pin (not just RX and TX). I had a converter that had CTS pins, so I had to buy a new one.

Finally, I spent around twenty Canadian dollars for components. I believe that I could have bought all of these things for ten to fifteen dollars, but I am not ready to wait a month for a package from China. In the case of BC Robotics, I got all these things in forty-eight hours.

In the next step, you need to find a schema for how to build your own Arduino from scratch. I used this one: http://shrimping.it/blog/shrimp/. I decided to use Protected Shrimp, but I simply removed the button from the circuit to save some space.

Just one piece of advice: assemble everything using a breadboard, because Raspberry Proto Strip Board has similar architecture. Once you have tested your circuit, it's possible to move all components to the strip board one by one.

In thirty minutes I got this:

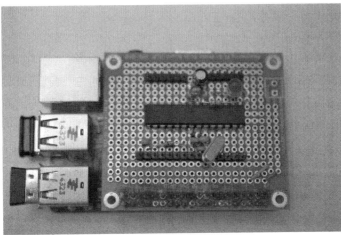

Now you can use the USB-to-serial to apply all needed software to your Arduino. This depends on the method you choose to make a connection between Arduino and Raspberry. For example, you can use the StandardFirmata sketch, which is installed with Arduino SDK, and you can use I2C or serial communications.

Chapter 35

How to Build Windows 10 Games in Unity3D

Visual Studio Tools for Unity

Lots of developers have used Visual Studio as the default code editor for the Unity engine for many years, and it looks like, since the Visual Studio 2015 release, integration between both products is stronger than before. Since Unity3D 5.2, Visual Studio Community Edition 2015 has been the default Unity3D code editor for developers on Windows.

First of all, both tools have cross-product installations. If you have a fresh PC with Visual Studio 2015 installed, you can find that the **New Project** dialog contains a new category—**Game**. You cannot use this category to create new projects, because there are just links to some popular gaming frameworks, including Unity.

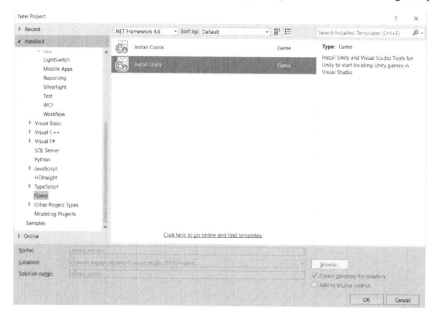

If you select Install Unity, Visual Studio will help you to install Unity and Visual Studio Tools for Unity:

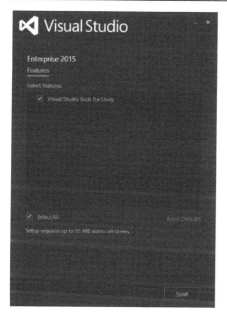

In the case of the Unity installer, integration is even better: users can select and install Visual Studio Community Edition directly from the Unity installer:

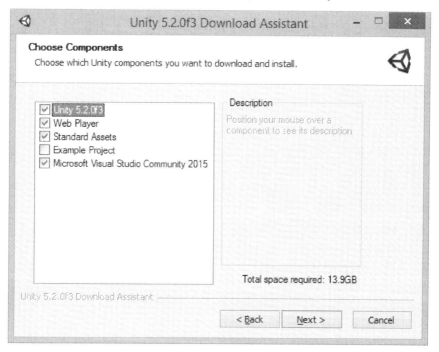

Note that since the Visual Studio Community Edition announcement, game developers have been able to use all-important Visual Studio features for free, including extensions (plug-ins) and debug features. If you want to download Visual Studio Community Edition separately, you can do it by visiting https://www.visualstudio.com/.

Visual Studio Community Edition has some licensing limitations. For example, you can use it for small teams only (up to five people), but if you work in a big company, you can use the Professional or Enterprise version of Visual Studio. In this case the Unity installer will recognize the existing version of Visual Studio and ask to install Visual Studio Tools for Unity only, which is a bridge between Unity and Visual Studio 2015:

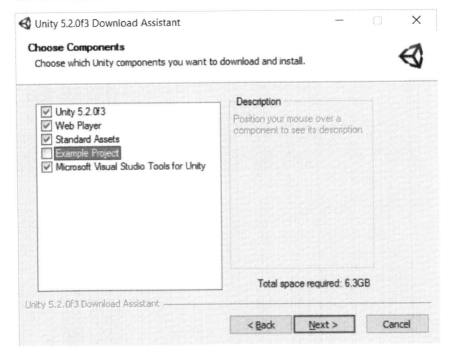

So if you use the Unity installer or Visual Studio, it's really hard to miss the installation opportunity for Microsoft Visual Studio Tools for Unity. Let's see how to use the tools themselves.

The good news that Unity3D 5.2 has native support for Visual Studio Tools. You simply need to create a new project or open an existing one. To make sure that Visual Studio is the default editor, you can call the **Edit→Preferences** menu item and open the **Unity Preferences** window, which contains information about external tools, including the script editor:

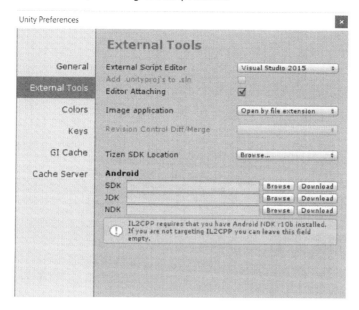

At this step, you can start working with your Unity project and create scripts in C#, objects, assets, and so on. If you want to open the project in Visual Studio, you simply need to use the Open in C# menu item.

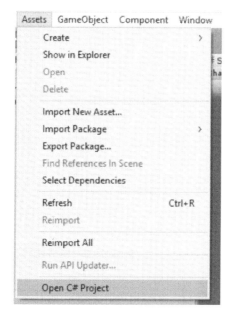

It's easy to do, and Unity will open your project in Visual Studio. Let's look at some important features that you can use.

First of all, you can use Unity Project Explorer (Shift+Alt+E):

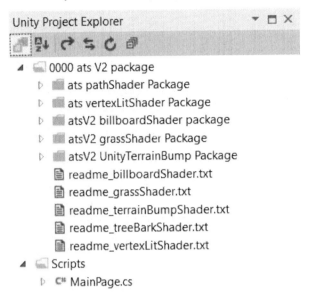

This window is similar to the Project window in Unity and can present project files in the same way. So if you need to find some files very quickly, you can do it in the same way as in Unity. Unity Project Explorer and Solution Explorer show project files in different ways. You can see that difference especially for large projects.

The next two windows allow you to override **MonoBehaviour** class methods quickly. You can use **Ctrl+Shift+Q** to call the **Quick MonoBehaviours** window. Just start typing the name of the method, and the window will help you select the right one:

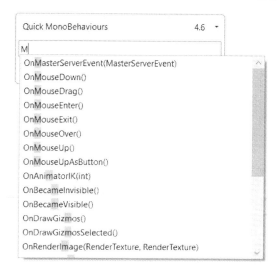

You can call the second window using **Ctrl+Shift+M**:

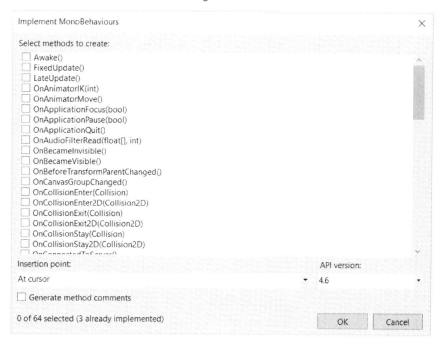

Using the **MonoBehaviour wizard**, you can generate several method stubs at once.

Two more features of Visual Studio Tools for Unity are support for shaders editing and integration with Unity output. Thanks to the first feature, you can see coloring syntaxes and formatting features if you are working with shaders in Visual Studio. The second feature allows you to see Unity errors and warnings in the Visual Studio error window.

Finally, the most important feature is debugging. You can connect to the Unity Debugger using the Debug→Attach Unity Debugger menu item. The **Select Unity Instance** window will show available Unity instances, and you can select any of them:

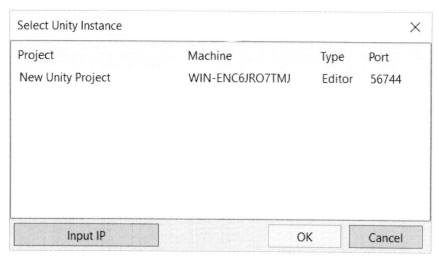

Or you can simply click the **Attach to Unity** button on the Standard toolbar.

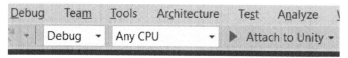

Once Visual Studio is connected, you can open the Unity editor and use the Play/Stop features. Of course, Visual Studio supports breakpoints, allows you to evaluate expressions and variables, and has other debugging features.

Publishing a Unity Game to the Store

If you are ready to publish your game to the Store, you can start with the Build Settings window in Unity:

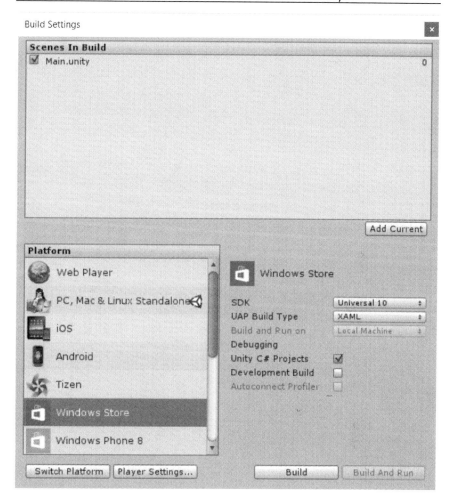

For Windows 10 applications, you need to select Universal 10 as an SDK and a build type between C# and DirectX. The project type shows which type of host project will be used for your game. I like to use XAML/C#, but you can select DirectX (D3D) as well.

The next important option is **Debugging Unity C# Project**. If you don't select this option, Unity will compile all code and create a new host project that refers to dlls with your game inside. In this case you will not be able to debug your game code in Visual Studio. But if you select this option, Unity will include one more project in the solution with the source code of your game, and you will be able to debug it.

Of course, some developers might ask why we need to debug code in the final solution, especially if we have Visual Studio Tools for Unity and have already tested and debugged the game in the Unity editor. The main problem is that the Unity editor uses the Mono framework for running the game in the player. But once you create the final solution for the Store and want to create and deploy a Windows 10 package, Visual Studio will use the .NET Framework for the debug version and .NET Core for release. That's why in some cases you need to tune your game by avoiding some namespaces such as **System.IO**, **System.Net**, **System.Reflection**, and so on. In some cases you can use the **WinRTLegacy** library as a wrapper for old functionality, but in some cases you need to change your classes directly (use **Windows.Storage** instead of **System.IO**, for example).

So debugging features are very important for the final solution as well because you can find potential problems in real Windows 10 applications but not just in the Unity player.

Before clicking the Build button, I would recommend clicking Player Settings and review the settings for the application that are relevant for Windows Store.

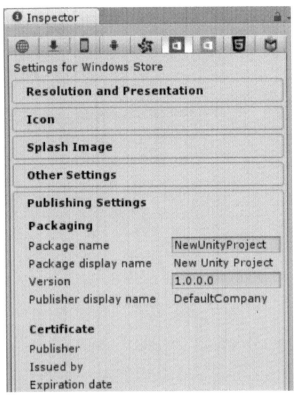

Using this window, you can assign lots of properties in the manifest file of the application. Of course, almost all settings you can assign are in Visual Studio. So you can select the best way for you.

Once you click the Build button, Unity will create the final solution for the Store and include two or three projects (depending on the debugging option): libraries, source code, and the Store project itself. Additionally, Unity will create three build configurations: debug, release, and master. In the case of the debug and release configurations, Visual Studio will use .NET CLR to build and run the application, but once you debug the application, you need to ship the master. This configuration supports .NET Native, and it's ready for the Store.

So in this step, you simply need to see whether the application runs successfully outside the Unity player. If you have some problems with the code due to migration from Mono to .NET, you simply need to find and use classes from Windows Runtime.

In the next step, you need to add some Windows 10–specific functionality. For example, you can use Live tiles, notifications, and so on. In the case of games, it should not take much time, but plan this in advance.

When everything works fine, you can check performance, test, and publish the application to the Store.

How to Create a Plug-In for Unity

Usually it's easy to prepare a package for the Store, but the most important problem here is plug-ins. If you have binaries that support Windows Store, it's not a problem, and you can simply use them.

But if you don't have access to the source code of a plug-in, and it doesn't support the Store, you have a problem, and you cannot do many things in this case: ask the plug-in developer to include Windows Store support or use another plug-in.

Finally, you can create a new plug-in from scratch or use existing source code to migrate it to UWP. It's a very common task, and I want to take some time to discuss the process.

First of all, you need to create a new solution that will contain at least a Windows Runtime Component project and a Classic Class Library project. Note that a Classic Class Library project uses the .NET Framework 4.6 by default, so you need to open the project settings and change the target framework to Unity 3.5 .net

Base Class Library:

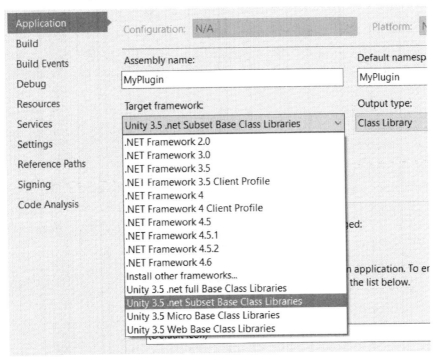

Don't duplicate your existing code (or new code) in both projects. Just add source files to one of these projects and use the Add As Link feature to add a reference to the second one:

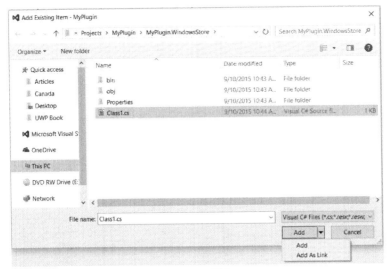

Then you can work with the same set of files for both projects.

Of course, in this case you need to use some preprocessor directives to enable conditional compilation. In our case we can use **UNITY_EDITOR** and **UNITY_WSA** as directives for the editor and Windows Store applications. Just visit the Build tab in the project properties and add the appropriate **Conditional compilation symbol**.

Once your code is ready, you can compile it and add all libraries to the Unity project. In the previous version, you needed to place the library in the special folders, but starting with Unity 5.2 you can place it anywhere. Instead, you can click each library and specify a platform using Inspector:

That's all. Of course, we didn't cover many topics such as diagnostic tools, communication between a Windows Store bridge and a game, and so on, but you should have enough information for a fast start.

About the Author

Sergii Baidachnyi is a principal developer evangelist at Microsoft. Currently residing in Canada, Sergii is responsible for working with the developer community and promoting client-development tools as a superior mechanism for creating cross-platform business applications.

The author was introduced to the .NET platform circa 2001, and since that time, he has actively participated in a number of .NET projects, developing, managing, and architecting financial, medical, and multimedia applications. At the same time, Sergii led Microsoft IT Academy, where he delivered .NET-related trainings on C#, Windows Forms, ASP.NET, and so on. He has published articles and reviews in multiple IT-industry magazines and several books on ASP.NET, Silverlight, Windows Forms, and Windows 8 Development.

Starting in 2006, Sergii allowed his passion to become his full-time job as a developer evangelist at Microsoft Ukraine and later at Microsoft Canada.

You can read more of Sergii's musings on his blog at http://en.baydachnyy.com. You can also catch him attending and speaking at Microsoft events around Canada.

Made in the USA
San Bernardino, CA
13 February 2018